PENGUIN BOOKS

LIGHTS C

'A riot of a book on I   inclair
blazes with fury. No o   uide to
London's cultural squalor' *Observer*

'These nine prose pieces – in which Sinclair "lights out" for his
Territory – form a powerful distillation of all that is best, most potent
and accessible in Sinclair's work. Here is a mind at the height of its
powers' *Independent*

'Anyone who cares about English prose cares about Iain Sinclair, a
demented magus of the sentence. He is a sublime archaeologist of the
present, and his dig has produced one of the most remarkable books
ever written on London' James Wood, *Guardian*

'As a stylist Sinclair is incomparable; he is the De Quincey of
contemporary English letters' Peter Ackroyd, *The Times*

'Crackles and fizzes with electricity' Ruth Rendell

'Many Londoners will see their city as they have never seen it before if
they have the good fortune to stumble across Sinclair's writing'
Ken Livingstone, *New Statesman*

'An exhilarating, funny, as well as visionary book' *The Times Literary
Supplement*

'Through polemic and travelogue and memoir, the cruel and seething
modern city emerges' *Independent on Sunday*

'A remarkable guerilla guidebook to a secret city' *Scotsman*

'Spot on. Ensures that the holy ground of London's streets, pubs and canals will never smell the same again' Roy Porter, *Sunday Times*

'A kaleidoscopic guide to London's sub-culture, to disintegration, a guide packed with information, historical detail, indigenous populace and character' *London Magazine*

ABOUT THE AUTHOR

Iain Sinclair is the author of *Downriver* (winner of the James Tait Black Memorial Prize and the Encore Award); *Landor's Tower*; *White Chappell, Scarlet Tracings*; *Lights Out for the Territory*; *Lud Heat*; *Rodinsky's Room* (with Rachel Lichtenstein); *Radon Daughters*; and *London Orbital*. He lives in Hackney, East London.

LIGHTS OUT FOR THE TERRITORY
9 EXCURSIONS IN THE SECRET HISTORY OF LONDON

IAIN SINCLAIR
WITH ILLUSTRATIONS BY MARC ATKINS

PENGUIN BOOKS

PENGUIN BOOKS

Published by the Penguin Group
Penguin Books Ltd, 80 Strand, London WC2R 0RL, England
Penguin Putnam Inc., 375 Hudson Street, New York, New York 10014, USA
Penguin Books Australia Ltd, 250 Camberwell Road,
Camberwell, Victoria 3124, Australia
Penguin Books Canada Ltd, 10 Alcorn Avenue, Toronto, Ontario, Canada M4V 3B2
Penguin Books India (P) Ltd, 11 Community Centre,
Panchsheel Park, New Delhi – 110 017, India
Penguin Books (NZ) Ltd, Cnr Rosedale and Airborne Roads,
Albany, Auckland, New Zealand
Penguin Books (South Africa) (Pty) Ltd, 24 Sturdee Avenue,
Rosebank 2196, South Africa

Penguin Books Ltd, Registered Offices: 80 Strand, London WC2R 0RL, England

www.penguin.com

First published by Granta Books 1997
Published in Penguin Books 2003
5

Printed in England by Clays Ltd, St Ives plc

ISBN-13: 978-0-14-101483-8

Keep the river road, all the way, and next time you tramp, take shoes and socks with you.

MARK TWAIN, *THE ADVENTURES OF HUCKLEBERRY FINN*

CONTENTS

SKATING ON THIN EYES: THE FIRST WALK

the magus dee dreams of a stone island in force, dying in poverty,
drunk on angelspeech, which paradoxically, he has not actually heard,
the scales of music tripping upward to evade him in perpetual deferral
to create open outward the place of definition.

RICHARD MAKIN

The notion was to cut a crude **V** into the sprawl of the city, to vandalise dormant energies by an act of ambulant signmaking. To walk out from Hackney to Greenwich Hill, and back along the River Lea to Chingford Mount, recording and retrieving the messages on walls, lampposts, doorjambs: the spites and spasms of an increasingly deranged populace. (I had developed this curious conceit while working on my novel *Radon Daughters*: that the physical movements of the characters across their territory might spell out the letters of a secret alphabet. Dynamic shapes, with ambitions to achieve a life of their own, quite independent of their supposed author. Railway to pub to hospital: trace the line on the map. These botched runes, burnt into the script in the heat of creation, offer an alternative reading – a subterranean, preconscious text capable of divination and prophecy. A sorcerer's grimoire that would function as a curse or a blessing.)

Armed with a cheap notebook, and accompanied by the photographer Marc Atkins, I would transcribe all the pictographs of venom that decorated our near-arbitrary route. The messages were, in truth, unimportant. Urban graffiti is all too often a signature without a document, an anonymous autograph. The tag is everything, as jealously defended as the Coke or Disney decals. Tags are the marginalia of corporate tribalism. Their offence is to parody the most visible aspect of high capitalist black magic. Spraycan bandits, like monks labouring on a Book of Hours, hold to their own patch, refining their art by infinite acts of repetition. The name, unnoticed except by fellow taggers, is a gesture, an assertion: it stands in place of the individual artist who, in giving up his freedom, becomes free. The public autograph is an announcement of

1

nothingness, abdication, the swift erasure of the envelope of identity. It's like Salvador Dali in his twilight years putting his mark on hundreds of blank sheets of paper, authenticating chaos.

Serial composition: the city is the subject, a fiction that anyone can lay claim to. "We are all artists," they used to cry in the Sixties. Now, for the price of an aerosol, it's true. Pick your view and sign it. Sign events that have not yet happened. (Take a stroll down somewhere like Catherine Wheel Alley, off Bishopsgate, and see the future revealed on a wall of white tiles. Superimposed fantasies. Scarlet swastikas swimming back to the surface. The Tourette's syndrome ravings of an outwardly reformed city. A private place, a narrow passage, in which to let out all the overtly disguised racist bile. The madness has to find somewhere to run wild. Obscene formulae incubating terrorist bombs. Runnels and enclosed ditches where unwaged scribes are at last free of the surveillance cameras.) Remember postal art, *Fluxus*? All that European and transatlantic bumf now consigned to a bunker beneath the Tate Gallery? Graffiti is the Year Zero version.

The tagger, the specialist who leaves his mark on a wall, is a hit and run calligrapher – probably young, MTV-grazing and male. His art is nomadic, a matter of quantity not quality. As often as not, the deed is carried out on the way back from a club in the early hours of the morning; the announcement of a jagged progress across home territory. Nothing too bulky to carry, a good black felt-tip pen in the pocket of your Pucca jeans will do the trick. The pseudonymous signature is rapidly perfected: Soxi, Coe, Sub, Hemp. Standards are rather more demanding than in Bond Street. Earlier efforts, already in place, if they are deemed inadequate, will be deleted with a single stroke. White boy business. Middle-class cultural diffusionism. The walls that have been set aside as open-air galleries, sites where aerosol activity is encouraged or at least tolerated, don't cut it. "Sign Park" in an estate off Tufnell Park Road, although it features constantly evolving monster murals, is not considered a serious option. Your tag will all too soon be worked over, obliterated. Taggers can be solitaries, but, more frequently, they hang out in teams or crews. The tag represents a corporate identity; not so much a gang as a studio or "school of". Battles are not territorial; the climate here is clubbish, mildly hallucinogenic. Inner-city impressionists who have moved on from the posthumous representation of light and pleasure. Everything happens in the present tense. No history, no future. There is no interference with subject. Fragments of London are perceived as Polaroid epiphanies; signed and abandoned. The tag is the record of a fleeting instant of inspiration. "Eas-y!" The more upwardly mobile careerists might attack a tube train, but most settle for walls and doorways, customised hoardings. Sprayed messages are meaningless, having no programme beyond the announcement of a non-presence. Night scrawls, minimal adjustments to the psychic skin of the city. The grander aerosol paintings, known as "pieces", are altogether too flash, baroque, an art in decline. They draw attention to themselves, thereby neutralising their greatest strength – invisibility. They solicit photographic reproduction, a collaboration with Warhol-tendency vampires. The plain tag is a purist's form. Satisfaction is derived from getting your hit into some high risk location, a dangerous bridge climbed in heart-pumping, post-rave excitement. The clubbing tagger's E-vision is an authentic urban experience: an enforced homeward walk across a lucid wilderness from Barking or Brixton, sunrise over the industrial alps of Stratford East. That's as near as they are ever going to come to it, unsolicited satori. Hemp, an American exile, who arrived here from New York in the wake of a 500 dollar fine, enjoys a toke, a session with the chillum. In reflective mood, he meditates on the relationship between tagging and skate-boarding. He drifts backwards and forwards, enacting complicated figures, over a South London parking lot: "If you're going to be around the city all the time, you'd better put your name up."

As newspapers have atrophied into the playthings of grotesque megalomaniacs, uselessly shrill exercises in mind–control, so disenfranchised authors have been forced to adapt the walls to playful collages of argument and invective. Not the publicly displayed, and quietly absorbed, papers of the Chinese, but editorials of madness. Texts that nobody is going to stop and read. Unchallenged polemics. My own patch in Hackney has been mercilessly colonised by competing voices from elsewhere: Kurds, Peruvians, Irish, Russians, Africans. Contour lines of shorthand rhetoric asserting the borders between different areas of influence. Graffiti could, I hoped, be read like a tidemark. In the course of our walk we'd find precisely where the "Freedom" of Dursan Karatas gave way to the "Innocence" of George Davis – OK. (Yes, George is still getting a result, the benefit of the doubt from the railway bridges of East London – long after being caught in the act during a raid on the Bank of Cyprus in Seven Sisters Road, Holloway. For over twenty years Davis has woken to find himself framed by DS Mathews. Thus proving that graffiti has a half-life far in excess of the buildings on which they have been painted. Broken sentences and forgotten names wink like fossils among the ruins.)

Walking is the best way to explore and exploit the city; the changes, shifts, breaks in the cloud helmet, movement of light on water. Drifting purposefully is the recommended mode, tramping asphalted earth in alert reverie, allowing the fiction of an underlying pattern to reveal itself. To the no-bullshit materialist this sounds suspiciously like *fin-de-siècle* decadence, a poetic of entropy – but the born-again *flâneur* is a stubborn creature, less interested in texture and fabric, eavesdropping on philosophical conversation pieces, than in noticing *everything*. Alignments of telephone kiosks, maps made from moss on the slopes of Victorian sepulchres, collections of prostitutes' cards, torn and defaced promotional bills for cancelled events at York Hall, visits to the homes of dead writers, bronze casts on war memorials, plaster dogs, beer mats, concentrations of used condoms, the crystalline patterns of glass shards surrounding an imploded BMW quarter-light window, meditations on the relationship between the brain damage suffered by the super-middleweight boxer Gerald McClellan (lights out in the Royal London Hospital, Whitechapel) and the simultaneous collapse of Barings, bankers to the Queen. Walking, moving across a retreating townscape, stitches it all together: the illicit cocktail of bodily exhaustion and a raging carbon monoxide high.

Graffiti is the only constant on these fantastic journeys; random codices, part sign and part language. Recording as many of these fractured compositions as we could find along a given route from Hackney to Greenwich to Chingford would be like editing an unpredictable anthology. The walk could become a phantom biopsy, cutting out a sample of diseased tissue without an anaesthetic. But, more importantly, it would also pay homage to a series of famous Lea Valley "temperature traverses", undertaken as part of a survey of London's climate, between October 1958 and November 1959. TJ Chandler, in his book *The Climate of London* (1965), describes the curious set-up:

> *The instrumentation of the orginal traverses consisted of electrical resistance thermometers housed in double-louvred radiation shields suspended from the roof-rack of a car so that the element in the lower shield was 4ft and that in the upper shield was 5ft above the ground and 6 in. from the side of the car. Temperatures in the first few feet above road surfaces seem, in fact, to be surprisingly uniform and the precise height of the instrument is less critical than might be supposed . . .*
>
> *Any warming of the elements by the car engine would naturally invalidate the readings. This problem has sometimes proved difficult*

*(Godske, quoted by Sundborg, 1952, p.53), but in the present
investigation the position of the radiation shield and elements in relation to
the engine and airflow over the car, plus a thick pad of glass fibre over the
car bonnet, prevented any warming. It was sought, in general, to keep the
car speed to 20 mi/hr . . . Except on a few noted occasions, speeds were
sufficient to secure adequate ventilation of the elements without being too
great to induce dynamic warming.*

This outwardly eccentric Dr Who-style progress, zigzagging by day
and night from Liverpool Street and Canning Town up the Lea Valley
to Ware, struck me as a paradigm for any visionary exploration of the
Essex fringes. An apparently scientific excuse for a glorious clandestine
folly, joyriding the trail of the cosmic serpent. As with alchemy, it's
never the result that matters; it's the time spent on the process, the discipline of repetition. Enlightened boredom.

Our proposed walk was far too neat. The implication of the vulgarity of the sign I intended to inflict on East London screamed for some
last moment revision. The project had nothing to do with Thomas
Pynchon ("He walked; walked, he thought sometimes . . . his only
function to want"). Pynchon's 1963 novel, *V.*, in any case, was always
followed by an assertive period. **V.** (I did once toy with the idea of col-
lecting an alphabet library: from "*A*" by Louis Zukofsky, through John
Berger's *G* and *The Story of O*, to *Z*, the novelisation of the Costa-
Gavras film.)

Arrangements in place, the evening before the walk, I was still worrying at the details of the scheme, hoping for some accident to bring
about a final revision. Rummaging through the chaos of my desk, the
bills, unanswered letters, unsolicited typescripts, fliers for last season's
poetry readings, I discovered an invitation, six months out of date, to
attend the inauguration, in Seminar Room 178, Technology Faculty,
University of Greenwich, of *seminaruim*, "a permanent site-specific
installation" by Richard Makin.

*Makin was given complete freedom regarding the site and the nature of the
piece . . . The piece is textual and is condensed from the site's appellation,
the artist working with the constraints of synonyms, associations and the
etymology of the compounded words* seminar room. *These served to focus
heterogeneous responses to the subject environment and its broader
surroundings and were instrumental in producing a poetic constellation*

evoking various motifs correlational to the function of that environment. The yield is an equivocal conjunction intended to instigate a pondering and contemplation of simultaneously the presented semantic arrangement and the functions of the host space, the receiver situated within this weave of locus and stream of words that have emerged from the nominative of a particular physical domain: a transparent and resonant superimposition of word and place.

How could I resist? Makin's artwork fitted so neatly alongside the theme of the moment. I *had* to go for it – sponsored graffiti of the most elevated kind. This character Makin, whose name I had previously noticed in the modernist periodical *Parataxis*, had been invited to creatively deface the wall of a new university. Here was graffiti of a previously unrecognised sort – indoor graffiti, premeditated spontaneity. A legitimate sibling of the invitations left on the doors of public conveniences, those capital-letter jokes trailing forlornly towards a puddled floor. It was unlikely, I thought, that Makin had got out his paint can, stencil set and ruler, to do the business himself. Could he, as a sponsor of secondhand graffiti, be included in our collection? There must have been faculty meetings, proposals, justifications, budgets, costings of material and labour. Then there was the style of the lettering: had some hireling David Jones or Eric Gill been found in the borough? Makin's room would be the pivot on which our route march would swing.

The bureaucratic comedy began as soon as I picked up the telephone. Making contact with the University of Greenwich, I was passed from department to department, secretary to impersonal assistant. It was that awkward time of the afternoon when the sun skulks listlessly over the horizon. I could hear tea-cups being pointedly clinked. I felt the uncomfortable warmth of the central heating, the flickering interference of strip-lighting that reduces humans to a species of desktop cacti. All knowledge of the mysterious Richard Makin and his art project was strenuously denied. The University of Greenwich, it was implied, was not that kind of place. I persisted in my folly. The Technology Faculty *did* exist, the clerks would go that far. But who was *I*? Who did I represent? What was the name of my company? I grew peevish. I quoted the original invitation. And the fact that Makin openly admitted that he was prepared to "read and talk about his work". "All are welcome" stated an official handout that bore the letter-heading of the School of Mathematics, Statistics and Scientific Computing; to say nothing of the

6

sponsoring names of Professors Mark Cross, DSc, CMath, FIMA, Martin G Everett, DPhil, Edwin Galea, PhD, Keith Rennolls, MSc, CStat, MICFor. Four professors were up for this and the functionaries were still giving me a hard time. The tea-cups were replenished. The clerks weakened. The room *might* be visited, between strictly regulated hours, but there was still no Makin in the computer. The man was a freelance, a floater.

By now, of course, *seminaruim* had become the quest, an absolute necessity. I must have sounded crazy enough for them to act before I turned up in their openplan office with a knapsack of gelignite. Makin rang me. He would be in Seminar Room 178 between eleven-thirty and twelve-thirty on the following morning, prepared to curate his achievement. This was a double-edged blessing. We had an achievable goal for our walk but we were lumbered with an unwelcome time-base. I never like that. Time on these excursions should be allowed to unravel at its own speed, that's the whole point of the exercise. To shift away from the culture of consumption into a meandering stream. Cut those wires.

The walk had received its arbitrary revision. There was a proper target, while the second stage, the return leg, could look after itself. (At this point, I dug deeper into the tilth on the margins of my desk and uncovered the typescript of an earlier Makin text, *the curve of forgetting*. I dived into it at random: "duped by the record of signs upon endless walls". Makin, back in December 1992, lived in the shadow of the obelisk of St Luke's Old Street. Home territory. Our conjunction was even stranger than I had supposed: we would both be travelling, twin arms of a compass, south-east across London, to meet in a transgressed seminar room.)

Another call. (Have you noticed how these things come in clusters? Like buses. The instrument, once activated, alerts other potential communicators, triggers off a chain reaction. Call it morphic resonance, or Secret State interference in the electromagnetic field, and switch on the answer-machine.) An audibly distressed woman, a writer, enraged by a sense of her powerlessness in the face of near-demonic forces, has to protest, describe, articulate her feelings about the M11 motorway extension. The battle of Claremont Road. What to *do*? The things that have been going on. Things she has seen. Dawn raids. Executed trees. Why is this unreported by the media? Why doesn't someone tell the *real* story? There's no specific request to make of me, no demand. But. Before it's too late. She will. Get it down. Herself. The truth.

7

Evening sunlight was polishing the grain of my grandfather's desk, bleaching the pinks in the John Bellany watercolour. It was my turn to abuse the phone, summon Marc Atkins from his darkroom. If we were to get to the University of Greenwich by late morning, we would have to knock off Abney Park Cemetery tonight. You can't visit the dead before 9 am. Already the "purity" of the **V** had been despoiled. Good. That's promising. If our pilgrimage is not to disintegrate into a marathon trot we have to walk out of the door without further hesitation.

2.
ALBION DRIVE E8. TO ABNEY PARK, STOKE NEWINGTON.
EVENING OF 24/10/94.

The important fact about urban living: the continued stream of second attention awareness. Every licence plate, street sign, passing strangers, are saying something to you.
WILLIAM S. BURROUGHS

Easily into our stride, I'm explaining the whole insane concept to Marc: on the hoof. No time for maps and bearings. He handles these feverish speculations with practised ease. God knows what he really thinks. Or who he is. Not "Marc Atkins", this much he will admit. Another volunteer orphan, a self-invented man with an interestingly labyrinthine personal life; postal systems that require a network of dead-letter drops. He's a shavenheaded vegetarian giant, a near-Brummie. That's already more than any reasonable person would want to discover. Give him a camera to frame out the rest of the world and he's happy. Promise him a free breakfast and the chance of running into a squall of long-legged black women and he'll walk through fire.

At the end of Albion Square, beyond the clutch of houses that have been built over the Nimby battleground of a fruitlessly defended green space, is a stunted obelisk set on a carpet of stone flags. Its octagonal base serves as somewhere to sit for those who take advantage of the Duke of Wellington's barbecue night, a stand for lager cans. The concrete shield from which the obelisk rises is patterned with a network of juvenile footprints. The site is shaded by a sycamore umbrella and frisky with the dance of leaf-light. The shadow of the obelisk, in the late afternoon, falls away from the house which the sculptor Rachel Whiteread and her partner are restoring – but points in the direction we have to walk. There's a cup mark or raised weal in the soft white stone, the explanatory text has been obliterated. Memorials are a way of forgetting, reducing generational guilt to a grid of albino chess pieces, bloodless stalagmites. Shapes that are easy to ignore stand in for the trauma of remembrance. Names are edited out. Time attacks the noble profile with a syphilitic bite. These funerary spikes, unnoticed by the locals as they go about their business, operate a system of pain erasure; acupuncture needles channelling, through their random alignment, the flow of the energy field.

Every obelisk has its acolyte. The undistinguished example that fronts the Duke of Wellington pub is serviced by the pigeon man, an elderly stooped figure dressed entirely in brown; from his flat cap, through his greasy raincoat, to his worn shoes, he is the colour of Daddies Favourite sauce scraped from a formica table. This pensioner progresses through the borough, each and every day, by his own eccentric circuits. He empties bulging plastic shopping bags of crumbs and crusts, ensuring that his feral pigeons will continue to splatter the same patches of territory. Action painting on a grand scale, bowel art. Where does all this bread come from? The man looks as if he lives on stale crusts dipped in vinegar sauce – and yet, by the quantities he slings over privet hedges and arranges on chosen squares of pavement, he must have the clearance contract from a chain of bakeries. He is never diverted by mere conversation, there's too much to be done, ground to be covered. He scuffles through, not bothering about who might be watching him, eager to get finished before the road walker starts beating her bounds. She's a creature of twilight, a tidy, middle-aged black woman who never shifts from the white line. There's something magical about the way she survives Queensbridge Road in the rush hour (it's tough enough in a car). No deviation, straight forward between the headlight beams, a journey to nowhere, but a journey that must be made. She has been heard to mutter: "The dirt, the dog dirt". It's canine excrement that keeps her off the pavements. Leaves her competing with kamikaze traffic.

Middleton Road and the Holly Street Estate: the horror nicely disguised (along with Shrubland Road, Lavender Grove, Mapledene Road, Forest Road) in names intended to invoke imaginary avenues of trees converging on London Fields. Hackney recalled as a market garden;

orchards just outside the limits of the city. The barrack blocks of flats with their colourful history in the process of being replaced by duplicates of precisely the same dimensions, better built versions that should last for years, tucked away behind a green barrier of temporary fencing. The nature of this present transaction subverted by the spectacular exhibition of a large black and white photograph, a presentation of what used to be here: the "truth" of dead bricks used to implant a false memory, an unearned inheritance.

CONTROLLED. **DANGER. DEMOLITION. KEEP OUT.**

Coalition against the/Criminal Justice Bill. RALLY.
Lobby of Parliament. WEDNESDAY 19 OCTOBER.
6pm Westminster Central Hall.

Socialist Worker. Build the resistance.

LAING

**Big Up/Miss Bounty Killer + Hype + Sweetie N
+ Killer Tits**

LAING: how that name, spread across town, reads like the announcement of a Sixties revival, Ronnie back on the rostrum like the Billy Graham of psychopolitics.

We march west: under the green and red railway bridge, once a mugger's wet dream. Escape routes into the flats, dustbin caves, or up the grass mound and over the wall onto the tracks. Handbags dumped in the hobo wilderness jungle where the elevated line used to run from Dalston Junction to Broad Street, a civilised shunt into the city for the clerical classes. A Euro-packet of loose change has hacked back the abundant growth, stamped out the campfire drinking schools, cleared the ground for future development – as car park or privatized railway. This dangerous but exhilarating walk with its views down between slats, and its secret glimpses into the backs of industrial premises, is no longer a possibility.

On the far side of the bridge, a number of haplessly optimistic survivalist operations hang on to the coat-tails of Kingsland Road. **TAILOR TERZI**. Silky disco waistcoats for citizens of restricted growth. Every night a Saturday fever, a blindman's wedding. SPECIAL

OFFER. MADE TO MEASURE TROUSERS. £35. No viable role has been found for this, the first shop, since the bag seller and boot-repairer jacked it in. Fantastic enterprises (designer hats suitable for Ascot or bar mitzvah), written up in listings magazines, wither and die before the cuttings can be securely pasted in the window.

Removals Anywhere in UK. ACCESS, VISA. Defunct. The sour stench of dog fear from behind boarded-up windows. Ex-rental washing machines that bark and yelp. A kebab slaughterhouse where all the dead meat has come back to life on a revolving skewer. The anarchists have their number.

LET THE
DOGS BE
FREE
OR OTHERS WILL

ALF. There is a persistent rumour floated by conspiracy theorists that Special Branch (and their competitors in Five and Six) have been forced to talk up the animal liberationist fringe in order to justify their munificent budgets. Sad-eyed veal calves have to replace Belfast outrages in the news reports. Beagles with a habit are the new Soviet. Hunt saboteurs are fifth columnists. Well-intentioned cells of Middle Englanders have been ruthlessly penetrated. Staged provocations orchestrate the latent hysteria of the tender hearted. After the iniquity of factory farming there's nothing left to pay for the upkeep of those mephitic riverside palaces. The graffiti on the grey door of the dog shed is so precisely aligned that it's hard not to suspect the trained hand of Secret State forgers.

Cooked Brawns etc. QUALITY DOG TRAINING. Noise, smell. A proprietary group, perfumed against the shrill odours of their métier as canine educationalists, block the doorway – not so much keeping their unbroken charges in, but keeping dubious citizens (non-owners) *out*. Dog training, surveillance, security: those are the growth areas, that's where to sink your redundancy packet. Very popular with villains who have managed to stay liquid and who fancy an indoors occupation. Security is the equivalent of the old time footballer's pub. The philosophy is homeopathic, treating like with like. Take a gander down the flank of the decommissioned hospital on the far side of Kingsland Road: vans. And they're all plastered with promises of heavy duty protection – alarm systems, grilles, trip-wires, locks, chains. Everything the upwardly mobile Ecstasy broker could require.

THE LONDON DOG CENTRE. The title says it all. A copyright on negatives. This shop openly declares itself the pits. The tributary corner, where Middleton Road squirts out into the stream of the old Ermine Street, houses a coven of visionaries who are hopelessly attempting to "train" the shapes of chaos, to discipline hot-breathed things that creep and crawl between human and animal worlds. Dogs. A window of cutely traumatised puppies, given the once-over in Fairy Liquid, busk like Amsterdam prostitutes. Professionally on show. Offering it. A pal for sale. A buddy who won't talk back. A baby-sized minder. A minder for your baby. (And there's a satellite trade, living off the woof-woof biz, photographing these beauties – so that they can be remembered when they are gone, in ripe colour, just as they looked in their prime. Oval snapshots to paste on a granite gravestone.)

Various meats are advertised on a menu board. Fish food. Sacks of bird seed. Doggy treats. A tray of stitched bootees in something that looks like waxed skin. Doll's house footwear for your pooch to gum. The shop has the atmosphere of an interspecies affray waiting to happen: the noise and the pong. But the Dog Centre co-exists in evident sympathy with the adjacent property: KENNY'S, THE BEST LITTLE SHOE SHOP IN TOWN. (Kenny's? Hard to shake off sinister echoes of Frank Zappa and pod people experiments.) Ranks of burnished Doc Marten boots. STEELS, DEALERS, COMMANDO STEELS: an army waiting for the word.

We swing out into the main drag (Kingsland Road) without paying our respects to the pub on the corner, the Fox, whose former landlord, Clifford Saxe, a commercial associate of the Knight dynasty, is said to have planned the £8 million pound 1976 robbery of the Bank of America from the room upstairs. Mr Saxe is one of the Famous Five (along with Ronnie Knight, Frederick Foreman, Ronald Everett, John James Mason) who opted for early retirement in the sun. So many of the faces are out there now it's like a time-warp, like having a poodle down Kingsland Waste in the late Sixties, before it went native.

Such disreputable myths have been airbrushed from the history of the borough in a punt at a minimalist gentrification programme. The idea is to propose, with a few green and white metal signs, a sense of place, local identity: that a strip of pavement can be something more than a headsdown charge after a Kentish bus trying to find its way to Liverpool Street. Marc can't believe the tasteful semaphoring arms that try to seduce you into a detour through KINGSLAND BASIN, STONEBRIDGE GARDENS, DALSTON TOWN CENTRE.

Dalston Town Centre, I love the chutzpah of that. Can a ghost have a centre? Dalston, coming into its pomp after a railway carve-up, as an alternative for those who couldn't afford the trip "up west", has all the buzz of a JG Ballard traffic island squatted by cowboys. Everything-Under-A-Pound bazaars rub shoulders with embattled chemists, off-licences, and the famous eel and pie shop with the blood-smeared slab. LARGER LIVE EELS IN STOCK. PLEASE ENQUIRE.

Conscious of the fact that we had to keep up a decent pace to reach Abney Park before they closed the gates, we didn't have time to give Kingsland Waste the close reading it deserved. We stuck to the line of shops on the east side.

The wall glyphs come straight at you. Low down, crude; increasingly frantic variations on the same logo. Written not sprayed. The signs defy instant interpretation. The most common one might stand, we decided, for EOKA. But that made no sense. The Cypriots were much earlier immigrants: like the Lambrianou family (coming to public notice through the criminal exploits of Tony and Chris) who had settled, a few years after the war, in Belford House on Queensbridge Road – effective (red brick and flowerpot on balcony) public housing which is still very much in service.

Away from its side channels, Kingsland Road was a furious river of competing voices: West African enterprise (an optician who doubled as a copier of legal documents), Fax bureaux, exotic cake shops, a mini-cab firm with a radio beacon tall enough to endanger lowflying aircraft, Turkish football club poolrooms, schmutter merchants, and the entire range of multi-ethnic snack bars and fast food emporia.

I had to copy the EOKA glyph into my notebook, so that I could have it analysed by someone more knowledgeable in the subtleties of Turkish splinter group politics. And then, looking more closely at the letters, I realised that I had got it all wrong. TOKi. The bandit penman of Hackney was a tagger. A juvenile smoker customising the word "toke". What I had taken to be an outburst of political sloganeering was no more than the territorial flourish of a peculiarly persistent dope-freak.

TIKB. STOP DIRTY WAR IN KURDISTAN. A professionally executed red stencil. The Turkish Workers' Communist Association. One of a number of groups busking for budget, hoping to upgrade their premises (by painting out the previous occupants' affiliations). Apparently, the Turkish hard left have only recently taken up the Kurdish cause, making gestures in support of the mountain people from around Malatya; farmers and herdsmen driven off their lands by rural poverty, and threatened by both central government and the incursions of PKK guerrillas.

The Kurds drifted in stages down towards the Mediterranean and then on, chasing some distant relative, to Dalston. Restaurant work, sweatshops, endless benefit applications. Streams of moustached and stubbled men in open-necked shirts queuing politely for their turn at the photocopier. Rumours also of protection rackets, extortion, prostitute outworkers. Husbands bringing venereal diseases back to their housebound wives. Rundown auction properties crammed with statusless immigrants.

The New Country Off-Licence and Foodstore in Kingsland Road is a typically modest venture: green vegetables racked on the street, the middle classes nipping furtively across the road from De Beauvoir Town for halvah and olives. Three or four men – no women – chatting behind the counter.

A twenty-nine-year old shop-assistant, Ali Ozturk, was standing in the doorway when he was shot. The event was scarcely national news but it made a splash in the *Hackney Gazette* – who suggested that Mr Ozturk was the victim of a hitman, or team of hitmen, dispatched from Ankara by the secret police. The local journalist, with evident ambitions to become the next Frederick Forsyth, pictured the assassin squatting, Dallas-style, in the flats opposite, waiting for his moment. To sustain this, it was necessary to find a more significant target. The shop's owner, Mafiz Bostanci, "a vigorous campaigner on trade union rights" and a senior figure at the Halkevi Turkish Centre in Stoke Newington, was the intended martyr. No shot was heard, no gunman seen. The incident made no particular impression on drifters cruising for kebabs, curries, battered cod, rice 'n' peas.

ANNMARIE

+

JACKIE

+

KELLY

WOZ

ERE

THE ALCOHOLICS

Dark sweatshop doorway leading back into unknowable regions hidden from the street. Storerooms, muscle gyms; striplight offices of lawyers paid to postpone extradition, smooth over motor frauds, front

"Jewish lightning" insurance scams. As I stoop to transcribe another concrete poem, three Nigerians trundle a monster package up the stairs.

A newsagent's window: the noticeboard of the urban village. TIE AND TEASE MASSAGE. MAGIC MOMENTS, DISCREET SERVICE. TONY GETS A BUZZ FROM DEAD BEES.

Closing on the junction, the crossroads, the epicentre of the notional Dalston Town, we spot, for the first time, a quirkier intelligence at work on the flagstones beneath our feet. The message has been stencilled, like the exhortations of TIKB, in blood-red lettering: WE'RE/[B]EHAVING/LIKE/INSECTS. And then by way of variation, in blue, STOP HISTORY. No half measures, these wandering philosophers are playing for high stakes. And with no embarrassment at self-plagiarisation. A thing that is true once loses none of its veracity in repetition. The stencil behaves better on the fresh white matte of Barclays Bank PLC. The previously absent B is smudged but clearly visible. The alignment of scarlet capitals, displayed directly beneath the bank's nameplate, is an obvious foretaste of poet Richard Makin's assault on Seminar Room 178 of the University of Greenwich.

WE'RE

BEHAVING

LIKE

INSECTS

The quadrivium, or meeting place of four roads, is the spiritual centre of the area through which we are walking: it's where suicides and vampires would receive their toothpick through the heart. On the east/west axis, the hobbled spurt of Dalston Lane, labouring gamely under the burden of cultural significance imposed upon it by Patrick Wright in *A Journey Through Ruins*, goes head-to-head with Peter Sellers' comedic Balls Pond Road. And to the north, Ermine Street, lightly disguised as Kingsland High Street (Stoke Newington Road, Stoke Newington High Street), makes a bid for Stamford Hill, White Hart Lane, Cambridge and other inconsequential destinations. This cruciform reef of shops, stalls and small businesses, has died and returned to life more times than RL Stevenson's Master of Ballantrae. Not so much a failed shopping centre as a car boot sale in an open prison, tactfully invigilated by security guards in peaked caps.

There couldn't be a more appropriate location for Doc "Papa" Williams to have launched Dark and Light, his walk-in, neighbourhood voodoo boutique. Dark and Light (The Foremost Source of Occult Books & Supplies) is part of a multinational franchising operation with branches in New York and Haiti. It's moment has surely come around – even if the shop has been dressed after the style of *Live and Let Die*. The statuettes have the authentically ironed-over, Roger Moore android look: charming but dysfunctional.

The doc, a softly-spoken Haitian exile, is always ready to pose with fat Cuban cigar and skull perched on top of his electrified hair. He can heal and he can curse. He can work on your barnet or drive out demons. He can put lead in your pencil or cleanse and bless your ill-disposed accommodation. Supplicants bring their warts and tumours from as far afield as Bristol or Manchester. He has the cuttings to prove it. Local spirits willingly dance to the command of this Dr Dee of Dalston.

Dark and Light dominates the crossroads. Travellers are forced to make a choice between lefthand and righthand paths. The window facing Dalston Junction suggests something between a clearance of surplus Vatican stock and the gnome reservation of a downmarket garden centre: runtish saints and Snow White virgins, dozens of them packed against feely pastiches of Leonardo's *Last Supper*, mowed out of felt. The left side of the shop, confronting the newspaper-seller's booth on Kingsland High Street, superimposes headlines of hysterical horror, reflected in the display glass, with potions, herbs, candles, chicken bones, feathers, roots, claws, cat-sized coffins. A tarot that has broken free of its box. Potential students of the dark side are encouraged to browse through the small library of books on display: *The Egyptian Secrets of Albertus Magnus*, *White and Black Arts for Man and Beast*, *The Story of Solomon the King*. I can never make my mind up – is this tellingly sited shop promoting the craziness, the babble, that has spilled over on to the walls? Or is it simply a focusing device, a shelter for all the unhoused definitions of the weird that stalk the streets of the borough? Dalston, twinned with downtown Port-au-Prince, has declared itself a voodoo republic.

Doc Williams' graffiti comes in the form of a quotation: a group of photographs of the healer in full spate, stogie clamped between teeth, straw hat, conducting a ceremony on his home turf. On the blue wall behind him is painted PLACE DES HOUNSSYS: reproduced words join the rest of the trumpeting exotica in the encyclopaedia of the city. That place becomes this place. If we do not cross to the west side of the street, we will be transported, trapped in the implications of an exorcism we do not understand.

In the revitalised air, the messages are coming much faster. All the special-interest groups want a piece of this. Out-patients, anarchists, cadres and weekend socialists. I have the uneasy feeling that we are pursued by a twist of Doc Williams' green smoke. Cul-de-sacs are dense with malign script.

TIKB. FUCK YOU. DHKP.
NOSTALGIA/IS/A/WEAPON.

SUPPORT THE PEOPLE'S WAR IN PERU (RC MAOISTS).

IMHOTEP, a Black Man, was a multi-talented genius
of ancient Africa.
MALCOLM X ON REVOLUTION

Death to the
Islamic Republic
of Iran!

NIGGARS RULE
THE World
Lady Sweetness

The occult configuration of the borough of Hackney is confirmed by an encased streetplan (one of Patrick Wright's numinous foci), a wayside shrine that has presumably failed to pay its electricity bill and had the power cut off. The map has been reversed, you'd have to stand on your head to orientate yourself. It's a Sufi meditational device that has fallen into disuse. The faster we walk past these things, the more ground we lose. There's nothing tangible for Marc to photograph; lifting his camera would be like trying to stuff fog into a bottle.

At the next turning on the road north is a young man with a barrow of paperbacks, trying to make a go of an all-weather bibliothèque. The broken leg doesn't help. He keeps his back to the wall, fending off the advances of deranged strollers who treat him as an unsalaried social worker or lay psychiatrist. (He *can't* walk away. He can't even hop into the caff without risking his stock.) He is forced to share the responsibility for adult literacy in the area with the Oxfam superstore and other less reliable charity bunkers. (It would be a charity to take anything away from them.)

17

The barrow is a canvas-covered cousin to the book vans that still ply their trade in remote rural areas. You can't be too elitist about the stock. Take what you can find and be grateful for it. Like one of the mobile libraries, the barrow is carefully, not to say obsessively, arranged in sections: science fiction/horror (no real distinction there), crime, posh Penguins, romance and her lightly-salted sister, pornography. It does what it can, this overstacked book tumbrel, to compete with the "open field" semiological excesses on the wall, which looms behind the barrow like the back projection of a middle period Godard film. The stock is unashamedly populist, but not quite popular. The hawker spends more time chatting, or struggling with his thermos, than he does putting coins in his pouch. His barrow is more of a museum than a shop; the units don't turn over, they remain on display. I toyed with a copy of Barnet Litvinoff's *The Burning Bush (Antisemitism and World History)* which had hung around at a fiver through spring and summer and well into autumn. Finally, I cracked. I had it in mind to write something about Barnet's less reputable half-brother, David, the much-mythologised lowlife conduit for the Nicolas Roeg/Donald Cammell film *Peformance*. *The Burning Bush* is an atypical sample of the bookman's wares (a ghost from an earlier era, when most of the broken private libraries of Hackney were Jewish – leftist, rabbinical, and in the original Middle and Eastern European languages). Hardbacks are barely tolerated on the stall, often kept in sealed plastic envelopes. They tend towards Book Club reprints of marketable crime and horror pros (I did once buck the trend by coming away with a fine first edition of *The Shining* by Stephen King); movie star memorabilia, militaria (especially Nazi), true crime photo shockers, and transatlantic fiction deemed too obscure to be worth remaindering. It's very unlikely that *Lights Out* will put itself around enough to claim a perch on the stall. Neither will any of the desktop pamphlets of modernist poetry that circulate entirely in *samizdat* form, unmolested by reviewers, unknown to bookshops (outside Camden Town). No place on the barrow for the disadvantaged, anything without a square spine is barred.

A nice sample of this postal art, Peter Riley's *Royal Signals* (Cheltenham, 1995), landed on the doormat to provide a welcome diversion from my laboured remembrance of the Kingsland High Street bookstall. In this slender composition, which I recommend, the poet tactfully edits the diary jottings of his father's North African campaign: an unexpected and effective collaboration.

Tent peppered with shrapnel
then ammo dump went up
and ½ shells and shell cases dropped on us
Had to keep under all morning.

Checking frequencies now.

Poor Jock, he was a good fellow.

Indeed he was. Jock the runner, the pornbroker and hedge scholar of the Waste. Riley's poem (along with the obituary notices for George Jeffery of Farringdon Road, received in the same post) put an elegiac bite into my musings on the vanished street-traders. George was the governor, the last of the line. There's no need to dwell on the legendary achievements of the ex-paratrooper with a fondness for recuperative breaks in Florida or the Channel Islands; it has all been spelled out in the *Guardian* and *The Times*. George was a time surfer: in his barber's blue jacket and his Three Stooges' tonsure, he oversaw the transfer of coded documents from the nineteenth century to the gutters of Camberwell. Forgeries that launched the Brotherhood of the Golden Dawn. Masonic passports. Maps of undiscovered islands. Pseudonymous novels by untraceable authors that inspired, in their turn, even more labyrinthine fictions. The mob waiting for George to unveil his first board would gossip, feed rumours, infect an entire underworld of book scouts, trash fetishists, bounty hunters. Here might be found the skeletal and preternaturally bright-eyed Martin Stone; the Corvine pedagogue Donald Weeks, who knew more about Frederick Rolfe than anyone alive or dead (including the man himself); the science fiction and fantasy encyclopaedist John Clute – a pundit who virtually invented his own field of studies (and amassed an important 20,000 volume collection in the process). And also less public eccentrics who peddled to the stall every day of their lives, gladly abdicating all other human possibilities in the quest for the cabbala of the unobtainable.

George Jeffery's chain of stalls, inherited from his father and his grandfather, was in recent times increasingly hemmed in by building work and the press of traffic, bottlenecking back from the plastic cones of the City's ring of steel. George's cash business, which belonged historically in the shadow of the dome of St Paul's, was marginalised out of existence. He had the luck, or more probably the good taste, to die at the right time. To take the whole magical enterprise with him.

I like to imagine a Viking funeral: George laid out on the barrow on a cushion of Saturday-special books, a comfortably-fleshed mound beneath the roped tarpaulin. At a signal from his son or daughter, the biblio-cannibals would be let loose, elbowing, scratching and spitting, forced to devour the great procurer, down to the last knuckle and curl. They should carry him away in their distended bellies to the obscure rooms where they have stashed their dusty treasures. George had, over the years, dispersed acres of country house libraries, Bottomley'd institutions: remorseless tides of salvage. Rare Victorian pamphlets, plump Edwardian bindings, railway fiction – he graded the lot, hemp sack or auction table. He kept the culture of print in flow. He served it like a pest controller, a water bailiff. Perched above the Fleet ditch, he shovelled the failed remnants, the picked-over dross, into the corporation's dustcarts. These Farringdon Road barrows were the court of final appeal. After the frantic ceremonies of the predators there was extinction.

But George Jeffery had his pilot fish, lesser figures creeping in from outlying districts of the city, to recirculate the scraps. Which brings us back to the Dalston bookman, Jock. There's a moody photograph by Cyril Arapoff (collected in the booklet, *London in the Thirties*; Nishen, 1988) that perfectly captures the atmosphere of the Caledonian Market in 1935. This is a visualised fragment of the Arcadia that still haunted Jock: alps of books, mountain ranges thrown across the old cattle yards. Pipe smokers content merely to contemplate the spilled plunder, treating the conical heaps like a visionary landscape. Scavengers icepicking a path towards some mouth-watering desideratum. The books were so much opencast slag, insultingly priced, happy to rot amongst the spoons and rags and horse manure. Jock was spoilt for plunder. He could scarcely summon the enthusiasm to wrestle with another elephant folio, parcel up a raft of colour plates, give shelf space to a conspiracy of three-deckers. "You wouldn't believe what was there. You'd weep if I told you."

His practical erudition, which was genuine and broad ranging, had been beaten into him with a tawse. He was happy to make an early escape from the old country, while continuing to hymn the brutalities that cursed him with book knowledge. Unlettered, he might have been in clover – a butcher or a car mechanic. Instead of this eternal journeying after texts which would never be investigated beyond the title-page. He had survived sixty years on the streets. "We're both foreigners here," he used to tell me. "It'll never change, no matter how long we stick it out." Aboriginal Cockneys were an inferior species, he'd never persuade them to anything better than tits and tommy guns. Let them call him "Jock" if they wanted to, his other names had disappeared with his birth certificate.

In the war years and just after, he made a decent living, so he said, taking a loaded taxi a couple of hundred yards from the trays of Foyle's Bookshop (which were replenished on a daily basis) to the indifferent antiquarians of Cecil Court. He shifted Poetry London publications by the tea-chest. Lucian Freud and Graham Sutherland lithographs.

In later days, George Jeffery became his most reliable source of supply. (Like George he haunted the Cheshire Street market on Sunday mornings. They would pass each other with an almost imperceptible Masonic nod, a cough of acknowledgement, or a signal to indicate that something rare and strange was reserved under the table. George, in civvies, made a leisured progress, sauntering through, picking up his fruit and veg, disdainfully examining proffered bindings, anything "old"; while Jock, who had a stall to run, soaked up congeries of paperbacks. Which I happily drudged for him, being granted a preview of the items that I would soon be polishing for display in Camden Passage. The hierarchy was safely in place: the psychogeography of retail. The same books might be found in any quarter of the town, only the prices changed with the zones. In Cheshire Street I made my William Harvey discovery about the circulation of stock, like heavy oil between the gates of the heart. And it was during these early walks, before the market was in spate, burdened with carrier bags of unsorted pb dreck, that I received the benefit of Jock's philosophy, a blend of David Hume and Frank Harris. Empirical exaggeration.)

Jock the Bookman was the direct precursor of the young contemporary with his stall on Kingsland High Street. But Jock's operation was more complex, both in terms of territory and of stock. On Sundays, Cheshire Street – alongside the caves of exotic animals in the railway arches; on Saturdays, Kingsland Road; and the rest of the week in Hoxton. He never engaged in the Saturday scrum at Farringdon Road, opting instead to take a leisurely and scenic 243 bus ride on all the other days, arriving in time for the exchange of gossip that preceded the eleven o'clock unveiling. He raked over the floor of rejects, the grievously harmed veterans, the optimistically described "reading copies"; prepared to embark on a rescue operation. George's dross represented the cream of Jock's stock, the posh stuff that could be displayed in an orange crate at the back of his stall on the Waste.

Picking out the splinters and razoring off the sticky price tickets, I upgraded first editions of James Joyce, Wyndham Lewis, WB Yeats (and lesser figures such as William Gerhardi, Gilbert Cannan and S. Baring-Gould): their achievements rapidly summarised by Jock as he engraved their present value with a fierce biro.

Jock enjoyed the patronage of a smaller and less psychotic bunch than the headbangers of the Farringdon Road circle. It was here that I came into competition with the late Peter Fuller, the essayist and art magnate, who was then enduring his grubbing-at-the-fringes boho period – a transitional stage between Bergerite Marxism and full-blown sunset Romanticism. (In one of our last head-to-heads, he advised me in that slightly sneering glove puppet voice to sink my entire wedge in Ruskin.) Fuller's take on Jock, a throwaway in his Dalston confessional, *Marches Past* (1986), was brutally dismissive. He sketched him as a lowrent pornographer. Which was both unobservant and unfair. Jock's living, its true, came from filth – more beaver than the Yukon, monochrome spankers creaking like pack ice, dog-love that would never win a certificate of approval from the RSPCA, as well as mundane periodicals that were safe to display out-front for a loyal one-handed readership. He did what he had to, so that he could pass himself off as a bibliophile, a conservationist of language. Jock was the only bookman in the whole strip between Shoreditch and Stamford Hill who *knowingly* retrieved vanished gems from the library of the lost. And who placed them where they would be best appreciated. For every book there was an ideal reader. I remained on nodding terms with the others, the modest shufflers who carried away their little brown parcels – secret scholars, incubators of fantastical projects.

Jock's juveniles, an ageing Fagin school of likely lads, took care of the physical work, the graft: dragging the stall on to the pitch, humping the crates, weighing the carrier bags of exhausted trade-ins – the castoff partners whose extravagant abandon no longer tickled the itch. Jock himself would have the final arbitration, converting smeared mistresses into future credits. The sex fiends never appealed his decision. They knew that it was as futile as asking George Jeffery for a discount. (George would look hard at the volume in question, then tear it, slowly and deliberately, into small pieces, before turning back to the serious punters.)

The lads could read a price ticket, but that was the end of it. They enjoyed a day out; made a few quid, great crack with their mates, product to take home. The business barely survived Jock's death. There was some haggling over his inheritance, and then, one by one, they dropped out. They weren't cursed with the obsession: books as objects, books as icons, books as a form of race memory.

It's entirely possible that I'm underdescribing Peter Fuller as thoroughly as Fuller patronised Jock. (The artist Ian Brightwell told me recently that Fuller was fond of a flutter and used to make a few bob turning in lively reports on boxing matches.) Who knows? I should have been able to overcome a prejudice against that customised drabness, the scurfy gymshoes and elastoplast spectacles that bore too close a resemblance to the charity shop uniform of the official chapter of the Camden Town bicycle mafia, the out-patients – who soured the street level booktrade for a generation by their adenoidal whining, their bleating about prices, their determination to break the elegance of the chain, to beat Jock to his sources. Dole bandits of the worst kind. Grant aid capitalists. Buddhist bully boys. You couldn't buy an Ace-Double from them without filling in a form in triplicate and listening to the lecture on Thoreau. This level of bitterness is corrosive. The books are a penance that customers have to undergo in recompense for all those unpublished poems on the walls of the office.

Perhaps Fuller merely looked the part, as he squirrelled away his cache of blue Penguins. Perhaps it was an ironic disguise. And Graham Road, Dalston, a convenience address, a stopover with grubby authenticity. A bolthole in which to plan the reinterpretation of the culture. Fuller was to emerge from his exile, debunking modernist heresies, the follies and excesses he had once championed. He would extol the spiritual virtues of epic Suffolk skies, motoring eastwards to apotheosize flint churches and English craftsmen. He would lead Sister Wendy Beckett from her caravan. He would found *Modern Painters* and an effective critical/commercial nexus, broad enough to include David Bowie, Howard Jacobson, William Boyd, AS Byatt, Grey Gowrie *and* Patrick Wright.

Abney Park was still waiting. I held back from the book barrow and dutifully copied the Boleyn Road graffiti into my Europa notepad. Then we legged it.

Stoke Newington Road stretches onwards like the rubber neck of a chicken. We drift past exotic minimarts, deleted cinemas, tributary nameplates with literary associations. The Hasidic foothills have always been disputed land: Jews escaping from Whitechapel sweatshops, early West Indian immigrants (as depicted in Alexander Baron's novel, *The*

Lowlife). Baron, troubled after the war, wandered the borough like a fetch: watching, listening, hungry for the clues that would allow him to reorientate himself. He returned to his mother's house in Hackney needing a safe place in which to heal the trauma of combat, familiar territory he no longer recognised (like the Neo-Romantic account of Mare Street produced by John Minton for the dustwrapper of Roland Camberton's *Rain on the Pavements*). Baron found himself criss-crossing the East End in a series of mazy traverses, eavesdropping on conversations in cafés, reading the reflections in the windows of tailor-shops. A landscape that had not yet been optioned: bomb-damaged terraces, wilderness gardens, green shoots amongst the rubble.

From the City, From the Plough, Baron's first novel, was published by Jonathan Cape in 1948. It was a success of a kind that is no longer imaginable; numerous impressions in hardback and paperback. Baron, a modest man, was inveigled into attending a celebratory party in Bedford Square. He took the bus from Dalston Junction, had a few solitary whiskys in an anonymous pub to steady his nerves, looked up at the lighted room, the buzz; turned on his heel, went home.

The Lowlife came at the other end of Baron's career, in 1963, a few years before he slipped gracefully out of print with *Franco's Dying*, to become one of the "reforgotten". *The Lowlife* featured Harryboy Boas, a Hofmann presser who works only as much as he has to, a gambler with an even more destructive addiction – the love of literature. Harryboy, true to genre (true to *Night and the City*, *The Small World of Sammy Lee*, *Killing of a Chinese Bookie*), keeps on the move, cheating fate, ducking and diving, a post-existential loser. He's pursued by a diminutive strong-arm man in a cylindrical coat, a literal torpedo. Flush, he makes expeditions to Soho for fat Italian meals, cigars, women – and secondhand bookshops. Then he hides out, stays in bed working his way through yards of Zola. ("I knew what my programme was going to be for the next few weeks. I can go off on a jag with books like some people do with liquor. Weeks at a time.") Stoke Newington is the perfect location in which to stay lost: limboland, London's Interzone. Large shabby properties that ask no questions. Internal exile with a phoney rent-book. Stoke Newington is the place where terrorists behave like unpublished poets, and poets cultivate a justified paranoia. Drinking clubs, spielers, anarchist pubs: they cluster around the nick with the worst reputation in North London. A permanent, on-going, death in custody protest.

FREEDOM
TO
DURSUN KARATAS

Hammer and sickle imposed on star. Karatas cartoon with raised fist in universal salute. Neat black stencil on blue hoarding. Graphic art with a budget. Karatas, the Dev/Sol figurehead, arrested in Paris. The most extreme of the leftist groupings; assassinations, militant action. Backing, apparently, from drug traffickers. An uncomic strip running north: the balding, moustached activist winning the war of the fences. An elegant, hard-edged gallery of the streets. Broad band of sky blue, narrow band of inky blue, broad band of scarlet. The aesthetics of provocation.

Collectable posters. **Qampanya Serkeftine**. Printed in the Kurdish colours – red, green, yellow; crowds and leaders making the shape of the mythical homeland. Suns and flags. Creased where the paste doesn't grip on plywood.

Sanctuary
ONE FLEW OVER THE CUCKOO'S NEST

By now we're cruising past the accommodation address (Box 15, 138 Kingsland High Street, London E8 2NS) of that mysterious and fugitive publication, the *Newsletter* of the London Psychogeographical Association ("35 Years of Non-Existence"). This anonymous, unsponsored, irregular, single-sheet squib is probably the most useful of all London's neighbourhood tabloids. And certainly the most entertaining. It has no fixed cover price and no distribution. If you need it, it finds you. It writes itself. It invents the rumours that it purports to discover. The deranged geniality of its prose offers the only accurate temperature chart of the city's fevers: reality as an infinitely accommodating substance. A fictional documentary, a retrospective prophecy. The *Newsletter* is unembarrassed by the knowledge that news is whatever you want to make it. News has no present tense. It's dead when you read it. Much better to trust fantasies that become fact through the sheer energy of the prose.

SMASH THE OCCULT ESTABLISHMENT (May 10th, National Maritime Museum, Greenwich). *The Queen and*

Baron Greenwich (aka Prince Philip) will be making a ritual visit to a site of key masonic importance – the Queen Anne House, Greenwich. The Royal Greenwich Observatory have published their expectation for an annular eclipse on this day . . . **PSYCHIC WAR in the East End** . . . **What are Ley Lines?** . . . **St. Anne's rededicated by former Gresham Professor.** *St. Anne's, Limehouse was recently rededicated after having over £1m spent on restoring the exterior. Eric Sorensen, chief executive of the London Docklands Development Corporation attended the ceremony at a key site on the leyline* . . . **NAZI OCCULTISTS SEIZE OMPHALOS** . . . *The election of Derek Beackon as a Councillor on the Isle of Dogs caused shocked outrage across the Establishment. Beackon is a dedicated Nazi occultist. He graduated to the British Nationalist Party after serving his apprenticeship in the British Movement. Beackon is an adept of Enochian magic. Devised in the sixteenth centuy by John Dee, it was the magical system which laid the basis for the conjuring up of the Brtish Empire.*

The matter of London, the refleshing of Lud's withered hide, is exposed by doctored maps, speculative alignments, black propaganda. The revenge of the disenfranchised. Improvisations on history that are capable of making adjustments in present time. Prophecy as news. News as the purest form of fiction. Subversion in splash headlines. The most corrupt of all forms, the tabloid, can be "turned". The psychogeographers are operating an equivalent of James Ellroy's novel *American Tabloid*, freebasing among archetypes and video clips, speeding through the image bank. A paranoid poetic whose lies are so spectacular that they have become a new form of truth. The Kennedys, Dean Martin, Onassis, Sam Giancana, Santo Trafficante, Marilyn Monroe: blood and sperm and money. Retouched colour spreads. Studio PR. Fixes. Bribes. Stone-crazy investigators who, after quarter of a century studying the same Jack Ruby hit photograph, find an earlier version of themselves standing next to John Peel in the background.

The past is fluid, a black swamp; dip for whatever you need. Stepping off the main road at this point lands you right in it: the psychogeographical badlands. Secret cells of counter-terror scribblers, dole bandits sub-editing propositions too manic for even the *Sun* to contemplate. This is where the Invisibles go to ground. Amhurst Road: a bent diagonal running south-east, one side of a dangerous triangle. The sloped back of a praying man, a homage to Nicolas Poussin. Stoke

Newington Road/Amhurst Road/Dalston Lane: enclosing, sealing off, the perceived drug frontline of Sandringham Road (twists of silver paper trodden into the cracks of the paving stones, the tesserae of the underclass); enclosing nests of poets (the Hackney ward that is forever Cambridge), avant-garde musicians, rogue cadres refining their rage, displaced Kurdish mountain restaurants.

Back in the Sixties, the area was asleep; plenty of reasonably priced accommodation available in large family houses, now split into separate flats and garrets and dark basements. It was from Amhurst Road that the poet Tom Raworth operated his revolutionary Matrix Press (later to become the Goliard Press, then Cape Goliard). The press was revolutionary in terms of its quality, its quick witted intelligence, the unfussy but enticing look of the thing. ("There were no mad men now on the streets, the harmless ones that would walk down the middle of the road, their hair long . . . We were living in Amhurst Road, Hackney. On the way back I passed a policeman on a grey horse . . Piero arrived first, a wilting sprig of marijuana in his lapel." *A Serial Biography*, 1969.)

Professor Eric Mottram told me that he visited Raworth around this time, or a little later, he couldn't remember where (North London, Finchley, Cricklewood?), and was amazed to discover a room filled with hooky electrical produce, cookers, fridges, hairdryers. All the elements of an abandoned, or yet to be composed, surrealist poem. Like a poet walled in by the objects of his imagination.

Also in Amhurst Road (at number 359) were another group, or temporary alliance, with Cambridge/Essex connections and a genuine interest in exploring the possibilities of kitchen-table publishing: John Barker, Hilary Creek, Anna Mendelson, Jim Greenfield, supposed members of the Angry Brigade. Their arrest and trial inspired many miles of precisely lettered graffiti – FREE JAKE PRESCOTT/WHOSE CONSPIRACY – that was to hang around for years (though not, obviously, the example on the side of the Old Bailey). Calligraphy of this quality betrayed a background in higher eduction, quality time in teaching practice. Work that the cuts in university budgets have ensured we will never see again. The communiqués produced on a John Bull printing set for the Angry Brigade's Moonlighters' Cell were, according to Gordon Carr (*The Angry Brigade, The Cause and the Case*, 1975), duplicated at Amhurst Road and composed, at least in part, by Anna Mendelson. Some of these texts, arranged in broken lines, read like rehearsals for the suppressed urban poetry of the Thatcher years. Communiqué 9 accompanied an attempt to destroy the police computer at Tintagel House, just across the river from the Tate Gallery.

> *secret files in the universities*
> *the census at home*
> *social security files*
> *computers*
> *TV*
> *Giro*
> *passports*
> *work permits*
> *insurance cards*
>
> *Bureaucracy and technology used against the people . . .*
>
> *to speed up our work*
> *to slow down our minds and actions*
> *to obliterate the truth.*

The originals of these documents are presumably bagged and stored in some Secret State facility, just as the relevant "little press" magazines have been examined by Wolfgang Görtschacher at the University of Salzburg or collected by Geoffrey Soar at the Library of the University of London. This material is of enormous interest to wealthy nostalgics (those who *were* there and can't remember, and those who like to play dangerously in retrospect). Counter-culture ephemera, throwaways, psychedelic posters, the "School Kids" issue of *Oz*, the Burroughs toy in *IT*, *Sigma* papers, situationist durables: all have their price-tag, their accountants and their archivists. Mimeo'd single issue chapbooks of free verse, or anarchist bulletins, they are fused in second generation melt-down. The hybrid form prophetically alludes to the coming state of English poetry, when the technical language of psychoanalysis and political rhetoric (plus Walter Benjamin and Theodor Adorno) would respond to the crisis in our cultural and social lives by striking a spectacular treaty with the imperatives of the gutter. So selfless and communally based was the spirit of this poetic that it was universally denounced as elitist and resistant to ordinary intelligence.

The Angry Brigade communiques were the only small-press publications to be thoroughly reviewed and debated in the nationals (author photos, long-lens snatches, reproductions of holograph letters). **DEAR BOSS**. It was like a replay of the Jack the Ripper frenzy. Stoke

Newington, like Whitechapel of the 1880s, became fixed at a particular point in time. Subsequent accounts would have to refer back to this burnout of flash-bulbs, doorstep excitement.

But the distortions of popular journalism are such that it's impossible to develop any sense of what the Amhurst Road group were really on about. Mendelson, it now appears, was essentially a writer, a poet. The further events moved away from language, the more obtuse and fragmented they became. The rhetoric betrayed itself in its attempt to strike a univeral tone, to speak for the disadvantaged masses. Private confusions mistook acts of public drama for insights and metaphors that should always insist on remaining theoretical. In other words, at that particular instant, the poetry wasn't good enough, true enough to its own difficulties. It solicited destruction.

Mendelson's subsequent reinvention as the singular and distinguished poet/artist, Grace Lake, is perhaps a revelation of the nature of her political acts. *This* is what was always true, the courage of her attack, the intelligence operating with and through stress: the achievement in her transcribed internal monologues. Hemingway justified at last, in the most unexpected place. "Grace under pressure." The rest, the tabloid stuff, was an accidental apprenticeship.

Stewart Home, "Neoist" or anti-Neoist, art guerrilla, is a marvellously untrustworthy (by intent) historian of this Interzone. His novel *Red London* (1994) documents, through programmatic fiction, the schisms, plots, affrays of anarcho-Buddhist-sex deviant street life. The large and unrestored pubs of Stoke Newington providing R & R for thirsty cells of Class Warriors. (Home, it must be admitted, is a prime suspect as second leader writer and provider of squibs for the Psychogeographical *Newsletter*.) Home's shtick is alternate history, subverting myths to rewire received accounts of who was there and what they did. ("Situated as it was on Stoke Newington High Street, the pub attracted the more presentable elements from among the Hackney anarchist community. While the punk-hippy-squatter axis would frequent less reputable establishments, members of the Class Justice Federation and all manner of syndicalists, bakuninists and impossibilists were to be found in the Tanners.")

Stewart was the man who would have picked up whispers about the present careers of the ex-Angrys. (If he didn't, he'd fake it.) He'd heard (he broke off from his longterm investigation of prolific novelist/historian, Andrew Sinclair, to tell me) that several of the males were now operating as writers, novelists, pulp fiction journeymen. It was just as I had suspected: the era of the small time dope-dealer, the used-book buff, was over. Survivalism and subversion had palled up with trash literature.

Thinking about the conjunctions of Amhurst Road, I recalled my first sighting of the magnificent Egyptian gates of Abney Park Cemetery – built under advice from Joseph Bonomi Jnr, the "great expert on symbolic decoration and hieroglyphics". Bonomi, who never practised as an architect, became the curator of the Soane Museum in Lincoln's Inn Fields. Another of those secret lives whose purpose and meaning seem to reside in their ability to encode some prescription, or unnoticed text, into the surviving architecture of the city. Agents who work outside time. According to Paul Joyce (*A Guide to Abney Park Cemetery*, 1984), Bonomi "contributed designs for the winged orbs emblematic of eternal life as well as their attendant hieroglyphic legends which translate as *The Gates of the Abode of the Mortal Part of Man*."

There was no time then, on that afternoon in the early Seventies, to make a leisured examination of the gates, or to stroll through the cemetery. I'd been invited to meet a couple of very jumpy fringe members of the Angry Brigade network who were hiding out, in quite an airy and well-sanded, pine floor fashion, in Cazenove Road. The man, it was understood, might want to liaise over the possibility of our shooting some 8mm footage of the Ron Bailey Redbridge squat. We went through all the paranoid interrogative, rambling cross-purpose chat – and later did the filming on outdated stock that made Redbridge look like downtown Bucharest. But what struck me most was the Habitat domesticity, polished mugs on hooks, cut flowers in jars, that went alongside the need to continually check out the cars parked in the street. A twitchy net curtain syndrome that would not have been out of place in Carshalton or Purley.

Kynaston Avenue, N. 16. Out with the notebook.

LADY

POSITIVE

IS A

UGLY MOTHER.

BAW SQUATING. FUCK YOUR EVICTION. **SHELTER is a basic human need – dont ban squatting. STOKE NEWINGTON GRAVEYARD 1st October.**

Now we must move, keep pace with the pull of the graveyard. The margins, the walls of alleys, the doorways of inactive commercial concerns, carry invitations. Abney Park outflow. Broken texts washed free from their headstones. Erased letters forming a new language.

ECO TEN   HAT

OEVE   BELLE

I   OULD NO   PB

Dates and times of assignations that will never be kept. Cruisers, sex vampires, occult geometers. You don't have to walk, you can slipstream. One of the expeditions in Patrick Keiller's film, *London*, took this route. Of course it did. Where else? The intention, to pay their respects to Edgar Allan Poe's boarding school, to the doppelgänger William Wilson, had been aborted. No visible trace remains, nothing you can catch on film. ("Let me call myself, *for the present*, William Wilson . . . I feel the refreshing chilliness of its deeply-shadowed avenues, inhale the fragrance of its thousand shrubberies, and thrill anew with indefinable delight at the deep hollow note of the church-bell . . .") Keiller's character, Robinson, settled instead for traces of Daniel Defoe, dissenter, double agent, eyewitness to events that had passed him by. Stoke Newington: the extramural settlement of Crusoe exile; a village where failure could be enjoyed in the grand style.

The glass-fronted police station is designed, head on, to present the illusion of openness, access for all. There are huts and cabins tucked around the back to take care of the everyday stuff, armed juveniles, purse-snatchers. Cautions are administered as casually as enquiries about the weather. The building is no more than an advertisement for itself, the new look doing nothing to eradicate the evil reputation that has hung over the place for generations. The photographs of the old brick hulk that stood in for any hard information about the arrest of the Angry Brigade still infect the ground. Pedestrians cross the road, fearful of searching in vain for reflections in the darkened glass.

There is a traditionalist Afrikaner aspect to the layout of the cells and staircases: they seem to invoke on sight an inclination towards suicide. Victim posters and announcements of protest rallies are always there on the street. Only the names change. The rumours multiply, heated by conspiratorial drinking sessions in the anarchist pubs, by disaffected informers, speed freaks; off-duty CID mythologists, addicted to fiction, denounce themselves to local press stringers, for the glory of seeing their names in print. Insider dealing in the drug squad.

Investigations permanently pending. Bad scripts for TV fillers: silhouette interviews, blood-red brakelights in a longfocus orange nightscape, talking heads disintegrating on impact.

The streets around the cemetery are orderly extensions of the necropolis culture. Muslin shaded windows. Avenues that stay shtum, that look the other way. Pre-dead. Victorian speculations that are of great interest to the archivists of the Hackney Society. These local-history buffs are keen to demonstrate that Hackney has a pedigree, something other than the mess of the present. If there has to be a human form in one of their illustrations, let it be colourful, old, reverentially peering at heritage. You might find a sketch of Mr Pooter but you won't come up against a single ethnic. I take a furtive interest in these glossy-covered publications, this lush pornography of detail: Italianate ostentation, scrolled brackets, decorated keystones, fragments of wallpaper. A lip-smacking pathology of connoisseurship. Catalogues of perverse refinement: quoins, string-courses, swags.

Locating one of the featured houses is like rediscovering a music hall star. Take Evering Road, for example. The way it poses for the camera. Michael Hunter in *The Victorian Villas of Hackney* (1984) features the front door of No. 245: "The paired columns and foliage capitals are typical of details derived ultimately from medieval ecclesiastical architecture." Get down on your knees (as the photographer did) and the diminishing perspective of the original diamond tiles pulls you rapidly in towards the dark doorway. That's as far as you go. The lives that unfolded within the house are untouched.

The agency snap (Popperfoto) of No.71 Evering Road, reproduced in Anthony Lambrianou's *Inside the Firm (The Untold Story of the Krays' Reign of Terror)*, is of a very different quality. It stands well back, spurning architecural refinement. It doesn't crop out the scrubby garden, the dingy basement window. It's a mugshot, not a portrait. The house itself is of no consequence, a drab disguise for the events that took place in Blonde Carol's basement on the night of October 28, 1967, when Jack "The Hat" McVitie was killed. Albums of photographs won't clarify the conflicting accounts of that grand guignol party. McVitie was a pill-popper, wild card, underdressed villain with an enviable reputation as a gilt-edged irritant. A sartorial disaster, he gave the faces of the Sixties (hoping for the call from David Bailey) a bad name. Barbers would go out of business waiting to give Jack a bit of style. His death, if it did nothing else, fixed Evering Road on the murder map of London. Lines of pain spread out from the black hole of that basement. The route his body travelled became a mantra, a reverse pilgrimage: Lower Clapton Road, Narrow Way, Mare Street, Cambridge Heath Road, Commercial Road, Blackwall Tunnel. A burial that was never recorded, the wrong side of the river.

Through those Egyptian pylons and inside the cemetery walls, Poe's wilderness of oak and chestnut, swamp cypress, thistle, Japanese knotweed, has been fiercely hacked back by community miscreants. An evident passion to reveal the paths, catalogue the broken statues. The sun low behind the trees; Marc Atkins framing the odd conjunction of stone and weed with no real enthusiasm. He's confused: is this our starting point or is it the finish? It's been too easy so far, no blisters, no insights. Abney Park has been demystified, it has lost its patina of obscurity. The locations and achievements can all be checked in the book: William Booth the Salvationist (Cyclorama photograph of his funeral, the crowds blocking the High Street, packed in their thousands up Stamford Hill); Frank Bostock, zoo-keeper, imprisoned beneath a sleeping marble lion; Edward Calvert, disciple of Blake, associate of Samuel Palmer, much of whose life was spent "in obscurity in Dalston and Hackney"; Thomas Canry Caulker, son of Canrah Bah Caulker, King of Bompey in Western Africa; Joseph Conder, bookseller, poet and author; William Hone, bookseller, prosecuted for blasphemy; Enoch Bassett Keeling, architect, surveyor and speculator who is "remembered for his series of extraordinary churches . . . in a wildly vigorous version of High Victorian gothic." He died of drink, his churches have all vanished or been "seriously mutilated". George Leybourne – alias "Champagne Charlie"; James Bronterre O'Brien, political activist, Chartist, imprisoned for "seditious speaking"; Henry Valentine Orfeur, lost with all his crew when the schooner *Invoice* went down in the Bristol Channel. A scuptural relief of the storm-tossed vessel: "The Sea Shall Give Up Its Dead". Evelyn Pyle, the last of the great horticultural family; Samuel Sharpe, banker and Egyptologist; Sir Edward Sievking, physician extraordinary to the Prince of Wales, afterwards King Edward VII. Author of medical works and water-colour illustrator of anatomical figures. John Swan, originator of the steamship's screw propeller and the self-acting chain messenger; William Tyler, police constable, shot by Latvian anarchists of the "Flame" group in Tottenham on 23 January 1909; Henry Vincent, political agitator, the "Demosthenes" of the Chartist movement; Rev. Dr Isaac Watts, poet, hymnist and moral philosopher.

We plod towards the chapel, its spire our compass bearing. Sinister drifters agitate the undergrowth. Sepulchres divested of their vegetation are targets for spraycans and felt-tip pens. WHO EVEN LOOK/AT THIS YOU MANS/A BAD FUCKING, COCK SUCKING/DOING RUIPPER ALRIGHT. "**WEED IT A HERB**" by Bob Marley. ROULES. **1. No wyfe. 2. No hotrse. 3. No mustashe.** ALL **hail** DISCORDIVC! Smell like old hay. Like a skinner's yard. A pit of rags and dead pigeons. Rubble and fire traces inside the unrestored body of the chapel.

While Marc climbs on the dead bones to find a good angle, to catch the green rays of the dying sun, I wander aimlessly around the back of the building. A window sealed with corrugated iron sheeting. In blue paint: the eye within the triangle. Pinkish white lettering spells out the obvious, that which does not need to be spoken: DOG. It had always been the architect William Hosking's intention that this should be an interdenominational chapel, a single "cell" betraying no bias towards any of the Christian sects who would use it. But this Special Brew occultism was pushing it, mocking the heritage of an antiquarian who had been invited to take part in the restoration of St. Mary Redcliffe in Bristol, and who shared with Joseph Bonomi a particular interest in the arcane Egyptology of the cemetery entrance.

We had brought ourselves to the heart of it, the vandalised chapel in the woods, and we were confronted by just the reversal we deserved. DOG. The word twisted our expedition back to its source. It established this site as the **X**, the given, the point from which the true walk would begin.

I call Marc over. The eye within the blue triangle is unstable (the eye of the window blinded by corrugated sheeting). Triangles multiply. I think immediately of the gilded triangle imposed over a circle of gold on the lefthand panel behind the altar at the east end of Christ Church, Spitalfields. The Christ Church triangle is a brand of liquid fire (you can see the red beneath the gold where the paint has flaked) imposed on a white, pupilless eye. It floats above an iconographically complex weave of studded flowerheads, chains of roots and branches. Responding to the camera's flash, it shines. It gleams out of articulate darkness.

Marc composes his black and white account. I snap a colour record. The pinkish white DOG. The triangle of concentration. A sense of this and of all the other triangulations of the city: Blake, Bunyan, Defoe, the dissenting monuments in Bunhill Fields. Everything I believe in, everything London can do to you, starts there. The theatre of obelisks and pyramids, signs, symbols, prompts, whispers. The lovely lies that take you out into the light. That bless each and every pilgrimage.

The v of our walk is no longer an open-ended proposition. The v is sealed. It has become a triangle. And the unblinking blue eye is the eye of the camera.

WALKING THE V. ALBION DRIVE E8 TO THE UNIVERSITY OF GREENWICH. TO CLAREMONT ROAD.

25/10/94.

Pyschic landscaping, drifting and free-association . . . he seemed to be attempting to travel through time.
PATRICK KEILLER, *LONDON*

Usual first light start; grey skies, the lid on our prospects. Useless for photography. Like wading through a fog of developing fluid. Ghost imagery without a border. Persistent slanting rain nibbling away at the white stone plaque set into the wall where Albion Drive is split by Queensbridge Road. **1893 HACKNEY/BOUNDARY/IF 41 SOUTH.**

Ballpoint scratches through damp blotting-paper of notebook. Inscription dissolves. I know these days: long and wet. "Soft" they call them. Like Dublin. In off the sea. I'm dressed to accommodate it: tweed cap, long green coat. Anti-sign weather. Weather set to erase all codes. All you want is to keep going, head down, get it done.

"They" (the ones who put up noticeboards to advertise their conspicuous interventions in the name of community) have recently been carrying out a purge of all the local sites that could be useful to free-lancers, aerosol bandits, copywriters of the unconscious. The Black Bull pub on the corner of the shopping precinct (always referred to as "The Triangle") was a prime target. The Bull, an unpretentious Truman's saloon, was a favourite drinker for Jack McVitie. (The Mildmay Tavern was another: roomy, no airs and graces, lively after-noon clientele, several exits to the street.) Jack shot up the bar once, when the horses weren't running to form, and the guv'nor was reluctant to serve him. "The Hat" was, as Tony Lambrianou says, "a sociable man", but he liked to expel his grievances before they turned sour. The Bull was a convenient meet for Tony and Jack, a stroll from Belford

House; hardly worth getting the motor out. It was a place where they could drink without front. Where Jack's sartorial shortcomings needn't be a peer group embarrassment.

When the whole area went down the khazi, they closed the Bull – pending redevelopment. Squatters moved in. It was a high renaissance for muralists, coiners of bold-type aphorisms. The Bull saw more action on its boarded-up windows than you'd find in ten years at the Whitechapel Gallery. Guys with pink mohicans, kilts worn over paint-splashed jeans, climbed out on a first floor ledge and got to work with the whitewash. Germans, Dutchmen. They brought some action to the local shops: bread, milk, cigarette papers. They were integrated into the general amnesty.

THE BLACK BULL. The gilt lettering became a unit of display, the announcement of a perpetual exhibition; a plywood screen of doodles and misinformation. An event to be grazed. The flowering that always occurs before the instant of extinction.

NO ADVERTISING. Big Brother's Advice: Consume. DECENT HOMES FOR EVERYONE. NEVER TRUST A POLITICIAN. Burn Flags Not Fags! BULLETS NOT BALLOTS. SHOOT THE RULING CLASS. A Pox Upon the Poll Tax. WHY?

The Bull was demolished, imprisoned behind green fencing. Shortly before the bulldozers moved in, a new cartoon appeared, a strange animal, a pink sketch on the blue/grey tiles. Inches from the pavement. The X-ray of a primitive horse, cave art. The spirit that manifests itself when it no longer matters. It faced west.

Cruder messages spread across the garages in the middle of the flats. FUCK OFF YOU. SOXI. ONLY WANKERS STEAL OFF OTHER WORKING CLASS PEOPLE! NF. The garages were blitzed, torn down in a day. Knots of disgruntled keyholders agitating officialdom. Entrances giving access to the shopping precinct were sealed. Control established, one path only. Drilling begins at 7 am. Helicopter overhead. The small businesses going under (bookie, grease caff, splat video survive) as the zone is gifted with a cosmetic makeover. The first act: the wiping of language from the walls.

As we slogged south/east, sticking grimly to our line, we confirmed that Victorian Hackney, patched and restored, had lost its voice. THE SHAMEFUL TRUTH OF DIRTY LONDON: the *Evening Standard*'s survey of Tidy Britain (22.2.95) "visited 14,195 sites to find out the truth about dirt." Mass Observation, Nineties style: rightwing diarists on the prowl, taking down ages and details of public school attendance. The horror exposed: Hackney was nowhere, not even in the premier league of "filthy boroughs". Our rightful position usurped by Havering, Islington, Haringay, Wandsworth, Lambeth. "People need a personal or communal ashtray", said Professor Ashworth. Hackney has lost its status as that communal ashtray. Islington is boss at graffiti and fly-posting: the Granita lefties have the self-confidence to compose, to hustle, to sign the chaos sheet.

Sad Hackney (leaving aside the heroic efforts of **TOKi** who has scrawled his way from the Waste to Mare Street) has bottled it. London Fields would have to go down on its knees to look Martin Amis in the eye. Studying the early maps, it's clear that the Fields were conceived as a jigsaw of tree-enclosed triangles – but now the dull grass is unworthy of fiction; a respectable dog toilet, a drover's patch lacking cattle. Lammas land, taken into public "custodianship" in 1872, this ex-common with its sturdy senior citizen plane trees has nothing going for it beyond its memories of use as a plague pit in 1665. Not a squiggle, not a curse; no conjuring symbols carved into the peeling bar of the still impressive avenue. Even the titular deities, a Cockney/Aztec pearly king and queen rendered in cement and multicoloured tesserae, are undefaced. Heritage populism after the heart of Raphael Samuel.

Minimal wall action outside the extant London Fields Primary School: parents exist ok. **THE DECS ARE FAB.**

I had more serious expectations for Beck Road, an artist-as-artisan terrace, famous in the supplements. We should be swimming down Hackney's cultural frontline, the epitome of the borough's claim to the highest per capita settlement of artists in Europe. I thought the street was sponsored by the beer. Washed clean by the rain, it looks like a row of commemorative labels. Like the credits for *Coronation Street*. (It has featured on TV as the scene of a bloody shoot out in *Between the Lines*; a bent cop, Secret State fantasy cobbled together by media Trots who can no longer raise the budget, or the clearance, for investigative documentaries).

Jane Gifford lived here June 1980–May 1983. One blue plaque joke. And the inevitable **CLASS WAR** decal on the side of the railway bridge. Pre-privatisation and Class War, they seem to go together: nostalgia for comfortable hierachies. The mob in the cattle cars knew where they stood.

It's terrifying to contemplate the slumbering dynamo of all this creativity, tucked behind drawn curtains (no early risers). What do they *do*, these self-confessed artists? How do they live up to it? The buggy in the hall, the street-parked heap. The bicycle on the stairs. The poster in the window. They can't all show at Flowers East. They can't all have a connection to Matt's Gallery or the Chisenhale. It must fester, boil and bite, cramp them with envy. A dim electrical impulse seems to flicker at the windows, make contact with the rain, expel us. Frauds, memory thieves. Con artists with our steamed lenses and wet pulp notebooks.

Going over, crossing into LibDem territory: Victoria Park. St Agnes' Gate and the "green lung", the idealised version, the salvation of dust-choked, slum-dwelling proles, is pictured on a board – a warning (check your flies and wash your hands before entering), a homage to the dominant ethic, the great green god. I like the park, visit it most days, circle it like a prison yard, but I'm increasingly uneasy about the way it presents itself. The park has begun to feel it is better than we are. Regimented flower beds are back. There's night security. Fences divide the park from the street.

Some vicious, antisocial element has pitched a pot of red paint across the muted park portrait (so that it looks like one of those Kurdish posters). The sticky scarlet gloss drips like a puncture wound, illicit tendrils scorning the official gold paths.

As transients (non-voters), we are here on sufferance. The park is a manifesto: life could be like this, disciplined leisure, controlled enlightenment. Uniformity, cropped grass and fresh paint on the railings. Vote for us. Give us your money. Better yet, give us *respect*. The whole country-in-town enclosure is stiff with sponsorship paybacks, boastful refurbishments, aspirations towards garden city status: the immaculate lawns that signal the rotten borough. Be wary of fountains. The frolicsome play of water outside some municipal temple is the gush of misspent public funds, dubious set-dressing. Victoria Park lake, which *was* once a lake, with boats and islands, is now the excuse for a fountain. Water foliage, tall spoutings lost in the sodality of all-over rain. The park had got above itself, this Versailles of Liberal Democracy, the *fons et origo* of the green chain, the secure paddocks (doggy exclusive) that shuttle south, alongside the Grand Union Canal, towards Limehouse Basin.

Zero graffiti. The park repels it. We keep our heads down and our hands in our pockets. We're trespassing on a canine sanctuary, ancient hunting liberties in which we are the prey. Don't expect an apology if some pooch gets its teeth into you, be thankful it's not a pit bull. Limp away before you're prosecuted for fouling the bitch's diet. (Nice old couples are the worst. They keep their beasts on extendable leads that grant them a comfortable fifty yard attack profile.)

If the live animals, the shit-machines, are bad, the divine archetypes we're supposed to worship are worse: twin white horrors, the Dogs of Alcibiades, raised on brick plinths. When they were blessedly removed, for months, my spirits surged – but, inevitably, this was no more than a truce. The frosty albinos are back, resprayed, restored (scrawny, loose fleshed, wolf-headed, genitally deprived): the gift of Lady Regnart. Posed on their red-brick chimneys, they howl in perpetual torment: as if fires had been lit beneath them.

Time to quit, to shake the raindrops from our caps, and exit through the grandiloquent boast of the Bonner Hall gates. Snatch a sentimental glimpse at the canal. Then south past the London Chest Hospital. CLOSED CIRCUIT TV IN OPERATION. Marc and I have been caught so often in our wanderings that I'm thinking of putting in an invoice. You could edit a feature-length film from these clips, our stuttering progress across town. We're perpetually hustling to stay ahead of our video ghosts. Surveillance is another form of erasure.

On the south side of Roman Road, beyond the sorry huddle of stalls, and out behind the low and middle-rise barriers of public housing, is the relic of Victoria Park Cemetery (VPC 1845), one of the most notorious bonepits of its era. They folded whole streets into the clay, stamped them down below the grassline as they were later to stack them above. Ground lucky to call itself contagious. This is where the Australian Aboriginal cricketer "King Cole" was buried, lace-lunged, and where a commemorative eucalyptus tree still struggles for life. Meath Gardens is a favourite of mine, one of the extramural city's most numinous (unvisited) locales. Rain is a given here, even when the surrounding streets are ritzed with sunlight. Trees, fat with the arguments of the dead, take on the most extraordinary shapes. They dominate otherwise undistinguished turf. They repel dogs. Silence is a specific quality; it deafens you, nourishes the imagination, irritates with a joyous madness. Talk in tongues, if you will, but keep your lips buttoned.

Showtime, Marc swabs his lens. The severe arch, the entrance to the gardens, is a whalebone collar: **NF KRAYS/Dont Fuck. NAZIS OUT.** Ronnie should have been planted here. Anonymously and in powder form. Shafted with a suitable spruce.

Under the railway bridge and follow the wall into Bancroft Road. We're soaked to the bone, shivering in our thirst for text. But Tower Hamlets stays dumb, anti-language, pro-grass. The library with its local history bias, its dusty files and boxes of documenation, is an obvious substitute for the script that has been eradicated from the streets.

In the grand entrance hall (which obviously embarrasses PC elements who have done their best to neutralise it with racks of leaflets) is a bizarre and unexpected exhibition of pebbles and broken tiles. Glass cases packed with beachcomber plunder and explanatory cards. *You never know what you might find when the tide goes out on the Thames. Walking on the foreshore, George Bradenell found three-quarters of a ton of coral. The pieces ranged from tiny fragments to 30lb. The coral originated in the Caribbean according to experts, but how it got to Wapping is a mystery.*

Outside: Indian students, arms full of books, laughing, rock a car. Queen Mary's College. BLACK & WHITE UNITE/T.U.C DEMO/19TH MARCH. **SMASH THE BNP.** Cartoon hammer and sickle. TREACLE PEOPLE.

On Mile End Road: The People's Palace. *The original People's Palace, built between 1887–1892, provided facilities for recreation, culture, amusement, sport, training and education for the people of East London.* Panels in relief, executed by Eric Gill, depict Drama, Music, Fellowship, Dance, Sport. One Gill-carved inscription. Reclining male, oyster-eyed, hand outstretched. Loincloth nappy.

UNTO/LAST
T
H
I
S.

One of those signatures that fill the pages of London's stone library, books read by statues.

Then nothing that is worth entering in the notebook. Not a sentence, not a tag. The Peasant's Revolt Mural in Bow Common Lane: post-Guernica, cinemascope frame. Graffiti worked into the design: SERFDOM, BONDAGE, FEUDALISM. **600 Years**/FESTIVAL/**1381**/SATURDAY/ JUNE/**13th**/**1981.**

Matt's Gallery (ex-industrial). Poplar Neighbourhood, Ragged School Museum. *Remembering our Past.* We have to trek all the way to Limehouse Church, blasted white, winner of a John Betjeman award for tower restoration, for our next entry. In one of the alcoves, so well adapted to resting vagrants, the cheerful slogan: GOD BLESS YOU ALL!

No choice now, we have to go through it to reach the river tunnel: The Isle of Dogs. Anubis land, a reservation of jackals. Death's promontory. The whole glass raft is a mistake, glitter forms of anachronistic postmodernism (the swamp where *that* word crawled to die). Instant antiques. Skin grafts peeling before completion. The seductive sky/water cemetery of Thatcherism, cloud-reflecting sepulchre towers: an evil that delights the eye (the eye in the triangle). An astonishingly obvious solicitation of the pyramid, a corrupt thirst for eternity. (Climb the true tower of St Anne's Church, and stand among Hawksmoor's crumbling Portland stone lanterns, pyramids set above catacomb arches, designed to be seen *through*, to keep vision alive; the river, all points of the compass – even the futile bluntness of Canary Wharf's phallic topping.)

The planners have dabbled in geomancy, appeased the energy lines (while attempting to subvert them), and have achieved nothing beyond futile decoration. A city state built on self-regard. A colony where news dies (Fleet Street in charge of its own obituary), and where VDU screens play back electronic wavelets, green lines filling the machines with poisoned water, responding to the tides outside the window.

You can't walk through the island (Mudchute with its Toy Town menagerie is a reprise of Marie Antoinette's sheep). It's a surveillance net. A spaghetti western ghost with serious, multinational co-production budget. Each time a camera pans to catch you, your life is peeled of another layer. We thin as we walk. There's nothing to be said. Marc is terrified of the shaggy cows. I say: "Give it back to the herdsmen." These were the fattening fields. Traces of ancient orchards can still be found. Turn the cattle out into the empty avenues and boulevards.

Dog Island repudiates graffiti. There's no surface rough enough to take the pen. We're trapped in an isthmus of signs, not language. A field of force deliberately set up to eliminate the freelancer, the walker, the visionary. Public funds for private roads. Systems of control based on necrophile geometry: underpasses, barriers, security guards. Minor pyramids misaligned with the boss tower. Meaningless stones thrown by people in glass houses.

Even Class War have jacked in the aggro. No pronouncements. No threats. Leave the disgruntled dock fringe to Derek Beackon. The anarchists haven't bothered to defile the billboard poster that boasts of its heritage, dead dockers queuing on this ground for a day's work. (They can't compete with the Ronald McDonald clown nodding on a traffic atoll of petrol burgers.)

Island Gardens, fronting the river and Greenwich, where Maze Hill, shimmers in rainlight. The relief: a return to language. The blessed continuity of rage. ELECTRIC FIX ANL SCUM. It no longer matters *what* is said; after the Isle of Dogs, we're grateful for crumbs. That the city's argument with itself should not be discontinued.

The tile hoop of the foot tunnel is visible on a giant TV screen in the lift, silent floaters. The merciful release of imagery that doesn't cut on impact, that isn't out to explain itself away. Random pleasures, a camera that edits to the rhythm of the breath. I could happily stay here all morning, but I'm pulled out of my reverie by the need to transcribe a handbill.

HAVE YOU SEEN HIM? DANIEL CHARLES HANDLEY. BORN 27/4/85. RED BIKER SUIT.

The lift chamber is sheer old-fashioned luxury, roomy and well-benched. The teak and polish of pre-war steamers. There are uniformed operatives, pitched by the mechanical repetition of duty into secret mindscapes. Passengers are no longer a reality. The cage has become a time-travelling module, connected to the outside world by a surveillance window: it's a Nautilus on wires, lowered into depths far stranger than Brother Thames can provide.

When it's our turn to perform for the camera, to walk down the narrow bore of the tunnel, to contemplate the tons of brown water above our heads, we remember that, of all London, this is PD James' worst nightmare. For that reason, if no other, we relish it.

Pleasantly disorientated: the south side of the river is much more than a simple culture jump, it operates on an entirely different pulse. The citizens of Greenwich have no choice, a north-facing consciousness (the brass rule of zero longitude in their spines): Canary Wharf as the inescapable point of focus.

We were due some breakfast and a reappraisal of our goals. We're so wet now that this posh rain, sharper and cleaner, seems to improve our general condition – sluicing off the sooty deposits of Old Ford, Limehouse, Poplar, Millwall, and stinging us until we glow. A pauper's sauna, a complimentary birching. It's coming straight down, no argument, bar-code blocks of it – driving us into the shelter of the nearest grease caff. No time to be picky, to choose somewhere rough enough to feel comfortable with our patronage.

NO DOGS ALLOWED. We steam in the window, knees rattling the formica; affecting the biosphere with our transported weather systems. Melting the plastic plant life. When I recite our orders, I notice the inscribed photograph in pride of place above the counter: Arthur Daley, *genius loci*. The small trader's small trader: TO LUIGI ENZA & FRANCO PETRILLI TERMINUS CAFE BEST WISHES GEORGE COLE.

It's beginning to fall apart. The University of Greenwich isn't actually in Greenwich, that's a courtesy title. The gaff is four hard miles downriver. But the University of Woolwich doesn't have the same ring. (Even Arsenal Football Club found Woolwich too lowrent and relocated to Highbury.) The ascent of Maze Hill – contemplated as we try to pull our spoons out of the Sicilian coffee – is losing its appeal. We'll never make our appointment on foot. We'd like to hop a riverboat to the Thames barrier, that would be within the spirit of the exercise, but the boats are not running. Wrong season.

It'll have to be that charity wagon, the bus. Can't keep Makin waiting in his cave, with nothing to sustain him: his composition on the wall like a permanent rebuke. Yesterday's inspiration. A single sheet anthology. A one poem collection. It was bound to pall.

Back out there, in the monsoon, we are obliged to take a sabbatical, to dry out in a primitive shelter, forget text and concentrate on numerology – as we wait for a bus brave enough to open its doors in this weather.

The minutes are ticking away. Should we abandon this folly and take to our heels, run it? We can't even enjoy the intermediate, half-sodden state: rain blows straight into the open-fronted shelter, cascades from the roof and down our necks. We're sitting on wet timber, shivering *and* sweating, precipitation fogging my spectacles. We know that we will, all too soon, be drenched again.

They leap to their feet, the potential commuters, stare out into the darkness. The shelter is like a game of bingo for the blind. Arms waving. Up and down. Curses aimed at non-stopping vehicles. Packs of empty buses, "on test", "on trial". Step out there, trying to attract their attention, and you risk the contents of a displaced puddle; a puddle that throws itself at you. Or, play safe, stay back on the bench, and you'll never stand up before the airpressure doors seal with a self-satisfied hiss. We're unpractised in the etiquette of public transport. We make the novice's error of leaping onto the first vehicle with "Woolwich" credited in its destination window.

A true adventure, this compulsory leisure, pitched from side to side at the rear of the bus (the flight out of East Germany in Hitchcock's *Torn Curtain* comes to mind: fellow passengers all frauds, actors acting, back projections you're not supposed to believe).

A Faustian bargain: we've signed away all our rights with the purchase of a ticket. (We don't even collect the things. No books in which they can serve as marks.) We turn from all hope of Woolwich and head into the interior, uphill. Logic is suspended with your acceptance of passenger status. At last, Marc has something to photograph: our fellow victims, travellers hooked on travel, the willingly bemused, a troop of dope-swollen moon faces, the sort usually glimpsed as they stare out of yellow special needs minibuses with lifts at the back. I'm sure that we've infiltrated a secure-hospital delivery, a round-up of sectioned carpet-chewers, white line walkers, parrot imitators, biddable psychotics, folks who live with the daily horror of seeing things as they actually are.

Once we relax, let it happen, it's quite pleasant (a post-operative morphine cocktail high). Washed-out streets, without shops or garages or action of any kind; a literally mindless progress, on the drift, floating in a soup of putrid breath and steaming gabardine; stopping and starting without reason, nobody gets on or off, deeper and deeper into the narcosis of the back country. Lost foothills to which only commuters return. After the archipelagos of cloned housing: scraps of parkland, tolerated forest. I can't connect any of this with the elegant fiction of my map. (A girl I know tears the pages relevant to her day's excursion out of the *A-Z*, throwing them away as she advances into fresh territory. The serial city is a manageable concept. She's in control, never tempted to go back to where she has been before.)

The migrants we've got on board are uncatalogued. They're quite unlike anything on the streets. They're fixtures. Nothing will tempt them out into the weather. They all have huge bags of food. They nibble and slurp; on board for the duration. Stateless, but content, they've solved the riddle. Time ignores them.

As walkers, we're here under false pretences. If we ever make it through the automatic doors, we'll find ourselves lost in the middle of Kent. The paranoia of travel is delightful. And still the wristwatch account of time races on – until, the hour of our meeting being passed, the bus relents, swings away from the prison colony of tributary streetlets, and into the mainstream; downhill, gathering pace, Ha-Ha Road, Woolwich Common. Woolwich the port, the barracks of Empire. Grog shops, whores, sodomy, the generating of ordnance, the temples of artillery: laid out before us.

We're released, pedestrians again, scoured by the storm. We take to our heels, bullocking lunchtime dawdlers, hunting down Makin's seminar room.

The bureaucratic complexities of the University of Greenwich are child's play to someone who got his start navigating the mile-long rubber corridors of the NE London Technical College (and School of Art) at Walthamstow, hunting down day-release rockers and razor-scalped trainee racists. Or so I thought, as I dragged Marc, for the first half-hour, up and down flights of stairs, in and out of deserted offices. Confused and gasping, we were soon back at the entrance hall with a new set of questions. Out: across bleak courtyards and into fresh towers, security doors with grander and grander titles, covering up for less and less action. Circles of plastic chairs for unattended séances in earth science or human geography. The energy is in the corridors: *Metropolis* zombies endlessly processing from non-destination to non-destination.

Finally, on the giddy rim of dementia (recognising that hum of bad electricity, saccharine coffee on an intravenous drip), I found myself in the room I had been connected with for so many hours in telephonic argument.

Uncanny: with no effort on my part, we're straight back into it. The dialogue picked up on the beat by my opponent. The woman I bad-mouthed is courteously resistant to our quest. There is no such thing as Makin and Room 178 doesn't exist. But I was free to take a cup of cof-fee and dry out under the striplight. (I was beginning to suspect that Room 178 was the ultimate Orwellian fantasy: a mirror, a door that opened on a door, that opened on another door, that . . .)

While I raged, Marc wandered off, fearful that he'd be forced to experiment with the obviously drugged coffee. Room 178 was his first discovery. It shared a wall with the office in which I was trapped. The man Makin, his back to the corridor, was waiting at the table (a num-ber of smaller tables pressed together). He looked like a permanent fixture, an installation representing "The Writer", "The Philosopher"; the last flickering flame of an intelligence distilled from the sullen, multicellular building. He'd still be here when his wall text had decayed into gnomic incomprehensibility.

With the author so abundantly "in residence" alongside his work, it took nerve to step forward to examine the exhibit. These words, this fixed arrangement, were what we'd carry away with us. We'd never make it back for the seminar, the explanations. No justification was nec-essary. Today, now, here: this was *it*. Worse than a poetry reading: having to engage with the script while the poet watched us. Just eight words to play with. How long can you stretch *that* out? Eight words and a set of close-fitting parentheses.

I shuffled down the length of the composition, towards the window, playing for time. There was plenty of white space (and the dread of the mathematicians in their tutorials, staring distracted, in their terrible isolation, at words like those uplifting tags on the walls of Victorian operating theatres).

germinal   storm
                    (driving towards the harbour)
empty   chamber

Storm Chamber. And we were the carriers, transporting rain news into an antiseptic laboratory. Wanting, before we had stepped over the threshold, to drive on towards the harbour. I muttered something about Ian Hamilton Finlay. Which was clearly a mistake. But the weather words were shaking themselves free, targetting us as future hosts: **arbour, germ, wards**. Snap anagrams: **mort**, **re-malign**, **beach rm** . . .

Our walk was "explained" by the lines of attraction between Makin's separate terms. **Germinal** travelling south-east to **chamber**. **Chamber** labouring under **storm**. **Chamber** casting us back, west, towards the **empty** quarter. A storm in a chamber pot. The drive towards harbour, we carried within us, in those broken umbrella brackets.

I don't want to make it sound as if we discussed and debated Makin's wall for as long as the intensity of his involvement merited. A wall is as good a place to publish as anywhere else, but it's difficult to browse. Annotation is out of the question. My take on the affair was over with the nod of acknowledgement. If the poet hadn't been around, we've have been back in the corridor in seconds. Fine, got it, nice plot; check out the photo at home. (George Davis, D/S Mathews and Dursun Karatas aren't sitting under their names ready to debate the proposition of their innocence.) This is more in the nature of a private view. No disinterested Courtauld girl to stand you off while she fiddles with the telephone; just the man himself – his words spilled out behind him like a speech-bubble in a post-Alan Moore comic strip.

We are the ones forced to come up with an explanation, to defend our presence, as we stalk the table, dripping puddles across the floor. Spoken aloud, put into words, our journey sounds insane. It *is* insane. What's the purpose of the photographer? Why Woolwich? Why the **V**? The truth is that we're in different stories. Atkins, Makin: the names begin to shapeshift. Each containing dominant elements of the other: kinship. Atget the Paris photographer of streets, the maker. Kinma, some primitive version of cinema (lacking the "I").

The solution is to fuse them, subject and object. Atkins bluffs his way into another part of the building, poses Makin in the widow, the inscription visible beyond him. Snaps from outside.

Makin had waited so patiently for this, at the table's end, a substantial paperback gripped in white hands: Gilles Deleuze. Something about scepticism and schizophrenia. Now the portrait clinches it, an act of separation; a definition of difference. We're free.

Woolwich tips everything loose down towards the Thames. We're shepherded, wind-pitched, between charity shops. A Dieppe, lacking the booze warehouses, but with its literary exiles in place. LOW PRICE BEDS. LAST FEW DAYS! WHOLESALE. A window of giveaway books: **THE DEFINITIVE DIANA, WHITE TIE TALE, GUIDE TO GOLD MARKS OF THE WORLD**. Faces to the north, the river, we're back in a graffiti culture: THE MOONIE BOYS. **FRANKIE GOES TO HOLLYWOOD IS SHIT**.

Townscape in a liquidiser. We're so far off the map that nobody has found it worthwhile to close down the free ferry. Work boats that are always off-season; passengers responding to the limited elation of being out on the water. First-time voyagers sprint around the decks looking for the bar, the duty frees. Old hands take up the position that will let them off first when the moving platform swings into place on the north shore.

Downriver of Silvertown, wind carrying the stink of sugar away from us; the coated tusks of the Thames Barrier. The illusion, from which we all suffer, of midstream freedom, choice – to step ashore or stay on board for the whole cruise, out of time, backwards and forwards between South and North Woolwich. The curdled Bisto swell of the river, its width under racing black clouds.

MISSING: **Daniel Charles Handley, 9 years old. 4'2" tall. Blonde short hair with a pony tail, wearing red bike suit with the word "racing" on front, brown boots; in possession of old silver coloured BMX cycle without a saddle. Information room 071–275–5732.**

The boy had been playing, as I remembered it, around the Beckton Power Station; a rubbled wilderness that Kubrick and his crew (ex-Nazi rocket technicians) had turned into Vietnam for *Full Metal Jacket*.

The river is emptying itself into the sky and the sky is chucking it back. Shlepping ashore, down the long drag of the bridge, we're on the point of letting the day go. Marc can't operate in this weather and my notebook is a wedge of sodden pulp at the bottom of my pocket. The

wall tattoos have become stale and listless: AS WILSON **081–459–8113.**
BNP NAZI SCUM. It's over, the **V** has closed its legs. We can take
the train from North Woolwich to Hackney and write the walk off to
experience. (Like hell we can!) But it's politic at this point to allow Marc
to think we *might* abort the mission. And, meanwhile, there's the Royal
Pavilion opposite the station: THIS IS WHERE THE BIG LAMBS HANG OUT. A
couple of Guinnesses and something to eat. See how it looks after that.

The vast bar (two regulars in) represents good times known. And
paid for. They must have had a decent crowd the night the *Princess Alice*
went down: newspaper men, disaster gulls, hopeful relatives. Stout's off.
No food. Not on Tuesdays. A packet of stale crisps, autopsy scratchings
stiffened with vinegar, will have to fill the gap. An abominable cigar, presumably salvaged from the wrecked paddle-steamer. DIAMOND WHITE
EXTRA STRONG WHITE CIDER. PEEL AND REVEAL. Life is creeping back into
the veins. Marc sneezes. Steam rises from our coats. Get in another
round. The edge has been taken from the afternoon. Maps mean nothing now. We're up for it: the smoking apocalypse of Silvertown, the sun
breaking through behind the sugar-smelting mills. Script on every available surface. We'll walk for as long as daylight holds.

That single track alongside the railway, from North Woolwich to
Silvertown, before we cut past the City Airport and over the Royal
Docks, is an ecstasy of transcription: the first true language-contour
we've discovered since we left Hackney. We're back into the rhythm of
striding out, pausing, shorthanding the graffiti, swooping on to the
next cluster. Movement under these skies and through this responsive
dereliction is pure excitement. It's evident that Marc's portraits of the
steaming factories – he scampers up on railway crossings to get them –
will work. As a photographer that's all he needs. One good shot to
freeze the universe.

RED ON GREEN WAR
SILVERTOWN BACK NO MARKET
JOHN PEARSON + PALUNDER KULAR '94
PAUL DICK-HEAD N BUSHY READY
TO SHAGG SORT **I.D.S.T**
KENNY + ANGEL/ NO NECK/ WUZ ERE
SAXON + STUMA WELL HARD CHAZ
I WOZERE/ ABOUT NOW I'M/ NOT SO I LEFT/
MY NAME TO TURN/ YOU ON. PS 40 UP

A delirium of coded information, hot text: cancer-grey lampposts frantic to declare their allegiances. Scribbles stacked like battle honours. Scudding clouds, an avenue of disappointed nautical ambitions.

ALEX JOHNSON SOLICITOR – **REPENT!**
FRANCIS IS A DOPE OWNER AGAIN
STOP TORY IMMIGRANT CUT/ VOTE LABOUR
CARS WANTED FOR CASH/RUNNERS
& NON-RUNNERS/SMASHED OR CRASHED
STEVE PETERSON 94 SILVERTOWN BOY!
WHY DON'T YOU BUILD UP A SPLIFF/ MAKE ME
A JOINT/ SUCK MY ARSEHOLE

Through the unselfconscious ordinariness of Prince Regent's Lane (Greengate Street, Plaistow Road), we're comfortable, pushing on; sustained by voices that never let up their attack. These streets – all one street – are operational, with no hidden agenda. They are content with disaffection. Resigned to something less than mediocrity. The shops don't make much profit, but they survive. Sticky buns (yes, we sampled them), burgers, cauliflowers still coated with earth. Mechanics prepared to take things to pieces.

ANN IS A SORT. **Don't Vote Nazi**
DELICIOUS HOUSE/ FISH & CHIPS/ CHINESE FOOD
TO TAKE AWAY
IT'S THE YEAR 200! BNP WANKERS
EAT SHIT BNP/ SUPPORT ANL/ LICK SHIT BNP

You can walk here without appearing freakish. The streets don't give a damn. A modest leavening of dirt and rubbish. This is where the weather visionary (cloud definer) Luke Howard had his factory. A Plaistow boy who had the sense to look up. Check the sky.

JANE VICTORY IS THE SEXIEST GIRL ALIVE – YES
TANYA + CARVY/ MEGASORTS
RICHY BENNETT CANT KISS TO SAVE HIS LIFE

The 12th century church of All Saints is locked and bolted. We detour respectfully around the churchyard. As we close on Stratford, we pick up intimations of a centre, a place that must once have been of some significance – a staging post on the way out. Civilization is represented by a narrow boutique filled with fetishists' gear: rubber, PVC, zips. Only marginally different from the shop supplying protective uniforms for industrial wear. You can't have decadence without first having a culture.

MODELS REQUIRED, *SHIATSU*, SCALP MASSAGE
DONT BUY THE SUN
DO NOT ASK FOR CHANGE/THIS IS NOT A BUS
DEFEND THE LEADER OF THE REVOLUTION IN PERU
DG IS MINE! I DREAM THAT HE IS/ LOUISE

Working a route through the confusion of the Broadway, we are safely delivered to known ground: climb into the cabin of any of the heavy cranes and you can see Hackney Marshes. A few scrubby acres and broken sheds alongside the shunting yards were once known as Chobham Farm. I worked there (with Tom Baker, scriptwriter of the film *Witchfinder General*) through an autumn and long cold winter: loading and unloading containers. Broken pallet boards burning in oil drums. Cheap scab labour (under £25 a week) brought in to circumvent the union stranglehold on the docks. The docks were finished. Chobham Farm was the final dispute: pseudo-dockers, marooned inland, defending their jobs against the restrictive practices of a labour elite – whose bases were being captured and destroyed, even as they left the river to defend them. The Chobham speculators, hard-hats and chalkstripe suits, were the forerunners of the LDDC pirates, the cardinals of the Isle of Dogs. Their fantasy cities, container units stacked on mud, were a trial run for the real thing, the republics of glass.

This was the era of power cuts, the three day week. We filled the pockets of our overalls with broken wax, with which to make candles. We smuggled out tins of outdated foodstuffs, thermos flasks topped up from punctured drums of wine. Days spent humping slippery sacks of talcum powder, anthrax-enriched sheep casings. Once we were issued with axe handles and ordered to reduce a loading bay packed with industrial washing-machines to powder. Yells of manic laughter. "Damaged in transit".

Heartbreaking sunrises as we drove to work, chill autumnal mists over the Lea Valley. Lunchhour picnics among the sunflowers, effluent-fed weeds. Trains shunting in the background. Talk of travel, gossip with the drivers. Letters from Tony Lowes in Kabul.

★

The day was exhausted. Chingford Mount would have to wait. We weren't going to get much further than St Patrick's, Leytonstone, that slumberland development with its forests of white statues. St Pat's, and its icy acreage, its yearlong winter, would take the temperature of the project down. Bringing Marc in through the gates, I was conscious of stepping back into the Prima Donna episode of my novel *Downriver*, into the psychotic topography of local mythologist John Morrison.

John, in his set of shoebox rooms, packed with their cargo of fabulous documents, was a self-hypnotised *voyant* – who, with the aid of sweet sherry transfusions, had circumvented the inhibitions of historical time. He absorbed pulse signals of the late-Victorian period, fondling scraps of graveyard cloth, rusty blades, ribbons, a twist of straw from a summer hat. He wore away at the tedium of the present. He "went over". Travelled freely through places and events that more prosaic folk understood to be available only on prescription, through a good library or a bad trip. Refraining from any gesture of intervention, he spoke with the dead; conscious that one misjudgement, one action to prevent the horrors he was witnessing, and he would never return. He would be stuck between worlds, a mute presence, a quality of light hovering over the rank vegetation of an unfrequented burial ground.

John's particular sweetheart was Marie Jeanette Kelly, the final victim of Jack the Ripper. (She gave him the tip about who murdered the three Brontë sisters.) There's a pathetic tale behind the memorial to Kelly that Morrison paid to have erected in St Patrick's cemetery.

MARIE JEANETTE KELLY

AGE 25.

THE PRIMA DONNA OF SPITALFIELDS

AND LAST KNOWN VICTIM OF

JACK THE RIPPER.

MURDERED FRI. NOV. 9TH 1888.

DO NOT STOP TO STAND AND STARE

UNLESS TO UTTER FERVENT PRAYER

(MARY MAGDALENE INTERCEDE)

DEDICATED BY JOHN MORRISON

DEC. 3RD 1986.

The tale involves a pair of brothers who, fronting a monumental mason's shop near the cemetery gates, established a connection with Mickey Rourke who was hanging about the graveyard, ready to shoot his *Prayer for the Dying* exteriors with Mike Hodges. (Alan Bates was also involved, tossing his hair, rolling his eyes, going through the motions as a "flamboyant racketeer who doubles as a mortician".) This turkey was no *Get Carter*, Hodges' celebrated exploitation of the photogenic elements of Newcastle gangland: betting-shops, boozers, slot-machine and child porn rackets. Plenty of bite in rusty landscapes. He even recycled John Osborne as a campy crime boss, but his hands were full with this one. Bob Hoskins as a priest. Belfast shifted to East London. Mickey Rourke's accent.

Rourke, while he was sweating himself up for it, waiting for tracks to be laid through the broken statues, fell in with John Morrison. This Ripper yarn (Morrison's from the horse's-mouth solution) sounded like a winner. The mason brothers brokered the deal as Rourke took out a cash option. The boys would stand Morrison a marble headstone showy enough to pass muster with Rudolph Valentino – and, in exchange, he'd sign away a major chunk of his screenplay and seed money.

The movie caravan moved on (to oblivion). Rourke tried for a celebrity boxing career. And Morrison duly got visiting rights to a grave of his own design, with Odeon-sized text. A loud stone page that very soon alerted the cemetery authorities – who insisted upon its immediate removal. Morrison, and the younger (more pliant) brother, equipped themselves with spades and a handcart, and prepared to dig Kelly up, take her into safekeeping in Morrison's chambers. An altercation at the graveside. The Old Bill summoned. Morrison had to content himself with substantial portions of the broken headstone for his private museum.

The tomb has subsequently moved several more times, at Morrison's expense. Less script with each flit. Not much more, now, than name and date: a postmortem tag. A long correspondence with Douglas Hurd and other functionaries has brought the truth home: "There is no Mary Kelly". Kelly's bones had been taken out of their paupers' pit, in the remotest corner of the cemetery, crushed and burnt. The headstone stood above seventeen layers of unrecorded East Londoners: cats, rabbits, pigeons, pebbles and rings, all impacted in the heavy clay.

The gates at the east end of St Pat's are chained. In the twilight, we're back where we were at the start of all this, dodging among tombs. We have to climb the fence and work our way down Cathall Road towards the railway. Maybe we'll get lucky and bump into John Morrison, out with his lantern, about to indulge in some nocturnal archaeology.

Claremont Road catches us unprepared: the barricaded remnant of the M11 motorway extension protest. £20 million has been pissed away in policing this obscure railway cutting. A thousand people have lost their homes. It has to be a major perversion: that anyone could have targeted this terrace with a prime view of the cemetery as a significant element in the blacktop revolution. As the chill of the evening clamps down, the conflict is totally one-sided – the invading forces are palpable in their absence. The barbarians huddle around small fires, or ready themselves for the next bout of journalistic interrogation.

Claremont Road is pre-electric, it has blitzed itself backwards; finding the spirit of resistance in a conceptualised self-trashing. It is defended and open to all comers at the same time. Clusters of communards sit in the middle of the road on battered sofas. Furniture that was once private, kept for best in front parlours, is left to the mercy of the weather. Outside is inside. There are no secrets. The road is closed to traffic by a number of contrived barriers and mini-henges of roughcast concrete. It's doomed, they know that. The situation would be insupportable if it wasn't finite. But for now the tribes are in occupation; painted faces, funny costumes, invocations of Lewis Carroll. "NO, NO!" SAID THE QUEEN. "SENTENCE FIRST AND VERDICT AFTERWARDS."

Claremont Road is the destination for the missing graffiti that has migrated out of Tower Hamlets. FORCED EVICTIONS/ARE A GROSS/VIOLATION/OF HUMAN RIGHTS. RED–UNITED NATIONS. HELP SAVE CLAREMONT ROAD/PHONE 081–558–2638. EAT MY(AN) PEANUTS.

Masts rise against the darkening clouds, crow's-nests into which the protesters can climb when the bulldozers roll. The road has become an adventure playground of treehouses, dens, hideaways: a confederacy of the gratefully dispossessed. Alliances have been struck between ancestral enemies. They are no longer opposing motorways, they're celebrating a forgotten parade of houses that would otherwise not be worth a glimpse out of the car window.

LOCK ON THIS/WAY. THIS TREE/IS ALIVE, HOUSES/AINT LOVE/THE FLOWER POT TRIBE. BENDER HOUSE: TSG BATTER CHILDREN/BE AWARE! OUR MOTHER IS WATCHING NOW. NO FORCED EVICTIONS! LOCK-ON BARREL/FILL WITH/CEMENT/INSERT ARM. DOWN WITH BOSSES & FOREMEN. WARNING THIS BUILDING IS FITTED/WITH A BUNKER.

Walking through is like visiting, on sufferance, a closed film set;

some Godard essay from the Sixties – *Weekend, Les Carabiniers, One Plus One*. The encampment has evolved to the point where it looks staged, a forum for bored journalists. But it's real enough for the people who live here in a state of semi-public siege. Claremont Road, by its sympathies, announces itself, in the manner of Derek Jarman, as "The Last of England". A ruined terrace overlooking a railway and a graveyard. The squatters flitter through the twilight, busking for energy input, wanting to complete their narrative, move on to the next battleground.

SEX IS SACRED. YES/ TO THE M11.

Ground is captured, inch by inch, in a weary process of encroachment. Board fencing surrounds the territory that has fallen into the hands of the developers. Africans, rumoured illegal immigrants, stand at intervals, protecting (for a couple of pounds an hour) the integrity of the fence. As Marc approaches, they cover their faces with their yellow hard hats. Performance art. Beuys waistcoats, doffed helmets. Too bright boots. One hand in the pocket. Mute minstrels at the end of the pier.

WE ACT WITH/ANGRY LOVE.

29.5.95. A letter from Richard Makin. He heard me deliver the opening section of this essay in a Cambridge church. His quote has been transformed, he tells me, and should now be amended:

> *the necromancer dee dreams of a lapus linguae island flying in force dying in poverty drunk on angelspeech which paradoxically he has not actually heard.*
> *swift scales of music tripping upward to evade him in perpetual deferral to create open outward the palace blueprint of reflexion.*

THE DOG & THE DISH

Oh keep the Dog far hence, that's friend to men,
Or with his nails he'll dig it up again!
TS Eliot

This small-brained animal, primed to hate, straining at the end of a short leash, is universally recognised as bad news. And the dog, his yellow-eyed, drooling familiar, the killing machine, is not much better. The relationship is a mistake, a dangerous misconception, a perversion of actual needs. The dog as protector becomes the very thing that must be protected against: squat embodiment of threat. It is of course a truism that beast and man come to resemble each other; an odd couple wearied by compromise, tissue manipulated by shared embraces. Man curses his creature, thrashes it with a chain in a ferocious show of love. If it were possible, he'd wear that burnished pelt like a new vest, the dog's snarling mask in place of his own. He'd zip himself inside the hot skin and take the world by the throat. The dog channels, gives sculptural form, to prodigious spite. Jolts of electric tension pass through the links of the chain, atavistic fears. The man believes he is tethered to an heraldic cartoon, his own courage expressed in meat form. He is pulled forward by an intelligent muscle, a growling machismo. His phallic extension has achieved independence and swaggers beside him; twins that would put the Krays to shame. The dog is a prick with teeth. Its balls are so heavy it rolls from side to side in a ruptured waddle. The ultimate carnivore, incest's glory: the pit bull.

My wife has taught for years in a borderland school. Its catchment area includes some of the worst estates in Hackney and a number of the tower blocks they blow up on Sunday mornings for the benefit of TV crews perched on the far side of the marshes. But other schools in the neighbourhood pick up the coverage: "Headmistress in Lesbian Love Tangle with Governor". That stuff. "Romeo and Juliet is Sexist Propaganda." Otherwise the area is invisible, one of those zones where inner-city crimes slink away to be buried. Public housing that incubates, and provides refuge for, child pornography rings, drug poverty, lives of petty fraud and tranquilised rage.

The school-yard is surrounded by a storm-fence, and other security precautions, designed to keep out the less determined and more obviously visible spectres of threat. (The real danger lies with the parents, extended families who use their freedom of access as an excuse to have a pop at a teacher, or to encourage their kids to get their retaliation in first. "Kick 'im back," they scream. "Fuckin' nut 'im, you little poof.") In the mornings − as the children straggle in, with mothers, sisters, grandparents, keepers, or alone − the fence begins to resemble the hitching-post outside the OK Corral. Pits bulls are leashed at regular intervals. They stand, stock-still, flanks heaving, gleaming bronze in the pale sun, staring with eyes of incomprehending anguish at these potential feeding-grounds.

Dogs confer status, even at the bottom of the heap. Especially at the bottom of the heap, that is where status is most needed. There's not much else to aspire to: respect. Diss these honorary members of the Kennel Club and you've got a dog clamped on your vocal cords. The pit bull is twinned in desirability with the possession of a satellite dish (even if the machine that goes with it will have to wait). Ugly lids, each one representing a flattened dog head, creep like barnacles across mildewed properties that are waiting in the queue for demolition.

The dog and the dish, they hang out together, chummy as a pub sign. Dog protects dish, and also basks in its addictive glow − a sort of lowrent tanning bed. The activated dish feeds doses of liquid *Sun*-light; dopamine substitutes that induce a paranoid trance-state, in which the only possible reaction to programmed inertia is a wolf howl of madness − fire images of violation, apocalyptic seizures. Satellite TV is a longdistance heart attack, incremental cancers: the narcoleptic trauma in which the dreams of the dog and the dreams of the man (lager, sport, steroids, blood and sawdust) meet and mingle.

Experimenting with Murdoch's electronic ecstasy, his stage-managed highs, is a risky business. ("I'm cool, man. I can handle it.") Recyled imagery is pumped into your home, disbelief is given a general anaesthetic: you see dogs everywhere. Nerves frayed by envy, the urge to consume; we summon up the things we fear most. PIT BULLS. A visible investment. Cash on legs.

Everybody has their favourite pit bull story; yarns that pull the community together, like V2 myths in wartime. The Cypriot tailor in Dalston Lane, who operates in the ambiance that sent the Krays to the

Old Bailey looking like Romanian secret policemen dressed for a wedding, recalls the incident in an adjacent property that was guarded by a pit bull import. (American dog, German motor, second home in Spain: don't tell me we're not living in a multicultural society.) "Credit where credit's due, he gave her fair warning." The police wandered across the road in response to several complaints of unexplained "noises" at night. (The dog that didn't bark, it keened; it wailed as if it had caught its wedding tackle in a mincer). The door was broken down. The dog had been in there for a week or ten days, unfed, unwatered; nobody seemed to know if the absentee landlord had done a runner, or if he'd finished up in the boot of a car after a commercial dispute that had got out of hand. But when the policewoman effected an entrance – brave, direct, as trained, looking the beast in the eye, holding out her hand, palm upwards, for the lick of acknowledgement – the dog sprang straight at her and "took off her face". They secured the place and came back later, when things had quieted down, with a gun. (Pit bulls will growl a warning, that's the fable, but Rottweilers, guard dogs used to patrolling perimeter fences, go from drool mode to frenzied assault with no perceptible change of gear.)

The stories have been around for years in the local fright sheets. "Crazed Devil Dog Thrown Off Balcony" is one that caught my eye in the *Hackney Gazette*. Nkrumah Warren invited a couple of mates around to his second-floor flat for a cup of tea and a natter. His pit bull, a rare white costing £2,000, did not altogether take to the intrusion. In fact, the wretch tore the trousers from one man and tried to perform a full-frontal tonsillectomy on the other. This was taking the breed's reputation for liveliness too far. Mr Warren locked the animal in the kitchen. But the dog wasn't finished yet; he hit the door so hard with his head that he reduced it to kindling. Wanton destruction of council property can have unforeseen consequences: Mr Warren wrestled his pet to the balcony and threw him over. The pit bull sucked air, caught a brief, privileged view of Hackney, and hit the ground, suffering a broken back. The family, who had gloried in an expensive accessory, did not give way to grief. "I've got another," Mr Warren remarked, "who is absolutely fine with the baby."

Dog news works its way on to the walls of the borough, portraits of mad eyes as a signature of rage. The eyes are the only warning you're going to get. "It was when his eyes glazed over, a smoking white film over the gold, that he became dangerous," wrote Scott Ely in his novel *Pit Bull* (1990). The eyes that mark out the doomed buildings of the Haggerston Estate are red. I remember walking through these unoccupied hulks, in winter, just before they came down. The constant gush of water from broken pipes had frozen into icy cascades, solid blue floes dressing the dereliction. Mad red eyes glared out from a helmet of rime. Discontinued shrieks of graffiti: FUCK THE RENT, HOW MUCH LONGER MUST WE LIVE HERE, HILCOT HOUSE SALUTES BOBBY SANDS.

Closer to home, I can watch from my back window the procession of jaunty supplicants as they climb the stairs of a lowrise, redbrick block, to the metal-shielded door of the free-market pharmacist who operates (under franchise) his top-floor dispensary. Trade is on an upward curve, but the dealers haven't made it yet to their first pit bull. Their pride and joy is an Alsatian, an embarrassed anachronism, as sorry a confession of status on this turf as cruising in a two-tone Zodiac. (It's a toss up between a first-time pit bull and a BMW with 40,000 miles on the clock. Talk terms, guy, with John at Mildmay Motors.) Alsatians are good for nothing except barking, bouncing impotently against the mesh fences of scrapyards. They're like flares and kipper ties and talk of "blags": they belong in Seventies television, in *The Sweeney*.

Now the wholesalers, the tomtoms with the Ashanti gold reserves around their necks, the ones with the customised motors, who ride into the precinct like an armoured car into the Bogside, *they* have a pit bull. They've got a pair of them; a Cerberus monster advancing towards you, two heads on a single trunk. When poor old Lassie sees this mob, is dragged over to pay homage to the eyepopping, trunk-necked guys in the leather hats, she develops a sudden interest in cigarette packets, burger cartons. She contracts a devastating incontinence problem. She thinks wistfully of those golden days – back around 1985 – when pit bulls were mere pack animals; when the product was carried inside their collars. And the suss laws were cast into temporary suspension.

Writing gifts the hack with Dutch courage: if the worst happens, it adds colour to a dull tale. As an act of research, I risked stopping to take a look at a pit bull that was panting, at ease, unprimed, on the cool stone flags of the Regent's Canal, right opposite the gasworks. His oppo had interested himself in what was going on across the water. The man had a razor-cropped skull and no neck. His small flushed ears (crusty blood blisters) were stapled with rings. I expected him, if he moved too suddenly, to jangle like a wind-chime. The pit bull, disconnected from his master, was disconnected from the world. It was an alien life-form. It didn't belong here. If it strayed too near the canal bank, it would probably perish by attacking its own reflection.

The dog's ears, ragged purse flaps, had been stitched together with black bootlaces. The needlework was amateur. Flesh wounds festered and scabbed in the oily sunshine. On the far bank a man in a multi-pocketed flak jacket was dangling a rope into the water, from which air bubbles rushed to the surface. The little team were taking a leisurely afternoon, searching the canal's pungent mucilage for the weapon or weapons that inflicted "multiple stab wounds" on Hector Anthony Slaly (aka "Mike"), whose body, tied up in a blue plastic sheet, and weighted with a toolbox, had been recovered on the previous day. The victim lurked, half-submerged, for between "one and three days". The atmosphere, as the sun dipped behind the gasholders, picking out the gap in the fence and flashing against a burnt-out van, was unhealthy. I was conscious of the triangulation developing between myself, the man and his pit bull. Nothing was happening, and happening slowly. I had to summon up the noblest traditions of documentary reporting to stop myself shifting to a fictional mode, planting this pair with guilt by association (association with me).

The canal path has an affinity with sour luck. It provided the habitual evening stroll for the late James Moody, a longterm escapee from Brixton and an associate of the Richardsons. He thought his trail, along the canal to Victoria Park and into the Royal Hotel, was anonymous, mundane, unworthy of notice. But he grievously overestimated his invisibility. The man stood out like an Hasidic Volvo in a skinhead rally: *he didn't have a dog*! Curtains. Soft wages for the hitman.

What worries me is why, at this period in the evolution of our city, we need to invoke the dog, the "prime secret" of Robert Graves' druidic triad, one of the creatures of the White Goddess? The dog runs wild at the very moment that the Roebuck, that votive pub on the corner of Durward Street, is being gutted. Why, by granting it attention, do we indulge this elemental whose jaw, once locked, has to be broken open with a specially-contrived wedge? We have created a totemic animal we can openly hate, an animal that hates back, that *is* hate. Selective breeding in the good-old-boy, peckerwood, white sheet, lynch-mob states have brought about a monster that can be sold to the world. A dog that is auditioning for the apocalypse, trained until it is "viciated", as Romain Gary expresses it in *White Dog*, his case-history of a German shepherd schooled to kill blacks on sight. Can it be that we require some "viciated" thing, powerful enough to represent all the hurt that is loose in the landscape? In previous plague times, recorders of folklore interpreted the sighting of dogs as a warning: Padfoot, Trash, Shriker, Black Shuck, Pooka, the Beast of Bodmin, the Hound of the Baskervilles. Messengers of death, dark familiars with "streams of sulphrous vapour" issuing from their throats. Seeing such things now is an indication of our sickness. We are too demonised, too greedy for novelty, to repress this band of eidetic imagery. We have granted pit bulls a franchise to haunt us. They will populate our urban myths – until we can invent a worse toy, a pest whose breath poisons our children, whose eyes are as cold as our own.

"Black dog" is the mood of bottomless, suicidal despair suffered, most notoriously, by Winston Churchill (himself a kind of bulldog in nappies, a logo for Empire; growling and dribbling, wheezing smoke, swollen veins fired with brandy). It's the dark hole, the pit from which mania bounds. This dog is the alchemist's *nigredo*, black outside and white inside, like lead: the element that must be transformed. Pure nightstuff, uncut horror; it howls in tiled prison corridors to keep suspects under interrogation from their dreams. It fits like a flesh hood. Pit bulls do not howl. Their silence is a greater threat. It signals the pre-crisis plateau on which we have now arrived.

Our best hope then is to identify, and name, the opposite of a dog, the pit bull's contrary. We have connived at too much darkness, turned our backs on misjustice and abuse, judicial assassinations, social engineering, the wilful destruction of care. We know more than we can absorb. The "dog" is our totem: it is the term bookdealers give to the least desirable items of their stock, the definitively unsaleable. There is, as far as I am aware, no colloquial term for choice desiderata. Even the map has to be circumspect in its exhibition of canine tags. The Isle of Dogs has always been perceived as an unlucky and ill-favoured swamp. Pepys shunned it. Blake anathematised it. Ben Jonson's first play took that location for a title and it landed him in prison. The text has now vanished. For writers, the "Isle of Dogs" is a phrase that is never to be whispered; it's the equivalent of the luvvies' "Scottish play".

And so the contrary, the dog's opposite, must have a special quality; a quality that by its nature will be impossible to define. We can look for movement in the air, an unpredictable shift in the intensity of light. Whatever is not infected by being dragged over the ground. A music. A ravished inattention. Whatever resists being listed in a newspaper. Whatever is unregistered by surveillance cameras.

If we do not find this thing, if we fail in our quest, we will be left with the vision of that prince among paranoids, Franz Kafka, when he brought his avatar, K., to his conclusion – when he identified and illuminated the meaningless and futile instant of death:

> *But the hands of one of the partners were already at K.'s throat, while the other thrust the knife into his heart and turned it there twice. With failing eyes K. could still see the two of them, cheek leaning against cheek, immediately before his face, watching the final act. "Like a dog!" he said: it was as if he meant the shame of it to outlive him.*

2
KRAZY DOGS & PET PORTRAITS
"Dogs should be considered a natural hazard," he said stiffly. "Like werewolves."
IAN THOMSON, *BONJOUR BLANC*

My pit bull notes were begun, as a commission, in May 1990; ancient history, "another era entirely", as "Kray boss" Tony Lambrianou would say of his pre-prison years. Pit bulls were a significant element in the two fingers for culture, union-bashing, *Belgrano*-sinking years, the future we have hopefully left behind us. They were showbiz, Yankee-lifestyle imports to be laid aside with the gas-guzzling limos, the weaponry and the Mafia tailoring that characterised the aspirations of *The Long Good Friday* gangland. Hackney-born Bob Hoskins had by now declined from a pit bull performer, spitting venom, conjuring with dreams of redeveloping Docklands, into a global Cockney, a charmless dwarf for hire. From a riverside Mussolini, with Shakespearean tragicomic potential, to a softshoe shuffler cosying up to cartoons. (*The Long Good Friday*, like *Performance* before it, by plunging recklessly into the profane stew of London, defined its moment; being, by temperament, both analytic and prophetic – making intelligent withdrawals from John Pearson's Kray document, *The Profession of Violence*, and also anticipating the hubris of Canary Wharf. The genius of the film lay in its ability to satirise events that had not yet occurred. To muzzle the totemic pit bull before it had taken its first bite. Both films earn their place in social history by pulling off the difficult trick – producers will fight to strangle it at birth – of polymorphous perversity, the intermingling of high and low, past and future, entropy and ecstasy. Borges and Bacon can go slumming with the Krays and the Richardsons, the Elizabethans and Jacobeans with rogue cadres of the INLA; psychedelic psychotics can vamp the sado-masochistic pretensions of protection racketeers with red paint hair. The famous photograph of Ronnie Kray on a lemon-coloured sofa with Lord Boothby and a bleary-eyed rentboy is brought to life in a fiction that is beyond the reach of our cynical libel laws. These films, more than any works of literature, float the dance of archetypes in such a way that the collisions are wholly unexpected and perennially rewarding. The list of works of a similiar stature, if extended to America, and to other periods, would include John Boorman's *Point Blank*, Robert Aldrich's *Kiss Me Deadly* and Sam Fuller's *Underworld USA*.)

Like Maggie and Ron (last seen as the sugar daddy of conspiracy villains in Don Siegel's remake of *The Killers*) cruising, thigh to thigh, in their motorised golf buggy, the special relationship with the pit bull was off: Alzheimer's heaven. Golden days misremembered. Bill Sikes Thatcherism, with the pit bull as its proud emblem, had yielded place to John Major's Forrest Gumpery: the idiot savants of twilight Toryism. A tyranny of the suburbs insisted that fighting breeds (inner-city class warriors) should be castrated or quietly put down – by lethal injection, not public barbecue. No emotive canine executions were required. No reporters camped outside the compound of Battersea Dogs' Home. No last minute stays of execution. No humbling phonecall to fatally weaken Major Minor's law and order stance.

Pit bulls were forced underground and the landscape was freed. That was the theory. Horror headlines ("Mad Dog Rips Off Toddler's Leg") gradually dissolved to "Heartbreak of Condemned Family Pet." Muzzled beasts never made it as style accessories on the street. They were as anachronistic as Norman Tebbit tattoos. Chaining yourself to a pit bull that couldn't bite would be like sniffing for pussy in a stocking-mask condom. The point of pit bull investment was aggro: "Step aside, pal. Diss me and you diss my meat weapon, my holocaust toy." The charge from acquiring a fighting breed was the buzz the Richardsons got from purchasing the special services of "Mad" Frankie Fraser. "Like China going nuclear."

Now you could stroll through Victoria Park, down the Bow Heritage trail, without fear of demented bowwows. Or so I thought – until I penetrated the north east corner, beyond the obelisk, the rarely visited war memorial, which is sited at the point where an invisible barrier is crossed, and you move out of Tower Hamlets (Old Ford) into South Hackney. It was here, in the twilight of an early winter evening, that I came across the Dog Tree, a small republic of the hanged. A pair of police horses, leaking gusts of icy breath, were not diverted from their leisurely circuit. A young woman, with stridently bleached and cropped hair, receiving minimal protection from her expensive leather jacket against the chill dampness that was setting in, detached herself from her two male companions to act as lookout. The men clamped their pit bulls to the lower branches. The dogs leaped obediently, hung on, veins popping, while their handlers lit up their cigarettes. The tree drooped with strange white fruit – genital clusters, no sign of enforced emasculation. In their flash/casual gear you'd take the gang for off-duty cab drivers; there was no attempt to disguise their training rituals. They were all career smokers, fags cupped in their fists like candles flickering in halloween lanterns. No fear of intervention by the park authorities.

I moved on, carrying this disturbing image away with me, leaving them in the thickening dark, this silent trio with their suspended killers. The power in the dogs' jaws would leech the tree's sap, outlast the patience of the London plane. They'd hang until they ripened. Until some monster hybrid had been hatched, a new species to defy the feeble prohibitions of the bureaucrats: dogs suckled on wood blood, yellow fungus and recycled soot.

As the savage imports vanished from sight, so did their cropheaded keepers, the hurt-addicts who had sponsored them. Dogmen: they couldn't exist on their own, they were a dependant lifeform. A mingling of salts was required. Without the pit bull, a certain breed of warrior was incomplete, unfinished, half-cock. Without combat, how should he synthesise his courage?

Gerald McClellan, the super-middleweight who suffered "cumulative and concussive damage to the brain" after his ferocious title fight with Nigel Benn, had a hobby, a domestic interest to take his mind away from the brutal disciplines of his profession: he bred pit bulls. His training for the Benn fight was tapered off in territory that was profoundly sympathetic to his double life, a gymnasium in North Woolwich. (Doors closed for one day to honour the passing of Ronnie Kray, "The Colonel".)

McClellan was a short-fuse assassin, he dispatched pretenders inside three rounds. "Pound for pound", the Fancy rated him as, debatably, the most destructive hitter on the planet. The intimate association with pit bulls would give him stamina. He'd never quit. Cut his head off and he'd chew your ankles. Benn was going. He was marked timber: that was the word in the betting-shops. Benn was refusing interviews. He'd climbed down into a sweat lodge of his own devising, to ingest some lurid cocktail of narcissism, self-hatred, tribal courage and disco blast. He'd out-dog the dogman.

The battle, when it came, in the London Arena, Docklands (where else?), had all the futurist primitivism of techno-combat snuff movies. It hurt to watch. This was what Sky TV had been invented for: a nation of dishes to catch the gore. Virtue from the spilled blood of warriors, irradiated by the cable light of satellite violence, should feed generations of fighting dogs. This was a battle to peep at from behind the sofa. A Wagnerian smoke opera – trumpets, spotlights, tributes to ex-heroes – enacted in the perfect setting, Frank Warren's grandest (doomed) speculation. Frank, who was climbing fast to the top of the heap (courtesy of ex-numbers racketeer, convicted stomp-killer Don King: the motor-mouth prophet with the hot-seat hair). He had sweetheart deals in place with Rupert Murdoch's emissaries.

Frank had this vision: an arena in Docklands. Frank Sinatra. Liza Minnelli. Tyson. Bruno. Las Vegas without the mob. Off-shore investment. The acid rain of lights on water. Electronic haiku. (Frank had the balls for it. He'd got his start promoting unlicensed shows in partnership with the notorious street-fighter, Roy "Pretty Boy" Shaw, "The Hardest Man in London".) Frank had shrugged off the bullets of the jogging hitman: case unsolved. Now he had the ultimate gladiatorial match, two men who would elevate the refusal to quit into a philosophy. McClellan didn't know what it felt like to lose and Benn, who had been there, suffered the shame, the disrespect of the media, and would die before tasting it again. When the brain/body refuses to accept telegrams of pain, the world is stood on its edge. Anything can happen.

The circus battled its way onto the Isle of Dogs (heavy budget tunnel bringing them up on the roundabout where McDonald's have colonised the prime site: inflatable clown on the roof nods in premature parkinsonism, punch-drunk in the wind from the river). The island is divided against itself: its lumpen fringe, in manipulated fear of the alien, had resumed an earlier flirtation with populist racism and the BNP (remember the last dockers marching on the Houses of Parliament, chanting in support of Enoch Powell's "rivers of blood" threnody?); while its hollow centre was busy trying to flog empty units to dying newspapers. Here was a battle at the end of time, the last hurrah of pit bull culture. The American, the dog breeder, cool and controlled, would take on (and destroy the pretensions of) the unpredictable Essex man, the ex-squaddie with the flair for drama. Benn was a throwback, pre-dog; a dangerously lisping, James Brown showman. He flaunted customised accessories, but he could take them off and leave them outside the ring. He made no treaty with his animal part.

After five rounds McClellan was travelling through *terra incognita*, his gumshield hanging aslant like a secondary cubist mouth. Seeing double, he had two of everything: he was twice the target. Half-blind, blinking in shock, he was a drowned man forcibly returned to life on some dazzling mica beach; television lights fusing into a dwarf sun. When he remembered Benn, he hit him. Hurt him. Punished him. Benn's jaw was horribly swollen (no bite left, a liquid diet). The inherited bravery of the pit bull kept McClellan on his feet, kept Benn punching – in fear, knowing there was no way to stop the American's advance, to break free from this hallucinogenic tango.

When McClellan finally dropped (dropped away from himself), and started to work his passage, on the seat of his pants, back towards his corner, it looked – to those who hadn't been there for the Rod Douglas and Michael Watson fights – nothing worse than exhaustion, dehydration, the trauma of disbelief. The two fighters, when the referee stepped between them, were divorced, in different films: McClellan trapped in the slowmotion of involuntary autism, and the victor, Benn, raving at the unsteady cameras, to deliver a triumphalist monologue that was too swift for language. Bruised, sweating, a misshapen mask, the champion was a scene-of-the-crime photograph blessed with speech. Speedy with a natural mix of combat chemicals, he ranted in tongues: a Rottweiler soliloquy. He would take days to wind down, to unravel the tangy weave of hurt and self-justification. To pay his genuine respects to a man who was no longer there. McClellan travelled west in an ambulance, away from the unlucky island, back to Whitechapel: "on the point of death".

This was still the "golden hour", the first hour after the collapse, when there is still realistic hope of drawing the mind back, out of darkness. Recovery is a long and painful process. Rod Douglas speaks of being blindfolded and passed various objects which he was required to identify. A slim 5p coin, squeezed in his fist, felt like "a big rough stone". He had been initiated into the terrifying world of the damaged shaman, the shape-shifter. Objects no longer had names. (Is it any wonder that the futures market took a plunge in Tokyo? The future had been called in to describe the geography of a present divorced from its memory traces.)

The ambivalence of this suspended time – bulbs flickering and flaring, at the point of failure – affects the aura of the Royal London Hospital. The building loses its firm boundaries: gauze windows tremble in gaslight. Strangers, unaware of McClellan's floating presence, are drawn in from the streets: solicitous and talking in whispers. (My editor, out for a weekend ramble, described how he found himself, with no fixed purpose, climbing the steps, joining the crowd in the reception hall.) The hospital had developed its own microclimate: weather fronts racing down the rubber corridors, tropical rooms, thunderheads incubating in stairwells. Everyday vision was filtered, bruised. Like slate that had been polished until it was translucent. The wards were loud with the pulsing silence of dogs with their cords cut. The anomaly that alerted Sherlock Holmes: dogs that refuse to bark. The damaged boxer, the pit bull breeder, is here and not here. The battle he endured remains unresolved while the zone around the hospital plays host to a plague of dream dogs, summoned to heal, to call their sponsor back. Former fighters shuffle through, not quite knowing how to behave at the sickbed, awkward with flowers. Witnesses to a sacrifice they do not begin to understand.

Muzzled and castrated, the pit bill is meaningless. Disenfranchised. An embarrassment. His place at the end of the super-strength leash has been given to the bull terrier, that long-nosed plodder. The bull terrier is an expensive, hi-wax version of Bill Sikes' abject Bull's-eye: "a white shaggy dog, with his face scratched and torn in twenty different places." A dog living on its past reputation, pampered beyond its gift for retribution. A dog with its nose in a jam jar and the look of an iron-pumping minder shoehorned into tailoring he has done nothing to deserve. Sullen, sulky, with ears pricked in pretend alarm. A mercenary of the worst kind. The sort of pooch that gets to pose with James Ellroy, the pulp Dostoevsky, on the back of *American Tabloid*. The accessory dog that proves a writer's status, that confirms the leap from Los Angeles lowlife ("I was homeless before it was in vogue") to Connecticut landowner.

The blokes who had dragged their chairs into the sunshine, outside the London Dog Centre in Middleton Road, were extremely courteous and helpful when I pitched around there with my copy of the Ellroy blockbuster, and asked them to identify the breed of lounging lapdog. "Bull terrier," they said, with evident approval. "About £300 a throw. Handsome indoors. Good as gold with the kiddies. Lovely animal." Of course, they saw through me at once. They smelled it. I wasn't in that league. Twenty years of hack work and I might make the down payment on a secondhand goldfish.

Ellroy merits the full studio treatment, the Marion Ettlinger portrait. Flecks of grey in the cropped hair and moustache, tailored seersucker jacket and a wet-nosed dog the size of a small reindeer lolling across his lumpy bits. Man and animal have the same quizzical/psychotic eye, the same sheen of achievement and earned repose. The bull terrier has a jangle of keys and disks around its neck (dog tags?) – as if it were the keeper of the estate, a butler in white fur. The whole set-up is, consciously, reminiscent of Stubbs, Reynolds, the classic country house portrait: dogs first, women and children to the rear. New money defined by its livestock holdings. The bull terrier was the bite manifest in Ellroy's driven prose, but it also possessed an iconographic gravitas. It repudiated Ellroy's "reputation for strangeness". Domesticity, the acquisition of property, and the selection of animals, all came together. "I got married in December," Ellroy told the journalist John Williams, "we've got a dog now."

The physical bonding between owner and pet can be genuinely spooky, especially when the pet not only mimics its master's facial expressions and moods, but assumes the persona of a phantom child. Ellroy, reminiscing about his time in the Los Angeles of the late Forties, recalls a sighting of the connected mobster who was to resurface in his novel *The Big Nowhere*: "I remember meeting Mickey Cohen in a barbershop on Fairfax Avenue; he had a bulldog named Mickey Jr . . ."

Such is the sentimentality of these old villains, the dog fancying gerontocracy, that they surround themselves with surrogate children. (Non-speaking parts leading, all too soon, to a flowery grave. Rivers of mercury tears.) It's quaint to compare Ellroy's cover portrait with the offering at the rear of Frankie Fraser's apologia, *Mad Frank (Memoirs of a Life of Crime)*. Ellroy, unnervingly tall, haunted, catching the light on the curve of his contact lenses, proudly exhibits his prize breed, his lounging bruiser – while Mad Frank (in a much cheaper living-room snap) gets his gnarled mitts around some tiny, woolly, no-eye, terrier thing. A lady's companion, a charmer, a catcher of crumbs. You can't tell if Frank's grown the wee scamp or if he's about to bite its head off. This pensioner of violence is working the opposite pitch. He's advertising his innate cuteness, his soft spot for the dinky, furry, perfumed parts of life. The Richardson's dental consultant is a solid citizen: "I've got a little import/export business now – glass, fancy goods." He lunches with the literati, with Peter Ackroyd in Granita. Like Ellroy, Mr Fraser has taken a punt on domesticity, marrying the daughter of one of the train robbers. He's to be found in a little café, off Camden Passage in Islington, serving cappuccino to the antique dealers. With the Reaganised barnet, black brogues, four-button cuffs, he's old school, media friendly. "No one has been to see me about the Moody killing," he boasts.

Mad Frank fondles the terrier. No need for a caption, the picture says it all: "Only went after our own, good to mum, streets safe for grannies." Like an amateur ventriloquist, Frank's got his fingers around the terrier's throat. He's trying to make the dog talk. It would if it could. It would yelp about the wonderful work the boys did for charity.

3
THE BIGGEST STREET PARTY SINCE
THE DEATH OF CHURCHILL
23.3.95. BETHNAL GREEN TO CHINGFORD MOUNT.

Entry in the space reserved for "occupation" in Ronnie Kray's
passport: DOG BREEDER.

A crisp, clear morning, bright and fresh and cold enough to make the flaunting of anklelength black crombies no burden: the perfect day for a funeral. Walking towards Bethnal Green, through Haggerston Park and over Hackney Road, twirling my horn-handled cane, I am able to appreciate the unnatural, expectant stillness – dispersed by the fretting of traffic that is already beginning to snag up. Outsiders, transients, put it down to road works; an extension of the red cone hole that is London. But *three* helicopters to the south, somewhere over Vallance Road or Cheshire Street, that is unusual. One helicopter, ferrying traumatised meat to the Royal London Hospital, we wouldn't notice it. Helicopters tracking suspects through the Holly Street estate, you can set your watch by them. Strap down the furniture. They're as regular as the noon cannon in the tropics. Three silver choppers, remorselessly circling the same small patch, are worth remarking; an arrogant display of budget that speaks of royal visitations, the London Marathon, or John Major on walkabout, prospecting for inner-city blight. (Perhaps this lowlevel clatter was prophetic: the Prime Minister did, within a few days, appear in East London like a bloodless apparition; jacket buttoned, hands clenched to his sides, surgical smile. An understudy for Gilbert and George. He was, according to the *Hackney Gazette*, "glad to see the back of Dalston's 'eyesore' Holly Street Estate". Retreating rapidly to his limo, he delivered his verdict in a strangulated croak: "You can't throw money at housing.") But on this unearned, mint morning, the fuss is all about real royalty, indigenous royalty; one of our local princes of darkness, a cashmere colonel, is about to be folded into his box.

A mob of expectant necrophiles are packing the fringes of Bethnal Green Road, dodging motors, climbing on lampposts – and that's just the salaried media. They're here to give an elderly, Romany/Jewish business gentleman (who has been living out of town for 26 years) a decent send-off. It's a great turnout for a notorious homosexual predator whom Peter Tatchell somehow never got around to "outing". George Cornell's ad libs in that direction (both sexist and weightist) having tragically backfired. "Fat poof" was an anachronism that received a public riposte from the affronted pedagogue.

Say what you like about the doped inertia of the slacker generation, the timidity of pensioners, give them what they want and they'll still make the effort. Give them the biggest gangland funeral since the Albert Dimes do and they know how to show their appreciation. (The Twins set the benchmark in floral tributes with their wreath for Albert: "To A Fine Gentleman From Reg and Ron." At £25 a letter.) The point is that no other strata of society has such a sense of tradition, such a memory for previous plantings. Stanley Baker, in his trilby and three-quarter length, cashiered major's coat, never missed. The East End had its reputation to uphold: sentiment backed by strict discipline. Senior members of the Firm had been shuttling to Maidstone nick to go over points of procedure with the surviving twin. There'd never be another Ronnie Kray. "There's been nothing to touch it since Churchill," said Carole McQueen, florist to the fraternity.

Splitting the Twins, divorcing Reggie from his "other half", was like splitting the atom; it had done something to the sky, lifted the leaden cloud scarf, pitching us into a day when sharply-outlined shadows were printed on the asphalt. The clarity of the light teased out phallic clusters of lenses; telephoto stalks could be displayed without embarrassment. (One of the first public glimpses of Ron was as an extra in *The Magic Box*, John Boulting's film portrait of William Friese-Greene, "the inventor of the movies". In a still photograph taken from the television version, he is dark, sallow, serious. In his flat cap, he looks unnervingly like a ghetto child marching away to a darker destiny.)

The merely curious, the event junkies, packed along the pavements of Bethnal Green Road and Vallance Road, on the route the hearse would take from W. English's funeral parlour to St Matthew's church, were tactfully backlit; tired hair scorched into seraphic aureoles. A frieze of witnesses to an El Greco apotheosis: the homecoming. One of those rare occasions when the crowd is as important as the central figure. The stature of the dead man has been weighed in the ranks of those who are prepared to stand for hours, mid-morning, to collar a few details of the final journey.

Ron had known for some time that his earlier fantasy, retirement to Suffolk, dog breeding, would never happen. He'd died without that consolation. Reg had been brought from Maidstone to take his farewell, a pinched, fit, close-cropped senior citizen, gold spectacles perched on the slope of a nose that had grown more prominent with the passing years. After the enforced separation, the physical resemblance between the Twins was no longer remarkable. Ron had shrivelled on his chemically-controlled diet, kippered in a fug of cigarette smoke, the battles with his paranoid demons. The Krays were anterior to pit bull culture, they'd always fancied German shepherds. There's a fine photograph of the teenage Ronnie with his dog Freda. (Caption: "Me and my Alsatian, Freda. We used to spend hours wandering across bomb sites in London. Our parents always encouraged us to be kind to animals.") Unusual name, Freda, I thought – until I remembered Erzulie Freda, the Dahomean divinity, the Mater Dolorosa of the Voodoo cosmology. A flirtatious Madonna with a soprano voice, recipient of gifts from men and women. Ronnie and his shaggy pet invoke the sepia East End of Wolf Mankowitz: Yiddish-spouting chancers, dewy-eyed urchins. The germ of sentiment goes with the territory, it's endemic. (I overheard a drinking session head-to-head between Kray foot soldier, Tony Lambrianou, and old Etonian novelist, Robin Cook, on the subject of favourite films. Cook raved about his 18 viewings of the Brian De Palma remake of *Scarface*, while Lambrianou eulogised Carol Reed's *A Kid for Two Farthings*, a Mankowitz confection, concerning the quest for a unicorn in Fashion Street.)

According to these hoary old villains, dog-love justifies everything. Ron and Reg never recovered from premature exposure to *Lassie Come Home*. It blighted their emotional development and helped to formulate the lodge rules for survival in the dance halls, clubs, spielers: never bad-mouth a Cockney mum and never harm a single hair of a dog's head.

That is the unchallenged doctrine of gangland, approved for post-prison interviews. Even wrong'uns, like Cornell and Jack McVitie, never went that far. They cheated, popped pills, did damage for cash, but they loved their families and patted Alsatians for luck. They were cursed for another reason entirely: they cost the Twins their lives. "It's because of them that we got put away." A nice piece of sophistry – to blame your victims for making you kill them.

The dog days were over. Ronnie Kray had been laid out in the back room of W. English's establishment at 464 Bethnal Green Road; painted, primped, pressed. The event, the procession, the crowds (many of whom didn't know who was being buried or what he stood for), took on the nature of a self-fulfilling prophecy. It meant something because the journalists said it did. It was important to be there because we *were* there. Ron's last rites were television, what more could anybody ask? A chance to recall better times; safe to go out at night, singalong pubs, coppers on the beat. Messrs. English were quietly ecstatic, soberly smashed by a rare chance to show what they could *really* do. It was like a bucket and spade mob picking up the contract to clear Hyde Park after the VE Day celebrations. These were the funeral rites of dog consciousness. Even their trade name fell in with the mood: English as the lettering on a stick of Margate rock.

Bethnal Green was one big street party: high ritual and low comedy, martial pomp, conspicuous expenditure. Helicopters, outriders, helmets and hand-sets. Newsreel crews, deals made, filmed the principal faces, while Secret State technicians panned the crowd. The press were caught in the confusion between burns of hyperactivity and almost intolerable wedges of boredom. Style scribes did their homework, thumbing through the gangland memoirs so that they'd recognise Frankie Fraser or Tony Lambrianou when they poodled into the churchyard. Researchers were busy inventing quotes, hammering golden nuggets into the carious mouths of bemused recidivists. Paparazzi risked life and limb, setting rickety ladders on traffic islands, dangling from stop signs. The Kray funeral was a major boost to the local economy: paydirt for florists, renters of black horses, firms that stretch limos. (Know-nothings asked if the Queen Mum had snuffed it.)

Even with Ron stiff as a starched dicky, the lesser faces were taking no chances with their floral tributes. They hadn't been privileged to get a peep inside the coffin. Rumours of death had often been exaggerated. The Krays had long since moved into the realm of mythology; youngsters, aping their dress code and hairstyles, thought that they were contemporaneous with Jack the Ripper. The Twins co-existed with Craig and Bentley and the Reservoir Dogs: natural born killers on the spectral plain. Brightly inked Terminator figures floating through a monochrome world.

The funeral cortège would turn into Vallance Road at the Cornwallis pub, where there are two street names: the shabby original and the new, Tower Hamlets-approved version. New signs, in my experience, mean trouble. The elegant green motifs creeping into Hackney (forerunners of the Major visitation) are accompanied by traffic meters, prohibitions on laissez-faire street parking. Cleanliness comes with a price. "Safe" neighbourhoods and restored iron railings have to be paid for by Kray era tithes. Eco babble and brass knuckles. Tony Lambrianou agrees: "Today, if I see anyone damaging a tree, or drawing graffiti, I go absolutely potty."

We have, up to now, misinterpreted the Kray philosophy: the pitch was Green, and the boys were the natural allies of the Goldsmith Brothers. Free market capitalists who cared about the environment, channelling excess profits straight back into high profile charity. Good housekeeping that isn't afraid, when necessary, to rap the odd knuckle. Animal fetishism. Anthropomorphism so intense that it verged on voodoo ritual. It's a shame that the Krays' political career was aborted so soon: the Twins were very active members of the Bethnal Green Conservative Association. Lady Mancroft, president of the Association at that time, recalls "a frightful row . . they attacked someone, threw him across the road through a shop window. The police were very close and the hospital managed to sew the chap's ear back on." It was providential that Geoffrey Howe, a coming man, was on call to provide free legal advice. High spirits, unexceptional in the House, were deemed to be wholly out of order in the East End. So the careers of two good grass-roots Tories took a different turn.

I pushed through the mob of voyeurs who blocked a path to Pellicci's café, where I had arranged to collect Marc Atkins. There was no way to dodge our outstanding contract with Chingford Mount Cemetery. The first attempt may have petered out in the millennial twilight of Claremont Road, but now the Kray funeral procession would complete the second arm of our proposed **V**. As dedicated psychogeographers, we had unfinished business in the Lea Valley.

I'd had an interesting time with Messrs. English trying to wheedle out the route that the mortuary cavalcade would take. The premises, down at the Cambridge Heath end of Bethnal Green Road, were under siege: a low brick shed with a sloping glass and lead roof. (That's the back view from the elevated entrance of the Bethnal Green United Reform Church: RESURRECTION POWER EVANGELISTIC MINISTRIES.) Elegiac light shimmered on the rails of the steps, projecting tree shadows through the meshed windows of the death shack, into the coffin store. Behind me, the church door was smothered in Haitian posters: "Beyond the mountain, another mountain." (A translation of the popular proverb, "*Deye mon, gin mon.*" Take away one problem, and you reveal the next.)

"*The poor are not gifts from the sky. They are the products of the structures of exploitation and those structures have their roots since the months when Columbus arrived in America.*" President Jean-Bertrand Aristide.

Yes, I had broken off my Kray investigation to check out the church. Primitive, naïf paintings around the hall: "Suicide of Henri Christophe with a silver bullet." The stock Doc "Papa" Williams had been trying to promote in his Dalston Junction shop for £75, before seasonal fluctuations brought on a permanent state of sale. Day-Glo martyrology. Madonna and Erzulie Freda statuettes that would soon be resurfacing as cut-price garden ornaments. The paintings were interspersed with colour photographs of poverty and squalor, inducing flash replays of Ian Thomson's "*Bonjour Blanc*" (*A Journey through Haiti*), which I was then reading. Thomson told me that he had spliced an extract from my novel *Downriver* into his text. Haiti/London: these strange circuits continue, the river that is all rivers, the jungle that wants to break through the paving stones. In Thomson's account of his stay in the Graham Greene-celebrated Hotel Oloffson, he is disturbed by a dreadful nocturnal howling. "Papa Dog", he is told.

English's funeral shed aligns perfectly, so I notice, with the gasholder on the canal, the spot where they fished out Hector Anthony Slaly. On the far side of Bethnal Green Road: LONDON LOOK, MANUFACTURERS OF DRESSES, SUITS. CITY VIEW OFF-LICENCE. COLMANS HAIRCUTTERS. Which struck me as a fair summary of Kray Kulture. SAY GOODBYE TO STAINS. PRICE STICKERS £2.53. SMOKING CAUSES FATAL DISEASES. Tactful product placement on the wall above English's saturnine operation.

The front entrance, on the main road, is a grander affair, sustained by a half-hearted attempt at rustification: bull's eye glass, sample headstones. N.A.P.F.P FOR PRE-PAID FUNERAL PLANS. VISA. ACCESS. English's clerk, nipping out to block deeper penetration into the mysteries of the autopsy cult, is superbly cast: coalblack jacket, pearl waistcoat, striped

trousers, bulled shoes, hair like wet tarmac. Initially, and with every justification, he is suspicious of us: your dishevelled, limping reporter (who
can produce no documentation other than a mangled bookdealer's card,
used for claiming discounts) and his stiff-necked companion, the Oxfam
skinhead with the complicated camera.

I can't help staring in admiration at the mortician's aristocratic pallor:
you'd have to live under a parasol to achieve it. The man is so stiff that
you'd take him for a secret tippler of embalming fluid, but he carries my
card up the steps to the glass-fronted office and has it checked out. His
superior, a woman of substance, follows him back to the reception area;
she stands behind his chair while he opens his book of maps. When he
does decide to reveal the route, he recites it with genuine enthusiasm.
This gig, he's smart enough to recognise, will put him up there with the
Duke of Norfolk. The funeral is a command performance, no expense
spared; it's the event by which the East End will be judged. There have
been telephone consultations and high level conferences in Maidstone.
Expenditure won't be showy, it'll be exhibitionist. The mortician's controlled excitement, the rush he gets, comes from his awareness that he
is not merely planting an above-the-title Sixties villain, but stage-
managing, perhaps for the last time, a great social tableau: library footage
that will run for ever. (But he's not too preoccupied with his report to
censor Atkins' attempt to snatch a portrait.)

Six plumed black horses, with 26 top-of-the-range limousines to
follow. Poland has been invaded with less. A dark oak coffin with gold
handles would be displayed in a glass-sided hearse, borne on a gun carriage – as befits the deceased's martial status. The dimensions of the gun
carriage would test out the ingenuity of Carole McQueen and her horticultural engineers: how to fit **THE COLONEL** on to such a narrow
border; how to heap the roof with such a profusion of blooms. It
seemed as if the corpse had flowered; as if the body's noxious gases had
exploded into spiral galaxies of red and white and blue. A wake of
pollen and steaming horse dung trailed behind the procession like the
wash of an ocean liner. Some of the cars had to be pressed into service
as wreath transporters; there were enough floral tributes to replant the
deserts of Nevada. Four pall-bearers – Charles Kray (North), Freddie
Foreman (South), Johnny Nash (West), Teddy Dennis (East) – would
symbolise the homage paid by the four cardinal districts of London. The
conceit was Blakean, the Sons of Albion "dividing the space of love
with brazen compasses."

The route too, as the clerk previewed it, came straight out of one of those odd, but effective listings in Blake's *Jerusalem*. Districts linked together by will, not logic. It was the path we would have taken on our University of Greenwich graffiti trawl, if the light had held and we hadn't detoured into St Patrick's, Leytonstone. From English's along Bethnal Green Road to Vallance Road in a stately progress (don't look at the camera towers, don't frighten the horses). The mortician, top-hatted like Baron Samedi, setting the pace, doubling as a mute. Pinched shoes effecting an expression of mournful solemnity. The caravan would pause (horses loosen their bowels) at the spot where 178 ("Fortress Kray") used to stand, then wheel into Cheshire Street, right at the Carpenters Arms and on to St Matthews's Church.

Expectant crowds had gathered early, blue jeans and brown leather jackets set against the long coats of the minders, the jewellery, coiffures and dark glasses, of the public mourners, local celebrities recognised only by their own. I decided to take Marc with me to follow the procession on foot. The concept of "strolling", aimless urban wandering, the *flâneur*, had been superceded. We had moved into the age of the stalker; journeys made with intent – sharp-eyed and unsponsored. The stalker was our role model: purposed hiking, not dawdling, nor browsing. No time for the savouring of reflections in shop windows, admiration for Art Nouveau ironwork, attractive matchboxes rescued from the gutter. This was walking with a thesis. With a prey. (The term "stroller" had in any case been discredited by its association with George Graham, the former manager of Arsenal Football Club. George was an Albanian stroller, a pragmatic dandy with a fluid sense of fiscal probity. "Stroller" here is applied in the sense that a dwarf is called "Lofty".) The stalker is a stroller who sweats, a stroller who knows where he is going, but not why or how. (Andrew Duncan, in a review in the magazine *Angel Exhaust*, reads the work of the poet/sculptor Brian Catling in precisely these terms: "The classic Catling theme is stalking; delicately, in a hush; as anxiety and hunger spiral out of control on either side." Catling's *The Stumbling Block its INDEX*, published by Book Works in 1990, is the stalker's ur-text; a somatic investigation of the interface of dream and memory, present tense anomalies discovered in the laneways that divide Whitechapel from the glitzy husks of the New City. Debt corruptions and creative poverty assault the narrator as he stalks his "pillar to the dispossessed".)

Following the funeral would prove a nice exercise in this new mode, the coda to our previous failure. There was however one minor drawback: both Marc and I were, in our different ways, crippled. Marc couldn't move his head. Fourteen hours a day in the darkroom had gifted him with a ridge of tension at the base of the skull that felt, so he reported, like a bolt through the neck. It wasn't just the repetitive strains and stresses, it was the inhuman concentration, the dredging of imagery (allied to maintaining a double and treble life of breathtaking complexity, more names and titles than a college of cardinals). Stiffness was an elective condition: eye/brain/hand in a state of perpetual arousal. Stalking London, early and late, in a feeding frenzy. A convinced vegetarian whose lifelong obsession was the analysis and celebration of meat, dusty metropolitan light nibbling at the unclothed female form. Generously vampiric, he'd butchered himself in pursuit of his project: the cataloguing of the city, its buildings, shrines, rivers, railways, writers, clouds and women. Marc's liniment blended aromatically with the floor polish, necrophile blooms, and fierce preservatives that were washing around W. English's reception area.

My own problem was pre-geriatric obsolescence: the medial ligaments of my right knee, worn away, shredded by years of misuse, pounding the pavements. I'd relied too much on theory, ignored warning twinges and had now to endure the grinding of bone on bone. Over the last year, scratching at this book, I'd walked everywhere – coming home from Notting Hill, with a cargo of books, I felt the knee go (played it off against the usual spasms in the back). I couldn't rest, there was too much to do. Meetings already arranged, permissions to explore. The Krays couldn't reschedule the funeral to a later date, any more than they could have held over the George Cornell affair until the start of the grouse shooting season. It was unfortunate that, in one rush, we'd climbed the tower of St Anne, Limehouse, right up the ladder to the crumbling Portland pyramids, and then the old Port of London Authority building at Tower Hill, to photograph the giant stone oxen; then – fees paid – wound up the tight bore of stairs, under the hollow spire of Christ Church, Spitalfields. I was now on a stick, limping and hopping alongside the photographer who couldn't turn his head to scan anything that wasn't directly in front of him.

This quixotic freakshow realised one of my fantasies, the lightest of them: that pressure on the spine, wear and tear on the joints, estrangement from language, would finally reduce me to the condition of a dog. Driven towards dizzying spirals, meanderings, shit-sniffing quests, I'd fur over, pad through shallow inner-city runnels, piss acid to scorch a track across the abandoned tenter grounds. No weapon but a consumptive bark. I was sure that I was on the point of discovering a talking dog, the one with the revelation: the one who had been there all along, in fiction and mythology. The company of mutes was an odd place to begin my search.

But a much worse fear nagged at me: the interpretation of this sudden pain in the knee as the consequence of my long obsession with the feral monoped Todd Sileen, anti-hero of my novel *Radon Daughters*. I was on the proverbial last leg, and it was failing, self-condemned. Novels are bad prophecy, they don't obey the rules: that which is most fraudulent, most "fictional", will come true. We flatter the elegance of our imagination by our subsequent behaviour. We fix the future to rewrite the past. The weight-lifter's elasticated support in which my knee was gripped made it feel like a peg of timber. Like Sileen's tin shaft. I awaited the advent of Sileen's carcinogenic visitations.

What a pair! A photographer who can't twitch without screaming and a correspondent at large for whom every step is a small agony. (I subsequently discovered that the problem lay in my having legs of different lengths. Botched from the start.)

Atkins was hanging around outside Pellicci's: NO DOGS ALLOWED/SORRY NO PRAMS. His was the only unmoving head lifted above a tide of rotating Cockneys, who were straining to pick up the first muffled rumours of the horses' hooves. There was no time to indulge him in a coffee and a round of toast. Pellicci's is a fine, step-down establishment; lace curtains in ice-cream parlour windows, shiny vanilla panels and the name spelled out in generously spaced Univers Medium lettering; an Italianate ledge of pot plants above; family portraits, mirrors and marquetry, inside. The short limp and drag from the Cornwallis to English's austere shed is like a précis of Ronnie Kray's career. Pellicci's was a key rendezvous – gossip, fashion updates, subsidised grub – for the firm in its earliest days. Tony Lambrianou remembers it with affection: "Pellicci's Café . . . was one of the places that the twins used to hold their afternoon meets . . . Neville, the guv'nor often jokes about the number of people Ronnie knocked through the window." A post-siesta trance of cigarette smoke and coffee fug. Evenings working the circuit of sympathetic pubs. The Old Horns, scene of a famous stand-up battle, had now diminished to a rarely-opened drinker. Its symbol: Jeremiah Bullfrog, a horribly weathered amphibian with a baseball bat. There's a lot of time-killing in the criminal life, GBH of minutes and seconds; a lot of slo-mo nights out – rambling anecdotage sheering into eruptions of violence. Hours can drift by, brushing ash from a starched cuff, getting the knot of a silk tie *precisely* so. The Twins had the advantage of a living mirror, a double to be checked for dandruff and excessive nose hair.

It was quite a trick blagging my way through the crowd – the jobless, the unwaged, the never haves, the ones who parrot the party line, and those who don't have the faintest idea what's going on today or any other day. A restlessness is abroad. They all feel the buzz, the tremor, this shocking beneficence of spring sunlight.

Beyond Pelliccis (No. 332) is the Musclework Gym: MENS WEIGHT TRAINING/KEEP FIT. BODYBUILDING. PERSONAL TUITION. WEIGHT LOSS. WEIGHT GAIN. SAUNA. SUNBED. Like a postcard from the Kronk in Detroit. The sign invokes America in the way that returned exiles will paint their houses on the Maltese islands with stars and stripes, a spiritual twinning. Some of the funeral cortège minders got their start here: a street style quite unlike that espoused by the Krays. These are clubs for Tarantino inflatables: black suits loose as bin bags, ties thin as brass rules, shaven skulls, combat stubble. A coven of steroidal warder types cracking their knuckles. All of them with big shoes, even when their feet are as dainty as those of tap-dancers. A machismo of size. Big feet, big dick. One hundred of these gladiators rented by the hour. It's not often you find yourself so close to that quantity of tattooed ear lobe.

Random hallucinations multiply: monopeds, amputees, skipping along like a mocking subtext. A girl who only needs to buy one stocking at a time being carried into McDonald's. An elderly adolescent, with an expression of profound cynicism, being hurtled through the mob in a customised wheelchair, his jeans stitched at the stump. A wino battering along on crutches, as if he'd just heard that Balls Brothers were giving it away. A festival of the maimed in which we were no more than pretenders.

Backing off, we're squeezed against the shopfronts: No. 350, Trotters Jewellers. TOP PRICE FOR GOLD. We'd located the inspiration for TV's Delboy. A trophy cabinet laying out all the relevant totems of the locality. A golden greyhound at £139, or a boxing glove at £115, a horse's head at £125. Best of all, on this day of the dead, a gilded voodoo skeleton with red jewel eyes at £179.

Moving on: Alex Johnson. CRIMINAL LAW. IN TROUBLE WITH THE POLICE SEE US. DIVORCE & FAMILY PROBLEMS. ACCESS TO CHILDREN. SEE US FIRST. No question marks, statements of fact that define the special qualities of the neighbourhood.

No. 408. Meteor Sports & Leisure. BOX CLEVER & GET YOUR KICKS. THE OXFORD HOUSE KICKBOXING CLUB. Heavy duty PRO pump. Airsoft guns. Bull bars. Weights. The impedimenta of defensive violence.

Jesters Amusement Arcade. Steak houses. Florists. The grey shed with the inverted V roof where the dead are laid out. It's all here, business as usual. Respect is respect and a dollar is a dollar.

St Matthew's is one of those typical East London parish churches with its own patch of grass, no particular ambiance, sinister or otherwise, and permanently locked doors. The churchyard is a useful walk through, a shortcut, a stool-carpet for dogs. The church with its dull red bricks and blackened windows has the feel of a surprisingly well-preserved library or tax office.

A notable incumbent, the Reverend RH Hetherington, earned his paragraph in the pulp histories through his long association with the Krays. Hetherington, a muscular Christian of the old school, was frequently called up as a character witness. He was also chosen to officiate at Violet Kray's funeral.

But the main point of interest in St Matthew's, before this great day, is that it wasn't a Hawksmoor – although it carried the taint of association, a project dreamt of, but unfulfilled. Hawksmoor, in his epic reimagining of London, had drawn up a site plan for a "Basilica after the Primitive Christians" in Bethnal Green, on ground that lay between Brick Lane and Hare Street (later Cheshire Street). The Church Commissioners were unable or unwilling to complete the purchase of the land. So that Hawksmoor's "septum or Enclosure . . . to keep off filth Nastyness & Brutes" exists only as a sketch, an ideogram, a mind construction that still floats over the undefined territory. What might have been overwhelms what is: Hawksmoor's "complete environment to guide the beholder and enhance his experience".

A moderate crowd, bareheaded, behind crush barriers watched nothing very much. Accredited media paced inside the fence. OB vans. Tripods on the pavement, trainee clipboard-directors letting their cameramen set up in any way that took their fancy. Production assistants plotted coffee runs. Small groups of near-strangers worked together, professionals of *ennui*. An outbreak of yellow cones and police in scrambled egg vests. Bethnal Green is *en fête*, a celebration that cannot quite declare itself. Freakishly stretched limos, cigar torpedoes, barely make it around the tight left-hander into Wood Close. These villains are so old they think they're being flash by giving two fingers to petrol rationing. The term "wide boy" underdescribes them; strident incognitos with coathanger shoulders. Parked up, hidden behind tinted glass, they're instantly recognised by a passing bag lady, a Carpenters Arms familiar. She hoots her derision.

One minor TV mouth, toasted to an unhealthy walnut tan by studio lights, fannies about inside the fenced arena, screaming into his mobile: "Where are we? Can somebody *please* tell me where the fuck we are?" Helicopters circling. Grey bullet heads in Brick Lane buffalo jackets bunch together on the west side of the street. Down at the far end, beyond the Carpenters Arms, you find the same knot of foot-stamping ghouls who used to wait outside Pentonville for the posting of the execution notice. (This cul-de-sac and railway crossing, Hare Marsh, deserted on weekdays, pitched by Sunday traders, has been featured in works by two notable East End writers. It was the location for Alexander Baron's *King Dido*, his homage to Arthur Morrison, and it was photographed as a background to the author portrait on the dust-wrapper of Emanuel Litvinoff's *A Death out of Season*. For Litvinoff the bridge and the railway arch had a peculiar significance – like a crossing point in Berlin, a rite of passage. Locations illuminated, as he points out in his autobiographical sketchbook, *Journey Through a Small Planet*, by memories of sexual initiation and battles fought.)

It's easy to forget: somewhere in the middle of all this is a corpse. The hard old men are closer to it, arthritic claws knuckled in sovereigns, throats goitred in gold. Faces last seen making up the numbers in night-club souvenirs: Eric Mason, Terry Spinks (a cortisone cherub). Ruthlessly ironed handkerchiefs peeping from the savage gash of a breast pocket. This has been a major killing for the car rental mob, the muscle agencies, the three-chair barbers. Who says London refuses to oblige major film productions? Roads closed off, police, colourful extras, banks of cameras: the funeral is a one-day epic with a Mitchumesque non-performance at its centre. Nothing for the uninvited to witness. 140 ticketed seats barely covers the worldwide media interest, the reporters booked in to be serenaded by Sinatra's *My Way* and Whitney Houston's torch song *I Will Always Love You* – before the reading of the honour role of those who have been prevented from attending, "friends from Broadmoor and the prisons".

Outside, on the pavement, we make do with miles of colour snapshots: the crowd taking its own portrait. (When I went back later, after it was all over and the churchyard was its usual bleak self, I climbed on a tombstone to get a better angle on the crucified Christ statue. A voice from beneath me. "You used to be a bookdealer, didn't you?" One of the honorary Jocks, an ex-seaman with a Cheshire Street used-book pit, sleeping it off in the graveyard. He scampered away, still cursing the inconvenience, the noise, the bullshit, the crocodile tears. For him, there was no percentage in nostalgia.)

The procession moved off so slowly – following the mutes, the black-plumed horses, back down Bethnal Green Road to the east – that, even in our distressed condition, we were able to keep up quite easily. I punted on my grandfather's stick. Marc, stiff as an ironing-board, sweated, giving off gouts of horse embrocation. The glass-sided gun carriage was soon out of sight. We were lost in the rabble, wondering where it all went wrong. Albert Donoghue, one of many routinely described as "the hardest man in London", had his own theory. "Ronnie should have been brought out like a pit bull." The younger Kray Twin was, Donoghue felt, incapable of forward planning, sensitive man management, trading in futures. He was a pure frightener, a force of nature, like the "night-prowling devil-dog with 'phosphorescent eyes', apparently in the service of Baron Samedi", as described by Ian Thomson in *Bonjour Blanc*. (Reg Kray had occasion once to shoot Donoghue in the leg, in the way of business. And the Krays were always wary after that. "How can you trust a person you've shot?" Infallibly bent logic.)

Over Cambridge Heath Road and down the Roman. Marc told me how he used to wander here at night. He'd leave a girlfriend in Heneage Street, make his excuses, and strike east. For this priapic navigator, London was marked out by the rooms where he had conducted clandestine affairs. Or, rather, by the walks between them: anticipation heightening sensory awareness, appreciation of stone and sky. His monologue reminded me of the Hackney Irishman I nod to, a lopsided pedestrian in white cap, raincoat, trainers – always out on the street. I was never able to satisfactorily explain his circuits until I met him coming out of the betting-shop. The routes he adopted were pure superstition, defensive magic, posts to be touched to bring him luck. Spirals that favoured the jumps, detours for all the different racetracks. He was going over the ground, firm or heavy, in his mind, converting the Curragh into Queensbridge Road, Haggerston Park into Aintree. His hikes had to be adjusted to the measurement of the course, a long preamble to the laying out of cash.

How far was it to Chingford Mount? Ten, twelve miles? The mortician, map open across his lap, had gone gloatingly over every inch of the journey. We didn't need an excuse to peel off to ask the florist

Carole McQueen (409, Roman Road) to help with our enquiries.

Tasteful corner premises, polished brass lamps (lily necked) swooping over a green awning. CHOCOLATES, CARDS, BALLOONS. A cheerful little team, very obliging – and with a sense of humour. "Florists to the Fancy", that was their bag. Competitive pricing. A proper discretion. Nudge, nudge. No gossip where none intended. A diamond operation. Ronnie's do had been a challenge. The Channel Islands denuded to meet the demand. Colour combinations like an explosion in a paint factory. Floral sculptors working around the clock to shape boxing rings, wreaths like dog tracks, hearts the size of Sri Lanka. (Cue another Atkins revelation: he'd moonlighted as a welder once, making the armatures for postmortem tributes.) Paula, Carole's daughter-in-law, reckoned she could knock up quite a showy display, with full lettering, for £150. Cashmoney.

Wheeling right into St Stephen's Road, the marchers know that relief is at hand; around the corner, in Tredegar Road, the big black cars are waiting. 26 of them, polished to mirror glass by English-as-a-future-second-language Balkan labour. The brilliant roof gardens suggesting a spring ritual: dead king, metal bursting into bloom. The permed heads of the last witnesses in the crowd support this conceit, blown dandelions.

At last, those top hats can come off; the mopping of sweaty brows. Ticket holders haul themselves gratefully aboard. This is the best of it, the cruise to Chingford Mount. The best for them. The flotilla pulls away. We know where they're going, but we've lost sight of them in the fury of the Blackwall Tunnel Northern Approach. We're stuck in a sirocco swirl of diesel fumes, grit and greasy paper, under the Bow Flyover, looking east towards Stratford.

No point in spelling it out, the long dusty purgatory of that tramp: swinging by Angel Lane on to the track of our original walk. Through Leyton to Walthamstow, without the encouragement of graffiti. The Baker's Arms. A meditation on mortality. Would it be worth coming home? We had been wrecks at the start of this: newsreel footage from St Matthew's was playing in the TV showrooms before we reached the end of Hoe Street. Pirate copies of the Kray funeral video would be on offer in Walthamstow Market by the time we reached William Morris' house in Lloyd Park. The borough was hideously familiar from my misspent youth, teaching in Waltham Forest Technical College and School of Art. Walthamstow is where prospects of gentility, the Epping arcadia, come to die.

We are now entirely on our own; if the procession came this way, there's no trace of it. No dislodged floral tributes in the gutter. No tearful crowds hanging about, caps in hand. Bethnal Green is a foreign country, it's where they're all escaping from. Outside the pre-war glamour of Walthamstow Stadium, we're reduced to straining to catch dog noise: humanity. The fixes and fiddles, the razor gangs and petty criminality of Robert Westerby's 1937 novel, *Wide Boys Never Work*. Greyhounds: they don't belong to the same species as pit bulls. They're money on legs. You see them out on the Marshes in all weathers, being trained by fit young women: nerves on a string, shivering on the hottest day. They must have been hunters once – of a peculiarly dim kind. Who else would be stupid enough to chase a lump of old fur on a wire? Not just the first time, but *every* time; tongues lolling, or muzzled, up for it as soon as the trap opens. They don't have outsides, these dogs, no flesh cladding. They're all ribs and innards, X-rays of themselves. Febrile, bred to be elsewhere.

If I make it to Chingford Mount, that's the finish of the stalking project. The rest will be libraries and armchairs. Strolling through the archives. Picture research. A black and white poster at the bus stop: **KILLER SERIAL** TWIN PEAKS. Chingford, the town centre, a parade of shops and a bus turnaround: it's every Hackney cab-driver's dream. Lea Valley suburbia, the forest fringe. It's the one move you'd never have expected from the Krays, they hung on so loyally to their East End roots (Hoxton, Bethnal Green, Whitechapel): they made a career out of it. Even when Ron hid out after the Blind Beggar shooting it was on Lea Bridge Road – where you can find everything from chefs' hats to the firm that supplies the Queen Mother with ladders. The real country, yes. Suffolk, I could understand that. A country mansion, breathing space where a true urbanite could learn to appreciate what he was missing; outhouses geared for dog breeding. But *Chingford*. Elbowing cabbies and market casuals aside to reach the sherry shelf in Tesco's. Chingford is for rate-payers with kids. Chingford is compulsory amnesia. It's where you eradicate slumland memories. Ron, give him credit, was anti-suburb. The aristocracy on its uppers, showbiz and villainy: hearts of gold. Nobody can spray a patina on childhood like a retired gangster. Recollections are perfect – names, faces, details – until they reach the years of maturity, those little episodes that haven't been documented on their record sheet.

I have to swing my leg, stiff as a plank, to climb the gentle declivity of Chingford Mount; to leave behind Churchills Club (no apostrophe, generous green awnings), the charity boutiques, steak and fish restaurants, the locksmith and dog training centre. A small town high street swallowed in ribbon development. With relief, we approach All Saints Church, and its splendid view back across the reservoirs and pylons of the Lea Valley.

All Saints, low, square-towered, with its brick and tile extension, its leaded windows, its bushes and creepers, is a feature; a village church on a hillock at the side of the A112. It distances itself from the too regular rows of the cemetery, the New Town of the dead. Marc and I sit on the stone wall. The mourners have departed, the crowds have dispersed. The graves and sepulchres on this well-tended grass tump are detached residences, scattered at random, resting place of generations with proper birth certificates. The great and the good of the parish. (Including, oddly, a white tub-shaped vault with curved sides, which is dedicated to the memory of Robert Boothby, Esq., "who departed this life December The I. MDCCXXXIII". No relation, as far as I know, to Ronnie's bow-tied patron from the House of Lords.)

Crossing towards the cemetery, we come close to being run over, the vision back down the hill is so grand and evocative; a distancing effect that grants the city its mystery, horizon blue as smoke. Canary Wharf is uncancelled. This is a site of transition; we're nearer to the sky than the town. Time lifts its finger from the pulse. Abney Park and Chingford Mount fuse, float. Our petty discomforts go into remission. We turn towards the peaceful avenues of the dead.

In at the gate. THIS CEMETERY IS A/DOG FREE ZONE/DOGS ARE BANNED/EXCEPT GUIDE DOGS. We both laugh. We've surely earned it the hard way, this "dog free" zone. But, going inside, we feel it's true. The dogs – with this burial – have been put aside, discounted. The **V** has been accomplished and the hellhounds dropped back into another dimension. The auld alliance was broken and the power of the Twins neutralised.

We're tired, hurt, mad enough to see symbols everywhere. Immediately to the right of the gate, alongside the William Alexander Hall memorial, a grey granite plinth, is the robed statue of a decapitated angel with a white spike neck and a bad case of creeping leaf rust. This was it. I didn't have to say anything to Marc, he was already busy with his camera. Unofficial mourners were still drifting down the long straight avenue, looking from side to side, checking out all the flower-decked graves, the cellophane bundles, the fantastic tributes – which included a donkey shaped from pink carnations and a football of giant daisies. We wouldn't join them. (I didn't witness, but I read later, how Reg Kray, handcuffed to one of the tallest policeman they could find, a man with a presentable grey stripe suit, touched his lips to his young wife's tombstone. The photographs caught him bending forward, supported by layers of large hands, cabinets of rings, heavy gold watches.)

The head of the stone angel had been carefully placed on the rim of the memorial plinth, just beneath the words I DO NOT ASK TO SEE. It was split cleanly in half, the divided sections touching at the hairline; a dark triangle between them – the perfect **V**. Waiting for Marc to finish, I realise what we have discovered: not the "opposite" of a dog, but the contrary of the ley line. Dog lines. Instead of direct paths of light linking significant structures (spires, earthworks, mounds), the "dogline" is a spiral – like the sorcerer's *vèvè*: a stool-sniffing, circling back on itself, avoidance of the shortest way. (I recalled the track of Stan Brakhage's camera in his 1959 film, *Sirius Remembered*, his elegy to a dead dog. The sympathetic magic of mimicking the beast's halting surges in a dance of loss. "Movement does seem," Brakhage wrote, "to be the prime realator.") London, we were convinced, was mapped by cued lines of energy, connecting buildings with natural geological and geographical forms; making paths available down which the more tedious laws of time could be aborted. Now there was another, wilder system in play: the improvisations of the dog. The retreats, spurts, galloping loops and pounces of the stalker.

I let it lie for a few weeks, then, on a pleasant Sunday morning, I cycled back along the Lea to Chingford. I'd had the ligament damage checked out (learnt about my legs of different length) and been told to do no walking. I gripped the bicycle for support – in the fashion favoured by drunks on Irish country roads – as I made my way from the cemetery gates, the Hall memorial, to the Kray family burial plots at the far end.

The freshly turned earth, and perhaps forty yards of grass behind the tombstones of Ronnie Kray's father, mother, and sister-in-law, were blanketed in dead flowers, gaudy colours fading to browns and mauves. The traditional "wedding cake left out in the rain". Ribbons and bunting gave the low tumulus the appearance of a place of pilgrimage. I had only to follow the crowds.

Fathers led their young children by the hand, so that they would get an early taste of it – mortality, fame. Old Hollywood, the faith in hereditary royalty that had been lost: the Kray grave seems to have replaced all that.

Young women with long skirts and shoulder bags. Some of them have brought small bunches of wild flowers, violets, which they drop without show on to the floral carpet.

The effect was both emotive and grotesque, an overblown rhetoric of grief. Self-aggrandising tributes to a man who had been, for years, a chemically palliated zombi; a man whose humanity had died with his victims. In a sense, he couldn't die: he was dead already, estranged from himself. Victim and servant of the voices. The endlessly repeated (and revised) fables of those few short months of glory, which left him trapped forever in a coffin of newsprint.

Dead ground that had burst prematurely into bud; the sweet-sick stench of home-brewed perfume, flowerheads rotting in water. RONNIE. THE COLONEL. **THE KRAY TWINS**. Spelled out in pink carnations, with scarlet tulip crowns for emphasis: lettering on the side of a neon gambling hell. Colour combinations too rich to stomach. Fresh pinks with broken veins. THE OTHER HALF OF ME: as if Reggie had been interred with his brother. (The crowds outside St Matthew's call for his release, an end to this unnatural punishment. Which can never happen. That would be like rewriting history, opening the grave to make us see the spectre of our past wasted by time, pinched, crookbacked, shrunken.)

RONNIE iced into a birthday cake of daisies, into a boxing ring. The sacrifice of thousands of carnations, pink and white and sclerotic. Puce roses sweating with shame. Eggy bundles of lilies, pinched at the waist by purple ribbons. Wreaths like the wheels of articulated lorries. Hearts and hoops and American flags. GOD BLESS. A plethora of tributes from Birmingham. ACTRESS & BISHOP. MULDOON AUTO'S (with traditional grocer's apostrophe). **FREEDOM AT LAST, FLANAGAN**. Showbiz signatures: Barbara Windsor, Roger Daltrey. Enough armatures to keep Marc Atkins in spot-welding for a month. A body woven from flowers. The East End loves them (heaped on the pavement at the site of a killing or a road accident). Monochrome lives recalled in hot flushes of colour.

Too much black coffee the night before; sleepless, I had got out of bed to read William Burroughs' *My Education (A Book of Dreams)*. Nobody has more relish for the dark, greater access to postmortem revelations.

A tunnel which leads into a large round room with a domed top like a truncated sphere. This the womb, and as I approach the far corner I feel a

strong magnetic pull, another few steps and I will not be able to pull myself
loose. I wrench free and move back to the tunnel entrance. Here I meet
Allen Ginsberg, who has a nosebleed. Now a cry goes up. "THE DOGS
THE DOGS!!"

The Mexican Day of the Dead: Lowry in Leytonstone. A nail-varnish scarlet BMW, engine running, leaking carbon monoxide fumes into the still air, cruises the cemetery path. A couple of black T-shirt, leather jacket tearaways slouch across to the grave, primed to pick up the vibes. Blatant herb merchants, mobiles in pocket, stepping forward to make the touch. "This Ronnie Kray, mate?" The five-foot letters spelling out name, rank, sobriquet, were not enough. They wanted confirmation before making the energy exchange, soliciting the blessing of the dead. An impertinence that would have the Colonel spinning through the clay like a drill bit: lowlifers dressed like vagrants, German motor, peddling drugs, no bowwow. The filth he'd spent the best part of his career keeping off the streets.

The smell of decaying carnations, reds and pinks and livid greens, left me in a state of visually induced nausea. Long shadows of leafless trees. I couldn't wait for the undergrowth to take over, the revenge of the ivy. A child, encouraged by her parents, let a bunch of daffs drop on the mound. The mother balled up the newspaper wrapping and tossed it on to the grave of some unknown.

I couldn't resist it. When they'd gone – and before the next troop arrived – I smoothed out the paper. *Hackney Gazette*, April 20, 1995: **PIT BULL SAVAGES FAMILY.** MUM AND HER TWINS ATTACKED AS UNMUZZLED DOG GOES BERSERK.

BULLS & BEARS &
MITHRAIC MISALIGNMENTS:
WEATHER IN THE CITY

"My friend," said the Gatherer of the Clouds, "this is what I think
best. Choose the moment when all eyes in the city are fixed on the
ship's approach to turn her into a rock off-shore, and let this rock look
like a ship, so that all the world may wonder. Then throw a circle of
high mountains around their city."

HOMER, *THE ODYSSEY* (TR. EV RIEU)

Walking through the City, there is no encouragement to look up at the
sky. Historically, for most of this century – from the time of TS Eliot's
"unreal City/under the brown fog of a winter noon", his upright dead,
to Robert Frank's bankers, photographed in 1951, uniform drudges
purposefully scuttling under the lee of tall grey buildings (the lids of
their polished top hats, their bowlers, shading the eyes from the heavens) – it has been forbidden to tilt back the neck. An unfocused stare
into the middle-distance has been cultivated; Adam's apples bobbing,
lips tight with swallowed secrets. It's forbidden to stop, to slow down, to
admit changes in atmospheric pressure. There's no weather here: lightweight suits, loose raincoats, at all seasons. The City never was a place
for through traffic – where else was there to go? Within the walls, it's a
zone of other-directed zombies, procurers of fog, scurrying ants who
shave flakes of ancient dirt from the high cliff walls of banks and bro-
kerages and temples of finance. The gargoyles keep watch: dragons,
griffins, lions, eagles. They check to make sure that eyes stay on pavements, on the legs in front of them. An enclosure of high heels and
extravagant stockings. Walkers who make walking impossible, a stunt.
The sexuality of the enclosure is concentrated entirely on the feet.
Shoeshine boys working their way through openplan offices. Shoeshine
women, on their knees, polishing away, while the serviced men talk
numbers. Foot and mouth. Women aren't women, neither can they be
temporary men. When a woman goes down into the pit, when things

are quiet, and there's time to notice them, a cry goes up: "Beaver!" Which, it seems, is accepted in the spirit intended, in good part. Sexual identity is objectified into target specificity, a general temperature of arousal and anxiety. The salty, generated electricity that puts iron into the cloud masses, fouls up the climate for the rest of London.

The angled umbrellas, canes, and rolled newspapers of Frank's grim financiers are non-functional, wands of office; they are used to measure distance, to maintain a decent interval between intimate strangers competing for the same destination. The City is termite territory: thousands of heads-down workers serving an unacknowledged queen, a fear motor buried deep in the heart of the place. A dominatrix with carmine lips. Which is why all those drones, wideboys, and compulsive hustlers, responded so feverishly to the imago of Margaret Thatcher. She made it all right: greed was good, work was holy, the clouds were frivolous nonsense. There was no such thing as society, no time beyond or behind the present – no cosmology, but the great darkness, the worship of her achievements.

How the planners laboured, with their pastiche statuary, their cloned modernism, to invoke the Gotham City of the graphic novelists, of Tim Burton. A totally controlled environment, a studio with the lid firmly on. In their fantasy lives they wished for nothing more demanding than Michelle Pfeiffer in her windowless apartment, uncertain whether she was a secretary or a personal assistant: a timorous and bespectacled single forced to get her kicks by stitching a catsuit out of an old PVC raincoat. Submission is what the City preaches. A phoney ritual of punishment, in which the economically dominant partner pays for his relieving humiliation.

And yet, even at the bleakest moments of this post-human hiatus, the need for it, for "skying", survived. The pressure of those towers, the sheer weight of glass and steel pressing into the dull clay, forces the pedestrian to respond. S/he is blinded by reflections, cloudscapes racing across mirror windows, intricate shadows casting a cool path down those tight gullies of permission. If they escape to the river, they are confronted by gymnasia, bicycles that go nowhere: the ability to travel hard without arriving. Stock jobbers can build up the necessary ridges of neck muscle. The sweat of narcissism, glass angled to exclude the world outside: self-addiction. It's impossible to walk along the north bank of the river, you are constantly dodging between building sites, locked churches, roads that have been closed off. You are hustled by joggers, manic exercise freaks, office escapees whose greatest desire is to smash the paving stones, suck in bad air. Hyper-fit onanists groan through ecstasies of press-ups, as if they were dry humping the flagstones. Like the Pope in overdrive, they orally hoover the dirt of another virgin airport. The gyms and sauna sheds are interspersed by pink-tablecloth restaurants with river views that nobody has the time to notice. These days businessmen take their cellphones out to lunch, instead of their mistresses. No booze. No hanks of bloody meat. Elegant blue bottles of carbonated water. Tables that seem to have been laid out for a perfume launch. The absence of cigar smoke.

The City has worked hard to earn this annulment from climate. Outside is inside: small forests "rescued" and tastefully arranged around atria. Real trees that look worse than fakes. Sick trees feeding their blight into a sealed system. The plashing of a plurality of fountains in mustard-brick courtyards, heavy with the ghosts of labour. Junk art: monster women, tortured wood, tin can horses. Bring back myxomatosis to save us from this plague of cocky Barry Flanagan hares: anthropomorphic cartoon pests granting credibility to every development scam piazza.

Essex is parasitical upon this mess. Into the shopping arcade of Liverpool Street – chocolates, cheese, perfume, knickers – come the trains of women who would once have been called "typists", and are now something more complicated: smilers, laptop princesses. Men who would have waited years for a shared telephone, effortlessly sink merchant banks. Number-crunchers treat the City like a betting-shop. The future is optional. Money is a cosmetic. Male and female are professionally attractive, available. There's no landscape outside the train window. It's too dark for that. They start early and drink late. You have to be able to out-breakfast the opposition. Night has been abolished.

The new City has exploited images of terror, wrecked buildings, newsreel carnage routines, as an explanation of its desire to seal itself off, to put up physical barriers at all the ports of entrance. Vague spectres of menace caught on time-coded surveillance cameras justify an entire network of peeping vulture lenses. A web of indifferent watching devices, sweeping every street, every building, to eliminate the possibility of a past tense, the freedom to forget. There can be no highlights, no special moments: a discreet tyranny of "now" has been established. "Real time" in its most pedantic form. It is only when there is no one to watch the watchers, when the machines are left to hose imagery on to banked screens in an empty room, that a melancholy futurist poetic begins to operate: visionary street scenes unrivalled since the birth of cinema. The delight of a thing that is simply itself, mechanical process in all its essential mystery; a train coming into a station, firefly lights from a river of slow-moving cars. A cinema that spurns the vulgar excitement of editing, the control-freak buzz of nominating the close-ups, moving the camera. The inner sanctum of surveillance imagery in Bishopsgate Police Station oversees this revolutionary movement, this new art form: the City is at last able to compose its own poetry, with no human intervention.

But the new City has a defining image. In the entrances of office blocks, just outside the revolving doors, on the fake marble steps (behind which can be glimpsed internal security personnel, pompous desks, escalators, hanging Jim Dine torsos) are these suits. Women in suits. Slightly shifty blokes. Insiders, badge-wearers, forced to taste the weather, to step outside – because they want to, *have to*, smoke. Addicts, social lepers. They don't care if they're caught by the steeply angled surveillance cameras. They live to defy the will of the building. They express themselves in this existential act; weed to lips, dragging deep. They belong to a sub-species. They're prisoner types, recidivists. They should be circling around some stone yard. Tobacco is a prison currency. All prisoners have to smoke. They're supposed to get cancer. That's what they're there for: they *are* a cancer. Prisons are cancer factories, beagle cages. Smoke is the product. Wistfulness, nostalgia. The old flannel about the great times that have gone.

City smokers, alone, or in couples who spurn eye contact, or women together, have an adulterous aspect: clandestine and brazen. They look like shoplifters waiting to be bussed to court. They're hooked and they don't give a fig who knows it. They're class traitors, flaunting behaviour you'd expect from a lowlifer, a boho, an unreconstructed writer. From Martin Amis. He's made a career out of smoking and tennis in the afternoon. Delivery men and labourers use the roll-up as an excuse for a break, it's their translation of Tom Eliot's coffee spoons.

> Shall I say, I have gone at dusk through narrow streets
> And watched the smoke that rises from the pipes
> Of lonely men in shirt-sleeves, leaning out of windows? . . .

They pace themselves, these fumblers with cellophane, with their cupped hands and fiery mouths. These mint suckers. They foul up the entrance to the place of business. It's like hawking on the steps of St Paul's. Gobbing green. It doesn't seem to matter. Nobody comes and goes, the occasional messenger with a flat package. Voluntary banishment. Smoke tastes of the possibility of another kind of life, remembered pleasure.

What the smokers never do is watch the sky. They can't even bear to look into the faces of their co-conspirators. This is a shameful but necessary act: like a whistling line in the Gents, they gaze at their feet, not at the things in their hands. Their thoughts are inward. If an angel, or a horse on fire, passed along the pavement, they would not notice. They would remain modishly unimpressed. Now that Ronnie Kray is off the scene, they are the sharpest smokers in London. The tailored elegance of the women smoking in doorways should call up the Soho of the Messina brothers, the spunky covers of exploitational paperbacks, Anna Karina in *Vivre Sa Vie*. But these bright Spring afternoon tableaux are nothing like that. Karina's cigarette was décor, a prop. She smoked like a charming amateur. The nicotine junkies have a much more significant role to play, they help to peg the City as a time-punished prison, terrestrial in its ambitions. They are puffing like locos to lift the "smoke values" of their area, to counter the derogatory remarks floated by TJ Chandler in *The Climate of London*:

> The relative purity of air in the City of London can be attributed both to its small resident population and smoke-control regulations. Pindard and Wilkins (1958, p. 7) estimated a reduction of 40 per cent in the average smoke concentrations over half the city's smokeless zone and at a time when it was surrounded by built-up uncontrolled areas . . . but others have expressed more guarded views and the figure must now be regarded as suspect for it was based upon readings from different sizes of stain.

The sullen knots of menthol-breathed renegades will have to put in heroic sessions to trouble the drift of cleaner air that rushes down the Lea valley and into Lower Thames Street.

The smoker is the contrary of the star-gazing romantic who thirsts to break out of the flesh envelope, mingle with the vapours. It's not a vagueness, a moony sense of elsewhere; it's a part of the English temperament to want to classify everything, including the clouds. They'd weigh them and measure them if only the buggers would hold still. Nothing could be further from Odilon Redon's centaurs and fallen angels: who confront amorphous floating socks, generalised cloud forms. Barrage balloons of melting cheese. The English disease is precision, Gradgrind facts. The ambition to quantify the ephemeral. John

Constable, out on Hampstead Heath, on the rim of glacial drift, looking over the huddle of London. He does not need to include the City, he frames nothing but a patch of sky. The City is there by implication. Nothing is left out. The swirling curvature of the heavens is a kind of mirror, a water bowl. Clouds are "influenced" by the layout of the streets, the pattern of rivers and parkland, the eccentricities of those who use weather systems as aids to meditation. "27 aug 11 o clock Noon looking Eastward large silvery (? Clouds) wind Gentle at S. West." Clouds nailed as they move through: the "chief organ of sentiment" in any composition.

Which brings us to Luke Howard (1772–1864), Quaker, meteorologist, and small businessman. Howard got his living as a retail chemist, operating from premises near Temple Bar. He is a figure for whom, I'd assert, you'd search hard to find a contemporary equivalent. He attended, efficiently enough, to the mundane routines of his trade; he prospered, finding the leisure to proselytize, to publish tracts sponsoring his religious prejudices (against profane swearing, in favour of temperance), as well as to make detailed observations *On the Modifications of Clouds*. A move east, to Plaistow, with a factory in Stratford, brought Howard up against wider skies: the cinema of weather, long before cinema was invented. Lyric spurts, leisurely rhythms, satires, heroic couplets, cliffhanger serials: they're all up there at the same time, chasing their own agendas. Constable sketched and annotated. Howard's work inspired him; he scribbled frantically in the margin of his second-hand copy (described by the bookdealer as "published at 10/6 scarce") of the second edition of Thomas Foster's *Researches about Atmospheric Phaenomena* (1815) – which included, as its first chapter, Howard's *Essay on Clouds*.

Howard had the passion to name, to classify cloud types – to search out their characteristics, their foibles. He became the Freud of "skying", the stern analyst of meteorological tendencies. The Quaker ethic, hard work and the fellowship of labour, required this antidote: the lifting of the soul, a libidinous permission of vapours, constantly metamorphosing skies.

Cirrus, Cumulus and Stratus were christened. The publication of Howard's long years of observations in *The Climate of London* (1818–1820) brought him a more than local fame. Shelley worked these exotic terms into his compositions. Constable had something to kick against, to inspire the cloud studies made at Hampstead in 1821 and 1822. But, most importantly, Goethe discovered the one Englishman he addressed as "Master". The greater part of the autobiographical "facts" we read about Howard's childhood and apprenticeship have been garnered from a famous letter sent to Goethe, at the poet's request. Goethe's considered response was the poem, "Howard's Ehrengedächtniss", and a description in verse of the chief cloud forms according to his correspondent's classifications.

After Howard it was possible to be precise about things which had previously been described in the loosest terms; to espouse a kind of pseudo-scientific terminology, a reading of omens, signs in the heavens, that was almost respectable. The sky became a spreadsheet, a curved screen on which intimations of the futures market could be sketched and interpreted. Disinterested observation came to excuse prophetic hucksterism, a gambler's climate: the computer terminal, with its advancing pressure systems, was an updated version of the gypsy's crystal ball. Howard's discrimination of cloud families mitigated the rhetorical excesses of Turner, and his epic British skies with their layers of psycho-dramatic narrative and allusion. Turner habitually carried his swift weather notes back to the studio, where they could be recomposed to some grandiloquent scheme. Long hours staring out to sea, sky pressing down on a rising tide, calm evolving to storm, prepared him for the furious present of the creative act. He wasn't satisfied with the passive role; lashed to the mast, he conducted elemental chaos – gifting placid galleries with future weather, feeding a rage of light into complacent art-historical bunkers. In the intensity of his engagement, he doubled for the fated captain of Bram Stoker's tempest-tossed vessel, the *Demeter*, as it carried Count Dracula's cargo into Whitby harbour.

Now it's too late, the fears are out. Weather/City: serious anomalies in the electrical force-field. Poets, those hiphop neurotics, got there first. Sensitivities picked raw: with jump-cutting, restless minds splicing together all the disparate signs and portents. Uncooked language. Ugly to handle. But horribly accurate. The state should fund these jokers, keep them around like canaries, hoping they'll pick up the first whiff of poison gas.

Take William Empson. The story goes, the gossip, that a group gathered in the old *Statesman* building in Clerkenwell to pay tribute to the Cantab poet/philosopher. To honour him: for being alive. For staying bloody-minded to the end. (Difficult to imagine which poet the current mob would celebrate. Poetry is off the agenda. No radio presenter worthy of the job can name five living British poets. The only employment for once famous versifiers is hacking out obituary notices for their deceased rivals.)

There were lengthy speeches, drinks; more drinks, longer speeches – a presentation. But when the moment came and they looked for the great man, the bearded sage, he'd vanished. They searched the building from the cellars up. At length, Empson was found. Under the eaves: trembling, head on knees, in a huddle – a book pressed against his face. One of those worthy review copies that can't be fitted into a convenient compendium, effortlessly summarised. A grand enough theme: an account of global warming. It was already the obsession of the poet's climacteric, this metaphysics of sweating ice-caps, peevish monsoons, big symbols in the hurt of chaos theory. Inundation, crushed lungs, steepling walls of white water: the City swallowed in a chilling rush. (Those other prophets, the science fiction visionaries, the Turners and John Martins of generic pulp, had been pushing the story for years before modernist poets caught on. S. Fowler Wright in his novel *Deluge*, published in 1928, described an England underwater, the Cotswolds an archipelago. Alternate world copywriters respected the spirit of Gilgamesh, that ancient epic. London was submerged beneath a great lake, surrounded by primordial wilderness, in Richard Jefferies' *After London*, or *Wild England*, a post-holocast fantasy of 1885.)

Weather as the cleanser of the City, as apocalyptic threat, was a popular message in the Sixties. It was delivered as doctrine from the platform of the Roundhouse by Gregory Bateson in 1967, during the Congress of the Dialectics of Liberation for the Demystification of Violence. His sobering philippic, preached with a smile, had Allen Ginsberg, RD Laing, Alex Trocchi, Stokely Carmichael, and other counter-culture luminaries, drooling. They *wanted* to hear the worst, the spidery voice of doom: grave prophecies delivered like news. Blake's voice as received, pre-*Howl*, by Ginsberg in Harlem. Unless there was a change in the level of global consciousness, the audience was told, it was over: Chaldean dreams of enveloping catastrophe.

> *The city was already old when the gods within it*
> *Decided that the great gods should make a flood.*

The City invoked the horrors that most excited it. It focused them, flatterered them, pleasured them – to the exclusion of the rest of the world. We become the thing we fear. There was, for example, a real sense in which the communal strength of the Greenham women –

votive priestesses circumnavigating a field of phallic toys – began to incubate the apocalypse; granting credibility, juice, to the evil on which they lavished their attention.

Weather's got a disease, it's sick. It's been infected by our inattention. It's always out there, restless, migratory, seeding towards some conclusion we don't have the nerve to predict. In the City, there simply isn't the time to notice these capricious shifts. Heads in laps, numbers on the screen. The gamblers don't understand that their moods, their small corruptions, affect the pressure, destabilise the thunderheads. Weather, sliding in from elsewhere, is a personal thing. No two people see the same cloud.

Eavesdrop across the City, scribble down the snatches of conversation that you hear: no meteorology. It's remarkable. Outside the walls, strangers meeting talk of nothing else. The City is immune. I wandered for three days without catching a whisper. "We-ll . . . I'm working on a worst possible scenario." "It's got thick security, iron gates you can't get inside without, you know . . ." "Paul Dickinson may not be the world's best advertising man, but he's been with us since he was sixteen, and his chances of getting another one aren't . . ." "The shotgun people have cabinets already made."

Writers, on the other hand, natural moralists, are obliged to tune in to random monologues, watch the gutter and the stars. Weather is what dignifies the cartoon monsters of Martin Amis's *London Fields*. His neighbourhood view is smeared by crippled cumuli, expectorated out of some graveyard in the skies. "I saw a dead cloud not long ago . . . The dead cloud came and oozed and slurped itself against the window . . . I thought of fishing-nets under incomprehensible volumes of water, or the motes of a dead TV."

Down below, in the garbage streets, the Amis stock company with its contagious glamour, is observed – as by an articulate surveillance system. The authorial presence sits at a window, smoking and brooding, while the plebs strut their stuff between boozer and bedroom. Urban clouds, with scurfy beer-guts, foul the glass. The writer's reflection is erased. He's part of it, a cirric pox printed across his profile. Looking up from outside, the journalist on the doorstep sees a clouded face: a thinker with an isobar problem. Fast prose puffs the anvils of moisture, the cloud streets, encourages them into ever more exhibitionist forms.

It's all become too personal. Weather can no longer be mentioned in polite society. As Peter Redgrove points out in *The Black Goddess and the Sixth Sense*, we are "so violently affected by weather changes . . . that it can easily become a clinical problem." Redgrove confesses himself a "Jekyll and Hyde to the weather." He suffers, both physically and spiritually, the fluctuations in the magnetic field, the minute shifts in air pressure, the seductions of pearly light above the morning ocean. We need our weather analysts more than our shrinks. Migrating depressions, "lows", wander like the Eternal Jew – homeless, restless, burdened with arcane knowledge. Cloud banks absorb the hurt from wounded psyches, mop up the frenzy of the City. Weather allergies stalk us like serial killers. The pressure of bad will can generate a sympathetic storm. It's tempting to claim a link between the great winds of 16 October 1987 and the panicked financial markets on "Black Monday" – when a loss of corporate nerve swept from Tokyo to New York, throwing the software into a critical condition. Consoles went ape, cocky columns of green figures drizzled precipitately from the screens: ancient forests, with their fossil hoards of weather memory, crashed to the ground. An interface of anxiety. Forecasters blustered and lost it. Paper fortunes dissolved.

And yet, outside the City, beyond the influence of the walls, this millennial fear persists, the flood at the end of time. There is a decayed Unitarian chapel at 49 Balls Pond Road; a ghost with an interesting history, hidden behind corrugated sheeting. Once this was the headquarters of Oswald Mosley's legions – from which they ventured out for acts of provocation in defiance of Dalston's long-established aliens: a skirmish in Ridley Road market. The kind of affair that was witnessed by the young Harold Pinter. The chapel became a source of charity in hard times, handing out free shirts (one colour only: black), sturdy boots, to anyone who would raise the arm in salute. Current rights of ownership are in dispute. A group of Sikh speculators, finding the cost of pulling the place down, dealing with the asbestos dust, prohibitive, turned a temporarily blind eye to its occupation by a nameless group of multinational boho artists. It couldn't last. They knew that and this sense of truce, provisionality, influenced their actions.

The gutted body of the chapel was invaded by a parasitical form: an ark constructed from the floorboards of the building itself. It's as if the host structure had woven a defensive module from its own entrails. Internal weather hits hard at the pedestrian, stepping in from the usual diesel-soup, pollution cocktail of the road outside: airborne motes, sawdust beams, sodden asbestos, wood-glue, coffee grains, cigarette smoke, discontinued psalms. The stink of latter-day creativity, art guerrilla revivalism: joss-stick madeleines from the decamped Exploding Galaxy.

This totally unseaworthy craft, this womb/ark, could have been a direct off-print from one of the Unitarian tracts that were still lying around in the chapel. It was a death ship, designed to sink, just out of sight of land (like the pleasure boats of old folk in Jack Trevor Story's *Little Dog's Day*). The polythene skin between the boards of the ark is encrusted with threads of living material: river-map outlines, worm charts, insects from Nineveh. The skin flaps loose, like the wrappings on a mummy working free in the dry air. You enter the boat by way of a perilous gangplank. No question of two-by-two on this trip. If the concept is to have any meaning, the rains *must* follow.

2.

London was, but is no more.
JOHN EVELYN

Returning across town from a disappointing visit to the gardens of Lambeth Palace, I decided, on a whim, to drop into the Barbican to book some theatre tickets. *Twelfth Night*: it had been ominously well reviewed, but I was in a reckless mood. I'd never seen the play performed and thought, why not, this might be the moment. Some out-of-character gesture was required to lift my spirits after the futility of the Lambeth experience. Years had been wasted quietly seething outside that wall, circumnavigating the private enclosure, cursing the lack of access, the ecclesiastical privileges. Much better to leave these mysteries unexplored. But, when the postern gate was flung wide – £2 in the bucket – for a single afternoon, I couldn't resist it. The "second largest private garden in London". The Archbishop and Mrs Carey had gamely allowed their grounds to be included in the National Garden Scheme, along with the ranks of proud suburbanites and inner-city Greens. Along with, for example, 3 Wellgarth Road, NW11 ("7 minutes walk from Golders Green tube station . . . swathe of grass with long border of bushes . . . herbs and mints, some uncommon plants"); or 15 Upper Grotto Road, Strawberry Hill ("33 bus to Pope's Grotto"); or 25 Albion Square, E8 ("on two levels with pond beside camomile patch").

A utilitarian grass carpet suitable for a WI cake sale with a good address. I bought a raffle ticket and won, to the mutual discomfort of myself and the size sixteen floral print, a small cylinder of "relaxing" pink massage oil from Boots. The garden had been renovated within an inch of its life. Washing lines with striped pyjamas half-hidden behind fleshy clumps. Concrete leisure areas. A refusal to engage with the rank and licence of this location: the view across the river to Westminster, the backdrop of Lambeth Palace. I should have felt like a dusty trespasser, or a mendicant, not someone being tapped for the church restoration fund. I wanted this enclosure to despise me and everything I stood for. I wanted it to boast of the millions the church's financial advisers could chuck away in wheel-of-fortune property speculations. I wanted the bite of karmic history: Lollards imprisoned in the Tower, martyrdoms, tortures, blasphemies, grand and glorious corruptions, fancy dress, gluttony, simony, high art. Not this poodle parade, with nothing to distinguish it from the park outside – except the absence of leisure-abusing citizens.

And so it was, on the fine and pleasant afternoon of Saturday 8th April, 1995, that I found myself trying to walk in through the front entrance of the Barbican Arts Complex and being treated like a Bogside bomb-carrier. This sensation is not uncommon in the new City. It's how they want you to feel, uncomfortable: the stranger in town. They want you to carry a card, with a photograph and number, that defines you as some sort of non-person lowlife. You don't belong. You're wearing the wrong clothes. You're walking with no destination. You don't have the credentials that will get you inside. Because the City – like a Dantesque module (or secular temple) – consists of three distinct zones. The Inner is available only to a hierarchy of workers, priests and functionaries. Its palaces are studded with defensive imagery, iron gates built on a fascist scale, heraldic beasts, pyramids, obelisks, stone quotations: the Bank of England, the Royal Exchange, Mansion House, St Mary Woolnoth. On the operations of this zone I can merely speculate: once they were run by a tight brahmin caste of families, carefully crossbred into the landed gentry, infiltrated and re-energised by Sephardic and Ashkenazic implants. The same names float through the generations. Anthony Hilton in *City within a State: A Portrait of Britain's Financial World* quotes the Duc de Richelieu: "There are six great powers in Europe – England, France, Russia, Austria, Prussia and the Baring Brothers." The Barings were hierophants who operated, on a global scale, a cult designed to ensure, for all time, the wealth and status of the City. According to Hilton, one member of the family, Lord Cromer, "took time off in the last century to run Egypt more or less like a country estate." The nexus of land, investment, exclusion of the uninitiated, insinuated its web from the government of the day, down through all the ephemeral quangos, to the money-minting failsafe of Lloyds. These bankers guided the Saudi oil coffers back into the embrace of the City, pimped for the arms brokers. They managed the CIA investment portfolio: their patronage of New American Art, tame leftists. Action paintings for drugs, drugs for torture catalogues. Currency hedges that are not to be penetrated by casual pedestrians. Thorns to protect the castle of sleepers.

The question of how all this was brought down by one rogue trader out East is still unanswered. Perhaps Ezra Pound's psychotic curses on the very name of Threadneedle Street, the damage it did him, have finally been brought to ground. But whatever happens, happens everywhere; visible, and out of sight. If I saw it I wouldn't know what it meant: the jungle of provisional statistics, the lush meadow of money. The private dining rooms are still at the top of the buildings, fine art in the corridors. Other ranks stay below decks, beneath lowered ceilings, striplight in marble halls, one swift shunt from the street. Which is the City's second zone, the outer: a permission to move through, to hike briskly from a to b. The second zone is motion, a treadmill of commuters to drive the invisible engines of business. You may not wander here, or pause to investigate, to unpick inscriptions in weathered graveyards. You can eat if you do it standing up. You must bleed your image into unappeased storage facilities.

The third, and most intriguing, of the discriminations is the interzone – which is neither office nor street. The zone where everything is permitted that is not forbidden. The zone that has no interior or exterior, where anyone can pause, and no one is at home. Broadgate Circus, with its borrowed amphitheatre, its cod New York ice-rink, its cafés and bookshop, its upended Richard Serra girders, is the most visible exemplar of this mood. Interzone aspires to the condition of virtual reality. It's lost the louche texture of the William Burroughs original: exile, predatory sex, shape-shifting drugs. It's a brochure, an unworkable proposal brought to life; a perpetual lunchhour. A place to painlessly kill time. Journalists are sent there on assignment to count the number of drinks the cellphone dealers are doing these days. The piazza is the interzone model: de Chirico and mineral water. Drudge surrealism for insomniacs. Random statuary, pissing fountains, imported cobblestones. The summoning of an entirely mythical past. Interzone extends to entrance halls and atria, fun jungles, ledges for sandwich fanciers and clerical assignations. Primary colour sculptures as a vulgar compromise between the aspirations of the architects and the innate philistinism of the developers. Art that positively begs to be exploited. The concourses of Liverpool Street and Fenchurch Street stations: shopping opportunities, impulse buys to temper the frustration of trains going nowhere. Pick-up points. Racks of hobby magazines, fiscal porn, to replace the grazing of newsprint in rationalized public libraries. Selections of perfume for the beneficiaries and the victims of career adulterers. Even the task of getting out, escaping, the luxury of pre-travel vacancy, must turn a profit. The Barbican, so I assumed until this shakedown, nursed interzone aspirations. An investment terminal, an honourary airport without the stress of departure; a culture pond at the heart of the labyrinth, the conclusion of every yellow line in the City.

Now the simple act of trying to purchase two theatre tickets was as awkward as checking on to the Tel Aviv shuttle with a collage of Syrian and Libyan stamps in my passport. With no apology or explanation, uniformed security personnel (boredom plus focused aggro, plus diplomas in paranoia) cranked into slothful action. Slightly too plump for their *Star Trek* leisure wear. Pat-searched, disinterestedly groped, channelled through the electronic hoop. "Empty your pockets, please. Sir." Keys and coins and furry mints. The multi-entrance Barbican, and all its levels, walkways, graded restaurants, bookstalls, display cases of avant-garde jewellery, has been commandeered by a conference of European Bankers, Rescue and Development section, with their twitchy minders. "It's the only way we can fund our operation," said the ticket-seller, when I eventually found him. "You'll love *Twelfth Night*, a marvellous show."

Held on the stairs, looking back down, over the water gardens to the newly-islanded church of St Giles (where John Milton was buried), to those torpedo tombs stacked in a neat line on the flagstones, I saw the terrace beneath me as a geometric design of black and white: dark suits at every table. Men and women, tailored, barbered, sweet-smelling, protected by a discretion of blue shirts with mobiles. An impressionist take on leisure in the City. No buskers, no vagrants. Not a single copy of *The Big Issue*. The ideal of urban living, as imagined by an architect who had never left the safety of the suburbs.

Piecing a walk together along the craggy remnants of the London Wall – ragstone blocks, brick bonding courses – is like retrieving a false memory, the visual evidence for truths we prefer to forget. The Wall defines the limits of the imagination of Roman London – and is, in this, an act of modesty. To try to get a sense of the original shape by tapping its accredited ruins, following the designated route, is futile. You are contradicted, misinformed, fenced out, overseen for every inch of your journey. But the perversity of that desire, to pick up on the energy field, is as strong as ever. I am haunted by a mythology of gates: as metaphors and as facts. Gates cut into the Wall's continuity, truces of going and coming: exchanges with the idea of outside, with the field and the garden. Instants of risk and betrayal, capture and farewell. Anticipations of journeys and pilgrimages. John Bunyan. Apertures between life and death: the path out to the dissenters' burial-ground. To Blake and Defoe in Bunhill Fields. To the madhouses, hospitals and markets that sustain, and give meaning to life within the walls. To Curtain Row, Shoreditch, and the first plays of Shakespeare and Ben Jonson.

Aldgate, Bishopsgate, Moorgate, Aldersgate, Cripplegate, Newgate, Ludgate, Billingsgate, with the Tower, the Barbican and Castle Baynard: eleven wounds in an electrical circuit. ("Hurt him in eleven places". Sir Toby Belch.) The City, as is proper, is one gate short of holy Jerusalem, of symmetry.

The walls of it were of a great height, and had twelve gates; at each of the twelve gates there was an angel, and over the gates were written the names of the twelve tribes of Israel: on the east there were three gates, on the north three gates, on the south three gates, and on the west three gates. The city walls stood on twelve foundation stones, each one of which bore the name of one of the twelve apostles of the Lamb.

Even the angels have been blinded and scattered. They are there but you will have to search for them: on war memorials, alcoves, stained glass, above the keystones of pinkish-grey riverside buildings. The London Stone, with its mantic cargo, is now kept behind bars, beneath the pavement; a trophy for the Overseas Chinese Banking Corporation Limited in Cannon Street. Grievously misaligned.

The meaning of the gates has been carted away with the brickwork. The Wall is no longer a border, it's a preserved feature: a well-scrubbed and biddable geriatric. But it remains an enticement to the urban stalker, the fragments of it, the excuse to be out there on a dull Spring morning, starting at Tower Hill and walking the westerly circuit, stopping – when possible, when the masonry hasn't been sealed off, or trapped inside an office development – to touch and sniff and photograph. As we progress, the City reveals itself as a confederation of petty mysteries:

102

no Square Mile, but a chaos of triangulations, botched mandalas, competing hieroglyphs. If the Thames is seen as a taut string, then the Wall is the curve of a bow, aimed at the north. When we climb into the elevated Barbican system, the waves and ripples, the contour lines of getting and holding, are visible. A haze of pollution and undispersed smoke from the sacrificial barbecues of Smithfield. Surges of current flow between the pattern of churches. The City destroys itself – fires and bombs and blitz – only to reassert, *clarify*, the essential manifold. Spasms of traffic, scurrying businessmen/adepts, reinforce the tidal imagery: systole, diastole. The City is London's sorry heart, the heart's intelligence. The Wall, broken as it is, directs the exchanges of energy; makes allusion to the sites where the gates once stood. Blue plaques confirm the votive presence of the great English poets: Chaucer, the controller of petty customs, with his house in Aldgate; John Keats, born at the Swan & Hoop, Moorgate, in 1795; Milton, who lived in youth and old age in the Aldersgate Ward – and Alexander Pope, misshapen, born at the centre of it in Plough Court, Lombard Street.

As someone congenitally incapable of accepting the notion of "accident", I interpret this conjunction, poet/gate, as significant. The gift of language that compensates for the "sickness vocation" of the poet's fated existence is closely associated with the liberties of the eleven points of entry to the City: fissures in the brainpan. Poets are never properly incarnated, trapped in their meat bodies. They are too canny to risk everything on a single system of time. It's my conceit to imagine their spirit bodies whirling in a vortex as they anticipate the shape of the traffic cones. They exist in an eternal present: meadows and orchards behind them, the pulse of human congress in front of their eyes. Mithras, the double god, the Manichee, was an early role model.

The quiddity of these eccentric architectural arrangements, the compromises and epiphanies worked out through the centuries, has been wantonly and mindlessly set aside by an attempt to turn the zone of the City into a privileged playground. Legoland with shoulder-arms and extendable nightsticks. A profoundly depressing system of new barriers – red and white cones, pyramids stamped with the name BIG FOOT and backed by squared sections of timber – has been assembled as a temporary (permanent) measure of control; a visible narrowing of consciousness. Aftershocks of terror can be replayed whenever required to excuse the imposition of this "ring of plastic", a ring with no gates or breaks. As the *Standard* reported on 15 February, 1995: "A proposal to be discussed next week will seek to extend the no-go area westwards, closing streets at one end and turning others into one-way routes . . . Existing plastic bollards are already being replaced with concrete and paving in a £1 million upgrade, and the new extension would eventually become a permanent feature of the City . . . Meanwhile, US police have thrown a tight cordon around Wall Street, braced for another terrorist outrage." Ironically, these repressive, anti-flow bottlenecks – introduced without consultation or democratic legislation – were being instituted at the very time when libertarian/Greenist factions were demonstrating in Camden Town and other parts of London in favour of road closures, barriers: an alliance of extremes. The surgically-masked, lycra-clad cyclist offering tacit support to the private armies of the money market.

Armed with Nicholson's New City of London Access Map (Security Check Points, Through Routes, Road Closures) and accompanied, as ever, by Marc Atkins, I set out to photograph this sub-system of checkpoints and barricaded bridges. POLICE SLOW. At Bishopsgate the traffic out of bandit country (Shoreditch, Hoxton, Dalston, Stoke Newington) chokes to a single line. A quorum of Afro-Caribbeans in over-ambitious German motors are discriminated to the side of the road. (Affronted owner-drivers lean against their vehicles, refusing eye contact, while one of the cops rings in. Taking-without-permission suspects back off, put distance between themselves and this car they are seeing for the first time.) Forests of surveillance cameras interrogate number plates. In Bevis Marks a vanload of brilliant cloth bales, bound for Petticoat Lane, is painstakingly sifted, while the driver grumbles at pedestrians. At the indifferent policewoman. Control freaks in sadistic gold spectacles are licensed to snoop by the Corporation. These intrusions into our freedom of passage are the "something" that must be seen to be done in the wake of a bomb scare; the species of arrogant response that provoked the initial assault. (Before the VE Day bingo in St Paul's Cathedral, squads of searchers and sniffers checked every manhole in the City. Secure lids were marked with a special seal. Rooftops were scanned. Dogs turned loose in stairwells and basements.) Bishopsgate is not remotely Belfast, but it is a useful rehearsal – for post-conflict investment: drug laundries, protection scams, lump labour. See the hard-hat lads caressing their Friday afternoon pillows of currency. The parodic courtesy of Vatican guards, uniformed hirelings paid to protect the most baroque crooks in the kingdom. Black magicians with a cure for Alzheimer's disease.

The New City is immune from threat, defended as it is by invisible gates, gates that can be shifted at a phonecall. By rapid response paramilitaries hotwired to vindicate their undisclosed budgets. Photographing each of the surveillance checkpoints meant that Marc and I were, in our turn, also photographed. Word was out by the time we limped up King William Street, north towards the Bank of England. There is a major complex of camera poles, cones, plastic building blocks (with long trenches from which small birds drink), sited between the gleaming gold thistle of the Monument and a pub recently rechristened as "Bulls Bears Brokers". I became so engrossed in effectively recording the four cameras, tilted at different angles, that I didn't notice the rapidly-approaching plod, with his City of London helmet badge and his fresh complexion. (It's only examining the snapshot later that I can report on the correct sequence of events.)

Being, both of us, professionally courteous (but philosophically opposed), we were soon locked in an ontological stand-off. He wanted an excuse to haul me back to the station. I wanted him to behave badly enough to make the incident worth recording. And, inevitably, we were both disappointed. I didn't see why I couldn't photograph, without permission, a thicket of cameras that were making a feature film about my wanderings in the City. Without gates or walls you were left to guess when you had broken free of the City's gravity. You had to make assumptions based on a decreased intensity of surveillance: the precise point at which you became a walk-through extra and not a featured player. The King William Street checkpoint was old Hollywood: George Stevens shooting *Giant* with a battery of cameras covering every angle, leaving his editors with enough footage to make the most tedious script look good. These mean grey boxes were actually *erasing* truth, disqualifying natural colour. And, worse than that, their interference, their unceasing attention, disturbed the time-stream, the dance of photons. Their alien consciousness was a mortuary dream, the dream of someone left in a coma after a road accident. A dream with no rage, no anxiety, no phallic dew. A dream without symbols or archetypes. Instead of coding these images to heal, the Watchers in their Bishopsgate precinct had to invent a subversive psyche to fit the crimes that trouble urban sleep. Surveillance abuses the past while fragmenting the present. The subject is split, divided from itself.

I didn't try to discuss my improvisations with the policeman; nor did he, give him credit, spell out his frustration – that he couldn't simply blow me away, stomp me to butter on the pavement. His sense, whatever that was, of threat, was sublimated into a choked politesse: Fenians in the sewers, dole-chasers strolling free in the midday sun, scuffed shoes kicking up the dirt as if they had a perfect right to it. This was a terri-torial ruck with – in his case – the gloves still on. He didn't want me to do whatever it was that I was doing, but he didn't know why. Couldn't quote chapter and verse. My offence was essentially one of distance: I was too close to government property. Properly respectful photographs, the postcard kind, *might*, under special dispensation, be permitted. "What distance then," I enquired, "was acceptable – precisely?"

Hard to say. Fifty yards and they'd turn a blind eye. Ten yards and it was a collar. And then he spotted Marc and the debate became techni-cal. My little Japanese toy was one thing, Atkins' sophisticated long-focus lens made a mockery of distance: he could sneak away to the other side of the river and still work in close-up. The skinhead's camera was a weapon, Special Branch issue. Sarcasm gave away to overt threats: one wrong word and he'd frogmarch us back to Bishopsgate for a "Section One Search". Would we fancy that? (From his heavy breathing it was evident that he did.) We were less keen, but it would make excellent copy for the book I was working on. And so the affair de-escalated into peevish mutters. The engagement was broken off before it reached the point of paperwork.

3.

A plumper and portlier bull, says he, never shit on shamrock.
JAMES JOYCE

Repeated walks, circuits, attempts to navigate – to get to the heart of the labyrinth – proved frustrating. There was no centre. The geometry had been botched, the alignments twisted to flatter false imperatives: the money lake. The City was an off-shore island surrounded, protected, by high walls. Walls that became more effective the less visible they were to the uninitiated eye. (On the edge of old Bedlam, the sign of the Eye, scalloped in scarlet, stands out from the premises of **MARCUS AND ADLER**.) We traced vanished rivers, the Walbrook and its threadlike tributaries; we logged the distribution of tribes of totemic animals; we hit every church, recording armadas of stone vessels. And all without the desired shock of revelation. The City resisted us.

On the morning of the 14th of March, 1995, we were given per-mission to go up on to the roof of the former Port of London Authority

106

building at Trinity Square, Tower Hill, to inspect and photograph what appeared from below to be a pair of white bulls. (Perhaps the energy grid of the Square Mile could be graphed by the scatter of bulls and bears?) Tower Hill was one of the sacred places of London, the Bryn Gwyn (or White Mount) of EO Gordon's groundbreaking 1925 triangulation: *Prehistoric London, its Mounds and Circles*. Here was hidden the severed head of Bendigeid Vran, crowned king of the island, his face "towards France".

And they buried the head in the White Mount, and when it was buried this was the third Goodly concealment; and it was the third ill-fated disclosure when it was disinterred, inasmuch as no invasion from across the sea came to this island while the head was in that concealment.

This elaborate white temple with its decoration, its Corinthian portico, its overwheening rhetoric, had fascinated me for years, but I had never before stepped inside. That would be challenging fate. Gordon asserted: "no single instance can be found of a Keltic king erecting any kind of building upon the site of a sacred mound." It was already too late for the PLA, they had decamped to Tilbury. We were the temporary guests of Willis Corroon plc, "one of the world's largest insurance and reinsurance intermediaries", specialists in "risk management". Just the boys we needed in our present predicament.

Bulls on the roof. Bulls guarding the river gate. Where else should we start our circumnavigation? Had not the city once been measured by the distance covered by a baited bull? The crazy pattern of the lanes and alleys in Whitechapel had to be a faithful tracing of the blood running from the side of a tormented animal. *White Chappell, Scarlet Tracings*: the "explanation" of the title of that novel is arrived at, long after the book has been published. And will not the discovery of a minotaur tell us when we have finally located the centre of the maze?

Bulls were run at Smithfield, where they now hang in European-approved naves of meat sculpture. Bulls were roasted on the frozen Thames. But were they also used to map the City, these animals dedicated to the cult of Mithras? Butcher's *Survey of Stamford* outlines the ceremony of bull-baiting, which was a regular practice in that town from the thirteenth century until it was suppressed, "after much local opposition", in 1840.

It was performed just the day six weeks before Christmas. The butchers of

the town, at their own charge, against the time, provide the wildest bull they
can get . . .

Proclamation is made by the common bellman . . . that each one shut up
their shops, doors and gates, and that none, upon payne of imprisonment,
offer to do any violence to strangers . . . Which proclamation made, and the
shops and gates shut up, the bull is turned out of the alderman's house, and
then hivie, skivie; tag and rag, men, women and children of all sorts and
sizes, with all the dogs in the town promiscuously run after him with their
bull clubs spattering dirt in each others faces, that one would think them to
be so many furies started out of hell for the punishment of Cerberus, as
when Theseus and Pirithous conquered that place.

London did not lag behind her provincial cousins. Bulls and bears
were regularly baited at Paris Garden, alongside the Globe Theatre, in
Southwark. Bears, such as "Harry Hunks", were as celebrated as the
actors. "Sackerson" is mentioned by Master Slender in *The Merry Wives
of Windsor*. The same audiences enjoyed, and participated in, both spectacles: the play with its kings and clowns, its songs and mimed deaths,
and the bear-pit with its wagers, champions and cathartic conclusions.
Diplomats and visitors to the court of James I at Whitehall Palace would
move from a ceremonial feast to windows where they could look down
on a square in which a tethered bull would be attacked by dogs.

Whitehall and the City (in its licensed satellite across the river) had
their special enclosures set aside for public entertainments: rituals of torture, disembowelment, execution. Of men and animals. The bull or the
bear, chained to a post, "represented" grounded power, protected by
walls from the assaults of bandogs and greyhounds. The dog, once
again, stands for darkness, unpoliced liberties, the forest. Initiates, tran-
scribing the pattern of blood loss, would divine the fate of the city.

Marc and I carried these dubious theories with us to Tower Hill. We
waited in the entrance hall of Sir Edwin Cooper's river-facing bull temple, "the nearest thing London has to the Vittore Emanuele monument
in Rome", while a search was made for a woman to shepherd us into
the lift; then through the directors' corridor, and out into the sunshine.
We tracked a succession of exquisite private dining rooms – crisp linen,
polished hierarchies of glass and silver. Starched waitresses making their
final adjustments. Soft cell silence, limited edition light. Not the tweet
of a telephone nor the dry rattle of a word processor. Dim corridors
pleasured with marine oils, allusions to the building's previous function.

Our guide, who confessed to mild vertigo, didn't have time to waste on casual tourists, but was indoctrinated with compliance, the subtle art of massaging the male ego. Effortlessly, she did the patter: the building was a square, its sides aligned with the cardinal points of the compass. The rotunda at the centre – the mandalic circle within the square – had been destroyed by a bomb in the Second World War. A bomb which "surprisingly" did no other damage.

Stepping outside, we were invited to sit for a moment in the area reserved for power breakfasts, leisurely coffees taken within sight of Tower Bridge and the Tower of London. A morning of fine heat haze softening distance, smoothing over an excess of detail. The drudgery of our walks, down there among the insects, under constant surveillance, beating against locked doors, was instantly appeased by the width of this visionary exemption. It was like moving from portrait to landscape formula. You could even sympathise with the arrogance of these Lords of the City, the ones who had traded their immortal souls for the bounty of this view. The sculptural representation of Father Thames, and his galleon drawn by sea horses, reared above us.

Our guide, short of breath, humouring her disability, stayed where she was, pointing out the walkway that took us around the back of the temple, the tower, and to the east, where the great white bulls guarded their portal. The alignment was unimpeachable. It didn't matter that the ritual chambers within the tower were no longer in use; the pensioned river demanded no government, no structure of control and sacrifice. Father Thames had abdicated his Homeric status, refusing to patronise grand and noble themes. Spenser, Eliot and Pope were off the payroll. The brown presence, shimmering beneath us, ugly and delightful, was diseased – but in remission. A tolerated transient to be fought over by competing millennial committees with ever more preposterous schemes: Ferris wheels, waterfalls, meteorological platforms to botch the Greenwich axis. What role could be found for a colonised temple? A magnificent husk. How could the geomantic powers be turned, tamed, put back into service? The new operators acknowledged the dilemma, highlightling the surviving symbols in their glossy brochure: in the south-east wing, formerly the PLA boardroom, carved motifs pay homage to Pepys and Chaucer, while others in the reading room commemorate Newton, Hogarth, Inigo Jones, Harvey. In the floor of the entrance hall is a mark that represents the boundary between the City of London and the civil liberties of the Tower: the distance, so it is claimed, of a bowshot from the Tower walls.

Edwin Cooper's glacial folly, commanding the City's river-gate, with its pillars, overblown statues, its quoins and masses, its sepulchral hints of darkness within, was as much a triumph of quotation and pastiche as any post-modern docklands ziggurat. Without the labouring PLA clerks, at their concentric counters beneath the dome, scratching away to record every ship on the river, the temple was a hollow shell. It suggested nothing weightier than a fully-realised anticipation of the set for *Ghostbusters*.

And the bulls, the ruby-blooded beasts, now that we were free to prod their flanks, stare into their lifeless eyes, were exposed as oxen with dubious hairpieces: syrups hooked over stubby cornet horns. These were slack-necked beasts of burden: the Oxen of the Sun. The drudges of the *Odyssey*. Titular spirits mocked by James Joyce. "Down in the mud of crocodiles, or medical students", as Richard Ellman had them. Hormone-enhanced inflations, they are unworthy of sacrifice, existing only to break ground. They have been constructed in segments; the joins are clearly visible, dotted like a butcher's card, ready for carving. Ox-dumb extras in the imperial circus, they have been bred to drag some winged female, a muscle-beach faggot with strap-on, pistol breasts. The whole parade suggests a TV club night, leper-white poseurs with wispy drapes elastoplasted over their naughty bits. The knees of the harp-ribbed chorus boy (aka "Husbandry") who leads the oxen are malformed pineapples. Photographing them reminds me of the state of my own ligaments, the quiet agony of crawling about on rooftops, squeezing into crypts and cellars. And Atkins, as I notice him, head bent, black camera moulded like a growth to the stubbled pebble of his skull, is also flattering future infirmity. The intensity of his concentration is an act of exclusion, eliminating extraneous detail, keeping everything that is not pure revelation out of the frame. Savage and repeated acts of will that leave him with his head twisted like a vulture; that burden him with the catalogue of the city, images he can never live long enough to print. The sharp pain in his spine is the presence of all this untreated brickwork, a gluttony of skyscapes, imprisoned light. (His project is stranger – no thesis, no lecture base – than the feeding, by the late Theo Crosby, of the whole of Whitechapel, every doorway and window, into his computer system. Piranesian reefs to snag the unwary surfers of the Internet.)

We're in the right place, every aspect lives up to EO Gordon's prescription, but these are the wrong animals. This is a roof on which it would be a blessing to be turned into stone. Any number of lifetimes could be happily wasted looking out over the reservoir of money, basking in the illusion of being exempt from poverty, disease, mortality. All sorts of strange notions drift across the screen of consciousness: what if, for example, I'd got it completely wrong about Lady Thatcher. She was always, it's true, the protector of this self-regulating kingdom – get, grab, squeeze – but might she not have been acting on behalf of another? Of Denis, her consort. She was the window-dressing, paraded to take the flak, while he got on with the real task, amassing wealth, shoring up the immemorial "liberties" of the Square Mile. Denis was a Wodehousian con; a brilliantly impersonated buffer, *Telegraph* man, decent cove, snaffling the directorships, shaking hands on deals while his statuesque figurehead wife excited the prurient fantasies of the backwoodsmen. A dominatrix's consort, he would be at his ease in the private dining rooms, down there beneath us. Gin and North Sea oil. Nick Faldo-autographed golf clubs and heat-seeking missiles.

On the trot again, gabbling, the bull still an elusive figure, invoked by tavern sounds, drinking sessions: the wind-rush of the bull-roarer. Invoked but not represented. The bull becoming a Papal prohibition. The bear was easier. The bear had decamped to the other shore of the Thames, to Bankside: Bear Wharf. The bear was out of it, back where it belonged, with the revived Elizabethan theatres, the stews and prison rubble. A stained glass panel hung across a window that overlooks Southwark Bridge. The bear, representing Arcturus, an astral form, belonged in Rotherhithe with David Jones; a shagy circus dancer, glimpsed by a sick child from a bedroom window. The bear has been banished: it is a skin worn by a quest hero who is under enchantment. (Echoes of *Twelfth Night*. "To anger him we'll have the bear again." Sir Toby Belch. Or: "He brought me out of favour with my lady about a bear-baiting here." Fabian.) The bear is deactivated, muzzled, waiting its time. It's the bull that has been driven into the wrong pen.

Reaching the end of the visible traces of the Roman wall, beyond Aldersgate – having checked out the head of Mithras in the Museum of London – we found ourselves in St Botolph's churchyard, the "Postman's Park". You could, being generous, call it a kind of solution, but this dim parenthesis would not serve as a place of revelation, the heart of the labyrinth. It was dominated by tall-sided office buildings: a place for suicides to sit and be sure they were making the right decision. A wall of tablets, suggested by George Frederick Watts, recorded serio-comic episodes of Victorian life, domestic tragedies: drownings, fires, acts of fatal heroism. Prompts for bad poems, sentimental woodcuts. Let the dead celebrate the dead. Such events, exposed to ceramic decoration, provoke a cynical amusement among strollers: those unqualified to take part in a melodrama.

The park also features a small mound, or grassy knoll, on which has been sited a Michael Ayrton Minotaur, a black and greasy bullman. This mute, blind creature is crouched in pain, struggling to comprehend the burden it has to bear, the constricting helmet of bone: upturned horns which transmit the contradictory messages of the serpentine City. Some spark of human consciousness has been trapped in this awkward, unbalanced deformity. The Minotaur is yet another avatar of the Elephant Man, one of those hybrid forms that lurk, disguised, across the web of London: a guilt-provoking bestiary. From the rough stone head of the monument above the drinking fountain, outside the entrance to the St Mary Matfelon Park in Whitechapel, you can trace these man/animal monsters down a path that leads directly to the Minotaur. The path will of course be emphasised and confirmed by attendant beggars, winos, cripples. Deranged messengers with garbled prophecies, misapplied curses.

The Minotaur was illegitimate, the "byeblow" of an adulterous act of miscegenation, Pasiphaë's lust for a god, for Zeus or Poseidon in the form of a bull. Ayrton narrated the episode from the point of view of Daedalus, ordered to construct the love-hide – the cowskin in which the naked queen would prepare herself for a furious assignation. The child of this self-induced ravishment would be a monster, hidden in darkness, a destroyer of virgins. Only when Theseus, the chancer, the playboy, was given a red thread to follow could the Minotaur be slain. The red line that offers one of the walks through the concrete maze of the Barbican.

Ayrton's Minotaur, without some act of possession, is nothing – a Neo-Romantic gesture, a botched fragment of autobiography. It has been excommunicated, left outside the walls, to be visited by occasional antiquarians, such as Geoffrey Fletcher who sketched the Postman's Park in 1967 for his booklet, *Offbeat in the City of London*. The Minotaur is another misalignment, an accident of patronage in keeping with the regular attempts by the City fathers to subvert and annul the original grid of energies. Everything was to be preserved that could be preserved, the proud heritage of churches and antiquities; but it was to be neutralised by respect, rendered meaningless, explained away in tactfully designed museums; or broken up and displayed as trophies in boardrooms and vestibules. Restorations and near-perfect copies further confuse the picture. The complexity of the whole, the unified City and the necessary dualities that operated as symbols of cohesion – light/darkness, square/circle, bull/cow, altar/mound – have been exploited, atomised, perverted.

Where is as important as why. Ayrton may have painted on the Isle of Dogs, in Rotherhithe and Wapping, but his maze, when he came to construct it, laboured under the name of "Arkville", and was sited in hills of upstate New York. Like a Jewish weekend resort. The form of the maze, Ayrton said, was "as impalpable as smoke."

Among all this plunder, much of it difficult to locate, squirrelled away, is a strange and wonderful gathering of Bull and Mouth inn signs, catalogued (alongside its "Bedlam Figures") by the Guildhall Museum in its 1908 *Collection of London Antiquities*. There is a sandstone tablet removed from the Queen's Hotel, St Martin's-le-Grand, in which a bull appears, trapped within the yawning mouth of a grotesque, whose beard is formed from hanging bunches of grapes. The inscription at the base of the tablet reads: MILO THE CRETONIAN/AN OX SLEW WITH HIS FIST/AND ATE IT UP AT ONE MEAL/YE GODS WHAT A GLORIOUS TWIST. The "twist" in the vortex is the one consistent feature, the doubling back, the super-imposition, the scratching away at layers of darkness. A notable variant on the Queen's Hotel design is the other major example in the Guildhall collection. This is described in the catalogue, without irony, as a "finely-executed" bull, standing foursquare *above* the grinning head. There is no doubting the authenticity of this bull, a Smithfield prize-winner – now shifted west, imprisoned as a quotation from "Medieval and Later Periods" in the Guildhall Museum. And the mouth? The entrance to hell, no less. The bull is on parade, rampant, ready for sac-rifice. It was retrieved in 1887 from Angel Street, Aldersgate: the road that runs immediately to the south of the Postman's Park, but safely within the protection of the City Wall. This is the beast for which Ayrton's fearful Minotaur is a substitute. The grotesque head is then both mound and altar.

If the residual traces of bull-sacrifice offered a metaphor that was worth pursuing, then it was important to establish the place where these ritu-als were enacted. The temptation, as always, stood firm: to inflate a day's wandering, out in the weather, into something that could be described as a "quest". Rigby Graham, the Leicestershire artist and print-maker, a man whose work derives directly from the tradition of Graham Sutherland, John Minton, John Piper, was a cynical Romantic with a hyperactive bullshit detector. He wrote the introduction for an Ayrton show at the Goldmark Gallery in Uppingham, demonstrating an evident sympathy for the maze-maker as "a man of stress and strain and struggle". Graham also produced the image that was a keynote for our walk. His multi-coloured monotype, *The Ritual* (1994), depicts a bull's head hanging from a rope: wide-open pink eyes, lolling tongue – and blood, of the same colour, filling a chalice or grail-cup beneath. The impression persists, when the picture is no longer in front of you, of a deliberate act of blasphemy – an iconoclastic blending of Iberian paganism out of Picasso with the most sacred device of Christian mysticism. Blood of a grail that would scorch rather than cure the dead ground.

Yet again we tracked the submerged Walbrook, from the well-watered bowling green of Finsbury Circus, through gates with the sign of the triple compasses, HONOUR GOD (was there a missing L?), around the bulk of the Bank of England with its battery of niches and alcoves and tall iron doors; to a bookshop advertising PERFECTLY LEGAL TAX LOOPHOLES; to the Mansion House and the site where the Temple of Mithras was uncovered by Professor Grimes in 1954.

Moving south towards the Thames, down the street which preserves the name of its most notable tributary, the presence of the river is palpable. Stone reverts to water. On what would once have been the eastern bank, Wren's church, St Stephen Walbrook – whose dome he designed before that of St Paul's – asserts its claim to the ground once occupied by the Temple of Mithras; even though the interior embraces an entirely contrary spirit, being filled with light and centred on a broad, cold, altar stone from the studio of Henry Moore. A smooth-topped block of cheese. This was never the place of the bull temple.

Mithraism originated in Persia, making its way out of Asia Minor to Rome, and then on with the legions to London. It was a cult favoured both by the military and the mercantile classes. The energising symbol was the slaying of a bull in a cave by an initiate possessed by the spirit of the god: Mithras Tauroctonos. The ritual act of slaughter, according to the booklet put out by the Museum of London, represented "the triumph of light over darkness". Like Manicheanism the cult was dualist, a balancing of contraries: a deliberate submersion in shadows leading to the clout of illumination. The design of the temples, with their colonnades, submerged floors, was intended to foster a proper sense of mystery and awe. The structure of the building sympathised with a cult organised through levels of initiation. Women were not permitted to attend the ceremonies. Water was an important element.

The act – Mithras cutting the bull's throat – as depicted on the votive tablet discovered near Bond Court in 1889 is one of the crucial icons in any understanding of the psychogeography of the City. The figures of the god and the bull form a triangle within the framing circle of astrological symbols. Mithras, in his characteristic curved cap, turns away from the animal, cutting the throat from behind with a right-handed stroke. Light, in the form of blood, will gush from the wound. And the point, where the blade touches the throat, will be a sacred site in the mapping of London. Here: the bull falls. Here: the maddened animal runs through the streets, the circling and charging, ends. Here: a special quality of light, wisdom, is invoked.

So the knowledge of *precisely* where the original Temple of Mithras stood is crucial – if we are to fumble our way back, if we want to uncover the subterranean mechanisms by which the contemporary City functions. And that is where our difficulties begin: the Temple was never part of the territory of St Stephen Walbrook. It was uncovered by Professor Grimes on the west side of the road, and a hundred yards or so nearer the Thames. It is no longer there, not a brick of it. In its place is another City watering-hole, a wine-bar/restaurant – the Mithras.

This was not a very satisfactory conclusion to our researches. It wouldn't be enough to crash through the glass doors, in our dusty boots and sweat-soaked jackets, and demand the biggest steak in the joint. But it wasn't quite over: the Walbrook temple, it has been suggested, was the lesser of two cult centres – a satellite development. A good place to launch a quest, no more than that. During Professor Grimes' archaeological investigations a group of statues was discovered beneath the floor, including a vast hand – "far bigger in scale than the hand of Mithras". The hand gripped the pommel of a dagger, the sacrificial blade. It was thought that this hand had been rescued from a larger and more important site, hidden away for safety when the cult was threatened. And so we did not have to retreat indoors, not yet. The stalking and snapping could continue.

Neither had the Walbrook's Temple of Mithras been entirely eliminated. It's fate was worse than that: it had been borrowed, subjugated, parcelled up and shunted to a more convenient site. It had been – as if it were no small matter – dramatically realigned, so that the skeleton now ran from north to south, instead of west to east. Everything that had happened within the shape of that building was loosed on the City as psychic interference, bad karma, white noise. Jumpy pedestrians, battling down Queen Victoria Street, took an additional hit of rage, as they looked west, towards Lord Palumbo's work-in-progress and the pomp of

St Paul's. (Marc and I, en route to check out the effigy of John Donne, came across a man lying in the road with his head split open; a small crowd of fascinated office workers munched sandwiches; a lowering sun twinning the two domes, victim and church.)

Londoners, workers with somewhere to go, simply don't notice the rump of the Temple. It looks like an unfilled paddling pool, a parking space. Roofless, exposed to the gaze of the office block, it is a shamed structure, an approximation. Its potency has been ruthlessly neutralised. If you need it, it can be found outside Temple Court, the headquarters of the Legal and General Group, the London base of Sumitomo Banking.

If the present Temple stands for anything, it is a symbol of how the City has lost it; corrupted the integrity of its founding greed, its pattern of ritual and sacrifice, decent human vices, by yielding entirely to secrecy, cynicism, surveillance. Unprepared to let the past go, the off-shore investors and short-term profit takers have deliberately enslaved every artefact they can claw out of the ground. Walks are permitted only on agreed paths. The ancient gates, energy sluices, have been replaced by tawdry plastic barriers. A policy of deliberate misalignment (the Temple of Mithras, London Stone, the surviving effigies from Ludgate) has violated the integrity of the City's sacred geometry; leaving, in the place of well-ordered chaos, regimented anonymity – a climate in which corruption thrives. Poisoned weather, sick skies, confused humans.

4

Not for a boozed Murphy's bull in curial-cursive and leaded
for the scarlet pontiff o' the West
DAVID JONES

The hunt was over, let it drift; we'd never reach the bottom of the City's obfuscations. Stay on the move, that's all that matters. There is no great theme that will not eventually turn back on itself. Time to chase fresh rumours, to step eastwards. It had been whispered in Limehouse that on the morning of Ascension Day, at 7 am, the vicar of St George in the East, off the Ratcliffe Highway, would lead a party of parishioners up into the tower to hymn the rising sun. And, gasping on Fisherman's Friends, we intended to infiltrate that group. Thanks to the ministrations of Mr Peter Mason of Purley, an osteopathic magician,

Atkins and I were restored to nothing worse than our usual moderately distressed condition, ready for a fresh round of ascents and investigations.

Thursday, 25th May 1995. It was all too easy, strolling without pain, light cloud cover lifting to the promise of a glorious morning; long shadows across the small park at the rear of the church; leafplay on the stubby pyramid. We climbed the steps and stood within the husk of that splendid fake. The body of the church had been destroyed in the war, so that we found ourselves in a private courtyard: the glass of the new chapel dramatically reflecting the tower behind us.

In ones and twos, they appeared; this benign congregation. All known to each other, too polite to question us – smiles of complicity. A couple of City suits and the rest, mainly women, in Christian casuals: reindeer sweaters, hooded sweatshirts, laundry room leggings. The parson, balding, austerely bespectacled, black-cassocked, led us into the dark bore of the tower.

The service was described on the hymn sheets that were distributed to the circle, the twelve of us, as "Ascension Day: White or Gold". Two croakers to botch their plainsong. Clubbable, welcoming: the fellowship of those who have come together to break the ice on the pond and swim before breakfast. Conspiratorial grins and friendly asides: the vicar's lady told me about the flats beneath the pepperpot towers. Marc Atkins is one of those of whom it could be said, as Edward Dorn wrote of Richard Brautigan, that "the only respect in which he was a Christian was the interest he shared with Christ in professional women". Now he was visibly drooling over the self-evidently saved creature who was placed opposite him in the ring – long hair blown over her face by a warm-breathed zephyr; legs spread wide in an alarming V, as she bellowed the first hymn: "Hail the day that sees him rise. Alleluya!" A late arrival, panting up the steps just before the reading from Luke – "And they returned to Jerusalem with great joy, and spent all their time in the temple praising god" – botched our numerology. A bearded, leathery-faced party with a heavy cross slung around his neck: the coal-bright eyes of an inquisitor.

The short service over, we were free to climb a metal ladder to the highest point, to look down on the vicar and his group, beams of light cutting in through the arches in the stone; or turn our heads to the panorama of London – Canary Wharf, the river, the City, the white blade of Christ Church, Spitalfields. To the west we were aligned directly with the clock tower of the Houses of Parliament, with the bell,

Big Ben, cast at the Whitechapel Bell Foundry in 1858. From our viewpoint the path between the two cities was unusually distinct: Whitehall and the City of London. Government and the creation of wealth: the rest of the landscape, in the lush sweep of morning, existed only to serve those principalities.

Churlishly, not wanting to be drawn into a discussion on the reasons for our visit, we declined the ecclesiastic fry-up, and headed north to snack at Pellicci's in Bethnal Green Road. The quality of this day was special, it had to be seized. The "White or Gold" motif suggested alchemy as our theme. I had a yellow packet waiting at home that might prove helpful. It had lain on my desk for a year, but its moment had surely arrived. The donor, John Hudson, was a neo-classical poet and antiquarian bookdealer based in Vancouver, with whom I had been in spasmodic correspondence for some time. Mopping up Pellicci's excellent bacon and eggs, seduced by the aura of family portraits, polished formica, marquetry panels, I decided that this was the moment when Hudson's cultural aid parcel would have to be activated. It was obvious that Ascension Day, its ceremonies observed, offered unusual concessions: church doors would be open, secret formulae spoken aloud. We were constrained to act on Hudson's papers or shut up shop. He had, I knew – I'd met and talked with him – been constructing, at a distance, his own psychogeography of the City, based on a close study of the life and works of Elias Ashmole, the seventeenth-century genealogist and alchemist. For Hudson the prime site was St Paul's Cathedral, his calculations began there.

Back at the kitchen table in Hackney, I laid out the various elements of Hudson's collection:

1. A 3pp word-processed letter, with holograph corrections and additions. Signed in red.
2. 8pp of handwritten quotations, numbered: 5, 6, 10, 11, 12, 13, 14, 15. Obviously extracted from a much larger manuscript. Typewritten extracts – "Notes from RYWERT" – had been pasted to the backs of several sheets. *(ie. a belief among men of goodwill that forms of communal practice of the inner life would help to override theological differences and attendant savage intolerance/ pythagorean-solomonic mystery/(Wren) a pupil at Oxford of a strange person who makes the link (to Dee and Bacon) explicit: the "Rosicrucian" Peter Stahl, who established the first teaching laboratory at Oxford/William Stukeley (admitted a master-mason) did just that,*

and transformed a temple into a rather eccentric version of Christ Church, Spitalfelds.)

3. Photocopied biography of Ashmole (DNB). 1617–1692. *"The greatest virtuoso and curioso that ever was known or read of in England before his time." . . . In 1650 he edited an alchemical work by Dr Dee, together with an anonymous tract on the same subject, under the anagram of James Hasolle. In 1652 he published the first volume of his 'Theatrum Chemicum,' a collection of ancient metrical treatises on alchemy . . .*

4. A photocopy of Wren's proposal for the reconstruction of the City after the Great Fire of 1666.

5. A hand-drawn geometric chart (circle within square, within triangle, within circle): as an aid towards the completion of the calculations set out in Hudson's letter.

Irresistible. The full monty: Invisible College, Dee, Ashmole, alchemy, Masonry, maps, graveyards, cosmic conspiracies. All we had to do was transcribe Hudson's thesis, from his letter on to the photo-copied sheets of *The A-Z of Georgian London* – which I had picked up at the bookshop of the Guildhall Library.

Hudson had written (24 February 1994):

I am sending you the enclosed scraps, scribbles and photocopies in the hope that they will not too much increase your burdens . . . I have drawn my conclusions on other evidence, but you may at least find them interesting . . .

The story, if it were true, would go as follows: Ashmole, antiquarian, astrologist, historian, alchemist and one of of the first Freemasons never to have previously wielded a trowel, is a man dedicated to preserving the learning, including the hermetic learning, of the past. Most particularly, he takes upon himself the task of this preservation during the puritan interregnum: the past and the monarchy are one – the Restoration relies on the preservation of certain knowledge and institutions. To this end, Ashmole forms the so-called Invisible College.

The notes on Ashmole substantiate his connections to Wren, via Oughtred, the Oxford Society, Wren's father and uncle, and the Order of the Garter.

Wren along with Oughtred's other pupils were founding members of the Royal Society, following the Restoration. The Royal Society is, for all intents and purposes, Ashmole's Invisible College made visible: the membership is all but identical.

After the Great Fire, Charles II (who maintained an alchemical laboratory under his royal bedchamber) laid the foundation stone of the Royal Exchange, at a date and time astrologically determined by Ashmole. Meanwhile Wren had supplied his plan for the reconstruction of London, only four days after the flames were extinguished. The plan – full of Italianate piazzas and wide European boulevards, the city that London might have become if the Romans had never left – was rejected, and Wren instead employed rebuilding what had already existed. He built his churches on the sites of older churches; like Ashmole, preserving the past for the sake of the future. Wren's London became Ashmole's vision, the reminder in stone . . .

The letter continued with Hudson's instructions for tracing out "one of the principal alchemical symbols" on to John Rocque's map: the figure he had provided in his geometric sketch.

Atkins worked with a pair of scissors trimming the photocopied sections, while I pasted them together – and then, over several jugs of strong black coffee, we laboured at the mathematics of the thing. We borrowed bits and pieces of my son's geography kit, meat-skewers, lengths of thread, compasses stretched to their limit. We spiked the map, doodled on notepads. Until we grew tired of it and I fiddled the evidence to "prove" what I had already guessed Hudson was suggesting. Marc's geometry provided belated agreement. The demonstration was wobbly, but it was visible: a line linking churches and enclosures associated with St Dunstan – who I remembered from earlier researches in Stepney as "a metal-worker, alchemist, & bearer of west country grail-force."

We were invited by Hudson to "draw a line from the most south-easterly corner of the triangle, up through the centre of the inner circle," and "to continue the line beyond the bounds of the outer circle until it connects with a certain churchyard . . . confirmation may be received by extending the line also to the south-east, until it connects with a certain church." Using Rocque our destinations were now revealed: we would walk first to the west, to St Dunstan's churchyard, off Fetter Lane. On, via St Paul's, where Hudson asserted that "what happens on the outside also happens on the inside", to St Dunstan's Hill, up from Thames Street. Entering Wren's cathedral we were informed that: "The first circle is drawn for you: the great circle Wren laid on the floor of the transept crossing. Draw within this the same arrangement of triangle, square and circle, and the same line toward the North-West. Just before leaving the bounds of the structure, the line connects with a chapel, named for a certain, by now familiar saint." (This excursion is available to anyone who wants to sample it. No calculations are necessary. A straight line to walk between the churchyard, off Fetter Lane, and the ruin of St Dunstan-in-the-East.)

"This," said Hudson, signing off, "is my contribution to your Invisible City. If you make anything of it, I would be pleased, if only because Ackroyd treated Wren so shabbily."

It was mid-morning by the time Marc and I located the churchyard of St Dunstan, having negotiated Robert Maxwell's hideous *Mirror* building with its splashes of red and tested various Fetter Lane tributaries. There was nothing to announce or to commend this site: another palpable absence. Church gates and iron railings around a small rectangle of grass. The oddity was that no development had taken place. Nothing had happened here and was continuing to happen. Marc took his photographs and I scratched at the soil to uncover a small plastic tablet: 5 SWORD-EDGE BLADES. In early summer the area behind the gate, where there would once have been steps leading up to the churchyard, was clogged with last year's dried and fallen leaves.

Dues paid to Hudson's scheme, we drifted south to Fleet Street to sample a church that was still very much present (if not an active part of the Dunstan line): St Dunstan-in-the-West. Here we rejoin the tourist circuit, officially approved and brochured architecture. We're back in the book, mingling with crowds who have to look interested – the ones who have bought their bus tickets and are now being fed rapid summaries, blitzed with culture-bites.

We're still outside the City, but inside – by thirty or forty yards – the protection of the now removed Temple Bar. The church has been rebuilt on an octagonal plan, Eastern Mediterranean Christianity, high and ripe: incense, painted screens, sounds unsynchronised with the speed of streetlife. It's good, for a change, to walk around a visible, tactile, cold stone enclosure – where individuals are praying or meditating or brooding on some peculiar detail that takes their fancy. John Donne preached here, so I read. St Dunstan-in-the-West has been associated with a clutch of poets: Bretton, Drayton, Cowley, Dryden. Another worthy, who takes my eye on the honour roll, is Thomas White (1575–1624), founder of Sion College and the White Lectureship at St Paul's.

Externally, the twin figures that excite the tourist cameras are Gog and Magog, bell-bashers in an elevated alcove: Hercules-clubbed, draped in loincloths, muscle-pumped. These gaudy puppets bear as much resemblance to the chalk figures carved into the Wandlebury Hills (that TC Lethbridge describes in *Gog Magog, The Discovery and Subsequent Destruction of a Great British Antiquity*) as does Steve Reeves in the Italian epic, *Hercules Unchained*, to the Cerne Abbas giant. Only the persistence of the names matters. Magog, according to Lethbridge, was "the great Mother of All, the bringer of life and also its destroyer. She was the moon goddess . . . her lunar symbol was found on the head of every horned beast and on the hooves of horses." Gog was connected with fire ceremonies, bonfires. "The ring dances were his, making the shape of the disc symbol." Lethbridge sees this "combination of sun and moon worship" as a part of the "perpetual war against the powers of dearth and darkness." The figures should therefore be intertwined, combining male and female: fire and ice. (In a letter to *The Times*, May 10th 1957, discussing the "epoch-making" discovery of the Cambridge hill figures, Dr Margaret Murray begins by asking: "What has happened to English archaeology that three major failures have occurred in rapid succession? . . . The first of these failures was when the 'experts' pronounced the excavation of the Mithras Temple in London to be complete. Then a boy of 15, totally untrained in archaeology, discovered objects of the utmost importance on the 'finished' site. Next came the discovery of the hill figures on the Gogmagog hills . . .")

The cycle of familiar names recurs, as the cargo shifts, as the balance of psychogeographical elements is shunted. But tourism has its benefits. A knot of casuals gathered beneath a stone effigy of Queen Elizabeth I tempted me to pay it more attention. The figure was a representation of John Dee's queen, ball and sceptre, ruler of Empire, crowned and cloaked, lifted above Fleet Street's traffic. A plaque explained that the statue had "formerly stood on the West side of LUDGATE . . . that gate being taken down in 1760." Another misaligned refugee, a fragment of the old plan: facing the Temple and the river, her place on the hill lost. She should be up there, seen by pilgrims making their way to St Paul's – while she stared over their heads along the path to Whitehall. The capture of the queen was a minor act of heritage piracy to set against compulsory rustification, the removal and reassembly of Wren's Temple Bar arch in Theobold's Park, Cheshunt. (Dyos and Wolff in *The Victorian City: Images & Realities*, 1973, describe this conversion of "the true embodiment of early-modern London" into a "suburban conversation piece.")

Elizabeth battles for dominance with a bust of the press baron Lord Northcliffe, a dark bronze against a white obelisk-outline set into the wall: another deranged empire-builder, with his Newfoundland forests, his attempts to boost the circulation of *The Times* by slashing the price to 1d. These figures at the side of the church repeat the male/female, Gogmagog dispute of contraries. Beyond them, dumped in a shadowy doorway, are a banished trio of even greater significance: King Lud and his sons. The founder of the City, the ruler of the gate, rotting in the shadows; cast out, reforgotten.

There is one minor detour to make before we can confront the focal point of Hudson's alchemical interpretation, St Paul's Cathedral. Patrick Keiller in the intersecting journey/quests across town in his film, *London*, planted his camera at many heart-stopping viewpoints: river-scapes, Arcadian upstream prospects, sun-dappled inner-city courtyards. These alignments were magnificently right (they agreed so closely with my own private catalogue: locations where, visited at the right hour of the day, light affects time). I recognised, and respected, most of Keiller's choices, belonging as they did to a fully realised alternate city – a version that floats above or alongside the streets through which we hustle about our business. Keiller's retrieved London, his architecture of sun-light, belonged to the stalker. But there was one particular lane, one vision of a dusty church window that I couldn't place – and it bugged me. For Keiller it seemed to represent a literal passage in time, a location where it was possible to step, not back, but *through*; laying aside the burden of our conditioned reflexes. In this place the past had somehow got ahead of him. It was uncontaminated, freed from its human ballast. The lane with its peeling wartime posters was somewhere in the neighbourhood of St Paul's. I'd come away from the film with the idea that the church window *was* part of the cathedral, a part I didn't recognise. Was it possible that Keiller had managed to photograph this sequence with a time filter, translating "now" into "then"?

Marc Atkins and I, separately and in concert, worked our way around the cathedral in wider and wider circuits. No window fitted the image in the film. We had no problem with the other bits and pieces of St Paul's imagery. We'd photographed the broken statues in the churchyard on the north-side, but we couldn't fit this obscure passage against the layout of the building as it now stood.

Not until Ascension Day with its special truce, its permissions. Coming up Ludgate Hill towards the cathedral, we branched off into the maze of alleys and half-forgotten streets with boarded windows, the ancient offices perched between failure and future speculation: a limbo of medieval prompts hiding as much from the Great Fire or the Blitz as from crass development. Pilgrim Street, Apothecary Street, Knightrider Street, Addle Hill, Distaff Lane: the birthplace of Thomas Linacre.

And then we found it, realised our mistake. The sequestered court of Wardrobe Place with its shaded trees prepared us; turning from Addle Hill into Wardrobe Terrace, we found Keiller's camera position. The confusion had been a simple matter of picking the wrong church. St Andrew-by-the-Wardrobe was the time traveller, magnificently removed from the City's weather – operating within its own microclimate. The light stopped down to the limits of the visible, an illumination that depended more on fossils in the brickwork, on memories of conflagration, than on gas or electricity or the position of the sun in the sky. And to my delight, putting the seal on it, as we emerged into St Andrew's Hill, we discovered an abandoned bookshop – the individual letters of its title, as they peeled from the glass, reflected on a shelf that was thick with dust.

I have to confess that I've never struck an easy relationship with St Paul's, which is why I contrived to postpone our visit to this, the most important of the City's focal points, until we had reached the end of our quest. John Hudson apparently shared my unease. "Much as I love St Paul's as a building," he writes in his letter, "I was never very comfortable with it as a place of worship. Its true emblem is not the cross but the flag, and its saints those who upheld the flag and carried it into the world: it is a national building, not a religious one. But this, I suppose, is as Ashmole would have wanted, making no distinction between temporal and metaphysical power."

Hudson's reservations strike me as being absolutely correct: the humpbacked dowager is too grandiose and self-satisfied, dominating the heights of Ludgate Hill like a baroque power-point. St Paul's is contaminated by ill-conceived ceremony: the Royal Wedding, Charles and Diana, a marriage made in hell to take the heat away from civic dispute, riot in the streets. A sugary public rape of the last aristocratic virgin, soft porn on an epic scale. War celebrations, the clinking of petty potentates in operetta uniforms and self-awarded medals. Deathmask generals. Funeral barges for senile thunder gods. David Lean's fictitious account of the memorial service for Lawrence of Arabia – remembered and replayed when the last witness is dust. Flags and drums and necrophile marble, the rhetoric of the charnel house. And security personnel in ecclesiastical drag manning the cash registers, hooking out fare dodgers. Staying faithful to the free-market flag of convenience under which Old St Paul's always sailed. In less queasy times moneychangers had to get up very early to secure their pitch at the side of the nave, where domestics touted for hire, commercial introductions were made, harlots cruised for trade, and runners plucked at the sleeves of potential punters they hoped to lead to a nest of pornographic bookshops. St Paul's was the Thatcherite temple: the blue and the grey, the arms deal struck in a congregation giving thanks for victory. The ultimate heritage operation. Fallen heroes, granite adventurers, pikes and swords and cannons: all gathered to put the bite on susceptible investors. A crypt stacked with plunder, grails and robes and effigies. Christ militant laying out his business plan. Swooning with reverence, the patsies buy their tickets for the ascent to the rim of the dome, the small circuit that offers up the entire city.

EO Gordon's Celtic superstition is unshakeable: no vainglorious structure should be erected on a sacred mound. The mythical Bladud – son of Lud, father of Lear – crashed to earth on this site; the British Icarus, having flown from Bath. Bladud, founder of a School of Mysteries at Stamford, a healer, a shaman, took to the air. "Alas! How short-liv'd sublunary joys!" His kamikaze flight was a triumphant failure, a suicide's dream: lunar necromancy brought to grief on the Temple of Apollo at Troja Nova. Wax melted by the rays of the sun. Seen as he approached from the west, by the gathered priests and initiates, as a shining disk. The hallucinogenic act of sacrifice symbolised the moment of transition between cycles of lunar and solar influence; Druidic knowledge stepping aside into symbol and rhyme and mystification, ceding public worship to the temple of the sun.

Even contemporary mythologists have pictured St Paul's as a fitting conclusion to an occult mapping of the city; the ancient taint still exercises a powerful influence on any imagination that allows itself to float over the streets in a willed discrimination of archetypes. The graphic novelist Alan Moore's prize-winning sequence, *From Hell*, a serial composition, neo-Victorian in scope and energy, is superficially a reworking of the Jack the Ripper murders in terms of pyschogeography. In fact, as the project develops, carrying along its own critical equipment – footnotes that make TS Eliot and David Jones seem tight-lipped, speech bubbles that sag like condoms filled with lead shot – it becomes clear that Moore is engaged in an epic deconstruction of previous Ripper scholarship, a sharp-witted collaging of existent narratives, a tapping of voices. The pictorial aspect (illustrations by Eddie Campbell) proved very seductive to the Hollywood dealmakers, who increasingly want product served neat. Naked storyboards. Instant breakdowns, glyph-strips that obviate the need for pages of tedious synopsis. Rumour had Oliver Stone aboard for the movie of *From Hell*, with Sir Anthony Hopkins slated to reprise his sketch of Sir Frederick Treves, this time in darker tones, as Sir William Gull. Mega budgets are brokered. Stone, busy exhuming the demonology of Richard Nixon, gave way to Ridley Scott – who decided to transfer Moore's untrustworthy geography from the streets to the studio. A steam-punk *Blade Runner*.

In Chapter Four, *"What Doth the Lord Require of Thee?"*, Moore launches Gull and his coachman, John Netley – X-ray spectres borrowed from Stephen Knight's transcription of Joseph Sickert's "memories" of his father's Masonic/Royalist conspiracy theories – on a fantastic criss-crossing journey between the needle-points of London's energy mantle; a journey which becomes, with Gull playing the tour guide and pyschic instructor, a brief history of the arcane, the chthonic, the illegitimate. A lecture tour of the lefthand path. King's Cross gives way, as Gull munches through a bag of black grapes, to Hackney. "Albion Drive. 'Twould seem auspicious in that we aspire to probe the ventricles of London, England's heart. Regard the London Fields . . ." Snippets of Blake, brief asides on the Dionysian ("the Mind's unconscious hemisphere whose symbol is the Moon"), and the cab rolls on to Bunhill Fields; Hawksmoor's obelisk at St Luke, Old Street (pencilled crosses on the map); then Cleopatra's Needle, the Tower of London, St George-in-the-East and Christ Church, Spitalfields; "and, finally, St Paul's."

(Christ Church, in the person of a representative of the Spitalfields Trust, was the only Hawksmoor church that charged us to climb the tower. After some bargaining I beat them down to £30 – which would also allow Atkins to take photographs of the nave and altar. When he turned up at the agreed time, the building was filled with smoke, cabalistic signs and calculations were outlined on the floor. A documentary was being shot in which Alan Moore realigned the church and its fellow East London leviathans according to some dangerous occult prescription. Nicholas Hawksmoor's flagship had willingly rented itself out as a set for Clive Barker's history of horror.)

St Paul's, for Gull, is the nexus around which any explanation (or exploitation) of the City must be constructed. It is the dark hotel, the library of malign potentialities. "Christ is clearly but the Sun God's latest guise . . . in our paintings still we mark him with a solar disc about his head. Apollo, Lud, Belinos, Atum, Christ or Baal. All one God, Netley." Gull, discoursing on the cult of Diana, leads his coachman to the centre of the geometric design: as if obeying John Hudson's Ashmolean instructions. The map is spread out on the flags (fortunately, the church in the late-Victorian period seems to be profoundly unfashionable, there isn't a single visitor to disturb their public demonstration of geomancy). "Keep drawing, Netley. Next, Battle Bridge to Herne Hill, through Hercules Road and Cleopatra's obelisk . . . to Albion Drive, through Horsleydown (*sic*), The Tower, and Christchurch (*sic*), Spitalfields . . . Draw bisectors 'til they cross. St Paul's is in the centre. We are the centre of this pattern now! You can't OUTRUN it, Netley. It surrounds us . . . This pentacle of Sun Gods, obelisks and rational male fire, wherein unconsciousness, the Moon and Womanhood are chained."

Netley, overcome – "Hwurrrr . . . urr urwulsh" – spews up on the pavement. The final panel is a longshot, a grim London nocturne, moonlight on the dome. The text: ". . . engraved in stone."

Now Marc and I are the dogs returning to Netley's vomit, bilious with overripe speculations, high with ascents, cod "discoveries", authentic blisters. We've gazed down on the prospects of the City from so many church towers, it's almost as if we have flown like Bladud in an arrogance of vanity and delusion; as if seeing a pattern was creating one. As if walks linking discrete sites could manifest some miraculous whole, compete with the gears and bearings of the secret machine.

We pick our way through the loungers on the steps, to join the crush of camera-heads steaming in towards the security bottleneck, the clattering tills. I'm waved straight through with a troop of Nordics on a group ticket, but Marc, gangling skinhead, is challenged and pulled out. It's pay up or piss off for the lower orders.

Fulfilling John Hudson's prescription is difficult because – unlike Alan Moore's Gull – I don't enjoy the luxury of a private view. You'd need a squad of SAS minders to get anywhere near "the great circle Wren laid on the floor of the transept crossing". But the NW/SE line is so graphically established by now that it's a simple matter to locate the side chapel to which Hudson refers. The problem is that the chapel is out of commission and back beyond a gate, a security barrier: back with the unticketed trash. With Atkins. I signal him to check this one out while I see what the Dunstan line offers in the crypt.

No surprises. A glass cabinet with a bust of hook-nosed Wren, "Surveyor to the Fabric"; his knife-case laid on the green felt, green and gold. His ceremonial measuring rod. His wand of office. Which is properly arranged, corner to corner, to flatter Dunstan's ley. Wren's white lard head, protected from dirt and corruption, dominates its micro-landscape, as his most ostentatious church dominates the City.

The way out of the crypt, through a shopping mall, drops me back in the fresh air. Atkins has found a painted notice, turned to the wall, which announces the closed chapel as being dedicated to St Dunstan (though formerly known as the Consistory Court). So it only remained for us to leave St Paul's, drop down towards the river and back east towards the Tower, to find our last Dunstan marker, the church of St Dunstan-in-the-East.

And of course, as with all the other sites to which we had been directed, this temenos revealed itself as an erasure, an absence. On the incline of St Dunstan's Hill, alongside Idol Lane, was a secret garden, somewhere for office workers to drop off the pace, refresh themselves. The Wren steeple was all that survived. It is said that when Wren was told about the hurricane of November 1703 which had damaged so many of the City churches, he remarked: "Not St Dunstan's, I am sure."

During excavations on this site, several relics of the church destroyed by the Great Fire were unearthed, "amongst them the fragments of an east window" – which served as a model for the construction of the central east window of the new church. At the heart of the design were "symbols of Hebrew worship", including the Ark. Images of fire and flood to reassert the City's exclusion zone, the weather apocalypse. From Dunstan-in-the-East to Dunstan-in-the-West, a zone within a zone; a cylinder of alchemical experimentation and manipulation of the light. Blocks of Portland stone tempered by the green and the gold.

Earlier that day, after a lunchtime pint in Bride Lane, we had found – just as we'd expected – that the iron door to the tower of St Bride, Fleet Street, the printers' church, was open: Wren's "madrigal in stone". (We'd tried it many times before and had only Stewart Home's word that it was *ever* possible to make an unaccompanied ascent.)

A panting spiral through the darkness gifted us with another of those miraculous urban prospects to which we were in real danger of becoming addicted. This interlude, a breather outside the Dunstan thesis, allowed us to let go, to glimpse the whole pattern, the London that was and is and will be. Scudding cloud streets drifted in from the west, the kind to delight Luke Howard with their extravagant metamorphoses. Sunlight breaking through the flocculent quilt caught the golden cross above the dome of St Paul's. Beast faces on the rims of soft stone bowls were eaten away; toothless mouths wide open, cursing folly. All the private roof gardens, the satellite receivers, gargoyles and elective monsters, the lush green corridor running north from the Temple to Gray's Inn Gardens, were opened to us. The white spine linking the twin hemispheres – Whitehall and the City of London – was radiantly exposed. Blood-lights of stuttering traffic down Ludgate Hill, Fleet Street, the Strand. Twinned principalities in a treaty of power: Gogmagog or Ronnie and Reggie Kray (the "Other Two", as they were known to members of the Firm). The City is revealed as a naked brain, uncapped so that all its pulsing cells are offered for exploitation. The churches are needles, driven into the clay to bend the flow of current. Electrodes can be attached by any mogul with the price of a helicopter pad in his portfolio. The past is an unreliable dream. We know now that we know nothing.

We begin to impose fires and blitzes and millennial sunsets, to repeat heresies, to share the prophetic vision the Reverend Thomas Vincent published in 1667 in *God's Terrible Voice in the City*. "The yellow smoke of London ascendeth into heaven, like the smoke of a great furnace; a smoke so great as darkened the sun at noon-day; if at any time the sun peeped forth, it looked red with blood." We begin to see the gold of alchemy spread across the scatter of domes from St Paul's to the Old Bailey; streams of silver spurned in the gutters – as when the lead melted from the roof of the old cathedral and "the very streets glowed with fiery redness".

We are incapable of seeing anything as it is, without this haze of horror, these terrifying memories of events scorched into the stone. Future memories we are determined to provoke. My tongue is blistered by cinders in the air. I remember how the bookdealers packed the crypt of St Paul's with the pick of their stock, with the cathedral's own library; how they sealed away all the knowledge that was worth preserving. The church would repulse the flames of the Great Fire and London's memory would be secure in the cold vaults.

Nobody knows quite what happened. Perhaps one of the dealers, impatient to check his treasures, opened the doors too soon. Hot air reached the bundles of paper and parchment and they gleefully ignited. "They burned for a week until they were no more than a great mound of ash". And the amnesiac church was left to invent any past that took its fancy.

X MARKS THE SPOT

"If he starts getting mystical – hose him down"
DEREK WALCOTT ON AIDAN DUN

How about this? A middle-aged man in a black, defiantly grunge T-shirt and Sam Peckinpah long johns stalks barefoot into the crimson casket of the Royal Albert Hall to book it – one night only – for a monster celebration of . . .? He hasn't quite decided what. He'll think of something when the time's right, when the reality chill hits his system like the most luxurious of downers. He feeds on edge (with built-in survival clauses). The Zen tonsure (grape-smooth caput shaved to an Alcatraz fuzz), the Oxfam drag, the deep-breath, sixty fags a day, pyschobabble would be unexceptional if this sharp-eyed spieler were punting religious revivalism, the Second Coming of the Brick Lane Buddha – or if he were a heavy-metal impresario in civvies. The Royal Albert is simply the poshest church hall in England. A Kensington scout hut with budget. Every ego-tripping nutter in the land has gigged there: once. Every clown with an unperformed symphony in the bottom drawer. Every pub band whose income exceeds their talent. Every messianic conman with the price of a second sharkskin suit. Our boy doesn't faze the characters who accept the downpayment. They've seen them all: shaggy or bald as a stone, rabbiting like speed freaks or silent as the deeps of eternity. If they can make their cross on a cheque, they're in.

The awesomely hirsute arms and low centre of gravity prowl of a bouncer with a Hermann Hesse habit wouldn't rate this latest village hustler, hot from the sticks in a cloud of big city paranoia, a second glance from the doorman who was struggling to find some convenient flap or lapel that would accept a laminated pass. If he thought about him at all, it would be as a music business anachronism. A well-fed ghost. Professional eccentrics, dressed up, down, or out of it entirely, were the norm. But the pitch for which this chunky sadhu with the gold-rimmed accountant's spectacles is prepared to lay down £20,000, basic, is poetry. Madness!

Poetry: the hard stuff, the toffee of the universe. The antimatter that granted validity to the Thatcherite free-market nightmare by steadfastly manufacturing its contrary: a flame in the dark. There never was a better period in which to be unknown, off the record, ex-directory. With no chance whatsoever of mainstream publication, of becoming legislators, acknowledged or unacknowledged, the poets relished the freedom to take language for a ride. They squeezed it, surfed it, scorched it; fitted it with concrete boots and threw it into the river. Presses were no longer "small", they were microlite, singular – trade editions of one, mass market runs of thirty, giveaways, offers you couldn't refuse. This was the shift from the heady days of Pete Brown's famous poem *Few*, featured in the Michael Horovitz's anthology, *Children of Albion: Poetry of the 'Underground' in Britain*. Brown, the original poetry and jazz, on the road performer, "staggered into the bogs/at Green Park station/and found 30 written on the wall." "Surely," he thought, "there must be more of us than that . . ." In the Eighties and Nineties thirty is a mob, a sell-out. Thirty is a complimentary glass of Absolut Vodka.

Desktop concerns, run for love or politics, flourished in Cambridge, Brighton and London. Poetical Histories, Parataxis, Equipage, Angel Exhaust: gonzo outfits with marvellously pretentious titles. I treated each of their pamphlets, arriving as they did with the frequency of junk mail, like holy writ. Real news. The world compacted into a series of wafer-thin bites. Amyl nitrate snorts. Shamefully, I didn't always read them. Handling the pages was enough, letting the inky riffs burn through the skin. Furious compositions: it would take a ward of demented autodidacts to keep up with the pace and intensity of this output – lowercase, unpunctuated, long line, Adorno and Benjamin citing, dialectically lyrical, revenging song. Superb poets, who had published modestly for years, were energised by the pressure of disinterest, to achieve new levels of excitement and control: Denise Riley (*Mop Mop Georgette* and *Stair Spirit*), Barry MacSweeney (*Hellhound Memos* and *Pearl*), Grace Lake (*Viola Tricolor* and *Bernache Nonnette*), Brian Catling (*The Stumbling Block* and *Soundings*). Lines of heritage were vigorously asserted. Fresh voices, such as Drew Milne (*Sheet Mettle*) would, I assume, track a direct path through John Wilkinson to JH Prynne. A Vatican of periodicals came into being with no purpose beyond reinterpreting (muddying with exegesis) the minutiae of the Prynne oeuvre. In contrast, Prynne himself on his occasional trips to the Smoke (notably a lecture at the Tate on de Kooning's *Rosy-Fingered Dawn at Louse Point*) was luminously direct, practical and straightforward, dissolving from the pattern of paint drips on the canvas to Homeric mythology, by way of that mysterious lacuna, the empty zone at the heart of the composition. Difficulty exists only when you insist on it.

The solid citizen who marched into the Albert Hall from a twenty year exile in the East Midlands, with a mission to revive English culture, knew nothing about the subterranean nexus, the cult of the unreadable. He'd been taken up with survival and expansion. His genius – like Joseph Stalin's – lay in his ability to plot ahead in seven-year cycles. Future perfect is the tense with which he is most comfortable. It's not for nothing that he was a schoolmate of Stephen Hawking, back in St Albans. He understands as well as any physicist that time is a commodity, it's negotiable. History, private and universal, is rewritten by the man who owns the pen. He has the intuitive sense that the moment is swiftly approaching for poetry to go public. (If there were any doubts about the sanity of the Albert Hall gig, he assuaged them with a £20 phonecall to his tame clairvoyant: "No sweat, Mike. I see hordes storming up Exhibition Road." So that's OK. Plus which, his girlfriend had a prophetic dream with the same scenario.)

The Aquarian age had been announced by, among other manifestations, the *Wholly Communion* readings at the Albert Hall on the evening of June 11th 1965, with the release of what Alexis Lykiard called "God-as-total-consciousness". The much derided "British Poetry Renaissance, 1965–1979" was visibly launched. (And in typical style – with much of the huge audience barracking Harry Fainlight's hallucinogenic epic, *The Spider*, while signalling their approval for the simplistic formulations of Adrian Mitchell. What they wanted, as ever, was a protest prom. Poetry as CND sloganeering.) But no sooner were the photo-spreads of poets on the steps of the Albert Memorial surfacing in the broadsheets, than *Fulcrum* and *Trigram* and *Turret*, with their attractive and considered designs and their transatlantic lists of Beat and Black Mountain modernists, were noticed and distributed. Cape moved in on Goliard. The scrapdealer George Rapp approached Tom Raworth and asked him what was needed to form a mutually beneficial alliance. "Hand over the cash and fuck off," was the poet's reply (as reported by Jeff Nuttall). It was bound to end in tears. And it did – with sectarian strife at the Poetry Society, committee wars which wasted energy and duplicating fluid, and a widespread embargo on the whole tedious business. Poetry was blacklisted. Journos hate it worse than scabies. Pitch poetry at Channel 4 and Waldemar Januszczak will yawn in your face.

The man in the black T-shirt doesn't have any particular interest in those ancient squabbles. He recognises poets by their aura, by occult markings invisible to the naked eye. By serendipitous accidents. He prefers the quieter ones, the ones who have done it on their own, hermits with cast-iron egos. He certainly isn't going to involve himself with the kind of schmuck who zaps him with perfect-bound CVs, wallets of press cuttings. He hasn't read anything more recent than about 1650, but he has the quirk of liking what he doesn't understand. (He's no fool. He'll check every poet out with his coven of 24-hour standby telephone invigilators.)

So there are no names to put on the bill, not yet. And no title for the event, no hook. This mysterious conductor of chaos is not dumb enough to have signed anything like a contract – but when his squiggle does go at the bottom of the cheque it will read: "Mike Goldmark".

Goldmark. Mr Uppingham. Property developer, publisher (one book every eight years), gallery owner, healer, salesman: facilitator. Mike is a one man Arts Council (doesn't believe in public funding). An apostle of "can do". A patron of the reforgotten. He imported Gary Kasparov into the huntin', shootin' and strategic response deliverin' shires for a one-night chess blitz. Kasparov subsequently puffed Rutland on the Wogan Show. But he can't persuade the metropolitan art mafia to schlepp out of town for any of his exhibitions. Michael Sandle, Michael Ayrton, Graham Sutherland? Not interested. The openings are always well-attended – even when, as with *The Shamanism of Intent*, he turned his gallery over to a pack of clinically uncommercial, ley line-navigating, drum-tapping, crow-boxing, eel-weaving poets and sculptors.

Rutland, Goldmark's operation base, his flag of convenience, would fit comfortably under the lunar dome of the Albert Hall. It's nowhere, a Monty Python joke location. It doesn't officially exist – except in the memory sediment of Deepest England. A couple of public schools (one of which expelled Stephen Fry), a drowned valley, several hunts and a scatter of air bases. Landed and cash comfortable, rural decay mixing with service industry short-haul commuters and media dropouts. Every Englishman has at least one relative hidden somewhere within its theoretical borders. Even the hardcore Tory MP has had to come up with a bill to decriminalise cannabis to justify his continued representation of such a nest of weirdos. Rutland is a time-share gulag where damaged artists creep to reinvent themselves (with a little help from Mike).

The Goldmark Gallery/Bookshop on Orange Street functions as a networking centre, display case of sunset Romanticism, alternative health ashram – and command post for the revival of rural England (craft, cobbles, antique shops). Camden Passage, Islington, dropped into the middle of *The Archers*. A grandiloquent staircase – like a monument to the patron's DNA – sweeps the casual visitor on towards the upper deck, where a précis of postwar British art is always available on the walls. None of that reviled Bond Street hauteur, the well-connected Sloanes firming up their social diaries on the telephone. The Goldmark Gallery, in the person of the friendly and efficient greeter, Sally Jones, demystifies the whole schmear. A tiny pot – locally thrown – of decent coffee is plugged into your hand as you step in off the street, ensuring that, if you stick around, you'll require constant topping up: leaving you open to be painlessly pitched, drawn out, at regular intervals. A caffeine high soothed by piped Mozart. The only escape leads straight through a linking chamber into the bookshop. If Mike's crazy, he's crazy like a fox.

Accept the thimble of hot dark liquid and you've been initiated into the club. Within seconds you'll be introduced to other passing members: a puff writer from the *Telegraph*, a near-famous ex-Nazi set designer, a PR man undergoing a spiritual crisis, a serious art collector who hopes very soon to pass his Common Entrance examination, a prize-winning Quaker novelist with an interest in bondage, mendicants, hucksters, brickies looking for cash, depressed schoolmasters, waifs and strays, longhaired kids with drum kits and guitar cases, relatives of Tolkien, seekers and sellers, the guy who used to be Peter Whitehead. You don't even have to notice the art on the wall to get your fix of coffee and conversation.

The paintings and lithographs – John Piper, Graham Sutherland, the Nash brothers, Michael Ayrton – are all rigorously Tesco'd: priced and summarised on idiot-simple cards. Cecil Collins: "He consistently explored the mystery of consciousness. £2,450." Ceri Richards: "His mature work reveals his lifelong love of music and poetry. £650."

The taste represents a tradition in which Rigby Graham, with his interest in inventive printmaking, his compulsive logging (and debunking) of the sacred places of Britain, could be seen as a final spiky flowering. The cactus in the Bloomsbury garden. Graham's influence has been crucial in shaping the gallery's pitch: figurative, technically competent, enlightened conservatism. Which is not to say that Mike will not chance his arm. Nothing, at the time, would have appeared riskier than turning his first big show over to Graham, locally famous as the veteran of 42 disasters. The painter sold "fifty times more" than at any previous exhibition and his work has remained a constant presence in the gallery.

Mike effects his magic, as he explains, by watching the feet. That comes from his period as a double-glazing grifter. He worked the bookshop (essentially flogging "seconds" from the Cape/Chatto/Bodley Head warehouse) by day, and going out on the road at night. He'd get husband and wife together on some dormitory estate outside Peterborough and focus on the choreography of their shoes. When they settled in a certain position, he knew he'd hooked another prospect.

But all that Jack Trevor Story stuff is in the past. Now Goldmark is supervising the meltdown of our urban pretensions. He is offering high art to the turnip-bashers in a discreetly showcased car boot sale. Everything on the walls has a value, cashmoney. He'll shift it by instalments for school kids or pensioners. He'll barter or trade or take part-exchange. Failing West End brokers, who can't lose face by ticketing their Matisse doodles, their iffy Picassos, at remainder prices, are only too delighted to have Mike punt them, somewhere remote off the A1. (You can't say "no" to this man: the only barefoot in the door.)

But there is so much more to Goldmark than the official Byron Rogers version which is recycled at regular intervals in the press – although that story has its charms. This is its outline: parents as refugees from Austria, scholarship boy St Albans, Board of Deputies interview, Jack the Lad with Marks & Spencer, blags a management job with schmutter hustler John Michael (one of those double Christian name rag trade Jews from the Sixties), corners the market in floral ties (centre spread in financial pages – the last time he hangs around in Piccadilly at 10 o'clock on Saturday night to see what they say about him); boom, bust; sells The Hall, the antiques and the wife's engagement ring (gives up wearing ties); banished to Uppingham, dark night of soul, double-glazing, outdated dog food, used books (first window display: a collection of Masonic directories); cash flow improves, buys town ("like Lee J. Cobb in all those old Westerns"), publishes novel, hand-set by Europe's finest printer (gives up wearing shirts); therapy, Xanax; opens gallery, plans to take over hotel and turn it into a multicultural palace beyond the wildest dreams of Arnold Wesker or Joan Littlewood (gives up shoes); books the Albert Hall.

The Goldmarkian orthodoxy feeds off a repeatedly stressed fetish: X marks the spot. Remain perfectly still and the world will beat a path to your door. London is deluding itself if it thinks it can continue to dominate national consciousness: the centre is anywhere and everywhere, especially Uppingham. The conceit is expressed in a fable that Goldmark is fond of telling. It involves himself and one of his sons.

Sometimes the setting is a railway station, or sometimes (as in a profile by Natasha Walter) it's the sea-shore. "I lost one of my kids on the beach. I started running around, but I couldn't find him. I got panicky. Finally, because I'm fat and unfit and smoke too much, I stood still. Then he went running past . . . I thought I would live that way . . . I decided I would stand still in this little town and just look very carefully in one direction, to see what came past."

If this emphatic provincialism were the whole story it would hardly be worth the telling; any cheese-stone town could represent itself as the heart of the matter. Whatever next? Something as fantastically improbable as Stamford being cast as George Eliot's *Middlemarch*? The Goldmark saga would then be the plot for a Jeffrey Archer novel rather than a CV that, in its twists and turns, its steady ascent, has parallelled the glorious career of the Sage of Grantchester. Constant strife, challenge, near disasters and dramatic escapes: more bounce than a cheque from Hay-on-Wye. Both men suffered an early traumatic reverse in business and used that as the excuse to relocate and to recompose their life plans. Both men opened art galleries that traded under their own names (while building up impressive, and eclectic, private collections). Both men took a punt on the Albert Hall. (Archer tried, disastrously, to double-book Bob Hope and Frank Sinatra. Who refused to perform in the same building. Goldmark's calls to Seamus Heaney were not returned. Ted Hughes wanted a percentage of the door. Derek Walcott was thought to be unreliable. Philip Larkin was dead. At this point, he decided to take casting advice.)

There is a photograph in Michael Crick's biography, *Jeffrey Archer, Stranger than Fiction*, of the Archers posing at the Old Vicarage on the occasion of their silver wedding. A grotesque caricature of Lord Archer, carved in local stone, has been set into the wall of the folly: text around rim, open book on head. This is an amiable but self-regarding jape. The very thing for the man who has it all. Just such a panel, carved by Mark Porter, is to be found in Orange Street, Uppingham, fixing the keystone of the Goldmark empire. Indeed, Mike's one recent failure, his conversion of the old International supermarket into a cod-Edwardian, striped apron and straw hat delicatessen, foundered partly on the meanness of the county set, who won't waste an extra penny on a fancy cut of cheese, and partly on the name he chose to give it: Archers.

This knockabout stuff sketches the public man. It doesn't begin to approach the real motor, the secret passion. Mike is, without question, a rabbinical visionary. An artist at promoting art. An artist at finding work in the most unpromising places. A PhD in telephone studies. Cigarette kippering his first two fingers, intravenous coffee drip firmly attached, he goes into action. Two hour séances are nothing. Listening to him on the blower, time stretches like Hawking's spaghetti; our end is our beginning. I've known hardbitten editors who have lost days and never recovered them. Who now wander the city like shellshocked veterans, tuned to this terrible, unbroken monologue. From the Outer Hebrides to Hackney, from Allen Ginsberg's minders in New York to Leicestershire carpenters and bemused metropolitan mandarins. A soothing hum, a litany of startling confidences: so that even the most implausible proposition begins to sound perfectly reasonable. A handshake on the telephone is better than an agent's three-bottle lunch party.

Mike can – and sometimes does – walk away from it all. Go on retreat. Feel the sand between his toes. He speaks of the cycle closing, of clearing all this matter. He speaks freely and openly and at length about the – almost Kerouac-like – sadness of being. ("Goldmark's a sad man," Byron Rogers quotes Rigby Graham. "Some people are naturally thick, but he's naturally sad." "The saddest eyes in the world.")

First it was Rutland, now he's ready for London. Barefoot for over a year, living above the shop in benevolent austerity, conditioned by a twice-daily regimen of T'ai Chi, even managing in good weeks to get a couple of hours' sleep, he has alchemised profound melancholy into fugues of imaginative action. His shrink is so fascinated by this development that he no longer charges. And I get the feeling that, very soon, he'll be paying Mike to come in. The tranquillisers have been replaced by Albert Hall night-sweats, the full realisation of what he has taken on.

But standing there on the stage, surrounded by plush and gilt, aware of the voices of previous poets and prophets, he successfully channels all that loose energy. One of the sound-baffles overhead shapes a perfect meniscus from the dome. He's got the city in his hand. The names come to him: Ginsberg, Lou Reed (maybe Dylan, or rumours of Dylan), a spare Beatle, Sorley MacLean, Brendan Kennelly, David Gascoyne. Put that lot together, or try for them. Mix them with a raft of others, whose intransigence and long-husbanded rage nobody in their right mind would risk. Take advice: find a couple of women and ethnics. Whozat rap geezer? Benjamin Zephaniah. The slaphead Irish chick? Sinead O'Connor. There's even a title to go on the poster, which should look like a boxing promotion: Return of the Reforgotten.

London is begging to be rewritten, but who would have thought that a chancer from the sticks would be the man to front it? Because Goldmark's second book, an epic poem by Aidan Andrew Dun, which proposed King's Cross as the epicentre for the spiritual rebirth of the city and the nation, was about to be published. The manuscript found its way on to his desk in 1988, recommended by Oliver Caldecott who edited the esoteric Rider imprint for Hutchinson. (Rider didn't go in for poetry. Their list was built around such cornerstones as Eliphas Levi's *The History of Magic*, or *The Prophecies of Paracelsus, Adam and the Kabbalistic Tree*. A portable library for urban mystics. I had a number of them on my shelves in suspiciously good nick.) Caldecott, hospitalised with cancer, rang Dun "to reaffirm his belief" in the poem and to encourage him to make contact with Mike Goldmark of Uppingham. Mike was not simply the last chance the manuscript had of being properly launched, he was the man who, all unconsciously, had commissioned it. Mike – like Dr Mabuse of old – was, from the safety of his bunker, casting a new chart of the labyrinth.

Dun's bulky typescript thudded onto the gallery floor just as the owner was recovering from the shock of publishing the first Goldmark title, a novel (*White Chappell, Scarlet Tracings*). He was lighting one cigarette from the dying stub of its predecessor and staring in horrified fascination at this new problem – when the synchronicity hit him. *Vale Royal* the poem was called, and the logo on the side of the new pack he had flipped open read: Rothmans Royals.

He passed the word-hoard over to me. I happened to be in the office at the time. I was, as author of *White Chappell*, implicated in the event – in this project, whereby sections of London would have their secret mythologies exposed and activated by a publisher based in Rutland and a printer in Verona. Untrustworthy history in the grand manner. I skimmed the first few pages, caught the references to the child Blake, to William Stukeley, to Chatterton, to St Pancras Old Church, and suggested that Mike try the book out on Peter Ackroyd. The principal figures in Dun's argument came straight from the Ackroyd stock company – or they soon would: *Chatterton, English Music* and *The House of Doctor Dee*. Ackroyd could be relied upon for a generous quote in support of work that dealt with the Matter of London. If he could be waspish in private, he never stooped to badmouthing his peers in any of his reviews, essays or public statements. He dutifully kicked in on Dun's behalf with a prescription that covered all that he himself was attempt-ing in his serial compositions: "He has an extraordinary, powerful and creative sense of the past. He's one of those people, along with Blake, Chatterton and others, who are like a divining rod for history." (Years later, *Vale Royal* still unpublished, Ackroyd asked me about what had happened to that "strange firm up North, whatsisname, Mark some-body?")

Goldmark was more than half convinced. It's one of his conceits that he never reads anything he publishes before it appears in printed form. (An honesty that sets him apart from other publishers. None of whom *ever* waste time on an unsolicited manuscript. But Goldmark is the only one who turns it into a boast. He doesn't have to pretend to be Teflon man. Letting no shit stick. Admitting no connection with a title until it's safely lodged in the best-seller charts.)

"Never glanced at it, before I shipped it off to Italy." This is what he frequently told journalists about *White Chappell*. It wasn't quite true. He did accept the typescript without checking it over – but we had dis-cussed the project pretty thoroughly for years. Mike had been victim to my oddball speculations over many a pleasant lunch in my bookdealing days. He had copies of my previous books – "can you seriously expect *anybody* to understand these things?" – and he'd met many real life fig-ures on whom the characters were based. The self-promoting book runner Driffield was a particular favourite. Mike had read his guidebook closely enough to indulge in a flurry of legal threats. And he'd gone through *White Chappell* – by whatever method – until he was able to put the kind of questions that would shame a textual scholar, long before the estimate came back from Verona.

These retrospective accounts can be confusing. Talking to Natasha Walter, Goldmark remembers the start of his publishing career thus. "A chap called Iain Sinclair . . . used to pop in to sell books. I wasn't really a friend of his. But he was a man of great integrity . . . I said . . . if you can't find a publisher for your book, I'll publish it." Byron Rogers gets the revised version. "Met an old friend one day, a London bookseller called Ian [*sic*] Sinclair. Told me he'd just had his first novel rejected by Cape. 'Right,' I said. 'I'll bring it out.' . . . I'd managed to pull £16,000 out of a property deal, and I whacked it into the book." And Walter again: "The novel had been turned down by half a dozen publish-ers . . . Goldmark sold his Jaguar and published it."

The footnotes of literary history are of no account, I was certainly given a launch that no London publisher could have rivalled – and within a few months this other clump of mystical geography, *Vale Royal*, found its way north to the Uppingham clearing-house. Andy Dunn, late of Notting Hill, Trinidad, and the Charrington Street squat, had amputated an "n" and gained an Aidan (the double A of the Golden Dawn). He arrived, draped in black, and slightly out of synch, in the Goldmark Gallery. A notable non-presence, a vitalist absence: finely-chiselled cheekbones, strong avian profile, spiky crop of hair. The classic troubadour with summer shivers, tendonitis – and a determination that had to be measured in megabits. He was the quietly regulated trickle of water that cracks stone.

Goldmark made sympathetic noises and sent him away. *White Chappell* had emptied the coffers – but the moment would come. Dun was not discomforted, he had been working on *Vale Royal* since 1973 – what was another ten or twenty years? It was 1993 before the revised version of the revised version was ready. The timing was again perfect, Goldmark had got the loan sharks off his back and was eager to begin another cycle. He'd considered sending a private eye "to scour the squats of North London for a poet called Aidan". But that would be like asking a skip-tracer to find a fart in a hurricane.

Dun sensed the vibes, cruised the aether, drove north. The text was set. Mike broke the habit of a lifetime and read it. Demanded explanations, notes, pages that would act like the prompt cards in the gallery. This wasn't a *Waste Land* number, padding out a manuscript that was too slim for commercial publication: an exercise in irony. *Vale Royal* is closer in spirit to Charles Williams' *The Region of the Summer Stars* or David Jones' *The Anathemata*. The notes form an independent unit, a parallel text. The theme is a contemporary reworking of the Matter of Britain – scrupulously parsed and explicated; an active project, rather than an antiquarian exercise; an attempt, no less, to swear allegiance to a spiritual centre. That King's Cross, or, more specifically, St Pancras Old Church, be brought once again to the sacred site proposed by William Blake, the altar stone enclosed within a psychogeographical quadrangle:

> *The fields from Islington to Marybone,*
> *To Primrose Hill and Saint John's Wood,*
> *Were builded over with pillars of gold,*
> *And there Jerusalem's pillars stood.*

***

> *Pancrass & Kentish-town repose*
> *Among her golden pillars high,*
> *Among her golden arches which*
> *Shine upon the starry sky*

Dun's argument, like the one Charles Williams sketches in his preface to *The Region of the Summer Stars*, is based on "the expectation of the return of Our Lord by means of the Grail and of the establishment of the kingdom of Logres" – though *Vale Royal* is not a work of Christian mysticism and Christian symbols are only one element in its helical structure. Dun's expectation is that the arrangement of the words, the long gestation and final coming into being of his poem, will signal the instant of renewal: an immediate reversal of the city's entropic energy field. (This begins to connect up with Dun's recent interest in Stephen Hawking. He rang me to ask if he should send Hawking a copy of the book.) *Vale Royal*, Dun felt, should be interpreted as a sequence of visionary equations: the physics of metaphor, the cosmology of blank verse triads. ("Seven long years spiral into the stellar void/leaving a hazy blue trail of light/around the blazing axis of the sun.") The elegant phrase, fitting perfectly into the scheme, brings about a change in the material universe. The miracle of seeing the poem through to its conclusion, up from the streets, had to be reflected by a quantum leap, a shiver in the fabric of the culture. Dun was one of the few people to be delighted by the construction of the new British Library in King's Cross, announcing, as it did, the migration of power and scholarship from its dark stronghold in Bloomsbury: from the shadows of Hawksmoor's misaligned church, St George, to the more benevolent ambiance of the child martyr, St Pancras.

The peculiar charm of Dun's poem is its anonymity: egoic interference is minimal, the poet wills himself to disappear into his text. He recovers it, rather than inventing it. He spurns novelty and shock effects. At readings – long-jacketed, loose-laced, tense and trembling – he whispers the riffs: as if some messenger had just, at that moment, delivered them. With no script to prompt him, he reads from a phantom autocue. Eyes wide and unblinking. The poet impersonating the poem.

What concerns Dun, much more than the launch of his epic, is the fate of a degraded, fought-over, post-industrial landscape. Publication, achieved after twenty years of struggle, he saw as merely inevitable. The book had to succeed. It wasn't his work, it was the present articulation of an ineradicable benediction: an incarnation of the numinous on the ground of the city.

I had as soon as Mike spoke of commiting himself to the *Vale Royal* project, to declare a special interest. I'd long held the fancy that the skin of London should be divided up by poets and seers as much as by families of gangsters. Poets didn't need brothers. Didn't need a conformity of suits and attitudes. Didn't need dogs. They would service the ground they stole from, haunt a particular territory, tune themselves to notice everything, every irregularity in the brickwork, every dip in the temperature. Chris Jenks in an essay on 'The History and Practice of the Flâneur' speaks of "alternative cartographies of the city". We have to recognise the fundamental untrustworthiness of maps: they are always pressure group publications. They represent special pleading on behalf of some quango with a subversive agenda, something to sell. Maps are a futile compromise between information and knowledge. They require a powerful dose of fiction to bring them to life. The Nicholson "Access Map" was a sop to paranoids. The City of London revealed through the distribution of security checkpoints (subject, presumably, to constant revision). The key to "Special Security Symbols & Instructions" uses a yellow line to enclose the "area protected by security cordon"; coy pink arrows for "new compulsory turns", and a reassuring black bolt for "blocked off" streets.

Jenks sees clearly how these multiple cartographies (the microclimates under which we all navigate) "represent just some of the many potential . . . versions of how the manifestly shared (or at least explicitly public) streets and buildings delineate fragmented localities and senses of placement and identity . . . In another dimension the Krays' territorial longings are both more bizarre and more sinister than other accounts . . . of minatorial geography."

Writers, wishing to "rescue" dead ground, will have to wrest it from the grip of developers, clerks, clerics, eco freaks, and ward bosses. We are all welcome to divide London according to our own anthologies: JG Ballard at Shepperton (the reservoirs, airport perimeter roads, empty film studios); Michael Moorcock at Notting Hill (visited by Jack Trevor Story); Angela Carter – south of the river, Battersea to Brixton, where she hands over to the poet Allen Fisher; Eric Mottram at Herne Hill, communing with the ghost of Ruskin; Robin Cook's youthful self in Chelsea, while his fetch minicabs between Soho and the suburbs (meeting Christopher Petit who is making the reverse journey); John Healy sparring down Caledonian Road towards the "grass arena" of

Euston; Peter Ackroyd dowsing Clerkenwell in quest of Dr John Dee; James Curtis in Shepherd's Bush; Alexander Baron in Golders Green (recalling his Hackney boltholes); Emanuel Litvinoff and Bernard Kops disputing Whitechapel and Stepney Green with the poets Bill Griffiths and Lee Harwood (author of *Cable Street*); Stewart Home commanding the desert around the northern entrance of the Blackwall Tunnel; Gerald Kersh drinking in Fleet Street; Arthur Machen composing *The London Adventure or the Art of Wandering*.

King's Cross was up for grabs and Aidan ("a man of remarkable gentleness, goodness . . . zealous for God; but not fully according to knowledge" – as Bede wrote of his Lindisfarne namesake) was elected. He had named himself for his task – in the liturgy and discipline of the Celtic church. His emblem was the stag: the stag trapped in a thicket of facts, a forest of contradictory promptings. Aidan Andrew Dun. A.A.D. His homage to David Jones.

I have watched the wheels go round in case I might see the living creatures like the appearance of lamps, in case I might see the Living God projected from the Machine. I have said to the perfected steel, be my sister and for the glassy towers I thought I felt some beginnings of His creature, but A, a, a, Domine Deus, my hands found the glazed work unrefined and the terrible crystal a stage-paste . . . Eia, Domine Deus.

My prejudice in favour of Dun's task grew out of my own failure. I had tried, at exactly the time *Vale Royal* was taking form, to work on a long London poem, *Red Eye*. "Songs" in homage to the film-maker Stan Brakhage were interspersed with visits to such sites as St Pancras Church, an island shaded in torpor, heavy with melancholy, the drowned dead. I'd been working up the road for the Post-Office and spent time wandering the area. But the notes I made never achieved focus and were soon overtaken by a Limehouse project that evolved into *Lud Heat*. I'd like to include an extract from *Red Eye*, not because it has any value as an independent unit, but rather for its sense of the light-locked subterranean matter, the nigredo, that Dun successfully transmutes.

May 16, 1973:
at St Pancras Old Church. Drawn against the repetitive boredom of the pavements to investigate the building – its slight eminence.

It is unlocked (briefly) at this hour: 10.30 am.
I encounter
            the vicar
hobbling on a stick, a Powys ghost.
Empty.
            I study some of the relics.
A woman emerges, shows St Augustine's stone under
the altar drapes: Kentish Rag. She talks.
The curate
            left the church to work at the hospital
for nervous diseases. Suffered a brain haemorrhage. Now paralysed
down the left side. Has faith in a cure. Gower Street have
done all they can.
There is a subdued disapproval of the motions implicit in
his actions — as the woman describes them.
Today he is departing early, leaving her to lock the doors. He is to visit
the Bishop of Durham: on a mission that
has not been disclosed to this lady.
The church is part of that northern rail. It drinks
from ancient christian sources.

The helper
            worries about vandalism. Children
give her a "mouthful of language". Lack of god is
                                    her spider.
The place is cold & moulting. I purchase a leaflet.
Note several items:

About 6 feet down in the foundations of the old tower an altar
stone was discovered minus its relics but clearly marked with
five consecration crosses of curious shape. The form of the
crosses is said to be unlike any other but that on the tomb of
Ethne, the mother of St Columba, who died in 597. If this is so,
it would seem to date the stone as late sixth or early seventh
century, and point to a connection with Celtic Christians via the
kingdom of Northumbria which extended much further south than
is usually realised.
&
The young Thomas Hardy, then an architect's apprentice,
supervised the seemly carrying out of the last part of this work

and perhaps gained there his ever-recurrent interest in church-
yards.

&

Here PB Shelley, lodging at 5 Chapel Terrace (now blotted
out by the railway arches), first saw and fell in love with Mary
Godwin who was visiting her mother's grave.

3

He is mad by every measure of a standard man.

AIDAN DUN, *VALE ROYAL*

The saturnine, widdershins excursion of Alan Moore's anti-solar myst-
agogue, Sir William Gull, as revealed in Chapter Four of the graphic
novel, *From Hell*, begins, traditionally enough, with Boadicea: "She left
a stripe of ash, a cold black vein in London's geologic strata." Gull, representing lefthanded Masonry, the Scottish Rite, is a fraudulent
revenger: Sidney Greenstreet promoted beyond his station, Sidney
Greenstreet after a crash course at the Abbey of Thelema. A paternal
misogynist with a *tendresse* for "fallen" women (so useful for marking
out the pentacles of a perverse geometry).

Gull's journey – in which his coachman, John Netley, a lowlife
clown, dutifully absorbs a lecture on the city's occult mapping – begins
at Battle Bridge, described, with poetic licence, as being "below
Parliament Hill where Druids once made sacrifice to a Father Sun." The
site, now an undistinguished cul-de-sac, dominated by a crown of gasholders, is a condom gutter – the louche territory where the former
Director of Public Prosecutions chose, rather unwisely, to kerb-crawl:
the set operatically recreated for Neil Jordan's saccharine romance, *Mona
Lisa*. Tumescent predators, tax discs in order, willingly obey Gull's
directions. "Come Netley. Back to King's Cross, then down Pentonville.
Do you begin to grasp how truly great a work is London? A veritable
textbook we may draw upon in formulating great works of our own!
We'll penetrate its metaphors, lay bare its structure and thus come at last
upon its meaning."

Aidan Dun rather agrees, setting keel for his own great work of
urban alchemy from the same scar on the landscape. The X of the
buried queen. The stations of the Cross in their "mystical geography".
But Dun is playing for higher stakes: he is soliciting the re-enchantment

of the "cone of high land", Blake's "pillar'd rectangle", the place of the Pan Cross. He abdicates from the tyranny of "transience" and begins a measured survey of Old St Pancras' alternate history. He was inspired from the start, as he says, by a sense of recognition: what was happening had happened before. He would transcribe the unwritten and write over whatever was incomplete. Modernist notions of "originality", language games – speed, synthesis, atomisation – did not concern him. Reading, late at night, alone in the Charrington Street squat, he convinced himself that the prose-poem, 'Promontoire', one of Rimbaud's *Illuminations*, was a "metaphoric description" of the part of London in which he had come to live. He knew from Edith Starkie's biography that Rimbaud and Verlaine had shared a room in Royal College Street, a short walk from the churchyard. He pored over those incantatory formulae, sympathetic as they were to the derangement of the moment: fractured reality, the trembling of the veil, mild hunger pangs, life on the third floor. The pages became sheets of coloured glass, an interface between the shrouded buildings and Rimbaud's once-and-forever translation of them.

L'aube d'or et la soirée frissonnante trouvent notre brick au large en face de cette villa et de ses dépendances qui forment au promontoire . . . Des glaciers, des lavoirs entourés de peupliers d'Allemagne, des talus de parcs singuliers . . . et leurs railways flanquent, creusent, surplombent les dispositions de cet hôtel, choisies dans l'histoire des plus élégantes et des plus colossales constructions d'Italie, de l'Amérique et de l'Asie, dont les fenêtres et les terrasses, à présent pleines d'éclairages, de boissons et de brises riches, sont ouvertes à l'esprit des voyageurs et des nobles, qui permettent, aux heures du jour, à toutes les tarentelles illustres de l'art de décorer merveilleusement les façades de Palais Promontoire.

Golden dawn . . . slopes of singular parks . . . St Pancras railway station as the hotel of dreams. Dun's hallucinatory triads lift from this vision, the spikes and turrets of the promontory standing out against the dreary flood plain of the city of darkness. Dun would confirm, recompose, Rimbaud's imaginative seizure. The poem had already been written, every finely balanced stanza; now it was Dun's task, his duty, to read and research, to set out on foot to make his "wide arcs of wandering". "To throw light on the great secret of London".

Vale Royal is unspectacularly traditional in form, regular three-line units of bardic verse. The triad which speaks in an eternal present tense of things which were and are and will be again. The poem, worked at over a twenty year period, became a spiritual autobiography (homage to earlier avatars, influences honoured as co-authors of the project), and also a mythopoeic colonisation of a sacred patch of ground: the disregarded X of King's Cross. This threadbare strip of back country, skulking between railway and canal, must achieve – so the poet asserted – the status conferred upon it by William Blake's *Jerusalem* prophecy. Dun could not see why golden pillars, emphatically planted in vision, should make any latter-day manifestation redundant. He conceived his epic in harmony with the cosmological speculations of Stephen Hawking (as he understood them). He associated the figures of Hawking and Nicholas Hawksmoor with Horus, the falcon-deity, the sky-god (and avenger of Osiris): "an Egyptian hawk in the willow-month". *Vale Royal* expresses London in terms of Egypt, believing that the old gods are not exclusive to their country of origin, but valid descriptions of a much dimmer climate.

Spirals and chevrons, living and existent,
move on the outer shafts, while a blank central pillar
rises into pyramids of spinning androgynous Godhead.

Hawking's revelations, worked out in an almost unintelligible cuneiform, predicted future motions in the star-field. What was thought, became. Dun's mingling of the speculative and the arcane achieved an intoxicating tension, somewhere between the New Physics and orthodox fantasy: a cross-pollination of *The Large Scale Structure of Space-Time* and Tim Powers' time-travelling, steampunk novel, *The Anubis Gates* – which opens not far from the source of the Fleet River, and goes on to trace the career of the early-Victorian poet William Ashbless; while taking the hero on a nightmare journey back to the London of 1810, where Egyptian magic invests a subterranea of tunnels and monsters. A parallel account of Dun's "burning ocean of ruined thought-forms and auras,/full of mathematical fermentations of mentality – the pit."

Vale Royal is composed in two unequal cycles, double-spirals, rhapsodic narratives that turn on themselves, go over the same ground, invoking the same figures: the sacrificial child (as Blake or Chatterton or Pancras), the old man or Archflamen (William Stukeley) questing among the willows. A karma of battles lost and nobles assassinated, mind control, psychic theft, alchemy, numerology, dragon lines,

Arthurian mysticism. Colours recur: gold, red/blue, black, and above all silver (of "acres", "rays", "metals", the "image", "precipice", "edge", "blade"). Place is emblematic. Silvertown is not its weary downriver self, the boarded-up ribbon of dust between the City Airport and the sugar-drench of the Tate & Lyle factory, but "a silent quay . . . a bale of cinnamon . . . in the night-air". "An Aquarian moon rises over Limehouse". The psychogeography of London is affected by the special pleading of the poem. Dun's sense of the archetype, of converting the specific into a shape-shifting universality, is at odds with the drift of English modernism as expressed, for example, in Allen Fisher's post-Olsonian South London epic, *Place*.

Fisher's Brixton is fragmentary, multi-voiced, schizo – openly invaded by a consciousness of "the other". He accumulates an almost unmanageable mass of contradictory documentation. The project is open-ended, "found" material can be set alongside cut-ups, columned against long stretches of quotation. The typesetting is explosive. The poem responds to the chaos of the moment, shapes a path only to abandon it. The past is given access when it can usefully make a contribution to our understanding of present confusion. The poem gathers its evidence like an enquiry into bureaucratic malpractice: when it is all assembled the poet can walk away. A luxury that is denied to Aidan Dun.

Dun, a "lucid dreamer", has no contact with fashion. He's resolutely unpromotable, refusing to work in convenient lyric bites. He's happy to play with a marked deck, take on a dead man's hand. The discoveries he makes are confirmations of previous knowledge: the church on the mound, enclosed by water, under a curve of hills. He polishes each cerulean fragment before setting it into the mosaic pavement. He affirms its heritage. The homages he makes are unconscious. "Night-fishing for rib-cages and skulls" might invoke WS Graham, but that doesn't mean that Aidan has studied the relevant publication, or is creating a modernist grid of references. "The sun born at midnight" summons David Gascoyne, without any awareness by the *Vale Royal* poet of the 1970 Enitharmon Press publication, *The Sun at Midnight (Notes on the Story of Civilization as the History of the Great Experimental Work of the Supreme Scientist)*. It's hard to believe, reading Gascoyne's book in conjunction with *Vale Royal*, that the spirit of the original has not entered the new composition by stealth, by morphic resonance. The illustrations – the Hermetic androgyne from the Vatican Library and "Nature as woman and tree" from the "Alchemical Manuscript" in Basle University

Library – read like missing pages of Dun's text; they are the emblems that would bring these columns of words into focus. Gascoyne, the most courteous of speed-freaks, the most informed of London's night-walkers, confesses that his addictive use of amphetamine compounds "seemed to make me more actively intelligent and interested in everything, by counteracting my seriously depressed normal mental state of lassitude and above all of *dispiritedness*." He recognised (echoing the experience of Mike Goldmark) that "all suffering, however borne, becomes an activating, energizing agent in the soul. '*L'Alchimie de la Douleur*', as Baudelaire . . . has clearly indicated, is one of the secret forms of transmutation, in preparation for a new eternity . . . The latent treasure of Love and Forgiveness in all who have known pain and grief is an incalculable reservoir of force which will now be gradually released for the rebuilding of the world we have nearly shattered."

(Chris Petit, Marc Atkins and I took a day trip to the Isle of Wight to visit Gascoyne and to record him reading a poem for the Albert Hall extravaganza. Out in the back garden, over the tea table, late afternoon sunlight falling in a sharp wedge on the poet's troubled face, he spoke of alchemy: how the Goldmark event, and the publication of *Vale Royal*, had revitalised him, brought him "back to life". "It's a miracle," he said, laughing; as Judy Gascoyne leafed through the albums of photographs. Allen Ginsberg in New York. Robert Duncan in San Francisco. Visitors to the island: Bob Dylan, George Harrison. He was writing again. He passed me his notebook, filled with black ink translations, notes and future projects. The inspiration back after a long silence that stretched into the Fifties. Now it came in a rush. He spoke of Rimbaud expeditions through Docklands, the battle of Cable Street. He recalled the sinister Dr Bluth, hammering on a white piano in his Notting Hill surgery, before shooting Gascoyne up with a mixture of ox-blood and methadone. Anna Kavan and Conrad Veidt – rescued from *The Cabinet of Dr Caligari* – were beneficiaries of the same treatment. All of them hitting the streets, bug-eyed and hot to trot.)

Like Gascoyne, Dun stands apart from the schools and schisms of the moment, his "spiral train of thought turns backwards." The pace with which the poem's narrative unfolds is disorientating: it seems to have been frantically composed, and then played back in slow motion. Drug dealers and station-haunting vagrants are noticed, but seen as archetypal forms. The away-day tart becomes a "Magdalen from the red doorways of Holborn". The heroic persistence of reading the world in this way, when interpreted by the "standard man", becomes a form of madness.

It's so selective, elitist. The poet confirms his occult possession by "allowing" the poem to flow unhindered. He is a self-confessed "outlaw" drawn to the ancient church "by the magnet of shadows".

Gascoyne in the prefatory poem to *The Sun at Midnight* writes of: "Grass, grasses, fields, the field, 'la terre', our home." Dun mourns the "lost world of meadows gone to seed". A wilderness in the place of enchantment. Fallow ground in which too many layers of the dead have been impacted. Curious promptings that have to be obeyed: "infernal, dynamic anxiety accompanied by auditory hallucinations and delusions of persecution." Gascoyne, in his entry for "May 1969", snatches at themes that might become poems; that might, through some form of transference, become part of *Vale Royal*.

1. *A voice from childhood. Buttercups. Butterflies. Gold: the Psyche.*
   Royalty incognito and children. A bee?
2. *. . . The cloudscape – grisaille de Seghers – ruins and desolation.*
   The Sunset . . . Vision of nocturnal London . . . Evil and civilisation.
3. *Birds. Pelican in the wilderness. London birds at dusk. Their*
   revelry among the cornices above the neon . . .
   Two other possible poems:
   > *—Jerusalem (and Athens?)*
   Cities of our civilization now.
   > *—Grass . . .*

In my own copy of Gascoyne's book he has written: "So glad you like this odd little book written during a period when I was more or less off my head." *Vale Royal*, a notable attempt to forge a London epic, to live up to the challenge sketched by Gascoyne, is perhaps weakened by its decency, its sanity. Is it mad *enough*? The argument, persuasive as it proves to be, is too evenly distributed. The sources on which it draws are too right, too unobjectionable. Is the poem undone by the safety of its status as an unpublishable work-in-progress: a position now challenged by the intervention of Mike Goldmark? The poet as a romantic outsider who opposes Masonic and Secret State conspiracies, the ugliness of the pit, is there to be admired. He is an elective alien pensioned by the sites he celebrates. His language is smooth and unstressed, it flows effortlessly like a clear stream. He reports on the vision, rather than suffering it. He stands back, commenting on the immaculately turned phrases as he composes them. *Vale Royal* could be said to have too conservative a programme. We want more spleen in our illuminati. We want to see them sacrificed, cut down. The flaw is our own. We have been too deeply corrupted to accept, without flinching, this heritage park where "lambs roll in the warm grass". We have been seduced instead by the compressed and driven language of works such as Richard Makin's unpunctuated monologue, *forword*, a "cycle" published in part by Equipage in 1995: "a treasure troth plight of/revenant diction geistraum aback of two beasts a batlle/diesel shunts the roge thanatoseros for its horme . . ."

It's worth comparing Dun's measured and stately account of Chatterton in "transtemporal flight" with the much more urgent and implicated sequence published by Barry MacSweeney as *Brother Wolf* in 1972.

> *Oh germ-cloud of tomorrow, Walpole*
> *was one, his*
> *illustriously fabricated ruby forehead glows*
> *off a U2 battery for the holy chair.*
> *Trees shiver with human condition &*
> *the temple is thick with smoke.*

MacSweeney's poetic mask is half-ripped from a pulped face; he spits, prances. He risks everything. He aims at possession, identification with the doomed poet/pretender. He reworks what Chatterton left unfinished: as Blake reworked Milton. He drags the doomed youth, the broken shaman, home to Northumberland; rescues him from geography. He cracks the shell of his own lyrics to scorn a "cheesy triumvirate of ghosts." Knowing as much as Dun, he feels able to subvert the tyranny of facts, and to damn himself in the process. He honours by exploitation. "I will have Fame". He wants it, the whole curse: the poem that is true only to itself. Nothing else will do. Fuck the consequences. The poet has a dual responsibility: to give himself over entirely to his work, and to stage-manage a career. Aidan Dun will have to face that now. He has joined the company. His project is a significant one, so modest and subtle that it almost eludes fate by delivering itself as a poem without an author. It could be discovered, scratched on parchment, in the tower of St Pancras Old church: that is a measure of its generosity and its achievement.

"Memory's not what it used to be"
JERRY LEE LEWIS

13/6/95. An afternoon meeting was arranged with Aidan in the churchyard of St Pancras Old Church, "the shrine on a hill". For both of us it would be a case of moving forward by paying our dues to the past, a nostalgic shifting and comparing of memories and belief systems. And so, with that sense of excursion and expectation, I walked west along the canal with Marc Atkins and his black camera-bag. I pointed out the still-visible lettering on the side of the old Gainsborough Studios – which Marc dutifully photographed. He'd taken, so he said, around 5,000 images this year. Enough to keep him in the dark room, perfecting each print, for the rest of his life (which he used to estimate at ten years – now, since I dragged him on foot through the Rotherhithe Tunnel, revised downwards to five).

"Adrift in the city of exterior light", we shuffled along, dodging the bikers, inaccurately clocking the wildlife (a heron spotted at Queensbridge Road), until we reached the City Road Lock and the canal slid coolly away, like a scintillating stream, into its Osiric tunnel. At this point on the map we are all Estuary Egyptians: like the Victorian cemetery designers, we want to dabble in a more exotic iconography. The white obelisk of St Luke, to the south across the City Road basin, is an hieratic intention botched by unplanned industrial development. That glyph of sun/water/stone remains securely in the mind's eye.

Following Dun's prescription we climb through Islington to "the good walking-country of the long curved crescent". On the lip of the dune, looking down over Vale Royal: "Glorious pedestrians on pavements of light". Or so we thought until we were rudely hooted, honked, gestured at through the open window of a car held in the queue waiting to turn out of Copenhagen Street into York Way: John Healy, the *Guardian*'s house vagrant. This was ridiculous, the one time in all these months of pounding across the landscape, that we get picked up and offered a ride – and it's a career street-stalker, ex-wino, ex-celebrity itinerant, at the wheel. He thinks we're on the skids, going down to the Cross to pick up some change. It's much worse than that. It's difficult to explain that we're out dowsing for poets, no hopers, psychic vampires.

Healy lives with his mum in a tidy flat off Caledonian Road, where he practices his breathing and works on film-scripts. He's got one in development at the moment, a sword and shield number featuring a mouthy Cockney/Irish William the Conqueror. Who knows? With the present state of the movie business, this could be a winner – especially if he can bring it out first as a comic strip.

John guns the smoke-coughing Rover, as Atkins folds his length awkwardly into the backseat. It would be much quicker to walk, but I wouldn't want to miss the way Healy drives with his elbows, handling the stop/start of London traffic, and rattling along, idea to idea, at the same time. He's heading for Hampstead, cruising for chess action to alleviate the boredom of the writer's life. He keeps a copy of his prize-winning autobiography, *The Grass Arena*, in a blatantly conspicuous position. It's his belief that when (*when* rather than if) he's pulled by the filth, he can produce this proof of his status as a published author and thus circumvent any awkward enquiries into the vehicle's documentation or roadworthiness. This expectation of the tugged forelock is a refreshingly old fashioned notion of the power of the printed word. In my experience the word "writer" carries the same negative resonance with customs officers or constabulary that it does with insurance assessors. Better far to travel hopefully as "husband of school-teacher". And as for holding your hand up as a denizen of a "world ruled by psychopaths and peopled by beggars, con-men, thieves, prostitutes and killers, where the law is enforced with the broken bottle, the boot and the knife" – you might as well throw yourself down the steps into the canal and save them the paperwork.

Still afloat on Dun's mesmeric triads, seeing London as a network of coincidences and cyclic collisions, it was salutary to be on the receiving end of John Healy's buoyant pragmatism. The machine-gun raps, shoulder-shuffles, sniffs; monologues with all the voices; impulsive generosity turning, on a misunderstood gesture, into violence. The drudgery of the wrong side of the Islington ridge, the sorrows of Pentonville, gave Healy a very different insight into the valley of the Fleet. He saw it with the eye of a veteran – childhood scars, binges, skippering, blackouts: absorbing and intensely realised memories (where they hadn't been extinguished) that precluded Dun's more aristocratic overview.

We tipped out at the churchyard steps – with Healy recalling a visit to Richard Boston, the bucolic *Guardian* essayist ("pisshead"); the ruins of another church in some Oxfordshire field. St Pancras, as far as Healy was concerned, was a piece of countryside that had not yet been found out. He waved us off, abandoned us to our self-indulgent antiquarianism.

Aidan was pretty much on the button – that is to say, he sauntered through the gates about fifty minutes later than the agreed appointment (the standard variation between the spiritual/metaphoric and mundane time scales). Which forced us to give the shady enclosure a thorough going-over: the Soane Monument, designed by the architect in memory of his wife, and the famous Wollstonecraft tomb, still tended by feminists, where Shelley met – and made love to? – Mary Godwin. A rectangle of buttery pansies. Marc is particularly struck by the Hardy tree with its cluster of surrounding headstones – like a school of grey fins circling the massive trunk, feeding on the secretions of the dead. Hardy's poem, 'The Levelled Churchyard,' recalls the clearance of this ground: memory field to spurned park.

> O Passenger, pray list and catch
>   Our sighs and piteous groans,
> Half stifled in this jumbled patch
>   Of wrenched memorial stones!

> We late-lamented, resting here
>   Are mixed to human jam,
> And each to each exclaims in fear,
>   "I know not which I am!"

The park repels humans. They slide away, slithering down Rimbaud's slopes. There are no regular drinking schools here, just the occasional disorientated solitary, benched and muttering. If the place is a potential reservoir of light, the heavy waters have grown foul with disuse. The incursions of cultists are there to be noticed by those with a taste for such things: rags of tree worship, candle and bowl set outside the sealed door of the Sacrament House (a Shrine to Our Lady of Walsingham). Most striking is the oval design on the monument seen to the south side of the church in the view engraved for *The New Universal British Traveller*. An angel, wings spread, is carrying a child through the air. A zigzag of trailing ribbon gives balance to the acute position of the angel's legs. But the implication of what should have been a pietistic commonplace has been transformed by some freelance occultist who has chipped away, in a rectangle, the angel's profile – leaving the suggestion of a devouring beast, an axe-headed monster carrying off a sacrificial victim. Perhaps this is an unconscious representation of Dun's "Sunchild surrendered in the Dark House of Chrome" in order that "the hidden city of the Royal Vale" might be revealed?

Then, when we had forgotten our reason for hanging about the park, the poet was with us, or almost with us – slim, upright, black jacket, spiky coxcomb of hair, elegant rather than threatening (more glam rock than punk). Meaningful handshake and a quiet "ummm" of recognition. Again that feeling – the fault is ours – of being slightly out of synch: as if Aidan might have been over-dubbed by some censorious other. Teasing information released in gnomic droplets. Dun's take on the churchyard is uninsistently proprietorial: the things that happened here are eternal. They're on a loop. He can see them now: Shelley stepping from his lodgings at 5 Church Terrace, out there among the railway arches beyond the south wall. The doomed Chatterton falling into an open grave. The Fleet River, down from its source near Kenwood House, sparkling in place of the Pancras Road. Nothing is erased. Boadicea. The elephants that terrified her tribesmen. This ground is holy: from its golden pillars a city of revelation will be built.

The sun on the horizon catching the skeletal gasholder crowns, the fantastic mustard hotel of St Pancras railway station, its windows and pinnacles and red brick balconies. So much hidden land, nature reserves, goods yards, allotments, between the railhead and the canal. Dun leads us out of the back gate, down some steps – a path he could sleepwalk – towards the room that Rimbaud and Verlaine shared in Royal College Street. He believes that Stephen Hawking is another version of his "child demi-urge": primary school Hampstead/Highgate, paintings of Kenwood House, jumping on and off buses in search of a lost magical palace. Hawking – and perhaps Rupert Sheldrake – should join with Dun and his earlier friends and inspirations, John Michell and Heathcote Williams, to found, on this site, an Invisible College; "a perpetual symposium", "the human face of the cosmological." The poet, speaking of his vision, says that he felt an "ineluctable urge to get down on my knees, take off my clothes and give thanks".

There's an alley – so moodily apposite that it must have been sponsored by English Heritage – that brings you onto Royal College Street right alongside the plaque which announces: THE FRENCH POETS/PAUL VERLAINE/AND/ARTHUR RIMBAUD/LIVED HERE/MAY–JULY 1873. From this magnificently peeling wall, an aerial map of seas and deserts and curling landmasses, the poets set out on their London wanderings. I spent so much time gazing up – from the back of the house – identifying, with Aidan, the right window, that I didn't notice the anti-vandal paint which now covers my jacket.

Chastened, we make for Camden High Street. I want to go to Compendium Bookshop to find Aidan a copy of Barry MacSweeney's Chatterton poem, 'Brother Wolf' – which was included in an anthology put out by Paladin. (The book, *The Tempers of Hazard*, was launched with a reading at Compendium. And then rapidly pulped. Rupert Murdoch's accountants saw no reason to tolerate low-turnover cultural loss leaders. Barry took it hard. More than any other British poet MacSweeney was possessed by the knowledge that, being one of those gifted with language, he was also cursed. His was a true "sickness vocation" – questing for the heats and silks of fame, firework effects, the dazzle of a Michael McClure shriek cut with French decadence. He fixated on spoiled heroes, stopped in their youth: Rimbaud in 'The Boy from the Green Cabaret Tells of his Mother', Jim Morrison in 'Just Twenty-Two – and I Don't Mind Dying', and Chatterton. He didn't sit out the dead years in comfort. And then, when it seemed that work such as his was being allowed back into the debate, the plug was pulled. Trundling around the small-press circuit, with its comfortable outcasts, its triumphally defeatist politics, had lost its appeal. Barry perfected the profession of being difficult, the gift of rage. Took it to the point of collapse, his life in hazard.)

Our progress was hobbled by the necessity of waiting while Aidan chatted to, and sometimes tithed, supplicants in shop doorways. But a brief biographical outline was teased from him: childhood of respectable bohemia in Notting Hill, from 7 to 14 in Trinidad where mother ran a ballet school (Marie Rambert was his grandmother), back to London, walks out of Highgate School after playing Aufidius, General to the Volscians, in a "leather jockstrap" production of *Coriolanus* – and getting rather carried away by having the last word. "My rage is gone,/And I am struck with sorrow . . . Yet he shall have a noble memory./Assist." It was pretty much out of the school gates and on to a motorbike. Europe. The hippy trail. Busking along the Mediterranean and down to Marrakesh. Meeting the usual people and picking up the usual imprints of communal culture: India, dope, mysticism, white magic, Egypt, the Grail, poetry. The ideal foundation course for life in the Charrington Street squat.

The Tempers of Hazard had gone – even from Compendium. An instant rarity. A book that began life as a remainder and was now less than a rumour. A quarter of a century's work for the poets: scrubbed, reforgotten. But the shop (how many ley lines must intersect here?) came up with human consolation in the form of the art guerrilla (one-man distribution service) Stewart Home – whose potato-head we could see through the window, bobbing and nodding, as he pulled out the mid-afternoon edition of *Re:Action (Newsletter of the Neoist Alliance)* with its splash headline: THE GRAIL UNVEILED. *The Grail can only be understood when it is viewed historically, that is to say as an unstable signifier of continuous becoming. On 20 February 1909 the Futurist F.T. Marinetti announced to a startled world that 'time and space died yesterday.' It was these words that ushered in the current epoch of avant-bardism. Likewise, it is said that the founder of the École Druidique was Max Jacob; cubist, poet, critic, occultist, hoaxer and notorious blagueur. Druidry was (re)invented in the aftermath of the Renaissance as 'educated' opinion became divided over the relative merits of the Ancients and the Moderns.*

Atkins and I stood off to watch this amazing head-to-head: Dun, the taller of the two, swaying back, away from Home's more animated ripostes. Seen from behind a stack of books, the debate looked like an aristocratic cockatoo dipping for apples. A floater and a foot-soldier settling the fate of the city. Aidan wincing from the violence of Home's delighted subversion, the barks of laughter. Home is one of those who is always knapsacked, always in transit. Aidan is perched, even in movement.

They have to disengage – Home retreating with a book to the canal bank and Aidan leading us back to St Pancras Old Church, which is due to open its doors at 6.30. Aidan worries about the aggressive nature of Home's karma: the wrong path. He has a friend, a martial arts expert, who lost it by dedicating his life to putting a psychic trace on crack dealers, breaking their bones and then healing them.

There's still time to wander down Charrington Street, to look over the legendary squat. (Expunging unworthy memories of the Mike Leigh satire, *High Hopes*, with its dope-smoking despatch rider.) The dimensions of this backwater boulevard are so gracious that we're forced to wonder how it has survived. It must be a front for something. There is virtually no traffic, plants and chairs have been left on the street. It's very easy to accept Aidan's account of his period here as a monastic retreat, attendance at an anti-university that required no fees. Some people had books, some cooked, offering free food from the house on the corner. It couldn't last. But Aidan was given his first taste of Catullus. He immersed himself in Rimbaud and set about uncovering the secret history of the church.

The dominant personality in the shifting commune was the South African, ex-Oxford don and hallucinogenic voyager, Robin Farquharson, author of *Drop Out!* – which was published, complete with psychedelic endpapers and Alan Aldridge dustwrapper, by Anthony Blond in 1968. Dun thinks he still has a copy of the novel somewhere, fondly recalling a scene where Farquharson, meandering away from King's Cross, enjoys a vision of Magellanic clouds and hears a voice telling him to drop his new coat. He does so. Walks on for 300 yards and is then tempted to turn back. The coat has gone. (John Healy? Or Samuel Beckett's *Murphy*? Too many ghosts to let a toffee-paper slip while there's half a lick left on it.)

Farquharson went through the changes, from messianic inspiration – the founding of a counter-cultural college with RD Laing, Alex Trocchi and other cardinals of the alternate establishment – to paranoid depression. BOSS, M16, dealers and double-agents: he moved down the road, took a room on an upper floor in a house with no occupants, other than a pair of hard-drinking Irish workmen. One night a fire was started. Farquharson received third-degree burns, was taken into the Hospital for Tropical Diseases, alongside St Pancras churchyard, and subsequently died. The Irishmen ("Michael O'Connor, 26, and Peter Hilditch, 18, both labourers") were charged with "unlawful killing" and found guilty. An episode which has never been explained to Aidan's satisfaction. (In other words, it was composed from particles that fitted very neatly into a conspiracy scenario, the end of an era).

We rattled at the church door and, after a few minutes, it was opened by a discreetly camp curate dressed in the full fig. He let us wander freely, while he got on with lighting up a rack of candles. This church, according to Aidan, was "the keystone of *Vale Royal*". He describes it in his notes, citing the Vatican historian, Maximillian Misson, as "the Head and Mother of all Christian Churches"; founded at "the time of the formation of the Grail Cycle, even with the time of Christ's actual visit to Britain". Can this dim and rarely accessible interior carry that burden of belief?

Nobody is breaking the door down to confirm it. The hour of the service – which will take place whether any celebrants arrive or not – is approaching. The curate offers us a sight of St Augustine's altar stone, which is preserved beneath a heavy cloth. A relic that provokes another debate, another scrupulously polite cycle of question, answer and counter-question, between Aidan and the hierophant. Aidan to the north of the High Altar and the curate, defensively, behind it. Aidan pushes for a spoken confirmation of the special status of the church, the building. The curate will go no further than canonical authority allows – but he indulges the speculations.

Finally, just before two old folk slip in at the back to take their chairs for the service, the curate brings out a supposed fragment of bone from the boy-martyr, St Pancras. Authenticated by Rome and purchased from the Vatican hypermarket – like taking a dubious Rubens from Sotheby's, on the say so of the auctioneer – this nail-paring chip is packaged behind a glass clockface, set in a tinny golden crucifix. It looks as if it might glow in the dark. The entire skeleton, properly rendered down and marketed with impressive certificates, would sanctify every church in South America.

The leap of faith needed to generate Aidan's "perpetual symposium" is as nothing when compared with the superstitions that bolster mainstream Catholicism. Marc has whipped out his camera and is clicking away – with the curate's permission. Aidan knows that the church officials are no more than tolerated caretakers, functionaries of a bankrupt concern.

I wait outside, toying with the notion that each essay so far written for this book can be assigned one letter of the alphabet. Obviously, the first two pieces go together, the journey from Abney Park to Chingford Mount: **V**. The circling of the City: an oval **O**. The history of *Vale Royal*, its poet and publisher: an **X** on the map. **VOX**. The unheard voice that is always present in the darkness.

On the 16th of October 1995 Goldmark's *Return of the Reforgotten* event, featuring Allen Ginsberg, Sorley MacLean, Anne Waldman, Benjamin Zephaniah, Alice Notley, Brendan Kennelly, and the usual suspects from the home team, duly happened at the Albert Hall. Two and a half thousand people turned up, the biggest audience for poetry seen in this country since the Wholly Communion readings in 1965. The press, where they noticed it, were sour and mean-spirited. They concentrated on the finances. The poets enjoyed themselves (one or two of them were paid, while others were so carried away they handed their fees back). The audience, in general, were surprised: they had a good time. Even Driffield, dragged there by a younger and hipper girlfriend, rang me to express his wonder (and to ask for Anne Waldman's particulars). The evening closed with Ginsberg duetting (the Chas 'n' Dave of the counter-culture) with Paul McCartney.

Goldmark stood in the wings pushing the poets on, pulling them off. Seven minutes each. It worked: even Mike Moorcock's failure to remember who or what Denise Riley was didn't matter. The audience took it in good humour. And Moorcock made a fruitful connection with co-presenter Howard Marks.

It was all somewhat unreal, too easy, too smooth. I found myself talking about Henry James' garden, the burial of his pets, with Linda McCartney. She and Paul lived near Rye and would check it out. She was clicking away, taking photographs of the bemused poets.

Mike Goldmark, bare feet on the pedals, drove home in the early hours of the morning. He was still alive, he wasn't bankrupt; it was over. (Or had it all been maya, an illusion?) Aidan Dun had enjoyed the most spectacular launch in the history of poetry publishing. What next?

"I've always served"
LORD ARCHER OF WESTON-SUPER-MARE

I approached Alembic House, Lord Archer's Lambeth gaff, with a pistol to my head and both hands tied behind my back. As it were. I had promised my wife that I would be on my very best behaviour, no jibes, no sneers, no cheap satire. None of the usual kneejerk, formulaic, picaresque comedy. This would be disinterested reportage, a nice blend of *Modern Painters* and *Hello!*. Footnoted gush. Discreet tracking shots across the Archer art hoard, admiring references to the famous Thames views.

I'd put my request in writing, explaining that I wanted to look over the collection and to weigh the pictorial values against the expressionist raids on this stretch of the river by the painters Oskar Kokoschka and John Bellany. I made it clear that I didn't intend to poke into any of the material recently aired by Michael Crick in his blue-chip biography, *Jeffrey Archer, Stranger than Fiction*: the allegations of insider dealing, plagiarism, conspicuous charity to prostitutes on station platforms, enhanced CVs, or any of that "inaccurate précis" froth. I thought I might experiment with the Alan Whicker treatment, tiptoeing across Persian rugs while Archer talked me through the glittering acquisitions. (Apparently, and I sympathise with this, as the novelist's weight has increased his short-term memory has started to go. But we could fill in the titles and dates, if necessary, with the prompting of a properly-primed researcher.)

For a sweetener, the postscript to my letter dropped the name (with her permission) of an in-law of mine, a close friend of Jeffrey Archer's from his Oxford days. This is why, where my wife was concerned, I was dancing on eggshells. Her family had no problem in drawing a distinction between the relative merits of blood ties and speculative literature. Their sense of tribal self-interest made the Mafia look like wimps with suntans. Fiction writing was, properly, a kind of hobby: unfortunate, but tolerable if it brought in cash or fame. In essence, it was an exhibition of bad manners. If such matters had to be performed in public, then Lord Archer came as close as anyone to managing them with the proper style – by divorcing himself from textual mess and running the operation as effectively as any other public company. There was a highly visible product identity and no author. A trick for which I felt immoderate envy.

Alembic House, 93 Albert Embankment, is one of London's worst-kept secrets: anyone who can pick up a newspaper knows that Jeffrey Archer has bagged the top two floors, and spent almost £2 million pounds refurbishing them. A show home for a social balloonist. Wouldn't you – if you could? If you had the bottle. If you were prepared to expose yourself to all that metropolitan magnificence: the Houses of Parliament, the Tate Gallery, the great bridges of London in perfect alignment. Nothing separating you from the heavenly dome but a few sheets of glass. You can't get more upwardly mobile without taking on oxygen. This is the ultimate "riverside opportunity", the one the estate agents pay homage to in their Rotherhithe brochures. All those tacky hutches, peeping out over sewage creeks and dried-up poultices of yellow mud, aspire to this. The New York callisthenics and the sweaty couples faking loft-living ecstasy in some chipboard-partitioned wastelot factory are replays of the Alembic House paradigm.

But there's still something odd about pitching your crow's nest, your glass box, on the thirteenth and fourteenth floors of one of the most visible buildings in London. Leaving aside the rumours – quoted by Michael Crick – of the building's earlier identity as an MI6 sleepover, a safe house, you'd have to be Howard Hughes and employ a team of doubles to live comfortably in such theatrical opulence. Maybe that was the secret of Archer's energy, his legendary "bounce": he couldn't be just one man and get into so much trouble in so many places. He was legion, showing himself at the window, while sound-biting the skin from our TV screens, while wearing suede shoes in LBJ's White House, while giving the good word on John Major, while popping up as an insert in faked Beatles' photographs. Which Archer was he now? Jeffrey or Geoffrey? They both wrote thrillers. Was he the one who doubled as a newsreader? Or the one who lent his name to the Powell and Pressburger film company? The guy must be an entire government department, a cloning experiment that had got seriously out of hand. Not for nothing did his personalised number-plate read: ANY 1. An obvious case of multiple identity: he'd change personalities like the rest of us change suits. (He'd change suits too, although they all looked the same.)

Alembic House was a throwaway secret, the headline kind, part of the package that came with its flamboyant neighbour – Terry Farrell's MI6 palace of the vanities at 85 Vauxhall Cross. An Inca jukebox so blatantly a hybrid of Gotham City and Alhambra fascist chic that you almost suspect someone somewhere, between commissioner and architect, of having a sense of humour. It has to be one of the most expensive piss-takes in history – and the joke's on us. Spook Castle open to the world, because there are no more secrets, only authorised denials. One of the three great riverine monuments to Thatcherism: along with the hollow boast of Canary Wharf and County Hall, the deposed GLC ghost barracks, through whose partly-boarded windows it is possible to view the stalled conversion that would convert London's seat of government into a Japanese piano bar (and then a shark tank). These three, taken together, give us a new definition of shame.

It's a strange business to live, by choice, in a film set – so that the memories you work with are entirely fictional. Alembic House, so they told me in the Tate, where they keep records of such things, accounts of the river, had featured in the first Sweeney film, which was imaginatively titled: *Sweeney!* ("Cops find political dirty deeds are behind a suicide in this successful spin-off"). The very word penthouse is a time warp: gang bosses, Billy Hill era, in glass coffee-table pads. (Stanley Baker in Joseph Losey's *The Criminal*, basing his performance on night-club research with the Richardsons, being double-crossed by Sam "The Snake" Wanamaker – who redeems himself, in real life, by using movie loot to recreate the Globe Theatre, thatch, wattle and all. In partnership with Theo Crosby. But that's another story.)

Penthouses go with the innocent vulgarity of the James Bond films (which is appropriate – Archer's property once belonged to John Barry, the best-known Bond composer, and he retained the 0077 telephone number). Exhibitionist paranoia, Chairman Mao boiler-suits from Savile Row, fluffy white cats: the penthouse is where Rex Mundi has his operational base as the latest avatar of Fu-Manchu. *Penthouse* is also a magazine, a style statement, a brochure for Nigels. ("A wanky name", Archer says in the Mike Ockrent documentary). But *Playboy*'s rival stood for wanking with a philosophical base (*Penthouse* included William Burroughs, Alex Trocchi and Colin Wilson amongst its contributors); wanking with privileged prospects. A bikini-line nude on the rug and the city spread out lasciviously beyond the panoramic window.

Alembic House was rented for Sidney J. Furie's follow-up to *The Ipcress File*, a Cold War turkey called *The Naked Runner* (starring Frank Sinatra – whom Archer brokered to appear in his "Night of Nights" charity bash at the Royal Albert Hall, and who graciously entertained Reggie Kray and Eric Mason in Stockholm at the time of the Floyd Patterson/Eddie Machin fight).

Next up was the Glenda Jackson and George Segal vehicle, *A Touch of Class*, made before Glenda moved over the river as Labour Member for Hampstead, and before her moviettes plugging the Hanson Group in all its global, asset-stripping triumphalism. Each advert shot on a budget that would run Channel 4's positive-discrimination film programme until the millennium.

The penthouse's credits provide a potted history of Anglo-American cinema. Special-relationship thrillers (Californian producers camped out in Eaton Square), spirited love/hate tiffs symbolised by New Woman Jackson and unredeemed Segal, dress-designer and businessman: then the descent into burning-rubber TV features (*Sweeney*), and finally TV itself with *The Politician's Wife*. By this time, it is no longer Lord Archer's penthouse that is rented, but a lower floor. And it's not even a film but a mini-series, blatantly post-modern, using our subliminal knowledge of just who lived in the flat overlooking the House, in the expectation of some convenient scandal coming along to hype the production. The politician's wife who starts out as an idealised Norma Major, background support, happiest in the country, is made over into a Jacobean revenger, a high gloss beauty like Julian Barnes' sketch of Mary Archer: "You could crack eggs on her."

All the prompts dropped in the film – except the leading man who fails to achieve the look of a cream-fed chipmunk – point towards David Mellor (once Jeffrey Archer's researcher, the man who handled his constituency work between 1971 and 1973). Mellor has windsocked his political downfall into a media triumph, so that he has been able to join Lord Archer on the river, commanding one of the three great prospects: Archer in Alembic House, Mellor in the old Dockmaster's House at the entrance to St Katharine's Dock, and Lord Owen in Narrow Street, Limehouse. Mellor and Owen are in some senses satellites of the Archer empire, the super-materialist world view: Mellor, fresh from Cambridge, given his start by the young MP – and Owen, whose wife Deborah was for many years Archer's literary agent. The monster-monster success of Archer's fiction underwrote Owen's political manoeuvrings, allowing him to conspire at his leisure.

(Finding out who has first option on the Thames is a useful way of checking out the social temper of an era. Published under a twenty year moratorium, nostalgic retrievals – Marianne Faithfull, Henrietta Moraes – hymn a period when the action was on the north shore, in Chelsea. Jagger and his mates in Cheyne Walk. Christopher Gibbs, a connected dealer in remarkable things, a salaried facilitator with a famously good eye, camped out in Turner's reach. Upstream sunsets in a cloud of African smoke. The name "Turner" drifting away from the visionary London painter to the wrecked rock star hiding out in Powis Square for the film *Performance*. And on again to a fictionalised disguise for Marc Atkins in my novel *Radon Daughters*. Axel Turner: a cheap pun to christen a compulsive punster.)

The view from Lord Archer's flat was never simply a production value to be leased, short-term, by location scouts; Alembic House was also a charming setting in which to breakfast film deals. Otto Preminger, who met Archer on a transatlantic flight, was soon toying with the idea of taking an option on *Kane and Abel*. ("One of the best novels I have ever read" brags the paperback – not realising that this is no compliment coming from a Hollywood producer/director: a breed allergic to anything fatter than a three page synopsis). The bald virtuoso dutifully turned up at Albert Embankment for the novel's launch party. (Maybe he thought he could garner some seed material for an English version of *Advise and Consent* – blackmail, corruption, telephone promises, political appointments set against a sensational backdrop, and parts for every alcoholic ham who could get day-release from the Betty Ford Clinic?) Archer product-placed Preminger's *Exodus* in *A Matter of Honour*, and Otto indulged the novelist by testing him for the part that eventually went to Nicol Williamson in his rather pedestrian account of Graham Greene's *The Human Factor*.

Despite liftloads of meetings, and high-level tipplings of coffee and fresh orange juice among the art works, Hollywood's interest never went deeper than air-kisses and fiscal foreplay. The novels worked on their own terms – shelf-fillers, presents to sick relatives who don't read, media jokes for production assistants who can boast that they actually finished one – but they refused to break down into viable performance elements. They didn't survive the X-rays of the script doctors. In truth, there wasn't much of a skeleton to be found and the characters wheezed in cartoon speech-bubbles. They were, at best, low Grade fodder: television that would make the commercial breaks look good.

Archer was a book man. His books happened. They understood, better than the rest of the fast-fiction conveyor belt, what the true function of a book was. An object, a brick of paper, good to handle, nice to have around. Inoffensive – except to whingeing aesthetes. The epitome of a good yarn (that was the pitch). A kind of bookie's wad with author's name in high relief: too fat for your pocket. You had to go steady with the product, practically announce your engagement, before you snapped the seal. But, more than any of this, the power of the novels lay in the fact that they didn't have to be read. The much-edited story was so user friendly it spoke to you. It talked back. The plot was so familiar that simply bending back the covers was enough, the thick black lines of text (virtually braille) did the rest. Ownership of one of the novels gave you a direct line to the author: he was incarnated in a way that his ephemeral productions never would be. Take any title from the shelf at WH Smith's, Liverpool Street Station, and you are shaking hands with Lord Archer. He's there, barking at your shoulder: compact, immaculately serviced, brisk. His presence is the antithesis of film with its untrustworthy light shifts, its fractured narrative, its altogether leftist sense of time. The Alembic House flat was cinema enough. Lord Archer was living theatre. He didn't need film, he had control of the finest set on the river.

2.

"You know this place is full of falcons"
ROBBIE COLTRANE (IN CHRISTOPHER PETIT'S
CHINESE BOXES)

2/6/95. I took this appointment with Lord Archer very seriously, so much so that I insisted that we drive down to Lambeth. We couldn't bring sweat and dirt, the road, into the antiseptic bubble of the penthouse. I daren't risk one of our walks. They tended, all too often, and like one of my less disciplined paragraphs, to take over with an agenda of their own. "Better to journey than to arrive" wouldn't work, not when set against Archer's known obsession with punctuality. He had the ex-NCO's proper respect for good time-keeping. (This episode now seemed so pivotal in the development of *Lights Out for the Territory* that I almost decided to sleep in the car overnight, beat the jams and the city road-blocks. I was checking that Marc had film in his camera and that he'd cleaned his nails, brushed his teeth and polished his head. I looked at my watch so often that people assumed I'd developed a nervous twitch.) Whatever else we got wrong – too creepily subservient, too bumptiously rude – we'd arrive at the door of the apartment absolutely on the dot of 10 o'clock. We'd walk in as Big Ben started to chime.

It was very strange after all those months of voluntary pedestrianism to be driving again. The run along Old Street and down Farringdon Road towards the river would, I suspected, be the only motorised jaunt in the book. I hoped it wasn't a bad omen, a blight on the meeting. We needed Archer to counterbalance the parade of shaggy scufflers, my stock company of anarchists, disenfranchised artists and petty criminals. (The thought came to me as we passed Bride Court – where I once picked up a very nice copy of Patrick Hamilton's *Twopence Coloured* – that in all my years dealing in used books, when I'd pitched most things, high and low, I had never listed a single work by ARCHER Jeffrey.)

I sat clutching the wheel, uncomfortably constricted by a black linen waistcoat and jacket (Burton's special offer) that gave me the appearance of a Mississippi mortician – while Atkins twisted himself up in an unresolved attempt to find room for his telescopic legs. He'd broken the habit of a lifetime and put on a second clean T-shirt in one week. And there wasn't even any blood on it.

We were early and had forty minutes to kill. An awkward interval: not long enough to explore the churchyard of St Mary's Lambeth (to search out Elias Ashmole's memorial stone), but just right for a strong cup of coffee.

Undecided which way to turn to begin our quest (I vetoed the place opposite Alembic House which I'd braved on an earlier walk), we stood on the embankment, looking up at Lord Archer's tower in its nest of scaffolding. The building seemed to have been sawn-off, amputated. It wasn't priapic enough. The pyramid was missing.

Chatting on the phone, a couple of days earlier, to the film-maker Chris Petit (who was delighted by the psychokinetic possibilities of this audience with Archer), he'd asked me if I'd heard about the two workmen who had fallen from the building and been killed. (He managed to give this information a quietly threatening sound. He had the right voice for it.) Petit, it occurred to me, was not unlike Jeffrey Archer's fictionally enhanced account of himself: a cerebral doppelgänger. Petit's first feature film, *Radio On*, ran Archer's life in reverse, a mysterious, existential journey – to Weston-super-Mare (with swathes of prophetic weather, future rock stars tending petrol pumps, and unconsummated adulteries). The anti-hero was as glum as an *Insight* researcher trying to tease out Archer's true family tree. But that lovely West Country burr was still a trace element in Archer interviews, an endearment to soften the rehearsed bluster. That a human, who once lived in a particular place, still survived. Petit was true establishment; his father had been well-placed in a military/political job of the kind that can't be openly discussed, and he received his education at Ampleforth and Bristol University (with kosher "O" and "A" levels and all the trimmings). After that, of course, Archer would have to look elsewhere, as Petit fell among journos and wannabe novelists. It was, from then on, a case of compare and contrast: Petit, the circumspect poet of suburbia, a man who could keep his own counsel, and Lord Archer who wasn't and couldn't.

The construction firms working on Alembic House were interesting and rang all the usual paranoid bells: Regalian ("Development of Exclusive Apartments with Magnificent River Views") and Laing of London. I got Marc to take a couple of shots of the advertising hoardings whose texts seemed to have been chosen with the penthouse in mind: **DANGEROUS LADY** (WHEN SHE WAS GOOD/SHE WAS VERY VERY GOOD/BUT WHEN SHE WAS BAD . . .). **Tuesday 8.30 pm. ITV. THE ARTFUL DODGER** (VAUXHALL CORSAVAN). **STAY IN THE BLACK.**

The south bank *was* another country. Angela Carter was quite right. I remembered driving down this road to find her place in Clapham and simply not seeing all this crazy detail. *Wise Children*, Carter's last novel, fingered it: London is "two cities divided by a river".

We backtracked to Black Prince Road where there is a notable red brick folly, all grapes and tiles and crafty art – now boarded up, for sale – where I once, of all things, gave a reading from *Downriver* to a gathering of Book Club reps. Which might explain the building's current dereliction. But further down the same street was a very welcome signboard: SIRENA'S. ENGLISH BREAKFASTS & ITALIAN SPECIALITIES. Our suspicions should have been aroused by the correct use of the apostrophe. But it was a siren song that we couldn't ignore, although finding the true entrance to the dive wasn't easy. First you had to state your business – "two cups of coffee and perhaps a round of toast" – to the uniformed security operative at the desk; then you were required to sign the ledger and clip-on a laminated card (No. 000002). This was as tough as getting into Penguin Books at the height of the Rushdie affair. But it was worth it.

Sirena's was another glorious set: the Italian restaurant of your dreams plumbed into the cellar of a functioning office block. There were no other customers. Traditional red and white checkered (plastic) table-cloths, pink cloth flowers, photo of football team, poster from Amalfi, Gaggia espresso machine, overhead brass fans, strings of onions and an ominous wall mirror with a selection of Mediterranean postcards arranged along its base. The atmosphere was so calm and seductive that I felt we must have been hit with an anodyne spray: Sirena's (Sans Ire).

The set-up was a fake. It had to be. A Secret State listening post, crawling with as many bugs as a rotten log. How else could it stay open? How else could such a feelgood ambiance be unrewarded? The proprietor and his wife – Walter and Silvana – were actors, convincing but too courteous, too prompt. Those waxy bottles are obviously miked. High frequency squeeks bounce off the garlic bulbs. Cameras whirr behind the long mirror. Not content with the entire river frontage between Westminster and Vauxhall Bridges the spooks had wired all the pubs and caffs. Debriefing came with the grappa. Ashtrays were snatched away for analysis as soon as you laid aside your sigaro for a breather.

Our unspoken fears were confirmed when we tried to sit down. The patron scuttled over: "Not there, please. Two gentlemen come every day." And this to an entirely deserted room in which there must have been fifteen or twenty tables. Low ceilings held up by exposed girders and great red pillars (like the boundaries of Aidan Dun's spiritual temple at King's Cross). The coffee is excellent, the service swift. The toast comes ready buttered, chunky with marmalade. We forget our-selves, gossip about the coming encounter with Lord Archer. The lid of the pepper-grinder glows, and starts – spontaneously – to spin.

The Alembic House lift was heavily quilted like a soft cell. It would absorb any cries for help. We were deposited in a panelled hallway, an antechamber with no obvious exit. A Graham Sutherland goat's head did its best to invoke the Goldmark Gallery. We felt as if we had blun-dered into the coda of Stanley Kubrick's *2001: A Space Odyssey*; the lift had been a rebirth and now we had to choose the right door. We scratched and tapped at the panels, conscious of the clock hands mov-ing away from the appointed hour – ready to start spinning if we took the "wrong" decision. Archer would be revealed in some past or future incarnation: as dung beetle or talking egg. Then, all at once, one of the panels swung back and an attractive young Sloane, crisp and efficient, appeared – to tell us that unfortunately Lord Archer was away working on a book, and his son William, the art-history graduate and archivist of the collection, was not available to give us the tour, but we could help ourselves to the views in which we had expressed so much interest.

Game, set, and probably match, to Jeffrey. He had demonstrated his magnanimity by allowing us to do precisely what I had requested in my letter – ponder the art collection and photograph the splendid riverside prospects. I was in his debt – but he had not presented me with the opportunity to indulge in any form of interrogation, however bland. Absent, he was immune to ridicule, while I was obliged to do the decent thing by tactfully listing his possessions. Flawlessly played.

The secretary – personal assistant – retreated to her gantry, leaving us to come to terms with this gobsmacking exhibition of wealth and privilege. It would be a strong man who didn't fantasise about having the use of this flat, the low London skies, the glittering river. A great place for hatching plots, planning coups, or indulging in cosmological meditation, but a hopeless place for hammering away at the keyboard. How could you compete with the panorama that enveloped you?

I've never been in a writer's home – if you could call this a home – that hit you with such a sense of its separateness. The qualitative difference that Scott Fitzgerald (one of the authors Lord Archer purports to collect) saw as dividing the rest of us from the seriously rich. This was wealth as a vocation. I was used to apologetic cribs, part inherited, part salvaged – book wrecks, uncorseted sofas – not so much lived in as resurrected. The writer's life as an unequal struggle with chaos theory. Provisional slums awaiting the big advance, the Finnish translation that would furnish a new set of curtains. Lord Archer, a born-again cad, not content with simply buying his own furniture, had the chutzpah to have it made in larger than life size. He'd perch on one of these striped satin thrones like a mosquito on a tiger's nose.

Before initiating a tracking shot as complex and convoluted as the dark opening sequence of Petit's *Radio On*, I pondered Archer's indulgence in allowing us to wander freely over his fabulous domain. I had written to half-a-dozen others with a stake in this stretch of the river – painters, archivists, businessmen, keyholders – asking for interviews, intelligence, permission to view. Universal silence. Legal and General Property Management, who now control Millbank Tower, where Kokoschka painted his 1962, god's-eye riverscape (*View of the Thames from the Vickers Building, Millbank*), were gracious enough to grant my request, that I should visit the spot where the painter set up his easel, but they were obliged to insist upon an insurance indemnity: £250 + VAT. Per person. Certified cheques in advance. An offer which I had, reluctantly, to decline. (Kokoschka's Westminster is a molten stack of flags and towers; unpeopled but alive. It's not a matter of hierarchies and architectural detail: a pulsing cellular sample under a frantic sky. UnEnglish, the excitement of a capital city lifting itself organically from the river's sediment.)

We were in Lord Archer's debt and it left us uncomfortable. Cynicism, bred of the times, had made us suspicious of altruism and the public charity of gangsters (which remains charity for all that). Perversely, it was the character who had shown most faith in our project (whatever that was) that we trusted least. The leap of consciousness required to calmly evaluate the penthouse was beyond us. We were almost obliged to demonstrate our integrity by throwing ourselves from the balcony.

The spacious L-shaped apartment is on two levels, with the river-facing office/study set above the reception area, and accessed by marble stairs, flanked with golden griffins (multiples of the Maltese Falcon). The design, by architect Anthony Collett (and Pygmalion Interiors), is, according to a puff in *House & Garden*, on a "Third Reich scale." Cornices and skirting-boards have been "exaggerated" and the furniture is operatically over-scaled. "We had everything made specially for this flat. Normal-sized furniture wouldn't have looked right." The eastern arm of the L faces downriver: the Houses of Parliament on the left bank and St Thomas's hospital on the right, with the three bridges (Lambeth, Westminster, Hungerford) diminishing in perfect perspective. Sitting at the end window, sundowner in hand, a tragic poet with a taste for sentimental elegies would have been uniquely placed to watch the *Marchioness* go down.

Photographs, however tactfully composed, cannot do justice to the civic prospect. The kick of visionary rapture outreaches Wordsworth on the roof of his coach as he jolted over Westminster Bridge: "The river glideth at his own sweet will . . . And all that mighty heart is lying still!" Mendacious and masculine, the khaki Thames is as much present on this day, as it was for the Cumberland poet: a mirror of clouds and shadows. The span of Thomas Page's cast-iron bridge doubles into a rank of caves. The low tide reveals steep gravel beaches. Bruised blue pebbles, flints, glinting bottle-tops against the fleshy pink of the bridge's paintwork. Poets can snatch at it, carry away their hasty illuminations for revision in tranquillity. Painters are forced to take their time, let the subject work them over. The poets don't realise, until it's too late, that they've been gulled. They've been programmed to celebrate all these domes and balconies by a peculiarly seductive electromagnetic field. Painters fall prey to epiphanies of light on stone. They bend and twist the shapes at the margin until the river is squeezed out of the composition, until it's a slash of reflected sky. (Marc's prints, when he emerges after days in the darkroom, are all river, all cloud: a sense of width and expansion.)

We've lost it, the way Turner knew that the Thames was everything. His earliest oil in the Tate's collection is a nocturne, *Moonlight: A Study at Millbank* (1797), sombre and melancholy – having no truck with the fiddle of place. The Impressionists wanted to compromise, perceive stone and water and sun as a shimmering stream of light, a drunken dance of particles. Kokoschka and the Expressionists struck metaphors for their own sickness, responding and exploiting: the soul's weather. Violent compromises – the kind for which I felt a residual affection – between art that is commissioned and art that is free to indulge wayward parabolas of insanity.

John Bellany in St Thomas's Hospital, undergoing a course of treatment and taking tests before his liver transplant, painted *London Scene* (1989), a furious seizure, upstream towards Alembic House – with Lambeth Palace as a trivial aside; the septic river draining like a wound. The sky's a botched lid, a sponge of blood. "They should think of the view when they build hospitals," Bellany said. "I was always in the ward for no-hopers and everybody around me was dying." He presented St Thomas's with the work that was, in his opinion, the best of the series. Which is absolutely right: that his canvas window should interfere with, and enrich, our perception of the external world.

These paintings belong to the city, they should never be removed from the river. I read somewhere that Lord Gowrie, on taking office in one of Mrs Thatcher's cabinets, immediately had a car sent around to Bellany's studio to pick up a clutch of works to humanise his office. Peter Wright in *Spycatcher* (1987) reports on a security meeting convened at the flat of Dick White, who had replaced Sir John Sinclair as head of MI6: "paintings from the National Gallery lined the walls". State art shunted from department to department, from civil servant to Secret State creeper, from desk-admiral to temporary politician: public trophies stolen from the public gaze. Glance at the map of the Thames, at all the territory along its banks, within the alembic, between Hungerford and Vauxhall Bridges – the ministries, military/political architecture with memorials to war heroes; Treasury, Foreign Office;

172

historic and contemporary bunkers and tunnels; abbeys, cathedrals, church palaces, Parliament, private and official residences of party functionaries; enclosed gardens, police surveillance, counter-terror. All of it funnelling back into the royal parks, the benches reserved for spooks to meet their controllers; art chat, the leisurely debriefing of Sir Anthony Blunt; the rare privilege of being allowed to pay to tiptoe among the lesser bric-a-brac of the somnolent House of Windsor. Immeasurable chunks of London have been swallowed. If we are not tithe-paying tourists then we are suspects, trespassing on our own inheritance.

The river moves through time, obsessively painted and sketched, shifts of light captured, so that it retains its special status as a ribbon of memory: a journey through a collection of these images becomes the best way of travelling back, discovering what we have done to ourselves. And yet how many of the Tate Gallery's dozens and dozens of riverscapes have we been permitted to see? The list is extraordinary, running from George Price Boyce's *Blackfriars Bridge: Moonlight Sketch* (1863) to Walter Greaves' *Battersea Reach* (c. 1870), to Whistler, Kokoschka, Paul Maitland, Victor Pasmore's *The Thames at Chiswick* (1943–4), André Derain's *The Pool of London* (1906), Claude Muncaster, Francis Macdonald, William Collins, Patrick NA Smyth, JMW Turner's *London from Greenwich* (exhib. 1854), Peter de Wint, Henry Muhrman, Samuel Scott, Charles Nappier Hemy, Daniel Turner, Cornelius Varley, William Roberts' *The Port of London*, William Marlow, David Bomberg's *St Paul's and the River* (1914), Joseph Axe Sleap, George Thomson, James Barry's *The Thames, or Triumph of Navigation* (1792), James Burnet, David Cox, Edwin Edwards, William Havell, James Holland's *The Thames Below Woolwich* (1843), Lord Methuen's *The Tate Gallery from the Surrey Side* (1940), Arthur Douglas Peppercorn, Sir Joshua Reynolds, Richard Wilson, James Duffield Harding, John Linnell, Charles Ginner, Francis Holman, George Vicat Cole's *The Pool of London* and another version with the same title by Matthew White Ridley. The Thames has been diverted into an underground channel, the darkness and obscurity of the reserve collection. A greater acreage of London views hangs in government departments, in elegant offices, than in all the refurbished salons of the Tate Gallery. A virtual reality river, in framed panels of oil and watercolour, has been broken up, suborned to flow across the stucco of Whitehall like a private trout stream.

The journalist David Lister reported that "more than 200 paintings have gone missing from Ministry of Defence buildings". These had been lent out by the Government Art Collection which "currently owns

15,000 works". "206 paintings . . . are unaccounted for" in one department alone. They have simply vanished from the corridors of those imposing white buildings, with their flags and blind windows and regiments of uniformed security personnel. They have slipped through the surveillance screen like all those other meaningless, self-important secrets husbanded by Group Four, the Ring of Five, and the Red Orchestra.

If the official catalogue of 15,000 potential space-fillers proves insufficient, then ministers can always raid the state hoard. John Major, for example, "sequestered" a Hockney double-portrait from the Tate, along with "five masterpieces" from the National Gallery. Kenneth Clark makes do with eight paintings from the National Gallery at No. 11 Downing Street, with ten others "squirrelled away" in the Treasury. This Goeringesque zeal for acquired culture trumps those plutocrats who still buy their own stags, waterfalls and dingy landscapes.

Covert redistributions put Lord Archer's collection ("one of the most valuable in the land...which some estimate could be worth around £10 million") into perspective. It begins to look a pretty modest proposition: an assertion of his own taste, displayed in a building which he has paid for with his own cash, and which he makes more readily available to students and busybodies (such as Atkins and myself) than the galleries that we have been required to support. Archer's current exhibition can look across the river at the Tate without blushing. At £10 million, if that random figure means anything, his holdings are negligible, no more significant than the meretricious trash amassed for Robert Maxwell's posthumous jumble sale. It couldn't be compared, for example, with the collection accumulated by the Dublin fertiliser magnate, Sir Basil Goulding – with his Expressionist portfolio, magnificent examples of Kokoschka and Jack B. Yeats. Archer is more of a Jacobean, an adventurer, a New Man confirming his status by exhibiting a cabinet of curiosities.

But the scale and the organization of Lord Archer's set – right down to the vases of dying lilies – is one we have previously encountered only in public spaces, hotels or boardrooms (glimpsed on our explorations of the City). And that is as it should be: because the penthouse is the headquarters of a public company, Jeffrey Archer, his works and thoughts. You can't sit here doing the crossword, clipping your nails, or scoffing a TV dinner. You are perpetually confronted by the unresting buzz of London, the challenge of all those centres of power and influence – the indifferent, remorseless river. This glass cage, whatever the indulgence of the toys on the table, the mirrors and the golden birds, must be hell for a man of ambition and unflagging energy who has been excluded from the inner councils of government. To be the first clown in the land, warm-up act, cheerleader, must be an act of peculiar generosity and well-disguised bitterness. To be left with the surrogate drama of prose – which, with each successive book, more and more material used up, becomes a harder labour. The brutal exposure of inadequacy that is any longterm literary career.

Choosing the art that will promote your own special quality of discernment (and also express, by analogue, your personality in the form of a pictorial autobiography of developing taste) demands specialised help: investment brokers, fabric designers, style consultants. You always end up – because, after all, you are the one who is footing the bill – with much more *stuff* than any one life can reasonably absorb. You're over-advised, over-exhibited. The room becomes a personal statement, a confession that belongs with your analyst and not on public view. There are far too many choices: lamps, chairs, rugs, chandeliers. Which Miró for the staircase? Which Picasso dove shall hang en route to the lavatory? Which Lowry should signal the common touch?

It was too much for Atkins. Cultural overload brings on a savage form of migraine. He asked to be let out on to the balcony, while I started to log the collection. Alembic House is the contemporary annexe, Archer's equivalent of the Bankside branch of the Tate – with whom he remains in constant rivalry. The domed building on the north bank, housing London's altogether inadequate apology for a survey of twentieth-century art, was the gift of Sir Henry Tate. Without this showcase (once a prison), an ungrateful nation was disinclined to accept the sugar trader's stash of dreary Victoriana: 65 gems from the original collection could be lost among the treasures that would accumulate over the years, as gifts, tax substitutes, or purchases. But, as with the British Library, the Tate has an impossible mandate; however much it expands it will never be able to fully represent either the fluctuating reputation of international art stocks, the story of British painting, or even the endless attempts to make some valid response to the shifting mosaic of city and river. (I always think of the gallery on Millbank as twinned with the belching treacle factory at Silvertown, a long haul down river – but the distance that measures the point at which all cultural pretensions are abdicated. After negotiating the flood barrier, it's every man for himself: the Congo is as relevant as the Thames. No one should be allowed to gawp at the Stanley Spencers, or lift the felt from the cases of Blakes, until they have completed a tour of inspection at Silvertown, licked sugar crystals from the web of their fingers.)

Private plunder, the discreet pornography of the tycoon, evolves towards institutional benevolence: departments of research and education, sponsorship facilitators, career aesthetes, well-bred diplomats schooled to talk money. Lord Archer's collection is still in the primitive stage. It will be left, so it is understood, when the time comes – and after his son William, the art historian, has taken his pick – to Archer's old Oxford college, Brasenose. The westward-stepping funerary caravan will nicely duplicate the twelve cartloads that carried Elias Ashmole's raree show, his alchemical exotica, his cullings from John Tradescant's Ark, out from his Lambeth estate to found the Ashmolean Museum. The Thames is like a thread of consciousness, a water spine between the two cities. Linked settlements: the getting of fortunes and the more measured pace of learning and contemplation. *All* museums, libraries and galleries, should be banished to Oxford. Let them be for the exclusive use of those who will walk there. London should be left to cutpurses, brigands, hustlers, ganefs, courtiers, actors, whores, and other creatures of business. It's speedy, crazed, murderous – but never speedy enough. There are too many artificial Deep England villages, too many smoke-free zones, too much repressive hypocrisy. Museums have got above themselves, touting for funds, when they should remember their origins as mere cabinets of curiosities. Boxes of tricks, bits of animal skin, fossils, plant freaks: blood cargo. You can't make this pillage respectable by enclosing it in a fancy public building – with an outhouse for the sale of postcards and embossed pencils. Lord Archer understood this: he would scavenge, bargain with gallery owners, play the market. (He also had postcards made of the prime items in his collection. But these were for promotion, not for retail.)

I took out my notebook and began, like a bailiff, to list the art works: two Lowrys down at the east end (art for those who don't like art, those who are endowed with a healthy measure of English cynicism – the visual equivalent of Philip Larkin). A weary and bloodless elitism disguised by technical competence. A 1958 seascape with jetty and trippers like burnt out match-ends. A steep flight of steps from 1961. Both genuine, I would say. Cannily modest, with plenty to be modest about.

To the right of this pair, in a position of prominence, is a much noisier affair, a Vuillard, a family group. An acquired set, not Archer's own family – although the woman, it can't be denied, has something of the hauteur of Mary Archer. Painterly virtues, colour harmonies, balance and composition remove this piece from the genre that comes to mind: the reworked Polaroid.

176

Moving down the passage that leads to the stairs and the private sleeping quarters, you glide along the inevitable anthology of political cartoons (reminding me, once more, of the clustered wall of the upstairs lavatory at the Goldmark Gallery). There is the exhibition, beloved by politicians, of a demonstrable sense of humour. But Archer's originals do not feature himself, they are more subtle than that, among the best of their kind: Vicky and Peter Brookes, as well as Steadman and Scarfe, EH Shephard and Max Beerbohm. These are, if it's not a contradiction, cartoons with gravitas, an unspoken programme. Searle's Churchill portrait and his Kennedy motorcade ("Kennedy for President") of October 1960. More Churchilliana (Lady Thatcher would feel completely at home): Churchill and Beaverbrook by Searle, Churchill and Lloyd George by Beerbohm. Disraeli. Not a lot of laughs in this most ephemeral of forms. The framed doodles fade like old copies of *Punch* with the captions erased.

Beyond the cartoons, at the foot of the stairs, are a couple of throwaway Mirós – and, at the end of the corridor, above a potted plant, a notable Leon Underwood: *Venus in Kensington Gardens*. This is a rather academic affair in which a nude sits in an openair café among Underwood's art-school colleagues. But it is a totem for Archer, a memento of his Grafton Street Gallery ("one of my rare failures"), which was featured in his first and most personal novel, *Not a Penny More, Not a Penny Less*.

Russell Flint, Lucien Pissarro, Sisley: works mirrored in the columns of art books gleaming on the low glass tables. Small sculptures that I fail to identify, examples of the almost familiar. Anorexic things that aren't by Giacometti. (I'm missing the Goldmark titles and explanations, the price-tags.) I summon Marc, bring him inside to help locate the Henry Moore bronze that I've read about – forgetting that he's an ex-Cheltenham art student with a first class degree and is therefore excused knowledge of precursors and rivals. I should have called for one of the hard-hat lads from the scaffolding.

Too much time is wasted on this quest – we've already been up here for over an hour – but I need to complete the Moore triangulation. The big bronze (that looks from the river like the figure 2) upstream of the Tate and the one on College Green that camera crews use as a shelf to park their equipment: I believe that they are wired, connected, a gauss-pulse racing between them. Late, factory-produced high art acceptable to the state, and useful for mapping, weighing down, the divisions of the city. Visible investments that are not easily dented or defaced. Cold metal surfaces to refract the whispers. (These Moores are the equivalent of the Wren churches. In time, all civic sculpture from the second half of the twentieth-century will be attributed to the Yorkshireman. If it is a church in the City, it must be a Wren. If it's a bronze, a shaped lump on the forecourt, it's a Moore. Owning a Moore is like hallmarking your property.)

On the west wall is a mirror that extends the conference table where salesman can be brought for pep talks, where deals can be struck, and potential glitches circumvented. This is the place to hang Albert Goodwin's monumental account of the Palace of Westminster. So that the painted version plays against the other, but around the corner from it, out of sight. The real world is duplicated. A spindly figurine, posed alongside the window, gazes down on her twin, held in the palm of the hand by one of A. Drury's massive female presences that guard the piers of Vauxhall Bridge – the one that symbolises "fine art". Microcosm and macrocosm: Lord Archer's designers have achieved a fine balance, a quasi-magical essay on the nature of power. Like a blindfold raid by Imelda Marcos on the Royal Academy Summer Show, the collection is driven but wildly eclectic – betraying no psychological profile, no theme, no compulsion. It is as anonymous as shop stock, an exhibition curated by a squabble of financial advisers.

We climb the marble stairs to the upper gallery, where the personal assistant is working at the keyboard and fielding telephone calls: "Just make the cheque out to Lord Archer. He'll see it gets to the right place". The low ceiling (with telltale damp patch), the wood, the rails, the light from the river: this is a purser's office on a cruise liner. No lightweight furniture. Everything bolted in its place. Uncluttered desk and built-in bookcases with some small part of Jeffrey Archer's collection of first editions – all by one author, himself. I've never before seen paperbacks bound in silver, books bright and shiny enough to satisfy the most fastidious of dealers. (Is it possible to re-read an Archer?)

"His" and "Hers" desks sit on either side of the stairwell, backed by a run of Raoul Dufy Thames riverscapes, liquid blue sketches recalling the posters in the café-bar on the other side of the road. Inoffensive emotional prompts – like the onion strings in Sirena's.

The PA is struggling, ringing round her mates for advice – without success. She's been asked to book tickets for a show with a title she can't begin to pronounce, let alone feed into the spell check: *Peer Gynt*. Having suffered through a misguided production at the Barbican, I'm reckless enough to help her out. To employ someone to take care of

Ibsen for you must be the ultimate luxury. It goes with the cricket bat inscribed by the English Test team of 1992 to the best captain they never had, and the Max Ernst sculpture (bookend size), the WG Grace caricature, the japed Coke can, the rebound set of Dickens with gilt-edges (books as furniture), the lamps and mirrors and framed photographs.

The PA was still busy on the phone – "Go to Harvey Nichols and you can't *look* at a summer outfit for under £2,000. Honestly, you need at least £50 for a T-shirt" – as we waved our farewells, semaphored our gratitude. One final track across the penthouse: gold, birds everywhere, glittering avian *objets* that link with the gilded acorns and pineapples and obelisk flames of Westminster and Lambeth, with the *Per Ardua Ad Astra* eagle on its riverside column. A wistful blend of alchemy and heraldry in the tradition of Elias Ashmole (established, Royalist, arcane). If the birds in the east window look as if they belong on the end of a Roman legionary's staff, then the griffins on the stairs and the long-necked creature, beneath the mirror on the west wall, carry us directly back to the mysteries of the Tradescant tomb in St Mary's churchyard, Lambeth. It's uncanny, Lord Archer's imperialist conversation pieces duplicate and extend the hermetic iconography of the family of seventeenth-century gardeners and collectors. The bombastic chamber that the novelist has assembled is the go-between linking a long-submerged alchemical cult with the MI6 complex and its heady brew of surveillance, computer-generated secrets and occult manipulations. We would have to extend our investigation, go right back to the beginning, to the churchyard – and on foot.

3
"SALOMON'S HOUSE"
The prison-contractors lay out plans
for Pentonvilles and grand Panopticons
The judges lay foundation-stones in the rain . . .
AIDAN DUN, *VALE ROYAL*

5/7/95. With so much to be absorbed, and the taint of car-travel to be exorcised, we set out early for a day's walk along the river. Hackney to Tower Bridge, then back upstream towards Lambeth. I was preoccupied not only with the after-images of our visit to Lord Archer's pad (and how I was going to tone down my report to a level where it would restore domestic harmony), but also with the concept of "Salomon's House": the attempts, early and late, to establish "a Colledge, instituted for the interpretation of Nature, and the producing of Great and Marvellous Works, for the Benefit of men." This college, incorporating the notion of the museum, the library, the herb garden, was always sited, in the imagination of its planners – its secret architects – somewhere along the Surrey shore. Dick Humphreys of the Tate Gallery's Education Department fed me a very useful essay on this subject by Arthur Macgregor – "'A Magazin of all Manner of Inventions' (Museums in the quest for 'Salomon's House' in seventeenth-century England)" – published in 1989 in the *Journal of the History of Collections*.

Macgregor traces the various attempts made to give practical expression to the visionary notion floated by Francis Bacon in his tract, *New Atlantis*, published in 1627. Bacon proposed a kind of secular community, sheltered from the world, which would have the space within its grounds to display inspiring objects and artifices from the past alongside inventions and prototypes from the best mechanics of the present. The spiritually-inclined herbalist would work in harmony with the astrologer-poet, the musician with the psychic geographer. By the establishment of this protected module, the health and potency of the commonwealth, the working city, would be safeguarded. The idea had its attractions. (Inspiration leading rapidly, through colliding egos, to incipient chaos: something like Black Mountain College, North Carolina, at the time of Charles Olson's rectorship. Or London's Laingian anti-university. Glorious in retrospect. Sacrifices made to sustain the culture at large. Those who feed for generations on the risks taken by better men.) Salomon's House, if it could be realised, would combine all the richest and strangest elements from the flotilla of museums on Exhibition Road, the Tate and National Galleries, the Chelsea Physic Garden and the Royal College of Surgeons.

Bacon's seed-idea germinated all sorts of shapes – but always in this part of London, beyond the bearpits, theatres and brothels. Robert Boyle and Samuel Hartlib were two members of a group that conspired to convert the visionary thesis into a practical form. Bacon's concepts were synthesised in a document that outlined a series of proposals for the establishment in Vauxhall of an "Office of Public Address." (Such grandiose – but convincing – moonshine rhapsodies are common currency to the Millennium Committee. Fantasies to mitigate the squalor of our banana republic lottery. A great gambler's wheel for the foreshore. London as Las Vegas. Virtual-reality towers to foul up the natural prospects of Greenwich, to blight the necessary wilderness, out there beyond the sewage farms of Beckton. "Capture the view", as if that excuses everything.)

Elements of Hartlib's memorandum – the housing of "rare Models and Engines", the creation of "a place of resort whereunto Artists and Ingeneers from abroad and at home may repaire" – would fit seamlessly into one of the many lavish brochures knocked out to prepare a sympathetic climate for the launching of the new Tate Gallery of Modern Art at Bankside. The chosen architects, Herzog and de Meuron, are keen to incorporate into the structure of the power station a "luminous glass beam", "a construction that simultaneously advertises the presence of the new gallery to the outside world, houses the air conditioning plant . . . and accommodates the glazing for the top floor." The sentimental strategy of featuring one or more of the defunct generators, as heritage ballast, was toyed with and rejected. An overhead crane, useful for shifting major works of sculpture, will be retained – and encouraged to oscillate "between the matter-of-fact and the mysterious, the substantial and the evanescent." Casting the future is now a simple matter. Computer graphics, laid into the publicity material, are as convincing as any of the tactfully lit illustrations. We can appreciate exhibitions that may never happen: Rachel Whiteread's *House* dwarfed and solitary in the shafts of light that flood into the vault where generators once howled. Richard Long's slate circle convened without a team of handlers. The magical art of the proposal.

Vauxhall, Lambeth, Bankside: favoured landscapes in which to locate the Invisible College, the House of Memory, the properly aligned set of buildings within a complex of orchards and gardens. The colleges founded on the other side of the river, protected by the privileges of the City, were another thing: a resource, a think-tank, generators of strategic intelligence – Gresham College, where Wren was Professor of Anatomy, and Sion College, whose name promises so much more than its overt presence can deliver. Gresham College was funded by the rents Sir Thomas Gresham received from the 100 shops he placed on the first storey of the Royal Exchange. Seven professors were appointed to lecture on astronomy, geometry, physics, law, divinity, rhetoric, music. Learning put to the service of merchants. The college buildings stretched from Old Broad Street to Bishopsgate, with Bull Alley and Wormwood Street to the north, and Sun Yard and the South Sea House to the south: ground now dominated by the Nat West Tower. (The college, a ghost of itself, has been banished to Holborn, where free lectures are still given. At one of these – 27/2/95 – Atkins and I found ourselves sitting behind the psychogeographers, Stewart Home and Fabian, at a dissertation on John Donne.)

ELIZABETHAN SECURITY. DEPLANTING BANKSIDE. We stopped for a moment to examine the Tate's candidacy for operating the latest mutation of the Salomon's House paradigm. "Deplanting" was the name of the game, getting the industrial evidence out of Gilbert Scott's power station without destroying its fabric. "Deplanting": the antithesis of the arcadian Lambeth initiated by the Tradescants. (I had been invited on a tour of this site, peeping in from outside, along with a gaggle of Swiss investment bankers, cultivated explainers, art diplomats – and even practitioners, such as David Medalla, once of the notorious "Exploding Galaxy" commune of 99 Balls Pond Road. I nibbled the canapés and heard the pitch, valiantly and persuasively delivered by Sandy Nairne. I understood how the demonic machines of Nuclear Electric were to be pacified and the entire South Bank re-enchanted: Globe Theatre, with its "Starrs Mall" left open to the skies, opera house, prison as museum. But others, according to the whispers I picked up, were already plotting against the conversion of this austere, light-swallowing monster with its crematorium smokestack. Acts of Steinerist counter-magic were openly discussed: bricks removed at night and substituted for duplicates, packed with the ashes of burnt formulae. Rumours of the K Foundation, their millions impacted into a tile that could be slipped unnoticed into the exterior wall.)

This blatant "deplanting" of Bankside was an assault on the energy field; meditative/explosive art consciousness would have to replace the generation of electricity. The skies above the tower, seen from the river, from some pitching craft, were a wonder: cloud-coral standing in for smoke. The river attracts futile energy-creating machines: the treadmill in the Millbank Penitentiary, or the proposed millennial Ferris wheel on the Embankment. Punitive circuits designed to impress committees.

Atkins and I made a hurried circumnavigation of the site, discovering, on the south side, a sunken grass arena, approached by ramp and by steps, eminently suitable for performance or ceremony. This, within a blood splash of the Bear Gardens, was where we witnessed a playlet dedicated to the area's transformation. Two bullet-heads were sprawled on the bank, drinking, and loosing their dogs, pit bull compromises, in fierce combat. The beasts were taking it in turns to see who could most effectively destroy a series of orange traffic cones. The non-owner would hurl the cone into the air, and as far as he could manage without falling flat on his face, then time his rival's pet, while it shredded the cone into pathetic curls of rubber. The grass looked as if it had been cropdusted by militant Buddhists. (Watching, I understood how terrorists would smuggle explosives into the road-blocked City. They would simply arrive with a lorryload of traffic cones, cones stuffed with lethal fertiliser.)

4.

"so poisonous an egg should have been laid, whence, one must fear, a most horrid basilisk, a great danger to very many people, will be born if it be hatched much longer and be formented with further bilious matter"

JOHN DEE

St Mary's Churchyard, alongside Lambeth Palace. It's far too early to get inside the church – which we still need to do, to locate Elias Ashmole's memorial (*"durante Musaeo Ashmoleano Oxon. nunquam moriturus"*). When, a few days later, this is accomplished, and we amble through the Garden Museum, read the prompt cards, study the maps, notice the duplicate of Powhatan's Mantle (original in the Tradescant Room at the Ashmolean), we are no further in our quest. Ashmole's stone is hidden behind chipboard, part of an administrative complex: to be laid before the eyes of the uninitiated at some future time.

The light is soft, sympathetic to stone. I summarise, in pamphlet shorthand, the Tradescant story, tune Marc for the photographs he is about to take: a family of notable gardeners whose estates were about a mile and a half to the south of Lambeth Church. John Tradescant the Elder (c. 1570–1638), grey-bearded, earringed, skullcapped in black like Dr Dee (according to the portrait attributed to Emmanuel De Critz in the Ashmolean), was a botanist and collector, a traveller, an importer of alien shrubs and plants. Tradescant was of Dutch descent, a man who was comfortable in Europe, making excursions on behalf of his patron, Robert Cecil, the first Earl of Salisbury, to acquire trees for Hatfield House: cherry, quince, apple, pear, walnut, lime. Then on to Paris and Rouen in search of exotic fruits: pomegranates, figs, peaches. The gardener, like the poet, the architect and the musician, served at the court of some great temporal lord, helping him to express wealth and political power in a visible form: geometric plantings as part of a system of metaphysics. Herbs to heal, sounds to soothe, curious natural objects to contemplate. Language in perpetual revision, fretted by the new

183

philosophy, the discoveries of travellers, reports of alchemists and workers of angel-magick.

Tradescant, who had only one defect as a botanical gardener – no sense of smell – compensated for this by his gift for forming relationships with those who could be useful to him, to his covert purpose: those who would allow him to make surrogate voyages of exploration. (In Elizabethan London it was possible to meet everybody, walk everywhere, be in touch with all human knowledge. Now we keep to ourselves, hide away, convinced that we know nothing – that each new discovery eliminates former convictions.) Captain John Smith was a friend, returned across the Atlantic with tales of the virgin forest. Pocahontas had aroused great interest at court. Tradescant invested – "adventured" – in the Virginia Company. He secured the Mantle of Powhatan, father of Pocahontas, for his Ark – his collection of curios at Lambeth. And what a thing this was for the coming mercantile city, the cosmological blanket stitched from four deerskins: with its split human figure, its totemic animals, its star-field of clustered shells. Plunder the equal of anything in the Egyptian rooms of the British Museum. Tradescant offered his map of intent to the river, placed it in his house (which had the name of a boat); let it remain when Pocahontas was sent back, returned to her death at Gravesend.

He progressed, after the demise of Cecil's son, William, to Keeper of the Closet of Rarities for George Villiers, Duke of Buckingham: a catholic collection that included an elephant's head, as well as that of a "River horse . . . the Begest that can be Gotten". Buckingham's proto-museum was the inspiration for Tradescant's storehouse at Lambeth, the Ark – to which the public were admitted on payment of 6d. A privatised culture-for-cash transaction that showed the way to future riverrine enterprises.

Recognition from royalty came with Tradescant's appointment as Keeper of Gardens, Vines and Silkworms at Oatlands Palace (on the Thames, between Walton and Weybridge). He was also able, during this period, to advise on the planting and laying out of Oxford's Physic Garden – while continuing to cultivate his orchards and experiment with bio-dynamic imports in South Lambeth.

Lambeth, Lamb of the River, damp pastureland, was blessed by the rudiments of a new Oecology, a tentshow rendering of Salomon's House. The kind of cottage industry that was to be attempted, in very different ways, by future residents: William Blake (naked in his Hercules Road bower) and Jeffrey Archer, assembling the treasures of his period, as he understood them, in his high glass cell, his pilot's cabin.

When the great gardener died and the bell of St Mary's tolled for his funeral, his son, John Tradescant the Younger (1608–1662), was in Virginia, carrying on his father's work: the pursuit of the rare and strange. He returned to England, to his inheritance, with "about two hundred plants as well as seeds and dried specimens . . . American Plane, Swamp Cypress, Virginian Bladder Nut, purple Pitcher Plant."

There are two fine portraits of the son, again attributed to Emmanuel De Critz (who may have been related to Tradescant's second wife, Hester Pooks). In one painting the red-bearded, open-shirted man rests a powerful hand on his spade. In the other, he contemplates a skull on which a mossy wig of curls is growing. (Sympathetic magic, like that practised by Sir Kenelm Digby of Gresham College, who suggested in his book *On the Cure of Wounds* that powder should be rubbed into the weapon that caused the wound and not into the wound itself. Digby according to his epitaph was "born on the day he died, th'Eleventh of June". And, since we share a birthday, I choose to honour his eccentricities.)

The significant and inevitable moment in the younger Tradescant's life, the convergence of streams, arrived when, in 1650, he met Elias Ashmole, genealogist, alchemist and fanatical collector. Ashmole visited the Ark, cultivated its proprietor, and even settled himself into a neighbouring estate. In the summer of 1652 Ashmole brought his second wife, Mary, to "table" with the Tradescants, so that the wives should become as close as the husbands. He insinuated himself into the household and was given every opportunity to examine the collection at his leisure. Wishing to be of service, he offered, with Dr Thomas Wharton, to catalogue the rarities. The offer was gratefully accepted and *Musaeum Tradescantianum* published in 1656.

Tradescant's only son, John, had died in 1652 and so, with no one to add to the holdings, or to safeguard the South Lambeth Ark, he began to fret over the future of the collection. The idea of willing the rarities to a university occurred to him. And Elias Ashmole was on hand to facilitate the arrangement. After a seasonal rout in December 1659, when heroic quantities of drink were taken, Ashmole produced a deed of gift which Tradescant signed in front of witnesses – granting the collection to Ashmole.

Within a month of Tradescant's death in 1662, Ashmole preferred a Bill in Chancery against the widow, a lady of insecure temperament. The case was decided in Ashmole's favour. (He was, after all, a lawyer and a notorious and well-connected litigant.) Hester Tradescant, entitled to keep the rarities during her lifetime, ceded them in 1678 – two years before she killed herself.

Ashmole, in retirement, extended his South Lambeth estate to absorb the Tradescant property, the Ark, its orchards and gardens. He had successfully assimilated whatever virtue lay in that patch of ground: the arrangements of plant beds, native and exotic, astrologically sympathetic allies, medicinal herbs – their texture, shape, odour. "Moses in the Bullrushes" sent back from Virginia, scarlet runner beans from the West Indies, the Lilac, the Cornelian Cherry and the now extinct Great Rose Daffodil (with its unique capacity for doubling).

The coins and seals that Ashmole assembled to replace those lost in the Middle Temple fire of January 1679 were brought to Lambeth, added to the Tradescant curios, the books and alchemical papers (including those of Dr John Dee). Ashmole pondered, but never accomplished, a history of Freemasonry and a biography of Dee. What he *did* do was to initiate an hermetic museum of the river: linking Dee's destroyed library at Mortlake (alchemised by fire, angelic dialogues lifted into the air) with the future cottage of William Blake, the Globe and Rose and Fortune Theatres (and their astrologically-inspired architecture), and with the Tate Gallery (with its dynamic Turner seascapes, its remembrances of an ideal London). All these structures, combining with the private holdings of successful men (the Owens and Mellors and Archers, David Lean's hidden arcadia in Narrow Street, Limehouse), pay homage to Salomon's House: gathering images and icons, laying out rooms and chambers that achieve an idiosyncratic quality of stillness, operate outside the reckless fret of the present. So that the removal of Tradescant's hoard to Oxford was an act of liberation: unseen, unexploited, the Ark would achieve its true potency.

And it is the light on this particular morning, coming up from the tombstones and partially erased memorials, the haze that promises a blistering finish to our excursion, the vegetable light, that links a chain of wild speculations, and motivates this excursion. We see the churchyard of St Mary at Lambeth as an uncovered gallery, an intriguing set of broken texts, herbal hints, signifiers, symbols to be touched and tested. We can't get at the Tradescant tomb which is in the enclosed garden that is now part of the museum. But we have seen this before (moored alongside the stone vessel that contains the bones of Bligh of the *Bounty*); seen it, photographed it, brooded on it. Mounted on granite slabs like another Henry Moore, the sepulchral chest is one of the undoubted treasures of our floating museum: it is coded in layers of pictorial narrative that will take many miles of hard walking to unravel.

The design for the tomb – was Ashmole with his passion for sigils, magical ideograms, implicated? – could be read as a whole, a widescreen tapestry, with thick, sponge-cluster trees masking the corners: or it could be divided into four discrete panels. The side which, according to the illustration from *The Thames & its Views*, now in the Pepys Library at Magdalene College, Cambridge, should face west, features a monastic ruin (perhaps a reference to St Augustine's garden at Canterbury where the elder Tradescant was employed by Edward, Lord Wotton). If the building, pictured in low relief, doesn't represent an incident from life, it might instead be a prophetic vision of Lambeth Palace: the land slipping away to a primal swamp, out of which crawl the crocodile and the snail, and whose muddy bank is decorated with ammonites, fossils liberated from Tradescant's Ark.

The eastern panel (inaccurately represented in the Pepys Library sketch) is the most remarkable of all: an urban apocalypse. What has this to do with a family of gardeners? The revenge of the plants? Vegetable life exposing the pretensions of stone, reducing the city's temples to an Aztec desolation? Broken pillars, tilted pyramids, tumbled arches. Floods and inundation: the river rising to sweep away all the potentialities of Nicholas Hawksmoor's baroque overview, his ordered mapping destroyed before it could be articulated. The Tradescant tomb is a monolith revealed by a retreating tide. It is both a retrieval and a warning.

The end panel, the panel nearest the church, clarified this climate of incipient millennial threat into orthodox alchemical imagery: a skull guarded, or threatened, by a seven-headed hydra. A creature that sends us straight back to the book of emblems, that invokes a place we have already visited: Alembic House and Lord Archer's gilded bestiary. The design of the penthouse exploited symbolic forms that had been in place for hundreds of years in the churchyard it overlooked.

Archer's temperament, like that of Ashmole, could certainly be described as mercurial. It was not only elements of the radical left (cited by Christopher Hill in *The World Turned Upside Down*, 1972) who took an interest in magic and the mystical world-view during the period of the Interregnum. There was also a tradition, with Ashmole as the most notable exemplar, of conservative, pro-monarchist investment in the hermetic canon. Ashmole's fascination with Dee, Queen Elizabeth's imperial geographer, and his lifelong obsession with alchemy (which included the publication, in 1652, of *Theatricum Chemicum Britannicum*), should be seen in the context of a profoundly hieratic notion of society. He was a careerist, a social climber prepared to marry, several times, for wealth and advantage. He believed that "the *Order* and *Symmitry* of the *Universe* is so settled by the *Lawes* of *Creation*, that the lowest things . . . should be immediately subservient to the *Midle*; the *Midle* (or *Caelestial*) to those above . . ."

Alchemy, with its catalogue of emblems, its system of correspondences – as above, so below – was the key to any interpretation of Lambeth Churchyard. Looking around the area that was open to the public was like leafing through the engravings in Michael Maier's *Scrutinium Chymicum*. (Maier, a proto-Rosicrucian, had lived in England, intermittently, between 1612 and 1616, and was known to Ashmole, Robert Fludd, and the alchemists of the Bartholomew's Court circle – Dr Francis Anthony and David Dee.)

Death and regeneration. The startling transmutation of the leaden water in the fountain's bowl, as the sun breaks cover, into a shimmering dish of gold. And beyond the fountain, back towards the river, twin obelisks supporting a pair of golden acorns. Pink and yellow hollyhocks climb against the grey of the church, against rough stone that has been set as haphazardly as crazy paving.

To the south of the porch is a monument which I have noticed on previous visits but never inspected. Barred from church and Tradescant garden, we have the time to give the Sealy Family memorial the time it deserves. An urn in the shape of a cosmic egg. An urn crowned with a tongue of flame and intertwined by a dentated snake in the act of swallowing its own tail. (As Atkins moves in with his camera, tenses with concentration, the pink tattoo on his left bicep repeats the motif.) The great serpent seems to have been adapted from Maier's emblem, *The Dragon and the Woman destroy one another and cover themselves with blood* (Epigramma L.). And the background in this engraving, the ruined masonry, the pyramidical spikes, refers to the apocalyptic panel of the Tradescant tomb. (Our excitement, rushing from grave to grave, standing back, photographing close-up detail, chipped stanzas of necrophile verse, is such that Atkins blurts out his middle name – Bryan – as an offering, a confession.)

The Sealy verse looks, in its use of random capitalisation and its twisted syntax, as if it belongs in Ashmole's alchemical anthology.

> *Lean not on Earth, 'twill pierce thee to the Heart.*
> A BROKEN REED *at best, but oft a* SPEAR*:*
> *On its sharp point* PEACE *bleeds, and* HOPE *expires.*

And, more than that, on closer examination, it can be seen that the ghost of another poem, or earlier version of this one, is hidden beneath; the letters filled in and partially obliterated.

I let the riddle lie for future interpretation, some more leisured occasion. Now we have to push on, to locate Tradescant's Ark in South Lambeth Road. We have a metaphor with which to work. A minor mystery to debate as we walk south – pausing briefly, at Alembic House, to drop off, with a note of thanks, two of Marc's best prints, taken from Lord Archer's balcony, classically austere river views, which the photographer has laboured over for hours in his darkroom. A small contribution to the London portfolio.

In the lobby, as we carry our package to the desk, we bump against a man stepping from the lift. Good humoured, unhurried, he smiles and nods. Dark, pudding-basin hair meeting the raised eyebrows. Someone who missed the news that the Beatles have broken up. A loose shirt and white (loafing on the marina) slacks. A beachcomber with a private income. The effortless manners of a natural gent. A cheery wave to the security operative and away.

I know the face. I've seen it in the press. I signal Marc to get the shot. He skips across the road, covers me as I set out to track our suspect on his westward route. It'll come to me. There are no civilians, no innocents, on this turf. From Alembic House to Tintagel House (the Met's base for covert operations, the building outside which Nipper Read and his team were photographed after banging up the Krays), the story begins to fall into place. This whole prime chunk of river frontage is Matter of Britain real estate. Archer's Alembic House named after a standard item of alchemical equipment, a vessel used in distilling. Tintagel House (the Met's gesture at Eastern European anonymity) and Camelford House (where BT does whatever it does, authorised eavesdropping): mock Arthurian, Tennyson-on-Thames. Mythical names ironically invoked for this exercise in neo-Fascist stacking. Three buildings so dull that you'd have to be out on licence to notice them. Tintagel Cliff imported to London: Uther Pendragon's stronghold, birthplace of Arthur. Nine floors of nothing with a spike on the roof. (Could it be one of those photovoltaic scanners that are currently exercising Chris Petit's imagination?). In the gauze windows you can see the reflection of the next tower block, of Camelford House. And in Camelford House you can see the MI6 palace. The three run into each other: the mercury, sulphur and salt of alchemy. Bad electricity: didn't something go wrong with the water down there, Camelford? Isn't that the part of the world where they have to apologise for excessive enthusiasm in the application of X-rays?

When the names of sacred places are applied to Secret State architecture, duck out. The mythology was suspect in the first place, edited to appease Tudor power brokers with dubious bloodlines. Or varnished by Pre-Raphaelites over Victorian squalor. It's the same scam as plastering the names of poets around prolapsed housing estates.

I've pegged our man. He ambles along without a care in the world. He's used to being followed. He doesn't give a toss. When he needs to, he'll slip from sight. Straight spine, minimal arm movement: an aura of unconcern that leaves him conspicuous. He's drawing us into a trap. That's obvious, because today for the first time it proves possible to sidle down to the river, on to the chequered walkway at the front of Terry Farrell's termite masterpiece.

ANOTHER LAMBETH ENVIRONMENTAL IMPROVEMENT. **Helped by Money from the Government's Urban Programme.** The tide is low, exposing a remarkably pure strip of beach. The MI6 palazzo looks like a marzipan sandcastle (like that memorable, cross-river shot in Patrick Keiller's *London*).

I've been reading Peter Wright's *Spycatcher* ("MI6 . . . never settled for a disaster if calamity could be found instead") as background to this walk. It's mostly turgid ghost prose: posthumous in a way that gives table-tappers a bad name. But it does, in its first few pages, spell out the system under which this bridge-to-bridge nexus operates. Wright was a technician, a degausser: that was his area of expertise, reversing the magnetic field, weaving cables around battleships. He was able to repel magnetic mines. And that's what these buildings, the triangulation of Henry Moore bronzes, the seven-headed hydras, the photovoltaic scanners, are all about: reversing the magnetic field. Fucking it up on a royal scale. Throwing a loop around secure territory. Wiping the tape of undesirable elements. Repelling intruders. Who scuffle over pedestrian bridges like a pack of zombies. Who drive west without noticing what is happening outside the car window. Who are checked and flustered by freelance sponge-wielders waiting at the lights. Spooks disguised as bucket carriers. Degaussing.

Staying inside the oval circuit blesses you with a better brand of paranoia: you pose, as the man we have followed is doing, at the epicentre of the small circular temple. He can't take his hands out of his pockets, can't begin to contemplate the enormity of this development. Get away with building this and you'll get away with anything. This is hubris on a scale that would embarrass Rupert Murdoch. The green and cream Spook Castle looks like the ultimate publishing conglomerate (which in a sense it is – pumping out disinformation, suborning journos, corrupting the already corrupt, funding dog fiction, lunching the culture). It's probably a more active concern than its cadet version on the other side of Vauxhall Bridge, Random House. (Spooks fleeing over the water to avoid drinking in the nearest pub, a rundown gay pick-up toilet, meet the work-experience editors rushing in the opposite direction in quest of a decent cup of coffee, and a few minutes' break from the madness of corporate self-publishing.)

Stand here too long, listening to the synchronised plash of the fountains, counting the tiles, watching out for Wright's "Watchers", feeling our guts for the bite of irradiated bacon from Sirena's, and this daffy ziggurat begins to make sense. It develops a kind of beauty. We must have been thoroughly worked over to say it – but, cover the mound in vegetation, and it would display an inhuman charm. We should move now, before we develop the giveaway stutter, the liar's punctuation that Peter Wright and Kim Philby exploited: a captivating, upper class mannerism brought to fruition by the actor Hugh Grant. The instant of hesitation confirms it yet again: everything that is not forbidden is compulsory.

The building is laid out with terrifying symmetry – from sharp prow to bridge and pseudo-funnel. Hierarchies of blank windows, portholes. We promenade the immaculate deck with a troop of uniformed hygiene operatives, identifiable by the usual laminated badges. T-bar pergolas belong in a catalogue of Il Duce revivalist chic. There are so many cameras they seem more of a design feature, artificial birds, than a serious attempt to log intruders.

We can't quit without approaching the beachcomber – who is now carelessly rolling a jumbo spliff. His white loafers were never intended for city walking. He has that Oxford insouciance, the steadiness of hand under fire. But, even as a beneficiary of those connections, he hasn't necessarily been visiting Lord Archer, or crashing in the penthouse. A Balliol decadent might not choose to acknowledge a one-year PE instructor, who managed to get himself attached to Brasenose on the strength of a bodybuilding certificate from the International Federation of Physical Culture in Chancery Lane. He could have been taking tea with anyone in Alembic House, the building was a nest of conspirators.

I knew who the riverside dope fiend was. He shouldn't be here. As the press had it, the books and TV documentaries, he was banged up for a couple of eternities in a top security American penitentiary. This was

Howard Marks, the biggest herb smuggler in the universe – and he was taking a leisurely constitutional through the heart of the Secret State; sitting in a phoney temple to enjoy an undisturbed draw. Howard was the example that had been made. And been seen to be made.

Reports of his famous Celtic charm have not been exaggerated. Listening to that rich, deep voice, I felt nostalgic for things I had been living in London for thirty years to avoid. I introduced myself as coming from Maesteg. Howard had grown up not five miles away, in Kenfig Hill. "Here we are then," he said, "two boyos from the valleys up to no good in the big, wicked city."

He was happy to talk. That was one of his gifts, instant confidentiality, a lack of pomposity and self-justification. You can see why juries, packed with females, swallowed any tale he told them. (Put him together with Mary Archer and they could have been caught with smoking guns in their hands, sacks marked "swag", and walked away without a stain on their characters.) Howard had been, so he informed us, recruited by MI6, shortly after coming down from Oxford. A college chum. Marks' chain of boutiques, spread across Europe, were used for laundering cash and passing information (among other off-the-record activities). Favours for favours. He liaised with INLA splinter groups as well as the Curzon Street mob. And lived, quite contentedly, under perpetual surveillance.

Prison had been all right, once he'd worked it out. As a high profile felon he was unlikely to be a target for random assassination by the extreme rightwing death squads who kill as a rite of initiation. Howard helped the cons to prepare legal appeals. He worked on his tennis. Hard drugs were readily available (as a means of control). Soft drugs were discouraged by regular test programmes. Cannabis stays in the bloodstream for thirty days. Traces of heroin disappear fast. There was a chance to catch up on his reading in philosophy and poetry. Meet anyone who can quote Alfred Noyes and you know they've been inside.

The worst of it, Howard admitted, backing away from the river, was that he had developed a phobia about water. He could hardly bear it on his skin. He shivered. We walked with him, up the steps towards Vauxhall Bridge. Nicely mellow, he was going around to the front entrance. Why, I wondered, had there been no major publicity about his release? He grinned. "You can't believe everything you read," he said. "Lovely to meet you. Catch you again sometime."

The bridge, with its squad of fierce amazons, is the borderline. Unlike Marks, we couldn't retrace our steps. It was time to cut inland, pick up the Tradescant trail, search for the Ark. My instinct, looking back, was that the MI6 complex was completely uninhabited. It had been made public so that the wet jobs and black propaganda could be carried on elsewhere without hindrance: above a betting-shop in Stepney, a suite of unlet offices in Holborn. The point of Terry Farrell's folly was to *induce* paranoia, keep the populace jumpy. The building, the entire complex of buildings, pumped out brain-bending white noise. Separate stations competed to create an electromagnetic field in which fears could be triggered at will, demons visualised. Implants in the nasal cavity or miniature radios concealed in the teeth would conjure up flying saucers over Chelsea Harbour, or politicians so bland, so drained of humanity, that they had to be the forerunners of an alien race, extra terrestrials. Yes! It was getting to me already. Radio hypnosis, mind control, voices in the head. If such a monster could be funded, then there were no limits to the arrogance of government. There was nothing we would not stand for.

We were grateful to escape into South Lambeth Road; a relatively unknown quantity, virgin ground. There could be no real expectation of locating a surviving bucolic redoubt, not here. The mysteries had been broken up. They had decamped to Oxford.

We had to choose our pedestrian tunnel. The first (spurned) ran in the direction of the Oval and was decorated with the single word **RITUAL**, the T being exaggerated into a tau cross. The other, a white tile number, was soon confirmed as the correct decision. An alchemical/Rosicrucian riddle was sprayed along its length: **WHO IS CHRISTIAN GOLDMAN?** (Composed by an initiate sufficiently overqualified to employ the correct punctuation mark.)

From that point on, travelling south, our interest was held by quantum weirdness: the British Interplanetary Society at Nos. 27–29 South Lambeth Road and, on the opposite side of the street, an aerial pyramid with a spray of **666**s. The omens were propitious, that familiar, teasing sense of things running away from us. The narrative fragmenting into a pattern so random that it outreached even our capacity for self-delusion. Once again our path intersected with Patrick Keiller's fictional London walks (his attempt to uncover Vauxhall's "famous association with Sherlock Holmes"). Could it be that we were inadequately degaussed? That we had been suckered into yomping down streets that existed only as a sequence of static camera positions? Right in front of us were the red brick gates which appear in Keiller's film as an unplayed musical score, the deep green of municipal grass running away behind them.

("Listen to the gateposts at the entrance to the park.") Walking, unprepared, into another man's film is an hallucinatory experience. We didn't know where we were and we didn't know how to proceed.

Between the park and Tradescant Road, the shops – their smell and feel – were Portuguese. Delicatessens, barbers, driving schools, travel agents: another country, another time. A substitute for the absence of Tradescant and Ashmole. Because there is nothing left of the Ark and its gardens. Plaster fruits above doorways, evocative street names. Unpollarded shrubs. A security-alarmed chemist on the corner of Tradescant Road. It's over, Salomon's House is off the menu.

The best we can come up with, before battling back to Vauxhall Bridge and the river, is a Tradescant totem pole, sanctioned by David Bellamy: a heaving wedge of polymorphous perversity, hacked out of wood, rising from a globe of multicoloured fruits and flowers. TRAV-ELLERS: the word picked out in ironwork letters.

At this point, I recall for Marc the story a friend, Carol Williams, related: how she had been part of a group, inspired by the research of Sadao Ichikawa, planting spiderwort in the proximity of nuclear installations. Measuring radiation by colour changes, clearly visible under the microscope, blue to pink – before any leakage would be admitted. The botanical name for these spiky plants was *Tradescantia*.

Carol, who was now back in Sag Harbor, Long Island, had written to me, enclosing a copy of Ichikawa's "The Spiderwort Strategy" in the magazine *Bio-Dynamics* (Summer 1978). Her covering letter explained: "Another name for Tradescantia or spiderwort is Trinity Flower (because of its 3 petals & other 3 flower parts) – which I'm afraid made me think again of radiation during recent markings of 50th anniversary of explosion of atomic bomb as the code name for its first test in New Mexico was Trinity. I was struck at Museum of Gardening (which I did love and the walk) by the list of Tradescants' I & II plant discoveries – how they found plants around the world that had a particular & helpful relationship to human life: like gelsemium, like these radiation mutations . . . I wish I had seen the first museum, the Ark!"

Ichikawa's article clarified the role of *Tradescantia*:

Lovely and tiny flowers . . . have been showing an excellent performance in fighting against the huge technology of nuclear energy . . .

The story to be described here is: Increased somatic mutation frequencies were found in the stamen hairs of a clone of spiderwort planted close to some nuclear power plants. Long-term scorings of the somatic mutations at those

194

power plants revealed that the increases occurred only during the operation
periods of reactors and mostly at the places located to the leeward of the
power plants. The scorings . . . not only could break the "safety" myth of
nuclear power, but also expose several important facts which have been
ignored and/or hidden from the public by the nuclear proponents . . .

It was the stamen-hair system of spiderwort (the scientific genus name is
Tradescantia*) that brought much more detailed information about the*
genetic effects of low-level radiations . . . The system is therefore regarded as
the most excellent test system ever known . . .

Back on Vauxhall Bridge, we prepared to break free from the line of
female deities, with their steel books, their admonitory fingers (visible
only from the river). Their gestures were a Dantesque prohibition. We
were finished with this cultural reservation: one more tour across the
domes and roofs of the Tate would do it, revealing the scale of the old
Millbank prison, the layout of Jeremy Bentham's *Panopticon* or *Inspection
House*, the traces of the military hospital. Bentham had anticipated
Terry Farrell with his own system of perpetual surveillance: "a circular
building, an iron cage, glazed . . . with the cells on the outer circumference" and a viewing point at the centre "from which every corner of
every cell could be observed at all times of day and night". The bird's
eye plan of Millbank Penitentiary from the "Descriptive Map of London
Poverty" of 1889 reveals a vast enclosure, a flowerhead, or rose, six
petals sharp as razors. A shape that, with the twin gasometers as eyes,
transforms itself into a hideous bug, impertinently burrowing into the
riverside. A beetle whose other sections are the Vauxhall Distillery (now
Farrell's folly) and the Oval cricket ground as the thorax. Underground
cells – "the dark" – were exposed during the construction of the Clore
Gallery. And, as Krzysztof Cieszkowski points out in his essay on
"Millbank before the Tate", "many of the current employees of the Tate
Gallery are graded as warders and keepers". Employed to watch the
untrustworthy public and not the art.

No need to report on the rest of our trip to Putney and Mortlake, the
evening return along the other bank, through Syon Park, Hogarth's
House and Hammersmith: it's there, if you want it, before the event, in
my novel *Radon Daughters*. The unlooked for bonus, the necessary thing
we didn't know, came with the identification of the three Mary
churches: Ashmole's St Mary at Lambeth, John Dee's unmarked burial
place at St Mary in Mortlake – and the new one, St Mary at Battersea.
A chatty verger clung to us, pointing out William Blake's window (he

was married here) and the chair Turner used to paint his riverscapes. The site was also, apparently, a popular film location. Blake's father-in-law had been a market gardener, the poet/visionary had a real connection with this place – even though he was, as S. Foster Damon points out, suspicious of Marian worship: "A Vegetated Christ & a Virgin Eve are the Hermaphroditic Blasphemy; by his Maternal Birth he is that Evil-One and his Maternal Humanity must be put off Eternally, lest the Sexual Generation swallow up Regeneration. Come Lord Jesus, take on thee the Satanic Body of Holiness!"

We promised ourselves a drink at the Duke's Head in Putney, in honour of our previous trip, upstream, as part of the *Radon Daughters* "research" – coming back from Pope's Grotto, Sir Richard Burton's stone-tent tomb, Dee's Mortlake. That afternoon, a hot one, we had flopped in a corner, to find ourselves disputing the bar with another literary excursion. The celebrated novelist and television impresario Nigel Williams had bagged the window seat and was plotting his *Two and a Half Men and a Boat* package. (The half being Alan Yentob and his cellphone.)

Williams was preoccupied, a couple of pints ahead of us, but I had met him once before (a lunch invigilating a documentary that would never be made), so I exchanged a few words. Dee and his relics were not of the slightest interest to him (Peter Ackroyd had not yet published his Clerkenwell novel). Nor did another JK Jerome, striped-blazer frolic do much for me. Our ways parted, definitively. Atkins and I were trespassing here on a media friendly slipway – the whiff of resting actors, softshoe operators who take two newspapers with their lunch; afternoons without definition, shaggy dogs lapping from ashtrays. It would take years I no longer had to achieve that strategically rumpled Putney look. I've seen it on certain poets (retired) and on one or two bookdealers who have successfully made the transition from stall to catalogue, and who don't quite believe it. It's a very English thing, the professional amateur churning out volumes, running the culture while appearing to be incapable of doing up his fly-buttons.

We indulged in a last look at Archer's patch, the gravy-coloured river, then we pushed on.

5

DEVIL: So you walk around London?
ARCHER: Oh all the time . . .
DEVIL: Have you worked with the security services?
ARCHER: No.

INTERVIEW, *THE PRINTER'S DEVIL*

4/7/95. London abandons itself to the mood of the moment: sleet skies for state funerals, garden party haze for the Conservative leadership election. Like the rest of us, the city has been conned into believing that something is about to change – that the whole miserable farce is ready to self-destruct. Even the half-employed office drones skittering up New Bridge Street are prepared to talk to each other, to give the finger to the helmets running the checkpoint. If revolution comes to Britain it will be disguised as a garden fete: heads of the monarchy on coconut shies, bishops in full fig telling fortunes, military bands playing the *Marseillaise* and the *Internationale*. It took a strategist of John Major's peculiar genius to announce that he was "resigning" just as the English rugby team lost to France for the first time in years, and with a performance so lacking in life and ambition that it could have come straight out of Jeremy Hanley's office. (I bet Rob Andrew and the boys all vote Tory. The ones who are not ex-land surveyors, now guesting in the City, are on extended leave from the military or the police.) It was a defining moment when that subtitle rolled across the screen of the portable in the Soho offices of Koninck Films, where producer Keith Griffiths – sponsor of much that's been worth watching over the last decade: Keiller, Petit, the Brothers Quay – was explaining why nothing was happening in television, and never would again. (Then here it was, in front of him, a surprise.)

They must have switched off the degaussing equipment for the day, people got high just walking down the Victoria Embankment, knowing that the most sophisticated electorate in the world was progressing through a set of arcane and ancient (since the '70s) rituals that would leave everything precisely where it was now. In safe hands. It was a master stroke, a non-event that would engender a few weeks' excitement in the silly season. Properly handled, the election could become an annual do like Henley, Ascot, and the counter-demonstrations by Class War.

The river had been gilded. The public monuments, obelisks, bronzes, relief medallions of forgotten Victorians (let's hear it for Joseph

Bazalgette, the sewage visionary), came into their own. Were *visible*. River-gates that let out underground streams. They responded to the general amnesty with a proper sense of their symbolic role in the scheme of things: they positively hummed with electromagnetic benevolence. You could put your ear to a damaged sphinx and listen to the Nile. Atkins and I jaunted towards Westminster as if we had shares in the place.

We made straight for Downing Street or, rather, the iron gates that keep undesirables out of it. (Bizarrely, they lay down the red carpet for the most worthless category of all: giving a warm welcome to the press, the snappers with their priapic lenses, Murdoch's jackals. Walk past the gate with one of those dinky sets of aluminium steps and they'll forcibly drag you inside. Why do they bother with these leather-blouson'd dwarfs when they could hire out Marc Atkins and save the cost of a pair of stilts?)

If they do wave you through it's probable that you're hefting an armful of flowers (celebration/requiem?), or wearing lycra and looking as if you've mislaid the *Tour de France*. Cyclists arrive at regular intervals, all carrying identical jiffy bags. Obviously, there aren't enough telephone lines: lines they can trust. A BT van is turned back at the gate. They've got paperwork, but not enough of it – the wrong signatures.

Our presence encourages the gradual formation of a crowd: if there are people looking at something, there must be something for them to look at. Euro tourists squash us against the ironwork. Germans gather around their leader who is holding aloft, as a recognisable standard, a rolled umbrella. You can watch it moving like Moses's staff away towards the Houses of Parliament. There's a schedule to respect, Downing Street only rates two minutes. Lens caps off! And on again! March!

Even government cars (cleaned every morning) are thoroughly inspected before they're waved through. And that's just the start of it: a metal barrier rises alarmingly from the ground and a functionary in overalls rushes out of a security hut to poke a mirror under all the hidden parts. The first of these is a very nifty woman who scoots around the vehicle on her hands and knees at a Grand Prix pit-stop speed.

The routine of these comings and goings – "bodies" with their plastic carrier bags, inelegant shoes, fielders of phone-calls, moppers of floors – is not deemed worthy of notice by the hubbub of cameramen. They share a single point-of-view, fixated on the closed door of Number 10. Sometimes a policeman emerges and there's a small shudder of excitement. He takes a few steps, then freezes, and never moves again. Are the photographers *allowed* to shift, try a different shot? Or is there a conspiracy to pretend that Downing Street is an immortal set, located nowhere in particular (like the Tardis), unconnected to the Cabinet Office and Whitehall? The door is exactly where it was when Thatcher was driven off in tears and when that prescient child, Harold Wilson, posed for his first photo opportunity. (Lately, the weather playing along, John Major has taken to using the back garden to create the illusion of a presidential style. No room for helicopters to swoop down. Barely enough for a game of French cricket. The "new" Cabinet would be paraded there when this business was all over, awkwardly hanging on to their tea cups while Deputy Leader Heseltine plunged purposefully towards them with that mad gleam in his eye.)

Everybody is having a good time. They know it's a fix. The best stroke Major has ever been advised to make. He can't lose. He's turned the game around by the simple act of forcing his opponents to reveal themselves: a genuinely scary gaggle of aliens in outlandish suits. (The hot spell has found them out, as they parade for the cameras in outfits that have the broadsheet essayists arguing over science fiction metaphors. Major, the retired geek, can chortle with the rest as his rival, John Redwood, is brought back from banishment – Wales – to have his Vulcan ancestry confirmed.)

Reluctantly, we move on. It's mesmerising standing here, and quite soothing in real-time boredom. It's like watching a 24-hour surveillance film. Any movement in the frame, after such epic foreplay, is a tidal orgasm for the senses. But we have to fake at being reporters: take on the shape of how the day develops, sketch in the lightning cameos, eavesdrop on other men's interviews. List all the correct ages.

A chunky minder-type TV journo in quality threads saunters down Whitehall towards the House. Head like a medicine ball. A brutally anachronistic moustache. This must be what they call a political heavyweight, a face. I even know the name, John Pienaar. He does the interviews on College Green. And possibly some bouncing on the side. We trail him, slipstream his wake as – hands in pockets – he gossips with the competition.

College Green, a threadbare rug of turf, has already been marked out by rival TV crews. Tripod encampments and wholly unnecessary boosts of cold, white light. Again, this is the only shot you ever see: the dead bone-coral of the Houses of Parliament like the label on a brown sauce bottle. And some sweating suit offering up his formulaic prescription.

The plinth of Henry Moore's *Two Knife/Edged Bronze* comes into its own as somewhere useful to stack camera equipment. It's the accepted smoking room for the greyheads who have seen it all before. Not a yard of grass that isn't claimed, but none of the politicos, even the most desperate publicity hogs, have breezed out. Ten-to-ten on the clock, another warm day, and nothing to shoot.

Atkins is mistaken for a mini-cabber on the Shepherd's Bush run and almost pressganged into doing a vox pop. If we'd hung around much longer we'd have been number-crunching for ITN, trying to put some bite into dull statistics. A neat Latin gent – immaculate from the waist up, jeans below – was rattling away in Spanish to a camera set so high on its pins that the operator, a Sanchez Vicario lookalike in baggy white shorts, had to stand on tiptoe. (Sandals and painted toenails.) The prize for performance art (Atkins got a shot of this) went to the striped tie who was, with pantomimed gravity, interviewing himself. (Could this be the notably strange Peter Bottomley?) A virtuoso routine that involved balancing his Sharp in one hand, while nodding vigorously to an interrogator who wasn't there, cutting himself off with the one-liners the rest of us think up on the bus home.

It's building nicely but it's not happening yet. The voices are pacing themselves. Opinions are hedged. None of the serious players will stick their heads over the parapet until they can go live, nationwide. We wander off into those shady, private streets that converge on Smith Square and Conservative Central Office. Here is discretion you can taste, invaded by OB vans and monster aerials that allow you to hear Jeffrey Archer sneeze. Even the blue plaques fit with the general colour coding: TE Lawrence and Lord Reith. Period survivals and basement areas with wartime notices intact. The whole web is an extension of government, a collegiate network of passages and stone-flagged paths and dusty doorways that link the Abbey, the public school and the leafy rooms where deals are done.

This is where Michael Portillo blew it (or was blown), setting up his campaign HQ in Lord North Street – before he joined battle. Photographers happening along to catch BT running in the extra phonelines. And this is also where John Major's re-election team operated, without fuss from No. 13 Cowley Street. A bright blue door with polished brass knocker.

A lesser squad of photographic layabouts took their chairs onto the pavement and prepared to wait. They could pick any angle they wanted, but they still stuck together like a flock of gulls. They had time and space to spread themselves, read the *Sun*, send out for coffee and sandwiches.

(It was later in the day, on our second or third run, that a complimentary car let out this silver-haired gimp with a stick at the end of the street. A person of influence, obviously – and unhappy at being caught in the neighbourhood. He bellowed at Atkins: "Don't you fellows have anything better to do? You're not going to get a story sitting on your backsides here." The checkered lightweight suit, the discreet motor, the proximity of Lord Reith's plaque made me think of Marmaduke Hussey. But that would be to fabricate all sorts of illegitimate webs of conspiracy. Or, more probably, pure coincidence.)

We headed back, ambling with the schoolboys on their break, into the dappled Abbey cloisters and through to the garden – where a marquee was being erected, tables and chairs carried out. You'd never know, but just over the ivy-covered wall from the madness of College Green is this enclosed sanctuary, with its meadowbank of wild flowers, buttercups, daisies, forget-me-nots, a dense quilt of colour: the paradise of the Assassins. Right down to the circular fountain in its mandalic courtyard. An exemption for which you drop a few coins into a box.

The lift to the Abbey roof costs much more, but for a wad of cash they throw in a hard hat. And the view is worth the price. 11.45 am on Big Ben and it's hotting up below. Crowds foam and break, disperse and form again as the next taxi arrives. Soundmen with their furry scythes surround the unlikeliest suspects in a carwash lynch mob. Ready to polish them to death. From our Hitchcockian perspective all this termite activity is grotesque and meaningless. We see, behind the plaster decorations of the great church, the rods that stop these white stone bosses crashing down on to the mob.

Michael Portillo's advent throws the pack into a feeding frenzy. He's the first of the frontline players to make a move. His Morse-red Jaguar saloon brings the traffic to a standstill by backing out, U-turning, to position itself in a favourable light. The minister, making the most of his last day, before being shafted with Bosnian visiting rights, milks the pack. The demented urge to get something on film. He goes for it and in a choreographed improvisation . . . *takes off his jacket*. Slips into a yellow sweater which – we subsequently discover – is blocked with the Imperial Cancer Fund logo. The buttery yellow plays beautifully against the scarlet car. Portillo hops onto the bonnet one beat ahead of the universal request from the photographers that he should. (Cynics might wonder if he was putting out the most effective signals: yellow, cancer, topped by that vulpine grin.)

They wouldn't let him go. Dennis Skinner, who had been hovering all day in salt and pepper tweed, flicking back his hair and offering his repertoire of unreconstructed socialist grunts, was upstaged. But it's not often you get to watch a suicide dance, the manic tarantella of a career vanishing down the tubes in fancy-dress.

I hustled Marc down the stairs and across the road to within a few yards of that unforgiving leer. Portillo's cheeks were pregnant with stretchmarks of forced laughter, but still he rapped at all the female interviewers in their little suits: as if promising them, personally, a big bad bite. The cameras and the furry sticks followed him to his car – imploring cries of "Mr Portillo, Michael, over here" – manoeuvring us back in the direction of College Green.

I'm sure that, at last, we'll run across Lord Archer. He has to be on duty, cracking the whip, putting himself about. It's the kind of day that's made for his special talents. And, sure enough, there he is, back to the Jewel Tower, hands clasped across his wedding- tackle – serious but perky – barking clipped statements straight at the camera. A pro at work. He doesn't require a feed, just switch the red light on and step out of range. "It's behind us now. We have only one choice. We *like* government."

This is not Lady Thatcher's royal "we", this is more clubbable. Party first. The insider formulating what shakier brethren are too slack to grasp. It's a boardroom "we", a blatant busk for office. Archer dresses well. He's got too many suits to be taken seriously. And they look as if he bought them, had them made to measure. They haven't been adequately distressed: not to a Cabinet level, tortured in and out of cars, up and down stairs, through long afternoon sessions. They are too deep a blue, too smoothly cut. In the flesh he's got the slightly caramelised appearance of those who can take holidays whenever they want them. Half a stone too comfortable, but fit, brisk, sun-ripened: dangerously alert. He finishes the first interview and moves seamlessly into the next. Is rewired. The peak of thin hair that has spilled down across his forehead is tidied away. His nose, in profile, is a formidable instrument, which seems to have been fitted on the wrong way around. The conk of a power-truffler. His thick sandy eyebrows are unusual to a degree that doesn't come over in photographs. Frowning against the sun, they mask his eyes. Close to, Archer is unreal, a manufactured effect, like the posters representing Anthony Hopkins as Nixon. His defects have been artfully husbanded to an extent rarely achieved on this side of the Atlantic. There's no question that in the USA he'd be a candidate.

"It's a good day. A victorious day. The markets will bounce back. The real enemy are the socialists." He speaks. Like. That. In soundbites that can be effortlessly edited. It's sad to think that, as with Portillo, this is surely his final stand. (The last of many.) He's got more spring than a squash-ball. To say nothing of wealth and property and wife. But he's too human, too much of a risk. He's just a little *too* eager to confront the press, tough it out. No android: when they cut the cameras and pull the plug from his ear, his light doesn't go off. He marches away, regularly pounced on by civilians, book buyers – and each of them gets the firm handshake and the upbeat message. "Major: good. Socialists: bad. Hold your nerve. It's a wonderful world." One of nature's redcoats.

I can't let this opportunity pass. It rounds my essay off so neatly. I wait my turn and grab his hand. He's discommoded for an instant: it shows in the eyes. We're too scruffy, too road crazy – even for press vermin. We carry a mephitic cloud. At a signing session we'd be recognised as trouble and ejected. He steps back. But there's no escape. Atkins has his camera lofted.

I explain who I am, the relationship with the lady who backed my application to view the penthouse. He gets confused, thinks I'm claiming to be her brother. "You can't be," he growls. "A terrible looking fellow like you couldn't have such a beautiful sister." I return some tribute in a similar vein. Which he takes in good part, a roar of sales rep laughter and away, at speed. As I mutter our thanks. But he's gone even before Atkins can give him a card.

That seems to cover it. Marc is convinced that luck is running with us. We can't miss. Go anywhere and the doors open, the faces we need appear as if by magic. He feels we ought to route our return to take in Duncan Terrace in Islington, where "Mad" Frankie Fraser is reputed to exercise his pooch in a small park.

We make the detour. And our luck does hold. There's not a sign of Frank. When I arrive unscathed in my kitchen and put on the TV to catch the result, there is Archer, lit like the National Gallery, parroting the same soundbites. "The real enemy are the socialists. The markets will bounce back. I am happy to serve."

The episode is closed – until, three of four days later, when a fiercely crushed envelope drops onto my mat. It's the remnant of one of the riverscapes that Atkins left at Alembic House as a gift for Lord Archer. It had been packed in a plain brown rectangle with no backing, and now depicted a Lambeth subjected to a Ludwig Meidner apocalypse. The bridges were folded and split, and the Houses of Parliament creased with shadows of coming doom.

There was a letter.

The Lord Archer of Weston-super-Mare
House of Lords

5th July 1995

Dear Mr Sinclair.
Many thanks for your letter of 3rd July and for enclosing the photograph. I fear that I have several paintings and photos of similar views and I am therefore returning Marc Atkins photograph.

It was very kind of you to think of me.

With best wishes.

Yours sincerely

Jeffrey Archer

Please reply to: Alembic House, 93 Albert Embankment,
London SE1 7TY

HOUSE IN THE PARK

This park belongs to the people of East London, if you harm it, you harm them.
Bow Neighbourhood signboard

"What did *your* street look like in the past?" One of the more seductive ephemerals of the heritage industry is the Godfrey Edition of Old Ordnance Survey Maps: a largely Victorian patchwork intended for those "who wish to explore London and its history". Canny merchandising that is fit to set alongside the repair and enlargement – in sepia – of retrieved family photographs (not necessarily your own family). I noticed a shop that specialises in this trade in Vallance Road: the acquisition of a fraudulent pedigree, the hard evidence of a past that never existed. Why not extend the tactic to the city and its spurious divisions? Why not exploit and redevelop properties that are in the public domain, vanished streets, lost rivers? Old maps, with all their fictions intact, are lying around like so much out-of-copyright nineteenth-century literature.

The neatly-folded scarlet reproduction featuring Bethnal Green & Bow (1894) uses, for its cover illustration, a postcard of the Royal Hotel, Grove Road. Which struck me as a slightly odd choice given that the pub is now adjudged to be in South Hackney, and barely ducks under the cut-off line at the top of the map. The district on display, when the document is smoothed out and spread across a table, is a black and white jigsaw of impacted terraces, burial grounds, canals, railways. It is seriously lacking in photographed structures with the required gravitas, sentimental triggers to recall the moment of Imperial glory. The chosen image is like a single frame of film, about to flicker into life; to bring back the stroller in the straw boater, the horsedrawn cart with its beer barrels. The triumph of nostalgia is completed by the inclusion of a functioning public convenience (Gentlemen only), the kind now converted into subterranean wine bars or sun-bed tanning chambers (on Rosebery Avenue).

It must delight the Parks and Amenities Committee of the Tower Hamlets Council to know that the Royal Hotel survives, freshly painted, draped in flower baskets, bright with petunias, keyed to the dark blue and gold colour scheme that makes a run down the strip towards docklands like a pan across a packet of upmarket cigarettes. Railings, ironwork gates with lilies and crowns, litter bins, plaques with heritage trail antiquarian word-bites: they all conform to a sense of urban revival, a retro future. There are so many of these plaques, so much loose history lying about, that Victoria Park seems to have been parcelled off by estate agents. This plague of information, on lavish boards at each entrance, mixes self-serving political rhetoric with pious revisionism: we are informed that the park "suffered from underinvestment and remote management" at the hands of the GLC and the LCC. A multi-million pound restoration programme initiated by Bow Neighbourhood – and funded by a list of private sector benefactors and Euro charities – made this a fit location in which to parade that most precious of icons, Elizabeth the Queen Mother, on her ninetieth birthday. A photo opportunity that linked the triumphalism of the restored park (its fountains and sleeping policemen) with newsreel footage of the old dame's previous East London excursion at the time of the Blitz. Wartime dereliction was smoothly twinned with the blight of postwar socialist planning. All that remained, if they had the nerve for it, was to rename these lush enclosures. No more talk of "green lungs", people's parks: why not go for it, the Royal Elizabeth? Wasn't there already a powerful association between the Queen Mother and the commissioning of gates?

Cruder boards warn the public that "guard dogs are in use" and that these "premises" are protected by Armour Security with their manned "24 hour control room". Grove Road is therefore secure; an avenue of hanging baskets, pristine pavements from which poodle-squirt is regularly hosed. The park is fenced off, secure, a leaf-roofed marquee, safe for the exercise of police horses, the exhibition of restored public statuary – such as the titular *Dogs of Alcibiades*. (Horrors, such as the trash alp aftermath of the Gay & Lesbian Pride Festival, when the park was "left littered with paper, cans, bottles and used condoms", were a future nightmare. 150,000 shirtlifters and muff-divers pissing on the carpet. **MUCKY DEVILS!** screamed the *East London Advertiser*, digging out the usual pix of Sir Ian McKellen, Lily Savage and "Ex-*EastEnders* star" Michael Cashman. Let the hordes in and this is what you get. "There were Durexes everywhere and my dog cut his paw." Councillor Kevin Morton, Chairman of Bow and Poplar Area, remarked, more in sorrow than in anger, that "The Pride Trust have queered their pitch somewhat.")

Every artefact within the kidney outline of the park must align itself with the gonzo concept of the "Bow Heritage Trail". This is not a path that can actually be walked, it's a metaphor, a conceit, meandering aimlessly from dog plinths to the Top o' the Morning public-house, with its gloating celebration of the first railway murder. Schizogeography at its ripest: crime, charity follies, eco fundamentalism, and bent ley lines that exist only to assert some deranged territorial piracy.

East End boozers have always been game to follow the market, adopting extreme measures to keep their names in the guidebooks: think of the Blind Beggar on Whitechapel Road, forced to install a conservatory, shift its ambiance from the Brothers Kray to the Brothers Roux. Early afternoons are a babble of suit-talk, punctuated by the crash of dropped names, as the art strategists chain up their bicycles and rush in to claim the seats of departing motor-traders. I've drunk away more failed projects (films of *Radon Daughters*, books of Marc Atkins photographs) under the restored George Cornell bullet holes than anywhere else in London.

Even the Royal Hotel managed to catch the wave and make it into Duncan Campbell's *The Underworld* (1994). A hitman – "6 foot tall . . . wearing a leather jacket" – having parked a stolen Ford Fiesta on the spot where the Victorian urinal used to stand, took advantage of the balmy summer evening, the open doors, the stroll-through layout; he ordered a pint of Foster's (a good choice not to drink) and ambled over to the table where "Big Jim" Moody, a face who went all the way back to the affray at Mr Smith's in Catford, was nursing his contemplative beer. Moody, a friend of the late lamented Cornell, had been on the run since burrowing out of Brixton in 1980. Both men, off their own turf, were destined to become markers on licensed premises, blue plaque victims. Famous for dying.

Moody, a keep-fit "fanatic", found Victoria Park as useful as Reggie Kray once had. The grass circuit, with its culture of sweat and repetition, evolved its own electrical pulse: a loop of focused self-love, discipline, meditated acts of violence. Thought forms to infect the unwary. A relaxed urgency of lycra, martial arts rehearsals, flying drop-kicks under the plane trees. Moody converted these spiritual exercises into a cult of invisibility. He was so much *there*, so much a part of the location, that he couldn't be seen. He existed only in rumour: webbed up with the Thursday Mob, stitching a gash in his arm that went to the bone with needle and thread, carrying out drug assassinations in South London.

Anyone who came into contact with him had to obey the rules, make a maze of every journey; double back, wipe footsteps, confound surveillance teams. Moody's son, Jason, speaks of stretching time, extending distance, "making U-turns" to throw off the Watchers. The mystification had the opposite effect: it made the tedium of pursuit interesting. The whole family was grafted to trained shadows. Moody was free, living openly in the limbo of Hackney: neither alive nor dead. Unregistered.

The malign tourist who stood over him that June night in the Royal Hotel was a kind of double, a fetch. Moody had grown careless, let his concentration relax to the point where a crueller version of his spite could step forth. He had conjured up a spectre to conduct an indissoluble marriage with place. There was no resistance, no instant of foreknowledge. The faceless unknown pulled out a Webley .38 and shot his target four times in the chest at point blank range. Four wounds. Gates in the park. The 1894 postcard has been tainted by this drama, crimson seeps into the border – like an apocalyptic sky, the city on fire. Hurt *can* be retrospective. Furious displacements of energy are capable of damaging the membrane of what we call "the past". The past is an optional landscape. We are gifted with unearned memories, memories on which we have no moral purchase.

It is tempting for the stalker striking south towards Roman Road to block out the civic tidiness of Victoria Park by invoking the spirit of William Blake, the godfather of all psychogeographers: "thro' Hackney . . . towards London/Till he came to old Stratford, & thence to Stepney & the Isle/Of Leutha's Dogs . . . And saw every minute particular: the jewels of Albion running down/The kennels of the streets & lanes as if they were abhorr'd." The Hertford Union Canal, itself a failed speculation, is banked by the gutted shells of "various mills and manufactories", waiting for investment to catch up with imagination. Developers have to hone their psychic powers, look into the future, envision regenerated husks, industrial ruin carved into the optimum number of units. Evocative names cancel brick dust. The right quarter-page photograph in the property section of the *Standard* projects a bucolic idyll in place of dank waters, gasometers, feral dog packs.

Take the effort (March 1995) on behalf of Empire Wharf, E3. "A lazy afternoon in the park, a short walk along the canal to Lock House Gate and over the bridge into beautiful Victoria Park. When you live at Empire Wharf you live in Zone two, its (*sic*) difficult to believe its (*sic*) only a couple of miles from the City." *Sic*: it's difficult to believe that "Zone two" punters still exist, couples likely to be excited by this brand of lazy Impressionism. The promoters of these canalside complexes have to be scryers capable of seeing – and making others see – a credible tomorrow. In other words, they have usurped the role of the artist. The models sprawled under a tree in Victoria Park, the reinvented bandstand behind them, are looking at the property pages . . . and laughing. Dappled shadows, big hair: the promise of a Renoiresque lifestyle, perpetual access to the park. You don't sell property by showing pictures of houses. You sell space, greenery, summer. And one bedroom, somewhere in the general vicinity: "from" £54,995.

The scavengers follow the predatory instincts of the sculptors who have already surveyed the ground, every underused loft and bunker. Developers become the poets of trespass. They are like possessed shamans. They "see" white gymnasium temples where the rest of us, pedants picking over our heritage maps, find nothing but serrulated blocks of poverty housing, dull grey coral packing the space between the Hertford Union Canal (to the north), the Regent's Canal (to the west), the Great Eastern Railway (to the south), the North London Railway (to the east). We are stuck with an island of exile known as Old Ford or St Mary Stratford (the "old Stratford" of Blake). A biopsy of Bow reveals an absence of breathing space, a mad tangle of termite ladders pitched hither and thither at the whim of industry. The canals and railways, carrying passengers through this picaresque desolation, also acted as barriers to keep the indigenous population caged. They reversed their supposed function, snuffing out all fantasies of escape.

The Tower Hamlets planners, to give them their due, were closet visionaries: they conceived the transcendent notion of a Green Corridor, connecting all the broken patches of grass between Victoria Park and the Isle of Dogs – a vegetal strip running parallel to the line of zero longitude. They would decant parkland and use it as an excuse to sweep away all the unsightly clusters of temporary housing. Grass, the spread of it, the lush green emptiness of a deserted pool hall, is what they wanted to celebrate. Over-cropped and over-fertilised paddocks. A fenced and locked chain of canine reservations laid out to the horizon. A corridor that it was impossible to walk without irritating expulsions into the road, the rage runs of local traffic. Rate payers rarely bothered to make the attempt. These small enclosures – more than a back garden, less than a park – were left as monuments to their innate surrealism. They were out of sympathy with the rest of the borough, shadow museums, earthed-over streets that always threatened to break through their provisional covering.

Wennington Green is the most northerly of these sanctioned gestures at the pastoral. Neighbourhood politicians have disguised the Joseph Beuys-like lyricism of their modest proposal by talking up the environmental benefits. Councillor Eric Flounders of the Liberal Democrats, unconsciously echoing Le Corbusier, asserted that "what people who live in tower blocks want is parkland". An Arcadia for the underclass (who in reality have a profound distaste for grass, and who are allowed inside the Royal Parks on sufferance to cheer the latest jubilee, or banished with their rods and maggots to the canalbank). The parkettes of the Green Chain have been close shaved, barbered to within an inch of their lives. Wood carvings and eccentric pathways represent a punt at a municipal version of Capability Brown. Arbours have been created, in which lurk strange men and stranger dogs. Rustic camouflage for exiled drinking schools. Hillocks for meths-crazed hermits. We need the downland monologist, Patrick Wright, to stride through, weighing up a landscape that is fit only for tanks or a rhapsody of Powyses. This is what's left of that Dorset dream, the old green roads of England. This is where authoritarian race fantasies strike their treaty with classicism. Wennington Green demands its own maker/priest, its Ian Hamilton Finlay. The planners conceived it in a rare and disinterested flight of fancy: a mental landscape for a culture of compulsory leisure. An enclosure in which care-in-the-community waifs can safely spasm and foam. It was an historical inevitability that Wennington Green, with its last sorry huddle of housing, should be chosen as the location for Rachel Whiteread's spectacular experiment in cryogenics.

The only entry to Wennington Green on the north side is the inevitable gap in the railings created by fishermen wanting a shortcut to the canal. Squeeze through and the immediate impression is troubling: avenues of sycamores trace the fault line where the back gardens of the former Grove Road terrace give way to tolerated wilderness. Negotiating moist casts of dog dirt, flung by the rotation of tractor-drawn "triples", you approach the badly fitted carpet of replacement turf that delineates the ground where Whiteread's *House* once stood. Wennington Green is otherwise a graveyard without any of the usual prompts, the slabs and angels that record the names and dates of those who solicit remembrance. All the specific visual clues that provoke memory have been deleted. This is a meadow of voluntary amnesia.

It was prescient of Whiteread, after months of careful searches through housing lists, and a collaboration with James Lingwood of Artangel, to arrive at the one site where her project – "a mute memorial to everyday existence and the pathos of remembering" – would fuse all the loose wires of potential catastrophe. The whole affair seems to have occurred with a dreamlike logic: obstacles were overcome, implications were ignored. Whiteread drove forward with the courage of a sleepwalker. *House*, seen from across the field, was a giant bone plug feeding current into the madness of the city. Feeding and receiving.

Grove Road had the lot: an end of terrace house with three exploitable sides (and a sitting tenant), a hyperactive local politico willing to play the heavy (Bob Hoskins as UK casting, Danny DeVito in the US), anarchist squatters, post-Situationist music business trouble-makers looking for the grand gesture, and peg-eyed pyschogeographers prophesying war. This terrace was in the wrong documentary. It was blatantly touting for millennial funds. It stood as an affront to the radiant blankness of the Green Way, an all too human shambles. High art had to be capable of making the transition, erasing the tape. The "old sweat" intransigence of the last inhabitant, Sydney Gale (as he was known to the broadsheets), or "Sid the War Hero" (to the tabloids), was the only thing keeping the ruin upright. 193 Grove Road belonged, through right of long occupation, to Mr Gale and his family. The ex-docker had nothing else to feel so bloody-minded about, to exercise his hereditary prerogative for cussedness. Even his surname seemed to allude, punningly, to the night of the Great Storm, the 16th of October 1987: a natural drama hijacked by the Parks Committee. The storm, with its tangled avenues of uprooted trees, was the perfect front for a strategic refurbishment, the sequestration of the Victoria Park Lido – as a car park (with no direct access to the grassland). Mr Gale became the incarnation of the wind, a self-generating hurricane of grievance. He was even ready to busk as a performance artist, to display his hand-painted banner: THIS IS MY HOME, I LIVE HERE. A tautology that was all too soon to be confounded.

Up to this point, before the work on *House* began, Artangel and the LibDem caucus, and even Mr Gale, held to their uneasy alliance. Contracts were drawn up. Mr Gale would be rehoused and Whiteread, no stranger to the area, would move in her team – forensically wrapped and masked – to commence the process of mummification. Whiteread's earlier Turner Prize contender, *Ghost*, had been exhibited at the nearby

Chisenhale Gallery, a traditional (ex-industrial) East London art space. The Chisenhale specialised in emptiness, absence: mediated gestures in a culture vacuum. Fetish objects possessing *just* enough presence to keep out the smell of the veneer factory, the echoing voices of the women who turned out Spitfire propellers. Vacuity is what these transitional structures promote: mind art. "Mute pathos" is their shtick. They set-dress minimalism, make it feel good: the least disturbed, the most effective.

Ghost, encountered unexpectedly (in company with Patrick Wright, backing away from the trash destined as a sculptural rinse for the Bow Quarter), was a revelation. Literally so: the cube of retrieved and imprisoned light illuminated the windowless gallery. The relationship between sculpture and containing space was dynamic. The piece did not dominate (or deny) the history of the chamber to which it had been brought. A lengthy period of solitary labour in the original Archway room, casting and reversing, had resulted in this mysterious monobloc: this icy and unforgiving depiction of the unconscious. *Ghost* outranked pathos, it was much crueller and brighter than that. The allusions are to Egyptian and Assyrian plunder in the British Museum, to the whiteness of an idealised past, not to the sentimentality of false memory, colonised domestic enclosures. The Archway room was not called upon to surrender the shades and movements of the lives it had witnessed: it was elevated to an archetype, demotic overwhelmed by hieratic. Whiteread's art was profoundly female, not feminist, responsive and shaping – purposefully limited, open to a biological flow of time. Set outside in a sculpture park, a corporate watercourt, the venom of *Ghost* would be dissipated. It would be as ineffective as one of those "period" rooms you can yawn through in the Geffrye Museum.

House, a few hundred yards to the west of the Chisenhale Gallery, exposed to the spasms of passing traffic, was a much trickier proposition. Whiteread, innocent of irony, remarks (in her video diary) on how surprised she was to discover that the park would not be secure: "I hadn't realised the gates would be open the whole time." She will be constantly under observation. The prolonged and silent hermeticism of the Archway room will not be possible. *House* from its conception was under sentence of death. It would never (except for the computer mock-up at the Tate) be brought inside. The entire process of conversion would be as visible as an act of public surgery, a virtuoso amputation. A bride stripped bare by her bachelors. *House* was front-lawn art, a sponsored bastard. The stakes were high enough to alert every demon in the dictionary: vampire aesthetes, strollers and stalkers, all those factions prepared to underwrite any challenge on the torpid energy balance of the Green Corridor. A freakish alliance of extremes. Come in the K Foundation, Brian Sewell, Stewart Home, Councillor Eric Flounders. Come in Class War, the BNP, and the M11 protest lobby.

After 92 searches through dusty housing records, Artangel and the Whiteread team were fortunate to nominate a vagrant terrace under the "protection" of a sensationally contrary LibDem cadre. A wild bunch quite capable of trashing the user-friendly rhetoric of upriver spin-doctors. Grove Road fell within the influence of an embattled cell of activists who, by brazenly championing the "local", could promote their own notion of village values in a horizon-to-horizon panorama of urban meltdown. Covert racism ("We have produced leaflets with Scotsmen in kilts"), boastful philistinism, immaculate streets: that would be the unspoken manifesto. The slashing of the Arts budget (curtains for the Half-Moon Theatre) was therefore twinned with the conceptual reinvention of this rubble of abandoned terraces as a Neo-Georgian park. It wasn't that the ward bosses disliked art, as such. No, they were themselves artists *manqués*, card-carrying opponents of the Europhile modernist conspiracy. Under this straw-sucking regime the Bow Neighbourhood became a reservation of Laura Ashley pieties, a wedge of streets lacking a centre, but blessed with pavements from which you could lick your dinner. The real achievement of Artangel was political: the drawing up of the contract for *House*, the acceptable parameters of toleration, while the most effective spokesperson for a philosophy of enlightened prejudice was out of the country.

Councillor Flounders returned to the *fait accompli* like a bismuth Cromwell, fizzing with spite. It wasn't just the name, Eric was a nautical troubleshooter by profession. It was his fate to spread bullshit on troubled waters. He had another life as a theatrically drab PR man for Cunard. The perfect choice to puff the *Titanic*, or explain away that disastrous Christmas cruise to the Caribbean; he had an exquisitely honed instinct for disaster. Flounders was an experienced news manager who "hit the headlines in the *East London Advertiser* when he announced he was gay". Quite why he needed to tout his sexual preference is unclear. Perhaps an orthodox career move for a fading thespian would prove a vote-catcher among the incoming pink community. Bow, if Flounders got his way, would redefine itself as a satellite of Bath. But it would take something more exotic than regular bulletins on his gender orientation

213

to keep him in the limelight: the Whiteread *House*, that postmodern Rubik cube, was a once in a lifetime opportunity, a media event not to be squandered.

Exposed as a cultural Luddite and political bother boy by a half-page spread in the *Guardian* (enough to resurrect humbler careers), the cornered demagogue's seal-cub eyes visibly moisten behind lifebelt-sized spectacles. His portrait threatens to reduce newspaper to soggy pulp. A plum-fuzz tonsure gives definition to a troubled head, which would otherwise be as shapeless as blancmange poured into a surgical stocking. He hunches his shoulders, trying to hide himself in a Methodist overcoat. His one gesture of decoration, an abbreviated moustache, invokes Peter Sellers (in Fred Kite mode) impersonating Peter Ackroyd.

House was a chance for Flounders to address a wider audience – to defend the eviction of 100 Bangadeshi families, badmouth Hampstead lefties, and tell art scum sniffling for alms to "fuck off".

In other words, Eric was a down-the-line traditionalist, quickstepping on the grave of blue collar concepts that been laid to rest twenty years ago. But you couldn't help admiring his bottle: the way he resisted the party apparatchiks, the vigour with which he notched up a record number of LibDem own goals – in the certain knowledge that he was never going to get to Westminster, that he was pissing his future straight into the river. Flounders, despite the ridicule of the trendies, stayed true to the spirit of *Passport to Pimlico*. *House* was still "crap". "The more people who want it to stay there," he told the faithful *Advertiser*, "the more resolute I become."

2.

Avant-bardists declare the letter "e" to be particularly contemptible.
STEWART HOME

Sorry, Councillor, but "Ric" Flounders sounds even more preposterous. It's just that when questions of aesthetics are debated, the most unlikely figures find themselves in agreement. "Crap." "Junk." "Moronic." The disaffiliated (or over-affiliated) class warriors who squatted 199 Grove Road were primed to take a special interest in an increasingly volatile situation.

One of those who lived (in the mid-eighties) a few doors from the future *House* was the self-confessed "representative of the avant-garde",

'Pride of London'. Found object from Kingsland Waste, E8
SKATING ON THIN EYES

Split head, Chingford Mount
THE DOG & THE DISH

Aidan Dun
X MARKS THE SPOT

Figure from Vauxhall Bridge
LORD ARCHER'S PROSPECTS

Howard Marks rolling-up outside MI6
LORD ARCHER'S PROSPECTS

Gavin Jones
THE SHAMANISM OF INTENT

Angel-tree, Kensal Rise
THE CADAVER CLUB

Clifftop celebration, Maryon Park
THE CADAVER CLUB

Stewart Home. Home is too modest: by 1995 he was essentially the *only* (unelected) representative of the avant-garde left. The others had drained away into utter obscurity or been forced to perform on request by the advertising/media/gallery/ fashion nexus. Home had his outlets. He was the Beaverbrook of the counter-culture: *Smile*, T*he London Psychogeographical Association Newsletter*, *Neoist Alliance* flyers, multiple identity black propaganda, squibs planted in the press, samizdat leaflets shot through significant letterboxes by the bicycling author. The man existed in a rush of paranoid, Masonic conspiracy excavations: the problem was finding new locations in which to have himself photographed. Home sustained a programme that would have exhausted a less committed self-publicist: readings, lectures, club performances, essays, postal art, videos, expositions of historical avant-garde tendencies, creative plagiarism, denunciations, feuds, schisms, occult investigations, postpulp novels, demolitions of those innocent mainstreamers who were getting more attention than he was.

It was a racing certainty that Whiteread's trespass on Home's territory, and the fuss it generated, would be countered by a raft of anathemas. "The Avant-garde and Fictional Excess" was a "talk" delivered at Trinity College, Cambridge, in the same week that Whiteread received the Turner Prize. "About a year before Whiteread began making her casts, I satirised the art world in a story called "Straight" . . . At the beginning of this year, I wrote a novel partially set in the terraced row of which *House* was once a part. I wasn't interested in universalising the situation I'd encountered there . . . I wanted to trade in specifics. The response from most of those in the book trade was astounding. The book, *Red London*, was considered too original to be published."

Stalking the city at Home's speed (Poplar to Stepney to Whitechapel to Camden to Hackney to Westminster to Greenwich to Hackney to Whitechapel to the Elephant to Southwark to Poplar) gifts the schizocyclist with prophetic infallibility. His fictions become the most reasonable approximations of the truth. Misheard asides mature to fullblown rumours. Pub whispers infiltrate gossip columns, feed back to the Secret State controllers. Impossible to say who funds Home, who has invented him. If he exists or if he is a regiment of clones and imitators. On my walks with Atkins we usually crossed paths, two or three times, with the overheated provocateur. He always palmed us a fresh leaflet.

So it's not surprising that *Red London* successfully analyses and deconstructs the background to the *House* scenario several months *before* Whiteread's initial conversations with Artangel. Home's anarchist fringe readers, unaware that they were supposed to be a figment of the author's heroically rancid imagination, were alerted to exploit this rare example of public art dumped on their doorstep by outside forces that knew nothing of their existence. (Publishers called for Home's work only to compete with each other in the composition of the most dismissive rejection letters. "Next door neighbour to Strasserism", said Neil Belton.)

The culture guerrillas, sex criminals, and entropic activists of *Red London*, would do anything to preserve the integrity of the pre-Whiteread terrace – short of actually living there. "Every Buddhist Octagon had offered to house in Grove Road turned down the accommodation." Home whizzing a wicked cocktail of disinformation, satire, score-settling, delivered a much more accurate survey of the psychic forces at play in Bow than any of the subsequent depth-researched reports of the telephone journalists from Canary Wharf. Every fictive excess would receive its subsequent justification. Written, it would happen. "The co-op was controlled by a secret committee of monks who'd been co-opted from the Teutonic Order of Buddhist Youth."

What was Home's background and how did he come to achieve such a grip on the Matter of London? He grew up on the southern fringes in Merton, then transplanted to Notting Hill (crucible of all the follies he was later to deride). As much an instinctive autodidact as that other notorious skinhead, the bibliomaniac Driffield, he was soon weeviling through bookstall fodder, from "skins" and "sorts" and bikers to the reforgotten illuminati of the Gothic, to *Black Mask*, *Up Against the Wall Motherfucker*, Dada, punk, Situationism, Lettrisme, autism, populism, surrealism – and any other "ism" that could be rapidly gutted and turned to advantage. The apprenticeship was over: "I ceased to be a Neoist and moved to Stoke Newington."

Hackney was the logical progression. Home managed a ten-year tour of duty and Hackney, in return, provided him with some of his ripest material. There were abundant squats, sturdy Victorian properties rotting into the swamps, unparalleled vistas of civic corruption, housing co-operatives scammed by Buddhist gangsters; beggars, winos, junkies and insecure hospital wards that would have given Otto Dix the shakes. Home had simply to open his windows and plug in his word processor. The books wrote themselves. They were anonymous, mediumistic, so rapidly produced that no single press could keep up with them. Other deranged *voyants* have equalled Home for pace, usually with the aid of performance-enhancing substances. Home had something better. Home had Hackney.

The art of the Thatcher/Major (bingo millennialist) era was, as Home recognised, the art of the proposal. The event or manifestation was usually no more than the excuse to break open a case of sponsored beer and indulge in postmortem documentation. We're talking audiences that could be counted on the hands of one of the X-ray martyrs. Audiences that were not sure if they'd witnessed a performance or blundered into a knocking-shop. Nobody remembers if they were there or if they simply read about it afterwards. An industry grew up for describing things that hadn't quite happened, epiphanies for empty rooms. Found objects, clippings of skin and hair, torn maps, cullings from pornographic magazines – the vagrant shamanism of the streets – were accepted, revered, as part of the defining strategy. Much of this activity, out on the eastern fringe, seems in retrospect to have been contrived for the promotion of the alien consciousness that is sometimes known as "Stewart Home". Think about that moniker and the picture forms: a Jacobite pretender, initiate of the Scottish Rite, the lefthand path. It's not for nothing that Home hides out on the Teviot Estate, or "Hither Scotland" as he calls it. The *LPA Newsletter* playfully suggests that the layout of the McIntosh estate at the entrance to the Blackwall Tunnel "obviously" represents the "dog head variant visible on stone 5 at Rhynie, Aberdeen".

South of Teviot the game gets darker, you're closing on Dog Island, that remnant overshadowed by the vanity of Canary Wharf: the end zone targeted by Derek Beackon and his lumpen followers in the BNP. This is where Home enters into a ludic contract with the demonology of the skinhead. Dangerous games: on the estate, he's been pelted with stones. The unsophisticated proles haven't managed to keep abreast of the latest recyclings from the Frankfurt School. If you skulk around in small-check Ben Shermans, slippery bomber jacket, Doc Martens, with a No. 1 crop glossing towards suedehead, then you *are* what you appear to be. They haven't grasped the niceties of role playing, gender jumping, street theatre. A wanker is a wanker. And he's soliciting a thoroughgoing, ironically anachronistic kicking.

Undiluted plagiarism not pastiche was Home's bag (in *Sight and Sound* they call it "selective quotation" or "homage"). Having toyed with the biker novelettes of Peter Cave, and the works of Mick Norman, Alex R. Stuart and Thom Ryder, he nominated the 18 volume Richard Allen *Bildungsroman* as his model. Delivered from any bourgeois neurosis about invention and inspiration (the demand for fresh "product"), he successfully took possession of the reactionary melancholy of

Allen's paperback originals. He subverted Allen's mechanistic cynicism with a parodic menu of hyper-violence and polymorphous perversity. The New English Library hack used his terse (never more than 50,000 words) fabulations as a vehicle for summarising all the excesses of tabloid horror: he fed on newsprint. He slashed into the fears of the moment, basting them with just enough narrative salt to link his petty fugues of urban mayhem. Boots and belts and randy slags. Allen was never more than a cod moralist, guiding his female victims towards relieving acts of sexual masochism: "the woman would be subjected to extremes of intercourse". The underlying programme was fascistic: having at the outset distanced himself from the furies he was arousing ("In the interests of sanity let no one be under the mistaken impression that the writer sympathises with anti-social behaviour, cultism or violence for the sake of violence"), he readily accepted the status that typing a "top ten" paperback conferred. His authority figures are remote but benevolent, doing it by the book, offering cups of tea to the cop-killing teenage psycho, Joe Hawkins. ("Seriously, though, I'd like to see what a dictator could do in this country. Slums wiped out, harsh measures to curb the grab-all boys, savage sentences for injury to persons, hanging for child rapists . . . the birch for young offenders like these skinheads.")

Stewart Home cannibalises the primitive energy of the genre, the page-turning punch, the deliberate absence of subtext: he subverts the impoverished form with tremors of perverse sexuality, he intercuts ritualistic orgasms with improving passages from Marx, Hobbes, Richard Jefferies – as antidotes to premature ejaculation. Home relishes the elements that more fastidious critics despise: "In my fiction, I use a technique known as the plot thins, what I'm saying is that I've adopted the easiest way of resolving what happens to my characters as a story progresses, which is to kill them off." He's in a fix of his own making: he's anti-language in a written medium. The intricate, layered sentences of a Martin Amis, with their sensuous conceits, their twists, their self-regarding cleverness, are clinker in Home's mouth. He aspires to works that are "conceptually, rather than verbally, overloaded." He trashes trash – to grant it a second life. He models his prose style on non-prose, tabloid journalism: that hybrid of pictograph and scored shriek. Speed is everything. The diminishing returns of serial buggery, coprophilia, mechanical masturbation, are spiced by rapturous passages read aloud from *Hartmann the Anarchist* – who strafes the Thames from his airborne dirigible.

Richard Allen, laureate of Plaistow (its most notable celebrant since

Luke Howard), struggled to bastardise the last croak of the London proletarian novel (which was no longer acceptable for publication). Former practitioners were now marginalised: Alexander Baron in Golders Green ("I don't know who the publishers are anymore"), Emanuel Litvinoff still at work, wondering if the latest reissue of *Journey Through a Small Planet* would find a readership, Bernard Kops knocking out radio plays. Allen could afford to contemplate these matters from a remoter perspective – his comfortable stockade in deepest Gloucestershire. With what the poet Paul Holman perceptively describes as "the genuine pulp writer's trance", Allen's cut-ups of newsprint did achieve moments of prophetic vision. The fireplay of a written-out consciousness at the end of its tether. His suedeheads of the early Seventies, boot boys travestied in mohair, progressed to the Stock Exchange. They were the first jackals of the Me Generation: "An anti-social, anti-everything conglomerate affecting status as their protective cover whilst engaging in nefarious pursuits more savage, more brutal than other cultists we have seen rise – and fall – in this past decade."

Yes, Allen is the one to blame, the magician who caused fiction to be brought to life, the man who envisioned the Savile Row knuckleheads of the free-market: Lord Joseph's scum progeny. Even the Cotswolds, where Allen hid himself away as a country squire with a secret life, suffered as its energy field was warped by the aural vampires of Cheltenham, the Listeners of GCHQ, tappers and transcribers obliged to record *everything*. This whirlwind of bad sound – interference, hot sheets, babble – went rogue, manifesting its venom in the corpse gardens of Gloucester, racism in local politics, a cult of Hell's Angels, unexplained outbreaks of meningitis and necrotising fasciilitis. The mythical anti-career of Brian Jones. The malign triangulation of royal residences.

None of this is of any account to Home. He has one client and its name is London. "The only character in my books is the place itself." He wants to drop any notion of impartiality. He's hot to fuck the city. But he is as frustrated as one of Buñuel's lecherous old dons, he can't find a centre: "ambling along London's numerous waterways probably provides the most gentle means of experiencing the sharp contrasts between the variegated zones that make up the city." The language, for Home, is unusually eroticised, tender. The author, succumbing to poetry, dreams and writes "about destroying whole swathes" of the territory that provides his inspiration, but he understands very well that "the hero undergoes psychic breakdown as the price he must pay for

219

acting as a cipher through which various oppositional currents can pass." Home feeds on restlessness, frustration, lists of trains and buses, rucks outside phone kiosks, conversations in grease caffs. The light is sexual. The smell of diesel and dogshit on thin grass: it generates arousal. His excitement grows as he moves from district to district, the very names are a mantra of lust. London is his bitch and his bride. He likes nothing better than to be between events, waiting, reading on a canal bank, watching. He speaks of sitting in a Soho coffee-bar, fascinated by the trembling hands of recently serviced businessmen, getting themselves straight for the return to the suburbs, scarcely able to bring the tea to their mouths without spilling it.

Which was why Stewart took the Whiteread *House* as a personal challenge: a house is not a Home. It was all to do with gender; he interpreted the art project as an attempt to compromise his city in a Sapphic flirtation. He had no truck with memory, the fetishism of domestic detail, shards of wallpaper, fossilised tiles. *House*, standing alone, was the solitary representative of all that Grove Road – a Stewart Home blue plaque – had once been. It mocked the destruction of so many hectares of East London; this self-elected survivor, ugly ghost. Home's *Red London* anarchists, separated from their author, began to behave in ways he had already anticipated. (Whitehead, as this craziness progressed, found that her behaviour was fictionalised by the press into modes that existed nowhere outside a Stewart Home novel.)

The Green activists felt that the famous white structure, like an immobilised military machine (the sawteeth of the missing staircases resembling tank treads), should be returned to active service in the battle against the M11 link-road that was being fought in Leytonstone. Solidity should imply solidarity. (Whiteread, making a spot-check one evening, bumped into a few of the lads, who had turned up with sledgehammers and drills to break into the interior of an exhibit that *had* no interior. That was its essence. If their raid had been successful, they would have reversed time and never been seen again in this dimension.) The house of memory, the tree freaks believed, should join cause with their cousins, the plank cabins perched in the branches. Having a Turner prizewinner in the frontline would be worth as many column inches as persuading Salman Rushdie to drop out of the book launch circuit to face the bulldozers.

Home's mates in the London Psychogeographical Association, strategic allies of the arboreal squatters, published an editorial, HOUSEY! HOUSEY! (*Newsletter* No. 5), that drew attention to a perceived irony in

Tarmac sponsoring the genesis of Whiteread's revenant while simultaneously ordering the trees of George Green to be hacked down by dawn-raid mercenaries, in order to clear the ground for more "motorway madness". The alignment buffs, sustained by their notion of the city as a living body, were discomforted by the proximity of *House* to the Greenwich/Limehouse Church/Meath Gardens axis: a shining path acknowledged – as the architect Katherine Heron asserts – by the planners of the London Docklands Development Corporation. "Surprisingly the LDDC in its first and only published guide c. 1982 chose to keep and accentuate the axis by not permitting any building along its length that would interrupt the view from one place to the other."

This was a nice theory – which lasted for as long as it took developers Olympia and York to ruffle the edges of their cheque-book, and cast a counter vision: the new Hong Kong, Venice, the Pearl of the River. The towers of Manhattan rising out of swampland. Unlimited, on-line credit. A city of electricity. A giant slot machine with clouds in every window. An *inverted* centre. A conceptual city. A centre that could be anywhere and nowhere. The definitive repudiation of the discredited philosophy of place.

Canary Wharf had the vulgarity to climb off the drawing-board. Claes Oldenburg's giant lipsticks were jokes that knew how to behave: they were never intended for the landscape of London. They stayed where they belonged, in the notebook, on the gallery wall. You were free to imagine them, you didn't have to suffer them every day of your life: like that blunt acupuncture needle, that dissatisfied glass erection. Perpetual arousal without coitus was a meaningless boast, but it warped the magnetic field. A false ley line was generated, boosted by the installation of an acorn/omphalos on Haverfield Green (the paddock immediately to the south of Wennington Green). The wooden acorn was yet another tribute to the Great Storm, part of a series of windfall carvings reminiscent of Glynn Williams or Lee Grandjean on a bad day. Ruralist romanticism capable of delighting the shade of Peter Fuller and attracting the attention of taggers and aerosol revisionists. Canary Wharf, Whiteread's *House*, and the roughly-chiselled acorn were in perfect alignment – rivals to the true path, significant debris to fuel the geomantic ambitions of the Green Chain planners.

Home's psychogeographers were as keen as the tabloid hacks to copyright the indignation of Sydney Gale, the token occupant. The man wouldn't go away. Unrequired on set, he hung around the edge of the frame, polishing his one-liners. IF THAT'S ART I'M LEONARDO DA VINCI.

The money was what got up his nose: the figure of £40,000 available for the construction of the artwork had been punted by the yellow press in an instant of uncharacteristic understatement. Mr Gale couldn't get his head around the idea that art money is funny money (as the K Foundation were soon to prove). You don't buy a new flat with this stuff. It's no use in the betting-shop. It's theoretical, more like a hall-mark – and as unreliable as Salvador Dali's signature. Money, in the universe of the reputation brokers, is the only guarantee of seriousness. It proves, if you heap enough of it on the table, that the art is kosher. If you are already famous, it's the material you work with – like the gold leaf of Byzantium. If you're an unknown, a non-player, and one of the Saatchis drops around with a credit note, you are promoted directly into the brochures, the essays of explanation. Money is credibility. It's better than a medicine show cure-all: good for pickling sheep, poking into bodily orifices, hanging pianos, making bricks. It's the ultimate concept of the conceptualists, the angel-aether of Dr Dee. But art loot is no more negotiable than Monopoly money: you can't actually *spend* it, although it's perfectly happy to be used to build toy houses on vacant lots. What pissed Mr Gale off was seeing his home as a haystack of unearned banknotes, like a come-on in the *Sun*. He was suffering from a bad case of the new psychosis, National Lottery rage. Suicidal despair at being forced to watch someone else walk away with your fantasy.

The guiding spirits of the K Foundation, Jimmy Cauty and Bill Drummond, were equally exercised by the paradoxes of cash and art. But unlike Mr Gale they had money to burn. (And, worse, they had the full support of Stewart Home, who eulogised their provocations in an essay entitled "Doctorin' Our Culture", first published in *G-Spot 9*, Winter 1993.) No wonder that K, that angriest of letters, came to represent Konfusion (in all its elements).

Drummond and Cauty were romantic millennialists, anti-materialists burdened with all the potential material that liquidity represented. Their success, critical and financial, with the KLF pop group, and with their music market japes (*What the Fuck is Going On?* to *Doctorin' the Tardis*) left them in an ethically perilous position. Having cracked it, they deleted the back catalogue and proceeded to disinvent themselves. It was much easier in the days when the cash went straight up your nose, or converted into fleets of limos and bottle-blondes in the swimming pool. They weren't really into rain forests or self-promoting acts of public charity. They had somewhere to live, enough to get by on, suitably distressed motors, combat fatigues; what was left over was shit on their hands.

They decided to go for the big one: ART. And their theme was money. Money was their art. Which proved to be an inspirationally unpopular move. "Been done before," said the curators. "Don't want to know." Burning a million quid on an off-shore island? So what? Peanuts. They had to practically kidnap a tame journalist to get the scam written up in the *Observer* colour supplement. It smelled of the self-indulgence that rock aliens had always practised: burn it, snort it, drink it, eat it – what's the difference? The gesture was boring. Cauty and Drummond were bored with it, these suitcases of dreck. They'd given it their best shot with the **MONEY** A MAJOR BODY OF CASH, a proposal for a thematic exhibition that nobody wanted. The truth is that people fear and dislike money. They're relieved not to be stuck with it, the responsibility, the need to consume, invest, recycle. It's dirty, it's ugly. It's covered with engravings of people you wouldn't want in your house. Dead people. Royals who are the experts in the silent acquisition of all the loose change in the universe. They're born to it. It doesn't embarrass them. They're not fazed by creeping Masonic symbolism. If there is a conspiracy, they're in it. The green stuff is like a family album.

The revelation for Bill Drummond came when he walked out towards the car on the Isle of Jura, in the Inner Hebrides, just before the bonfire: "This feels better, going out into the night when it's pissing down with rain." Let it all wash away, the whole weary mess of art pranksterism. It belonged in a forgotten Terry Southern novel. Leaving a dead sheep on the steps of the hotel where the Brit Awards were being held, instead of going inside to pick up their prize as "Best Group", wasn't a satire on inane bingo culture, or a comment on Geoffrey Howe, it was an anticipation of Damien Hirst (who they thought of inviting as the solitary witness to the money burning).

There's something bizarre about the way these prize ceremonies excite the imagination of counter-culture activists. Home organised a picket for the Booker (with no takers). The event had passed beyond satire into catatonic boredom. It is meaningless. The same nothing has happened too often. Any critical gesture only serves to jump start the corpse for one final spasm of animation. The K Foundation gave the Turner Prize its singular moment of global attention by doubling the cash on offer, running a TV and press campaign, and letting the "people" decide "who is the worst of them all." If it wasn't for the glossy press pack provided by the Wapping-based PR man, Mick Houghton, I wouldn't have remembered who, beside Rachel Whiteread, had been nominated for that infamous shortlist (Hannah Collins, Vong Phaophanit, Sean Scully).

The pack, which is destined to become a valuable artefact, primary art documentation, is one of the best samplers for the Karma of the Ks. Canny copywriting ensures that browsers (originally journalists) are hit by subliminal messages, emotive flashbacks: MAJOR RETHINK IN PROGRESS, **ABANDON ALL ART NOW**. The words change places on the board, the prime minister is dumped. STAND BY FOR/**MAJOR**/ART HISTORY/ANNOUNCEMENT/IN **30** MINUTES. Apocalyptic prompts that should have engendered a *War of the Worlds* panic. But nobody was watching Channel 4 at the time. The invitation to join the MOTORCADE was spurned, except by lowlife hacks who spoiled the purity of the design by stuffing their pockets with wads of cash that they were supposed to tamely nail to a board. A money/art questionnaire was provided as part of the complimentary kit. Nine questions, answers on a postcard. The direct ones won't have been any problem to the outriders from the Street of Shame – "Have you ever shagged somebody who works in a Bank?" – but the more philosophical probes will have been ignored. "Why is 'raw nerve emotions' not the correct phrase to describe the anger, jealousy, embarrassment, resentment, hatred, disgust, disinterest, love, admiration, laughter, lust and longing inspired by the sight, sound and smell of money?"

The result of the K Foundation's award of its booby prize to Rachel Whiteread was unpredictable. Fame of a kind that Whiteread neither solicited nor wanted – and anonymity for Drummond and Cauty. Whiteread had been passed the black spot. She was stuck with £40,000 which she then had the angst of redistributing. Like it or not, she was an unofficial Arts Council, hit on by every beggar in the borough. Her work, whose essence was its privacy, its slow-cooking, meditative acts of repetition, was stripped bare on the street: asked to explain itself, when any explanation would negate the enigmatic stillness she worked so hard to cultivate. Meanwhile, the K Foundation, who wanted to enter the catalogue as serious jokers, critics of society, Dadaist thinkers, were treated with the scorn and incomprehension usually reserved for the avant-garde, conceptualists, performance geeks. Their identity as ex-rock weirdos with more money than they knew what to do with was confirmed – even when that description had no base in reality.

So, it's business as usual. Drummond has taken his first steps as a vanity publisher by producing a lavishly-bound elephant folio, beautifully set – and schizophrenically decorated by an appendix of sampled, full-frontal pornography. The book is too expensive for anybody except collectors of *curiosa* and art speculators. It's a populist gesture that must, by its nature, remain unseen. A single copy, treated as a holy relic, has been exhibited from time to time; only to vanish again like the holy grail. There's talk of flying sponsored witnesses out to look at it in some Irish tower. And Drummond himself is to be seen, from time to time, modestly dropping in on obscure readings in East End synagogues, or sitting in the shadows of toilet clubs in Islington or Camden.

After one of these events, unknown to each other, Rachel Whiteread and Bill Drummond sat back to back at the bar of the Queen's Head in Fieldgate Street. Whiteread was still angry enough to regret a missed opportunity for unloading some of the pain she had been caused. But Drummond slipped away early, plotting the next coup. Whiteread was history.

3.

Rachel Whiteread kept a scrupulous video record of the process whereby her concept (her successfully funded proposal) was brought to life. It's obvious, watching this material, that the real winners were the industrial contractors, the plant hire combos. *House* was a great deal for the McGrath Brothers and Tarmac: peel off the brickskin, then return two month later for a day's graft knocking down (with high visibility coverage) the most famous sculpture in England.

The early video footage is heartbreaking: filtered October sunshine exposing the deserted shell of the Gale home to inspection, a honeyed warmth. Tableaux of arcane domesticity viewed for the last time: contoured floorboards, wallpaper collisions, breathy curtains of ancient dust. The furniture, the household appliances, the accumulations of bric-a-brac have been removed – as if in response to a death in the family. The house is in limbo. It's tempting to sentimentalise this privileged state, to claim that the soul of the building is still present: a special condition of the light. Whiteread's camera lists the accidental survivals that will be frozen and defined. These mild heats and small excitements will soon, when the windows are boarded over, be sealed in their plaster canister as a film of memory. The sculptor's power derives from her perception of this originating phase, the tapping and casting of the unpeopled space. She understands, in her handling of the textures of wood and cloth and chipped tile, that she is working a ceremony to exclude the mundane, the temporal. The blind room becomes a recording instrument, a machine for the implementation of a revised history. I am presumptuous enough to assert that this would be the best of it, a period of reverie, undisturbed solitude, before the arrival of her collaborators – and the bother of getting the job done, justifying the commission.

The pleasures of the chrysalis stage are visceral: brisk technicians spraying Lockrete (the substance used to patch the White Cliffs of Dover) across a grid of steel rods. The video records all of this, making the viewer privy to the secrets of transformation. The sense of how unpleasant it must have been to work in this environment is acute: the wetness of the walls, the morbid fur, the muffled pod life that will be obliterated by the brittle geometry of the finished structure. Inside the cube, invisible to the spectators, this larval, sticky, insect thing will remain: a living, angry core. But the masked assistants are like a SWAT team fetched to some tragic address, the mass suicide of cultists or the cellar of a psychopath. They've been landed with the task of building a pyramid *from the inside*, reversing nature's alchemy – starting from what is known and sliding backwards into the future. *House* is a time-traveller, regenerating itself from illegitimate evidence. Whiteread's forensic crew are the exterminators of normalcy.

The dermabrading concluded, *House* stood exposed in a shallow, rubble-strewn declivity. It was now an art object: it had died, its flaws and faults smoothed over with Lockrete (plus a splash of white to enliven the skull-grey of its complexion). The virgin walls positively begged for the attentions of unsponsored sign painters, spraycan poets: WOT FOR, WHY NOT and the airbrushed addendum, HOMES FOR ALL BLACK & WHITE, appeared in the first week. The unedited book of the city is filled with a cacophony of quotations, obscenities. WOT FOR is a statement, not a question.

The pre-posthumous structure that was *House* became an intrusion in the electromagnetic field, it brought disciples running from every rat hole – even those who knew nothing of the history of Grove Road. They were primed to sample this new source of interference. *House* was a grounded UFO, a sign. In the B-movie cycles of the Fifties it would have been a metaphor for Communism: a something that would definitively recompose defensive, small-town consciousness. The enigmatic object was circumnavigated, probed, photographed. In the twilight, it was fed by flashbulbs. Convulsive therapy. The white ghost was seen in negative, printed. Thousands of different images, different readings from different heights: a terrace of repetitions, a city of broken mirrors. Loss was multiplied. Loss, carried away, was confirmed as a general condition. Professionals, archivists, chemist-shop casuals: they snapped and snatched and pondered. *House* was broken into an album of fragments, longshots, close-ups, colour, monochrome. It was sketched, painted, remade by school kids. A dreadful autism of detail: nothing must be left out, nothing forgotten. The images, laid out, would stretch down the length of Grove Road, and beyond, repopulating the grass wilderness, as far as the railway bridge where the first flying bomb fell on London. (A local man, Clem Baylis, survived the trauma of being buried alive three times. First as a 16-year-old Artillery gunner in his trench at the Battle of the Somme. Then, twenty-eight years later, as a firewatcher on a roof in Grove Road, where he witnessed the "flaming apparition" of the V1, before his building and eleven others were demolished. And, finally, just a month after he had been pulled from the ruins, a doodle-bug hit his tobacconist's shop – also in Grove Road. This time he was trapped in the rubble, a "bloody great dog" alongside him keeping potential rescuers at bay. Long before Whitehead's experiment, Grove Road boasted of bad luck. It was twinned with Pompeii.)

The trick for the sponsors, needing an upbeat icon, was to find a viewpoint that would exclude all the mania, the mess of the streets. Head-on, face to face (and back to the Sheppard House, the old Dr Barnado's home on the other side of the road) proved the slickest solution. Cropped tight (no sky), the park was banished. A suitably formalist shot was achieved – which all parties agreed could be used for the label on the commemorative bottle of Beck's Beer (best drunk before February 1995). This icon had been so severely edited that it qualified for prosecution under the Trade Descriptions Act: the park railings, aesthetically incorrect, had been airbrushed by computer, allowing *House* to stand directly against the real paving-stones. No pedestrians, no graffiti. No anarchists, no K Foundation, no flying bombs. No dogs. A Mondrian composition of rectangles and ordered lines, nicely judged asymmetry in greys and greens.

Moving back and away and the shape of the artwork is much more chaotic: futurist zigzags, lightning bolt staircases, blue smears. The construction is as unlovely as a septic tank. **WARNING HAZART**. Night-trippers examine the corpse from all sides. Only civilians, out there in the street, on the wrong side of the railings, see anything resembling the Beck's print. But there aren't many of them, not yet. Most of the suppliants are bussed in, culture punters with affiliations. It's like a visit to the war zone. A Beirut excursion sponsored by Harvey Nichols: Gucci bags, Hermés scarves, leopardskin prints trip across the greensward to pay their respects to Whiteread's sugar-dusted skull. Nervously, they huddle together to catch the spiel, the explanation. They can't wait to get away from this fearful place; the cold, the reek of the canal. They can't wait to talk about it: afterwards. At home. But others, self-propelling anoraks, skitter around the circuit; darting forward to touch the plaster, to report their admiration for the fossilised fern-prints of ancient wallpaper, the cast of fireplaces that float in the air like the vertical coffins of children. There's a favoured distance – about 25 yards back – from which to indulge in prolonged meditation: the position at the bottom of one of the cancelled gardens. Human figures lurk in the half-dark, traced by the smoke of their breath, black against the powdering of snow that chills the peppery grass.

One of the strengths of *House* was that it repulsed those who were most closely associated with it. The finished work didn't have the feel of a "Rachel Whiteread". It had accumulated its own urge towards extinction, forgetfulness. At the death, it was in league with Councillor Flounders and his legions of confusion. "It was like holding a party I didn't want to go to," Whiteread said.

While the influential friends of Artangel were manoeuvring for time, and the western world was camping out for a final glimpse of the famous fetish (famous because *they* were there), Whiteread concluded her video diary. Knowing of the structure's death warrant, the pilgrims had a subdued air. Subdued, but also delighted: at being part of it, the protest, the fuss. Wennington Green was the preview of a public execution. Winter light. None of them would dream of spending the afternoon hanging about a corrugated-fence to watch an ordinary demolition. *House* allowed them to pay tribute to their own sensitivity. It was the last visit to a sickbed, a rehearsed bereavement. They were well-behaved, sober. They needed floral tributes to occupy their hands, wreaths to heap on the front steps. There were too many of them for Whiteread to risk stepping out of her car. She pulled up at a distance, bundled into a heavy jacket, peeping over a newspaper (which probably carried a dot matrix version of her face), to keep surveillance. If she started to walk across the grass, they'd have torn her apart in their concern; their need to touch, own, express solidarity. She fumbled for a roll-up, a whispered confession to the diary: "If I get out of the car, I'd get swamped by people." Marginal to her own creation, she found herself duplicating the actions of Bill Drummond and Jimmy Cauty, who watched from a jeep parked at the riverside, while their hirelings called Whiteread out of the Tate shindig to face the scrummage of the booby prize presentation. Peter Brooke, notable for his baroque eyebrows, one of the finest Tory Ministers for Disaster, was also present in Grove Road. A government Rover discreetly positioned for a quick getaway, while the warbling fogey tried to make out what all the bother was about. It was the closest any politician had come to art without breaking a bottle over it, or digging it up to take home with him.

Just then, by one of the correspondences by which the whole affair was characterised, an area of grass close to the property Whiteread was restoring in Hackney came under threat. The standard leaflet on the doormat. This unfenced green space had a history of compromise, nests of prefabs, "temporary" housing that lasted from the postwar reconstruction well into the Seventies. The yellowing rug of scuffed ground was a troublesome lacuna – scarcely a park, nor even a dogs' convenience. But it was nurtured and tended by the more civic-minded ratepayers, particularly those with an investment in Albion Square who aspired to parity with their westerly neighbours in De Beauvoir Town. With enough determination, and a wind from Islington, it was possible to see this raised corner as a village green. John Betjeman would have approved. It was an area for which he had a particular fondness. Former magistrates and professional persons weeded and planted the borders. Children played here on summer evenings, within sight of their homes, and large mixed gatherings (all ages, weights, inabilities) churned it to mud in their weekly "Big Match" rituals. Unlike Grove Road's Green Chain, this turf was in constant use. It served a purpose. It was a necessary breathing space. A harmless device for sustaining the illusion of community life. Which, of course, was seen as a provocation by a ruling Labour Council, as deeply entrenched in its prejudices and labyrinthine corruptions as the LibDem brothers in Bow. It was decided that a small terrace of houses ("eight maisonettes") would be shoehorned on to what the square dwellers, shamelessly signalling their aspirations, liked to call "The Green". The Nimbys (who were both surprised and delighted to see Whiteread show her face at their AGM) mounted an effective campaign of resistance: snippets of local TV, campouts, rafts of documentation, points of order, fighting funds, top of the range legal stationery. Middle England's version of the M11 ecowars. And with much the same result. They found themselves slighted in *Newslook ("We Always Tell The Truth!!!")*, the official organ of the Haggerston Labour Party, as "a vocal minority". Their achievement, after months of meetings, emotional speeches, threats and gestures, was modest – a few adjustments to the builders' plans that would have merited a wan smile from Gavin Stamp. So successful was this compromise that the scheme, in which the Sanctuary Housing Association co-operated with Hackney Council, was "nominated for an award" – as *Newslook* gloatingly boasted, before moving on to puff the invasion of a much grander space. PRIDE IN THE EAST END! "Labour and Liberal councillors in Hackney have welcomed the choice of Victoria Park as the venue for the annual Lesbian and Gay Pride event." They didn't allude to the fact that seven council employees would be delegated to clear the rubbish of 150,000 marchers and celebrants.

The final exchange was almost too neat: Wennington Green witnessed the premature abortion of *House* and the reinstatement of some purely ceremonial grassland – while the abbreviated lawn screened by Whiteread's new home was built over by houses which, in the long limbo of construction, stood as gaunt and empty as works of conceptual sculpture. The true "vocal minorities" were the councils whose self-conceit allowed them to speak for the people, to interpret howls of rage and frustration as ripples of applause. Petty despots, frustrated in their art (in the way that Mussolini was a failed novelist), take it out on the landscape.

Across the canal, and a little to the south of Wennington Green, is another agitated and reforgotten carpet of turf, a non-place now known as Meath Gardens. It is blessed by standing on the true path of the Blackheath/Greenwich/Limehouse Church ley line. Meath Gardens, in an earlier incarnation, was the Victoria Park Cemetery – a notorious bonepit, putrid with multiple occupation. A field of stench and pestilence regularly denounced in progressive journals, it was also the burial place of an Australian Aboriginal cricketer known as "King Cole", who died in England in 1868, during the first tour undertaken by a team from the southern hemisphere. A few years ago, watched by another squad sponsored by Qantas, a eucalyptus tree was planted to revive and commemorate this fable, and a brass plaque was screwed to a polished wooden block to record the event. Naturally, the plaque, along with the legend, disappeared within days of the ceremony. The empty block is useful for scraping off dog dirt. The totemic tree, leaning crazily to the east, and supported by a stave, has been bent and brutalised: a damaged dreaming. But the validity of the King Cole myth gathers momentum as all the prompts of memory weaken. That is the nature of riparian London with its cycles of deletion and resurrection. We are the fiction of the vanished lives and buildings. They have nothing but our lies to sustain them. *House*, as soon as the last bricks were cleared, joined that company – misremembered and ineradicable.

Whiteread's artwork belongs with the invisible church of St Mary Matfelon in Whitechapel, a removed structure from which that district took its name. An absence, a brick outline in the grass, that gave credence to the surrounding crush of business and development. The church appeared, disappeared, and reappeared in many forms, soliciting destruction: the Great Tempest of 1362, the fire of 1880 which gutted the Victorian building in an hour, the fire-bombs of 1940, the tearing down of the ruin in 1952 – and its reduction to the status of "garden" in 1966. All that is left is the skeletal tracing, a psychic barrier that repelled the vagrants who gathered around the solitary sepulchre – until the Rowton House in Fieldgate Street (Jack London's "Monster Doss House") was closed down, given over to its new identity as a fashionable derelict, a venue for performance artists and rap promos. The reservoirs of psychogeographical energy are identified by being resistant to the attentions of cameras and recording instruments. Only when the frame is blank can you be sure that something worth looking at is there.

Parks are like strips of blank leader attached to reels of lost memory film. Nothing is left on which we can get a fix: gravestones are cleared to decorate the borders of market gardens. Angels and emblems have been set over empty earth, bodies "snatched" for the hospitals and lecture theatres. Springs bubble to the surface through pits of putrefaction. At St George-in-the-East the vicar hung a placard over the water-pump: DEAD MEN'S BROTH. The narrative of the city is rewritten, scribbled over, revised: the "lost" earthwork of the Whitechapel Mound ("considerably higher" than the London Hospital) is unaccounted for, synagogues are discovered as Bangladeshi supermarkets. *House* aspires to the same provisional status.

4.

Eavesdropping on the conversations of those who came to debate the nature and central mystery of Whiteread's construction, it was clear that many felt, or wanted to believe, that *House* had been turned inside-out by some conjuring trick (like the ritual performed, four hundred years before, by John Dee on the Isle of Dogs). A vacuum had been created in which time itself was held prisoner, a solid X-ray. And this process of transformation, inside to outside, was also recurring across the map of the city. Sacred markers (stones, statues, gates, obelisks) were being stolen from the centre, reassembled in the suburbs – reversing polarity: so that Temple Bar finds itself banished from Fleet Street to a scrub wood in Theobald's Park, and Euston Arch is broken up and dumped in the River Lea. This has always been the way. Prison walls becoming roads, church foundations supporting office blocks. The quarries of Portland stone, out there on their Dorset promontory, hide all the cathedrals that Hawksmoor imagined, the unachieved London of the mind.

House, in its brief apotheosis as a public artwork, stimulated a network of parasitical activity: lavish books of tribute, articles, visits by investors and supporters, guided tours for the young and innocent. The educational co-ordinator at the Chisenhale Gallery, Rachel Lichtenstein (original family name reclaimed by deed poll in 1988), was an artist who specialised in not-forgetting, the recovery of "discernible traces". This process is quite distinct from memory-theft. Lichtenstein accumulated, retrieved, polished, presented: she was an archivist of the unconscious, constructing her own biography out of a heap of disconnected shards and images. Without the hard evidence of a past life, she would have no existence. She would be an unjustified survivor, a ghost with no substance, no veins of blood and suffering.

It was Lichtenstein's pleasurable task to conduct parties of local school children on site visits to Wennington Green, to explain how *House* had been made and what its history had been. Later, back at the gallery, she would encourage and provoke a wide range of responses. The children, like many more sophisticated tourists, favoured a fairy tale solution to the mechanics of construction: liquid concrete poured down the chimney. They painted and modelled their own versions, a mosaic in primary colours, a restored terrace in which every house was a portrait of the artist. (Stewart Home writing on the *Ruins of Glamour/Glamour of Ruins* event, which took place in the Chisenhale Gallery in December 1986, begins with a piece reinvoked for "those of you with short memories": Stephen Szczelkun's "felt covered and smoke belching wendy house". Provo art derived from child art derived from . . .)

Lichtenstein, the other Rachel, was obsessive, ritualistic in her procedures. The quest for identity, for a family that would confirm her essence and existence, took her on a series of journeys: to Poland, to

New York, to Israel – and, inevitably, to Whitechapel. Each exploration – interviews, recordings, buildings and contents listed and photographed – brought her closer to the point of origin. When it was all gathered (like the manic accumulations of holy junk in David Rodinsky's Princelet Street attic), she would cancel herself out. She would be free to travel in other dimensions. The moment she confronted the existential terror of loss came when, as a teenager, she set herself to photograph a wall of photographs, Holocaust victims, children. She couldn't look at what she was capturing. She convinced herself that she had identified a provisional account of her own face. Her 1993 installation *Shoah*, at the West London Synagogue, was, amongst other things, an attempt to appease this double. (In an earlier rehearsal, at Art School in Sheffield, she had covered all the mirrors in the college with printed sheets – faint impressions of the fated portraits. The gesture was unpopular. Lichtenstein replaced the white hoods as soon as they were torn down.) For *Shoah*, Lichtenstein once again used photographs from the eradicated Polish ghettoes, printed on torn strips of linen. She embraced difficulty, the stitching and sewing, the long hours that became a protracted meditation on the impossibility of her project.

She would let nothing go, not an envelope, not a lock of hair. There was a quiet ferocity which was not to be found, or looked for, in Whiteread's *House*. *House* was a concept, the human elements were the flaws: it was the husk of an idea, extinguished in execution. The sooner it was disposed of the better: only then could it work on memory, displace its own volume. Lichtenstein would have filled albums from corners of curtain, cabinets of splinters. She had grown up among antique dealers, shuffling through boxes of depersonalised stuff, optional histories, invented pedigrees. Pawnbrokers, jewellers, gold merchants: they are the true custodians of heritage, knowing both the price *and* the value of everything. Lichtenstein's art was inspired by a love of these indestructibles, residual whispers. From the temperature that remained in found objects, she constructed new ceremonies. Her interests led her straight to Whitechapel and the Princelet Street synagogue, where she obtained a residency – which allowed her to pursue her interest in the life and mythology of the vanished caretaker, David Rodinsky. Lichtenstein spent many hours in the attic room, where Rodinsky had lived, alone, or with his mother and sister, accumulating his library, making his translations, scribbling jaunty verses and satires. She took on herself the Herculean labour of cataloguing the mysterious caretaker's possessions: as postcards, they could be "re-collected".

Whitechapel had to be read like a scriptural roll, an album of unknown relatives. Lichtenstein became a guide, a lecturer, walking the territory so that she could learn by explaining. She would make discoveries by revisiting familiar sites. Talking to herself, she would catch the echoes of immigrant voices. In her travels she encountered, and struck up a relationship with, the patriarchal figure of the string and sticky-tape merchant, Mr Katz. STRING/TWINE/CORD/&/PAPER BAGS: the shop of CHN Katz in Brick Lane was virtually the last survivor of a great tradition. Katz – overcoated, bearded, black homburg on head – could be glimpsed through the window, bent over his books in the back room; marooned upriver, businessman and scholar, like an Hasidic translation of Joseph Conrad's Mr Kurtz. Balls of golden twine were always on display. There must have been customers, though it was difficult to remember seeing any. The closed door had been sprayed with an advert for a cowboy mini-cab firm. Katz didn't have to be here: he owned several properties in Princelet Street, making him, potentially, a wealthy man. Something that looked like a coathanger had been twisted into the loose wires that ran above Katz's window: an ancient television set playing back patterns of spectral interference? The paving slabs were glossy and yellow as beeswax. The twine shop was the right place for Rachel to hold her *Ner Htamid* exhibition.

As an act of retrieval, this was the antithesis of *House*: its discretion was shocking. You could walk down Brick Lane without noticing any intervention in the usual fabric of events. Lichtenstein exhibited twelve panels, "Eternal Lamps", against a white cloth background, in the window where the spindles of twine usually rested. The artist had recovered a collection of numinous curiosities from her grandfather's defunct watch-repair shop at the corner of New Road and Whitechapel Road, and set them in resin, before welding (another self-imposed difficulty) heavy metal frames. The images were recessive – steel-grey, ochre, candle wax: a frame of memorial photographs. They did nothing to draw attention to themselves. If the numerology was significant, or if the twelve frames represented particular letters, it was not obvious. A quiet flame. A three-dimensional calendar.

Lichtenstein had a direct relationship with the objects she had chosen. They had travelled only a short distance, less than half a mile west, from one long-established shop to another. They were not for sale, nobody was paying them much attention. Unlike Rodinsky's room, there was not enough information here to build a biography. Trade goods, intriguing artefacts. There was no encouragement to construct a fantasy golem from the clutter of a lost life. The arrangement of the frames had no particular aesthetic, no sculptural bias: they were like so many rusted tins on a shelf. The postcards Lichtenstein subsequently produced would have passed without comment in one of the shoe-boxes of Victorian and Edwardian memorabilia in the Cheshire Street market. Instant antiques: relics created by the act of selection. A small bayonet bulb, a thimble of inherited light. An unredeemed death-ring woven from hair: with its ticket, the number 6. A white eye that is the delicate face of a watch. The portrait of a mother with two infants: unknowns. A decorative fork floating in a cloud of lace. A brush, a buffer with the outline of Noah's Ark. Ivory tags. A galaxy of clock wheels. A key plate. A chart of numbers coated in resin. There were many more items in Lichtenstein's back-catalogue, her private museum; more than she could show. Houses had no importance, no perma-nence: it was the intricate machinery, the portables that mattered. Things that had been handled, touched, animated. Through them she would reaffirm the past-in-the-present, the eternal now.

Wennington Green, a year after the *House* episode, had retreated into its old complacency. The suspect brilliance of an Indian summer cast ribcages of charcoal shadows from the surviving trees. For a few stolen hours the Arcadian conceits of the politicians were manifested. The pal-pable absence of Whiteread's sculpture validated the "secret garden" aspect of the park. An ash tree confirmed the boundary of Mr Gale's property. The tree had a deep gash in its bark, a second skin beneath – like surgical dressing wadded into a wound. A flight of drunken wasps, heavy with autumnal liquors, struggled to maintain altitude above a heap of glassy white grapes, arranged at the tree's base. They were vile, these grapes, a tray of artificial eyes. Disguising this votive offering was an arrangement of bricks – and on the bricks, a collection of copper coins. In the long, lush grass, close to the tree, where thick roots broke the surface, and the motor-mower couldn't operate, was a broken bot-tle of Foster's Ice. Vagrant sponsorship. Random mementoes of some *déjeuner sur l'herbe*. Grave goods. There were no other clues from which to decode this ritual. We do not know, or need to know, who came here to honour the anniversary of the destruction (and confirmation) of Whiteread's vision.

THE SHAMANISM OF INTENT

Intentionality is all.
KATHY ACKER, *HANNIBAL LECTER,*
MY FATHER

I finished the Whiteread ruminations and decided to move straight into the companion piece, the urban shamanism investigation. I had some material to hand – the catalogue of a small exhibition/series of readings that I'd curated in Uppingham and a pair of essays for *Modern Painters* on Brian Catling and Gavin Jones; but I wanted to bring all that up to date, to find out what the boys were doing now.

I got Jones first, still in the same place, the old bunker off Devons Road, in Bow, East London. Devons Road runs parallel to one of the dankest sections of the Limehouse Cut. A waterway that has, so far, repelled the efforts of the most inventive landscape pirates. There isn't an angle to be found that will customise this sewer for the supplements. Nor is there anything in the outer aspect of Bracken House to suggest the mysteries of Jones' hermitage. A drab block of public housing set around some tarmac on which trashed vehicles try to gather enough spare parts to make it to the breaker's yard. Unless you have a crane that will lift you over the roof, you won't discover the secret garden, the sunflowers and exotics that disguise an underground shelter, left over from the Blitz.

The Bracken House inhabitants are a mixed bunch: Bangladeshi, community artists, administrators with nothing left to administer, potential artisans and accredited recidivists. Climbing the stairs to Gavin's workspace you step over catalogues of unclaimed objects, lumps chained under canvas. The structure is sound, and the views – back towards the green riot of Tower Hamlets Cemetery – are breathtakingly modest. A torrent of new work to be looked at: experiments in electroplating, racks of paintings. His underground shelter – the entrance hidden by an upturned fishing boat – was disguised by a sub-tropical garden, worked by teams of Bengali women and children. A miracle of recovery: this green plantation that had grown over the mud carpet that I'd first seen six or seven years before.

But I'd have to wait until mid-September. Jones was leaving, the following morning, for his tin shack, in the shadow of a lighthouse on a rock in the Outer Hebrides. This was where, in monastic seclusion, he sweated out the city, worked on cloudscapes, seascapes, recovered the energy for another winter in London. These visits usually ended in disaster: the roof would blow off the shed, rows with the landowner or the locals. Shotguns, booze, hysteria. And another group of marvellously fresh paintings, oceanic blues and greens, turbulent skies, were rolled up, made ready for burial in the ground. One of these gems, *Landscape* (1989), a cross-section of rock, sea, and sub-aquatic depths, was exchanged for the ruined Citroën in which Jones, unconcerned with niceties of licensing, insurance, driving tests, took off for the north. Unlike the artist, the car never made it home again – and has probably been fetishised into a storage vessel for unsaleable art, before being driven into a bog.

I was not much luckier with Catling. I could, I thought, rely on him to stick to the passenger's seat. To be free of ownership. He was one of those who confirmed the Martin Amis definition of a poet – as a person who does not drive. By choice, by conviction. (Ed Dorn, who composed *Hello, La Jolla* at the wheel of a car, cruising to work, was the exception.) It's all to do with pace and intensity. Catling is a master of synthesis, rapid-eye perception slowly simmering, building towards the formation of a crystalline structure. He used to write on trains, between engagements, in the way that Allen Ginsberg scribbled during intercontinental flights. Not driving ensured a kind of independence: the right to fiddle with the tapedeck, invigilate landscape, be creative with maps, take the odd snifter without worrying about the consequences.

But Catling, and not for the first time, threw me: he also was heading for the Isle of Harris – *in his own vehicle*. A Volvo, God forbid. The shamans were taking to the road in some kind of Chris Petit nightmare. Catling wouldn't actually be driving, but acting as paterfamilias and route-finder was worse: his neck usually responded to the intensity of concentration with a bolt of pain. They would have to carry him from the car on a board. Something major, in the way of psychic alignment, was afoot. Jones and Catling, independently, and at the same time, were converging on the home ground of the sculptor Steve Dilworth. (Catling and Dilworth were old friends, confederates, colleagues at Maidstone Art School: not so much hunter-gatherers of the Isle of

Grain as pick-up truck poachers, headlight bandits, familiars of Skink Tyree, the roadside scavenger of Carl Hiaasen's *Double Whammy*.) My only chance of seeing Catling before he left was to drive immediately to Oxford in the afternoon heat.

The tarmac was bubbling like black cheese. Traffic funnelled and stalled in the East Acton chicken run: nervous car-phoners couldn't risk opening their windows. There was time to read the whole of the *Evening Standard* with its dose of misattributed articles, its black propaganda, as copies were touted up and down the line. What a strange publication London's sole afternoon paper has become: from Jak's rabid and humorless pastiches of Giles, through book pages that offer grazing rights to squadrons of otherwise unemployable aristos, to the latest PR plants from Docklands. Road rage simmered in its primary form, before translating itself into the French version – *La Rage*, rabies. The insanity of JG Ballard flyovers: chrome porn, leather sweat, petrol highs. Blood, oil, semen. I'd been re-reading Catling's *The Stumbling Block its INDEX* that morning, but this was too much. I nearly turned back. The book rebutted the Sherlockian formula of Catling's early mentor, Conan Doyle: when the impossible has been eliminated, what remains, however improbable, must be the truth. *The Stumbling Block*, sequentially, eliminates the impossible, and at the end of the massacre what survives still defies all previous systems of belief. Worse than impossible, a wall of invisible glass. A bell jar dropped neatly over a section of the city. In protecting it, curating it, celebrating its anomalies, Catling removes this zone as a useful token, wipes the map clean. Driving to Oxford, I was completing a fictional triangulation (the curse of *Radon Daughters*), drawing a line between the Whitechapel and Castle Mounds, as Jones and Catling travelled north to their fixed point in the Hebrides. (He-Brides.)

The original *Shamanism of Intent* exhibition was generously sponsored by Mike Goldmark – even though much of the work (and several of the participants) went against the grain. It has to be said that neither he, nor Gavin Jones, were comfortable installing Jones' sculptures, his heron casts, on the upper deck of the Goldmark Gallery. The paprika circles spread across the floor, the inherent unsoundness of the structures, might have had something to do with it. Or the visit from the police, who were looking into a complicated kidnapping case. Jones took to dozing on the sofa, a bottle in each pocket – or slipping away to meditate in the yew-cool churchyard. Visitors, particularly those from Cambridge, who came on the day of the event, went away in an equally uncomfortable state. Not all of them, of course. But the younger, immodestly articulate element seethed with discontent. They couldn't stomach the rhetoric, the hyperbole. Shamanism smacked of the Sixties, dope-freak indulgence, unredeemed phallocentrism, Castaneda: woolly thinking, slack language. It didn't have the precision required by the new austerity, elite populism. The whole approach to the numinous was suspect. The last "shamanic" text that was in any way respectable was JH Prynne's *Aristeas, In Seven Years* (Ferry Press, 1968), underwritten as it was by genuine and visible scholarship. Simon Jarvis in his essay, "The cost of the stumbling block", speaks of how Prynne's text "demonstrates the possibility of taking up with this fractured and extensive knowledge, of not rushing to self-exile from its supposed impurity". Prynne's flight, his figure, is a measured risk:

> *And his songs were invocations in no frenzy*
> *of spirit, but clear and spirituous tones from the*
> *pure base of his mind; he heard the small*
> *currents in the air & they were truly his aid.*

There is a coherence here that the Goldmark day, with its suspect commitment to "frenzy", confusion, mixed metaphors, could not aspire to. And what the hell, if anything, did it *mean – The Shamanism of Intent?* Was there a current in the social life of the city that could be usefully identified with this conceit? Artists so stubborn, so ruinously estranged from the tribe, that their outcast status was something more useful than a disguise, a horn mask. Is it too preposterous to think of this delusion – that work is capable of re-enchanting place – as a reality, a significant marker on the chart of our culture? Such questions – and the need to pitch the show – provoked a kind of retrospective manifesto.

2.

. . . each shaman has a Bird-of-Prey Mother, which is like a great bird with an iron beak, hooked claws and a long tail. This mythical bird shows itself only twice: at the shaman's spiritual birth, and at his death. It takes his soul, carries it to the underworld, and leaves it to ripen on a branch of pitch pine. When the soul has reached maturity the bird carries it back to earth, cuts the candidate's body into bits, and distributes them among the evil spirits of disease and death. Each spirit devours the part of the body that is his share; this gives the

We have been walking too long in someone else's sleep. There is a nagging sense – we reward ourselves by insisting upon it – of having
travelled through a dark night of the soul, a lightless tunnel. Sick colours
spiral from the grey-mauve scurf of cathode-ray addiction, recessing to
some infinitely remote, infinitely cold region: dead stars. Any action,
however stupid, outranks contemplation. The Bird-Mother, a necklace
of skulls in her yellowing, equine teeth, returns from the battlefield,
some lost bog in the South Atlantic, ordering the tribe to rejoice.
Celebrate death. Drum with scattered bones. The Bird-Mother cannot
sleep. We are the residue of her waking nightmares, we are her pain.
Out of rage and confusion, whisky fumes, fantasies of revenge, emerges
the Radiant City: Docklands. Swamp creatures, hungry ghosts, shiver in
their oil slick suits. Chalkstripes strobe like migrainous bar codes. Hard
hats are clamped on expensive hair like prophecies of gold. Art, and the
making of art, has to explain itself to these pirates. Doubt is inexcusable.
Any future programme – prompts in notebooks – has to justify itself to
a cabal of accountants. Novelty (that tired old whore) is back on the
agenda. We somnambulate through a house of mirrors, rediscovering
painters and movements that have never gone away, showcasing entropy.

Certain artists – the ones you came across by accident, working their
own turf – began to look strange, otherworldly, out of it. Their behaviour, this remorseless pursuit of discomfort, this restlessness and fruitful
irritation, struck me as exemplary. Worthy of notice. The will to continue, improvise upon chaos, could be defined as "intent": a
"sickness-vocation", as Eliade has it, an elective trauma. The health of
the city, and perhaps of the culture itself, seemed to depend upon the
flights of redemption these disinherited shamans (there were women
too, plenty of them) could summon and sustain. They were associated
in my mind with other avatars of unwisdom: scavengers, dole-queue
antiquarians, bagpeople, out-patients, muggers, victims, millennial
babblers.

One of the most visionary and heroically perverse experiments in deregulated shamanism was undertaken in a blasted corner of East London, too far from the tunnelhead to have felt the first wave of dockland development, by Gavin Jones: painter, sculptor, earthmover, outlaw ecologist. The essence of Jones has been described by a young architect who visited him, in search of the secret generators of the city, as "incredible enthusiasm and determination driven on by sex and alchohol". (TV directors, picture editors, and the folk who attend exhibitions in boilerhouses, raved about the cheekbones, the way he photographed: the cover for *Cosh Boy* redrawn by John Minton.) Sensory derangement is a traditional shamanic tool. Jones felt no obligation to "make it new", or to make it at all. The art circus, give or take the odd night out in the Colony Room, could fuck itself. Life was a series of rehearsals for the kind of novel that is best left unwritten.

One not untypical evening, a contact of the painter's, pissed but benevolent, laboured up the complexity of steps and balconies towards Jones' bolt-hole studio, carrying a tray of live snails. Three – or was it four? – flights, then the weaving past obstacles, bicycle frames, bits of canoes, puddles that stuck to the plimsolls. A warty sun was dying in spasms, as it slunk across the windows of the barrack blocks of Devons Row and Bow Common. Gavin was not at home.

What happened next would have to be imagined by an investigator with nothing to work on apart from a small pyramid of blackened match-ends. The frustrated donor, denied access to the artist, burnt the snails, torched them in their shells in a ceremony of low cuisine – and posted the smouldering remains through the letterbox. The lurker's presence was noted by neighbours, who swallowed the stench, and refused to acknowledge the precise point at which the surreal goes into overdrive and offers itself as next week's lead in the *East London Advertiser*.

Gavin returned late, glutted by society and a little unsteady on his pins, to discover, by treading on them, a tide of distressed molluscs melting across his narrow hallway. His immediate response to this domestic crisis offers an insight into the singularity of his vision and the methods he employs to service it.

He procured a large canvas, forced the snail-kebab maniac to slink back to the scene of his crime, and to pose, as the incident was restaged. In purely formal terms, the composition was cropped in such a way that it could have been anybody's hand that gripped the spiral shell and the flaring match. The way Gavin operates, it *had* to be the original pyrotechnician. The thin yellow flame is ominously cool. The massive hand immobile, a meat hammer. The background acres of the stretched canvas – like the flap of a medicine-show tent – are lovingly "toshed" with a busy argument of English romantic motifs: razor-edged leaves, thistle crowns, blowsy dandelions. There is a willed invocation of nature demons. Jones has been driven to audit what he perceived as the inevitable acts of childhood sadism: memories of frog slaughter, meaningless cruelties. The directness of the child, the arrogance, the need to experiment, to discover the parameters of permissible behaviour: these were the constituents of Jones' art, as he investigated the rites of passage that have replaced a tribal initiation as hunter or killer.

At this time, in Mrs Thatcher's middle period, Jones had become obsessed with deep-focus distortion. Carmine friezes of hands dominated his foregrounds, as they arranged worms for the hook, or offered an unstable platform for the mating dance of snails. His canvases were kingsized bed sheets. (Jones confesses that in his early days it took only four or five lines of his handwriting to fill a page.) Once, retracing his steps from a *plein air* session in Tower Hamlets Cemetery, the painter was lifted into the sky when his latest landscape (a flesh tree executed in negative against a bed of Celtic crosses) became a kite.

The series, featuring hands and snails, was rounded up for an exhibition in Limehouse Church. Seen as a totality they suggested a new religion, fierce and masochistic (like El Greco macerated in the presbyterianism of the Outer Isles): the artist's cumbersome, self-constructed frames enclosed aquatic ceremonies, priapic gastropods, gulls, cliffs, blood red skies. The chill, baroque interior of Hawksmoor's church was an ideal setting in which to witness Jones' work for the first time. (I was an instant convert.) Gavin had an unerring instinct for place: where he could best exhibit in the grand manner with a guarantee of total obscurity. Previous attempts included a flooded air-raid shelter and a Smithfield slaughterhouse cellar, run by a flaky rag trade princess looking for cultural credibility. There must be, so Jones asserted, a treaty between site and displayed artefacts: a chance for something unexpected to develop from the collision.

Portraiture is another method of defining place. The Kokoschka catalogue, the rogue's gallery of artists, musicians, businessmen, is a handy way of summarising a period: the pressures of the time distorting the challenged faces. The paintings in Limehouse Church were portraits of landscape, as well as landscaped faces. The sitter with whom Jones had once fished the Medway also provided the deformed fish stored in the icebox as a future subject. He couldn't attend the show. He'd vanished, "fitted up" for crimes too murky to be discussed, but vivid enough to grace the painting with an additional patina of threat. The latent strength captured in these faces is "confirmed" by acts of suicide or self-mutilating madness. Being chosen to pose for Gavin Jones is like taking out a full page advert in the *Police Gazette*.

The Limehouse Church event had an exhilarating, but menacing edge. It acknowledged the final flare of the old, dirty, dangerous riverside community. The rector, who had allowed the thing to go forward in a vague and liberal spirit of reconciliation, was alerted as the pictures were manhandled up the steps. He had already been tormented by the impositions of camera crews and the vulgarly curious, guided onto his territory by best-selling gothic fictions. Who could forget Melvyn Bragg and Peter Ackroyd, deep in conversation, as they approached the stone pyramid sepulchre? Rumours of Masonry, child sacrifice, graffiti out of *The Egyptian Book of the Dead* continued to plague him. Even the vagrants found better shelves on which to bask. They wearied of media exploitation, being woken by lunatics poking the turf with dowsing rods, psychogeographic journalists taking their own editorials too literally.

No, this irradiated phosphorescence of snails was too much. The sky-pilot snapped, locked the candlesticks in the safe, and bolted the church doors until it was all over. Leaving Jones, alone, inside: stamping the wooden gallery like Captain Ahab. But the word of a Christian had been given. The show continued: a paradigm of hermetic modernism, a valid exhibition that nobody could view – a scaled-down version of the Canary Wharf skyscape (visible but impossible to reach). The intense displacement of energy generated by the arrangement of Jones' work was unaffected by the fact that it could not actually be seen. Bishop Berkeley was refuted. Work and church gained by this temporary alliance, this shotgun marriage. Pilgrims who had traipsed out into the riverine wastes of East London could circumnavigate the building, feel the benefit of Hawksmoor's image-generating time machine. You could sit on the wall, in the shadow of a beached fishing-smack, and watch as pathetic clusters of art buffs rattled the doors, stepped over the glitter of British sherry bottles – wondering if *this* was it? They were forced to make a new kind of communication, to imagine the paintings, brighter and stronger for their passage through the resistant filter of Portland stone. They collaborated with the artist. Nothing sold, Jones continued.

His career had relatively orthodox beginnings, at the Slade – where his attachment was a conveniently casual one. He spent time, under licence from Professor Gowing, in Shropshire. In London, he haunted University College Hospital – the Mortuary and the School of Anatomy. He sought a connection with the Great Tradition, where close observation inspired high risk strategies, taboo breaking: cadavers split and analysed, the shadow line between life and death brought back to his studio. Jones solicited unholy laughter. The chosen corpses received a brief remission, danced like Muybridge photographs.

He interested himself in colours particular to the postmortem limbo. He was fascinated by the shifting, settling mass of the naked bodies on their slabs. The dead are the most obedient of models. He observed the clotting of blood, the flowering of dull bruises, the rapid encroachment of grey. One canvas depicts the photographing of a headless cadaver, strapped in a vertical position on a revolving turntable. A student picks listlessly at the flesh of the legs. There are reasons for this curious behaviour, but the strangeness of the image, its weird perspective, overwhelms them.

Increasingly, as he is forced to debate with interviewers and busybodies, Jones sees himself as displaced, born at the wrong time. He fancies himself living in an age when pentimento has been spurned or squandered. He works with fierce attack, without quite achieving the concentration to resolve his contradictions, to define the springs of his obsession. He is all too eager to move on, shift into sculpture, dig river mud for some exercise in public relations disguised as patronage. (The piece in question, a heron in flight, attached to a tower of baked slurry, lasted only as long as it took to be captured for the brochure that puffed the event. But credit is due to the developers and their agents: without the hubris of Docklands, Jones' totemic oddities would lose some of their impetus, their justified dynamic. With nothing worth opposing there is no honour in being contrary.)

Balance is achieved in Jones' life by regular purges on the island of Scalpay in the Outer Hebrides. London is where he feeds his anger, talks, drinks, is actively engaged in conversation, argument, the social (not society). He stalks. Information can be effortlessly acquired in pubs or on the streets, bits of books abandoned by other people, exhibitions, private views, monologues in the back of a taxi, the endless parade of private lunatics and quotidian visionaries. Nothing is wasted. He is inspired by throw-outs, brochures from skips, X-rays, negatives, pornography, bones, rings, magnets, the skull of a lark, a snake in a bottle. The isolation of the Hebrides will blow away all this froth. Life there is all weather. The world slows and the punctured body is restored.

By deliberate choice, news is something Jones avoids. He spurns live newsprint and is estranged from television, which he treats as an entirely random scatter of disconnected imagery. His art remains uninfected: the brittle ironies of Pop have him sibilating like Brian Sewell. He has incubated a rogue ecology with which to handle the idea of the place in which he is forced to live. Rather than using his paintings to create an Arcadia (like the Green Chain), he has laboured, physically and hard, to achieve a site in which a fitting art might one day be produced. He dug out a wartime bunker, and developed in the process the strength to undertake the sculptures that the bunker inspires him to attempt.

This bunker, with no official status, no existence on the maps of the borough, was excavated with an irresistible combination of will power and taboo-defying nonchalance. The effort, initially nocturnal and covert, was worthy of Howard Carter or Schliemann; but no team of pot hunters, no cowed peasants, worked alongside Jones. Sentiment and heritage didn't enter the equation. The sculptor lived here because he lived here. His view of his vocation was suitably pragmatic, or elitist: "whatever I do is my art."

I witnessed the excavation at various stages: the spade pressing through coarse grass to find the clink of metal, the trapdoor, the descent into darkness. The bunker was constructed in four chambers; to clear it, make it usable, was a major undertaking. The mound above had to be converted, as a diversion, into a garden. Back-breaking labour, obedient to the prescription of the poet Paul Celan: "There was earth inside them, and/they dug." Jones scratched his way beneath the rubble and the dead ground. Something was down there that he had to reach, a cave of silence. If the world offered no space for his paintings, he would entomb them for future generations. His sacrifice would gift him with rough walls, an alignment with the masters of the Aurignacian: beasts of the hunt rendered in their own fat. Fertility returned to inert clay.

Energy spun in a vortex from this recaptured nowhere. The Bracken House project had greater validity than Whiteread's peeled shell – because it was secret, the restoration of a place of safety: "God's Corner" where the bombs never landed. The shaman without a tribe is still an active nib. Hurt is perceived as wisdom. The sterility of the Isle of Dogs was questioned by the sculptor's frantic acts, his predatory laughter. If the skyline was to be dominated by a crop of alien verticals, exclamation marks in mirror glass, then we must burrow like moles. We must eat earth. The life-force of the city is measured in the candlepower of its keepers, the activators of place whose follies must be as imaginative as those of the developers and despoilers.

Jones discovered the perfect hood for his bunker: a Hebridean fishing-boat, the wreck that had been beached for so many years on the fringes of Limehouse Church. Too far gone to be relaunched on the Thames, where it had drudged in the twilight of its career, the herring smack was about to be burned as an affront to the church's scoured makeover. Jones intervened. The boat was hacked into two sections, transported to the Bracken House garden, then nailed together – upended, set in place. A functioning shed, a yurt, and also a literary quotation (it had featured in so many poems and neighbourhood sketches).

While Jones clawed and sweated in the excavated space beneath his craft, a secondary presence, an elderly junkman/collector, trembling with Parkinson's disease, filled his allotted chamber with all the debris he could drag, with his faltering strength, down from the exterior world. Once, in his pomp, he had trundled doorless fridges, trunks of condemned beef, unidentifiable elements of fantastic machines, spokes without a circumference, books raked from bonfires, things that had fallen from so many lorries they had passed far beyond forensic recognition. Time had hobbled him. He was almost ready to vanish into the Schwitters-like accumulations of his den: another David Rodinsky, a ghost defined by his possessions. Rooms turn into men, men are absorbed into damp plaster and peeling wallpaper. The junkman was a patron of the spurned, a collector of the uncollectable, a stalker of margins. He haunted market stalls, gallery openings, theatres – led by a half-blind dog on a string. He soaked up envelopes, feathers, fluff, hairballs, broken plastic spoons. His pockets were sticky with complimentary sugar sachets. Often he was the solitary witness at unannounced performance events, the only man in London with the determination to find his way to some reading in "a warm room with sweet tea" near the Elephant and Castle. The dealer who does not deal achieves the status of an honorary artist. Jones' tolerated sub-tenant established a museum of memory from which another London, disturbing and demented, could be reassembled. A city of articulate engines and aboriginal robots. The junkman's selfless piety counterbalanced Gavin's casual iconoclasm. When the recluse and his dog were seen for the last time (lurching through a twilight Uppingham), he left behind him a collection that was incapable of dispersal, a single lump oozing acid: lethal to touch, dangerous to visit.

In the climate of atavistic rage and congenital stupidity we have wished upon ourselves, the climate in which Jones's work is perceived as a threat rather than a blessing, shaped objects are driven to plea-bargain for their very existence. We require inoffensive exhibits produced by artists with biographies that are extremely offensive in their banality. We want shocks that are not shocks, predictable outrage. Jones' birds and beasts, his wax casts of snails and heads, belong in the flooded bunker. They have always been present, they are retrospective: an arc of intention was launched long before the sculptor broke into the buried chamber and discovered them. The sculptor's work announced a return to Blitz consciousness: the era with which Jones was most comfortable.

"I have a nihilistic streak that seems incurable. I see millennial disaster as a cleansing of the surface." Entrenched on the rim of Canary Wharf's ice field, Jones waits for those glittering monoliths to be swept into the sea. He gleefully summons Scottish winds to "just blow all their crap away", so that the forms he models – the giant molluscs, rope worms, carcinogenic fish, hydrocephalic children, drinking club gargoyles – can take possession of territory that is rightfully theirs.

New ways of seeing have to be found to explain the horror. For a brief period, Jones painted in negative. It began when he was playing with a collection of slides – all the drained commonplaces, weddings, holiday beaches. He toyed with reversal: brides in billows of black, the voodoo of carnival. Soon, he trained himself to develop negative vision, to see everything that way. Landscapes were meat. Visitors were their own ghosts. Heightened imagery escaped from the easel into the garden.

For the great Max Beckmann there were two worlds, the "spiritual life" and "political reality"; worlds that, paradoxically, his paintings succeeded in fusing. We have been obliged by the temper of the times to feed such nice distinctions into the shredder. The heavenly (the angelic orders) and the mundane interpenetrate any part of the city that we hold for a moment before our eyes. Apparently occult acts are revealed as simple survivalist reflexes. Shamanism has developed its own realpolitik. The Bird-Mother in stiff peroxide helmet watches over us, her darker intentions hidden behind "the lips of Marilyn Monroe, the eyes of Caligula." She is primed to bite and gouge, to remake the fabric of our nightmare, but not to restore stolen bones. Deposed rulers, refusing public sacrifice, slink into a shrill and unsatisfied exile: powerless but congenitally incapable of remaining silent.

Without expectation of success in his own lifetime, Jones allows his reputation to rest with future archaeologists. He intends to roll his canvases into tubes, to seal them and bury them in the ground. The bronzes will be dropped into the sea. Let time and the processes of the weather become his collaborators. He will conduct strange experiments with the city as his gallery. A fortuitous flask of mercury recovered from a disused industrial site (soon to be turned into a nest of luxury hutches) prompted notions of malign alchemy: the sculptor would inject the substance into certain trees, granting them a foretaste of a coming heavy metal existence. He would prepare them for the apocalypse. As the expected mutations occurred, he could sketch these living thermometers. The landscape would not merely conform to an Expressionist vision, it would become one.

"I feel so divorced from the time I live in," says Jones, "that I don't believe in making work for people of my age. That's why sculpture is good, it's durable . . . I'd love to see a bronze after it had been buried in the earth for ten years, it would have a very fine patina . . . I feel artists should put things back for the future, that's what their task is. They're trying to buy some kind of immortality."

The constant presence of implied threat, the reckless urgency in Jones' work, invokes the climate of a city under siege. Living with the imagery of Blitz consciousness was one way of surviving the Eighties. If Gavin Jones could be translated to wartime Soho – the fable of austerity, blackout, chance encounters – he would be an acceptable figure, a hero of the supplements. There would be commissions from *Poetry London*, discreet homosexual patronage, a bit part in the memoirs of Julian Maclaren-Ross, a paint-smeared mug shot by John Deakin. He would have a role as a perfectly traditional artist: bohemian, romantic, the prematurely doomed wild boy. Forty years out of synch, Jones and his art are derided as self-indulgent and slapdash. It will take some terrifying accident, when the air freezes in our mouths and the light burns with a painful clarity, to let us understand the true nature of his achievement.

I had, in the course of our *Lights Out* wanderings, exposed Marc Atkins to a number of bad experiences. Jones's bunker, which we visited on his return from the Hebrides, was the worst of them. The long slog through the Rotherhithe Tunnel had peeled a few years from the photographer's life expectancy, but the bunker left him a virtual basket case. The march home had him hissing like a defective radiator. Lungs, weakened from childhood, were now about as useful as punctured tea bags. His complexion wasn't so much pale as colourless, drained to subterranean ash. He couldn't lift a camera or extemporise a single pun. I had found an art that refused to be captured on film. A place to which the photographer would never willingly return.

Jones, back from his northern retreat, was revitalised, up for it – whatever we could throw at him. There was no yesterday. The Hebrides were forgotten, he was off on a new hack. He had the look of a transported Elizabethan, of Dr Dee's nemesis, the visionary mountebank Edward Kelly. Lank hair to the shoulders, eyes mad as Manson. Pure intentionality: "the wanton serpent that conceives of its own seed, and brings forth on the same day." Weathered corduroys and a distressed tweed jacket that must have been liberated from some laird's game pantry. He floated through the rooms of his Bracken House flat. There was so much to show that he didn't know where to begin. He started in the middle of an explanation and left off long before he reached a conclusion. He gestured towards electroplated insects, pink and blue improvisations that busked at violence and obscenity. Odd knives used as stencils. The light danced from the polished floor, from Jones's forehead, the telephone, his gesturing hands.

The bunker, where he soon led us, had been much restored; a water-pump kept the floor almost dry, though the walls still sweated and dripped. The master plan had advanced: work that would be produced, stored, and exhibited on one site. A chamber for sculpture, a chamber for the paintings, and a chamber where the old collector's detritus remained untouched. Further chambers, still closed off and rubbled, would be excavated. When it was all done, everything made that had to be made, then the bunker would be sealed like an Egyptian tomb. It's existence was still a kind of secret. Jones could ship out with his grave goods and the world would be none the wiser.

I think it was at this point in the explanation that Atkins began to pant and stare longingly in the direction of the unlit steps. But his sense of obligation to the project kept him firm while Jones pointed towards a new series of paintings that curled from the damp wall. These seemed to be more of the pink and blue cartoons that we had glimpsed in the flat. Loose, swift, spontaneous. Sometimes he found significant shapes, animals, and worked towards revealing them; sometimes he preferred to break off, leave the canvas in a provisional state. His method involved flicking blobs of paint, then blowing at them with a straw, imprinting objects into the wet gunge. The process interested Jones more than the result. "It's coming," he would mutter, before putting his latest effort aside.

In the sculpture space he was playing with cans of high pressure wall cavity foam, puncturing them and building up chaotic shapes from the emerging spawn. One of these was already a magnificent creation: organic, bestial, impossibly balanced. A blind minotaur. A vegetal bull with scaly skin. The spirit of the bunker. Heaps of empty cans lay around like spent ammunition. The bloke in the DIY shop thought Jones was the ultimate bodger. Either that or he had a pernicious cavity foam habit. The sculptor bought his cans by the sackful.

We weren't allowed to dwell on any of these achievements for more than an instant before Jones swept us into the next chamber and the latest gimmick. The real excitement came with the electroplating tank. *Exchange & Mart* alchemy. A tribute to Hammer Films. He dropped his plates into the copper sulphate and threw the switch. The mixture was soon bubbling away and giving off acrid fumes, which had no chance of dispersal in the sealed bunker. Plans were afoot for something much grander: the goldfish tank would be replaced by a sunken bath, large enough to take a couple of human bodies. The sort of contraption favoured by John George Haigh. The notion that excited Jones was that *anything* could be electroplated: leaves, twists of wire, bats, biro caps, sardines, strips of skin. And it was so quick. He fished into the tank and hooked out a couple of examples. He was immune to the bite of the acid, immune to gas. He thrived on it. Frowning with concentration, completely absorbed in the limitless possibilities of his invention, he spoke with a voice of awful reasonableness. Dizzy, stumbling, feeling the blisters break out on our flesh, we nodded like automatons; agreeing with everything – in the hope of an early release.

Atkins, a claustrophobic, who could barely stand upright in this low-ceilinged tomb, survived by keeping his eye to his camera. Clicking away to maintain some faint connection with reality. Otherwise, the silence was terrible; not a whisper from the world above us. No sirens, no screams, no traffic. A place that had gone through the Blitz without taking a single casualty must be due some nobler catastrophe. Jones was doing his utmost to incubate it. Removed from the hope and desire for exhibitions and fastburn fame, he was free to go about his own business with renewed vigour. There was no one else to please, no one else to consider. He already had enough work for two or three retrospectives, all of it buried, secreted in unmapped locations.

Viewing this art, we became part of it. We could feel the lick of metal coating our lungs. We began to accept the Jones thesis: there is no borderline between maker and made. All nature was absorbed into the catalogue. Whatever Jones noticed or touched became a part of him. He was the final solipsist, his experiments cancelled the boat and the garden, Bracken House, Devons Road, and the rest of East London. Jones had achieved the inspired dogmatism of Edward Kelly's alchemical tracts:

Bodies receive their figure, lineaments, and temper from water, their fixation from the dryness of the earth, and are more or less matured according to the velocity or slowness of the inward fire.

The garden above us was now tended by other hands, troops of Bangladeshi ladies, urchins, New Agers. They nurtured Jones's freak hybrids, his spiky plant trials, his mercury-fed monsters. If we never emerged, no one would know. The bunker was a paradigm of intentionality. The dripping walls. The bubbling tank. The scorched hands and unblinking eyes of the artist. We were there, but we scarcely qualified as witnesses. And we had no other justification. We had better surrender and climb down, without complaint, into the blue bath.

3.
*and farewell for a space to the yellow key
of the Rosicrucians*
SAMUEL BECKETT, *WHOROSCOPE*

Brian Catling, who grew up in South London, and later lived (in the period when he was writing *The Stumbling Block*) above a decommissioned synagogue in Heneage Street, Whitechapel, has a very particular sense of location. "I could never . . . name the streets, name the people. I wanted it to be a shape-shifting place not an actual city," he told Ian Hunt (the writer and publisher who has taken it upon himself to become Catling's Boswell). Catling's pitch was always more feline than that of Gavin Jones: the summoning and articulating of "concerned agile violence". Retrospectively, it can be seen that he was, from the start, a master of strategy, exploiting faults and flaws until they became strengths. Quietly, and without fuss (it wasn't as smooth a progress as it appears from his CV), the man has achieved everything that he needed: a career curve that would put William Rees-Mogg to shame. Turning the darkest days for conceptual/performance art to advantage, Catling emerged from the Thatcher years in a position of fluent power:

publishers seeking his texts, academic status he could use to promote other artists, to organise high energy events; worldwide invitations, work displayed on the walls of the British Embassy in Dublin, film scripts in development, videos of his performances, an influential show at the Serpentine Gallery, collectors beginning to sniff after his drawings, thesis writers confirming the mythology. Food on the table was no longer a problem: he had dining rights and invitations from here to Christmas. He had access to the gym and the shooting range, the keys to libraries, museums and earthworks. No, the problem now was to sustain a sense of necessary risk, to work with an audience that had learnt what to expect: to provoke his oldest ally, difficulty.

Catling had taught himself to create situations from which he could effortlessly withdraw, to discover sites that were transmitting whispers he had sounded in a previous life. He gives the impression of being an old soul, of having seen it all before: his work is a series of recognitions, discoveries that act as confirmations of things already known. His primary intention has always been to excommunicate autobiography, which he regards as an "unsanitary condition". And yet, in its disguised and synthesised form, it is the most potent element in everything he attempts. From the early days at the North-East London School of Art in Walthamstow, he was equipped, as far as the work was concerned, with an enviable self-belief. (He had to be, in the time of loons and tie-dyed T-shirts, of suedeheads in boots and braces. He stalked the corridors in pinstripe suit and wing collar – like an asthmatic Mycroft, Sherlock Holmes' clubman brother.) The lesser business – of living – could, and often did, degenerate into farcical complexities worthy of his heroes, Laurel and Hardy.

This unconditional trust in the inevitability of his chosen track, the track that had chosen him, gave Catling the strength to fail, to stumble or botch. The pleasure he took in the workshop (in his days as a student or a recipient of fellowships and art scams) was the pleasure of physical work – welding, burning, scratching, hammering, scorching his flesh, tearing nails – and having the space in which to undertake it. Otherwise, when such indulgences were denied him, he molested his notebooks. These stiffbacked objects are a treasure store and should be immediately bought with a millennial cheque and turned over to the scholars. There is one book in which he outlines the ideas for the poems – words, phrases, sounds, shapes – before the seizure of the thing itself. Which might come at a rush, under pressure, or might require revision. Another book will have postcards, images, drawings pasted into it, doodles and cartoons, prototypes that might hang around for years before they can be activated. The collection of notebooks is the essence of the Catling career. The studio, when it is available, is an extension of the notebook. The cards and sketches can be transferred to the walls (with phone numbers, recipes, and bullet holes from target practice); experiments can be undertaken, trial and error, visits from interested parties. The studio is a useful space in which to sit and think. Notebooks are also valuable tools for interviews: when things get sticky, pull one out, give the invigilators a whiff of enormous projects in hand, research, documentation, shorthand genius.

I don't want to pre-empt Ian Hunt's inevitable biography by summarising Catling's career here (the large-scale pieces made at the Royal College of Art, the films, the books of poetry, the performances) but to concentrate on recent London-based manifestations: his Book Works publication, *The Stumbling Block its INDEX* and the ritual, *At the Lighthouse*, undertaken at Trinity Buoy Wharf at the mouth of the River Lea. They came at a point in his life when he recognised that elements he had been careful to segregate (poetry, performance, sculpture), and even to publish under different signatures, belonged in a single energy field. His sculpture had always included "voice" as an unstressed but significant component – while Catling's poetry was constructed with a certain formal stiffness, as if it were a second language, a vivid report of something overheard, but not fully understood. It was a technical language, a language for describing process, a language in which nouns frequently served as verbs: a language that could be read but not spoken. (Samuel Beckett's *Poems In English* have been a major influence; particularly the notion of translation – between tongues, grammatical constructions, media. The slate austerity of *The Stumbling Block*'s design was perhaps a final homage to the faded grey wrapper of the 1961 John Calder edition of Beckett's poems.)

Before discussing the achievements of the early Nineties, it's necessary to outline the somewhat uncomfortable period that came before: endless travelling between art schools whose funds were being savagely cut back, Jocelyn Stevens hyperventilating at the Royal College, residency as Henry Moore Fellow in Norwich – where he found himself estranged from a clutch of "life-modelling fundamentalists". Catling saw the situation in stark terms: "They didn't want me there, they didn't even see me as an outsider for the job. I wasn't making sculpture as far as they were concerned, I was a conceptualist . . . At that time I probably didn't know I was a conceptualist. The conceptualists I'd met at the Royal College were all people who sat on balconies with type-writers and then didn't use them."

Leaving East Anglia and returning to London, Catling discovered that his shamanic insistence on sticking to the high ground left him with no ground at all. His work was liberated from the studio and turned out into the streets: specific but unplaced. He went where he was asked to go: shuttling on ferries and planes to Scandinavia, Iceland, the Low Countries – like an Elizabethan Jesuit, a bearer of forbidden doctrine. His performances on home turf, minimally resourced, were private affairs attended by a ring of the faithful. He dowsed forgotten sites, staying one jump ahead of the heritage pirates. He operated with the recklessness of the dispossessed. It was evident that he had found a new formula for his work: iteration, transformation, erasure. Investigate, locate the essence, move on. Like Dr Dee, he played with the angelic tables. (A film with which he was involved – in the role of a surgeon or alchemical quack – was called *Maggot Street*. Unconsciously echoing the term "maggid", or teaching angel, from the legends of Rabbi Loew and Prague.) Carpets, books, and animal hides were found (or made) to anchor his installations. Tools of inscription – pens, nibs, feathers – became instruments of confession. He masked windows, bandaged his steel moons: what he was chasing was remembered light. It was not that he relied on metaphor for his effects – but that the boundaries were down; artist, place, objects, were in flux, exchanging identities. Catling had developed the skills of a ventriloquist, a medium: he didn't manipulate or impose, he allowed himself to be imposed upon. He curated his own performances, a man possessed but articulate, capable of shifting from mumbled incantation to prophetic violence, to grotesque comedy. He would move in and out of character at will. He was even prepared to accept the risk of a commission that apparently contradicted his entire *modus operandi*. Book Works, publishers of artists' books, wanted a text (or visual record) made in response to "what's going on in the world today". Madness: he scorned the notion, it was meaningless. And then he began to write.

The Stumbling Block was a pivotal moment, the author's most fully realised publication; a masterpiece of movement and intensity. It has an improvisational inevitability that fulfils, but goes far beyond, the scope of the original commission. The author, aware that he was working in the last of days – for the place in which he lived, and for the society of immigrants and grafters, protected for so long by indifference – set out to attempt a Henry Mayhew circumnavigation: a journey of possession, not analysis. The intention would be to discharge his undertaking by subverting it. Mayhew's insatiable curiosity, his proto-fiction, was never part of Catling's agenda. Catling gathered evidence, memories, fables, only to describe the obstacle that stood in the path of enlightenment and which, paradoxically, was also its principal motor. The repeated litanies by which the stumbling block is invoked have a delusive confidence. Mesmerised by their charm, we come to believe there is such an object, a grail of redemption for the blasted territory. This obstacle, floating like a Magritte anvil, receives its necessary obeisance from a parade of Mayhew stereotypes: the knife-grinder, the dubious medium, the cranker of barrel organs, the dog catcher, the miner with a basket of rotten fish, the street magician, the bookseller, the vagrant. These sentimental engravings, the heritage London we are supposed to recall, are wrenched from their dreamtime into a fatalist scenario constructed with the vigour of a Tarantino. Catling smears them with bad food, slashes them open, in order to withdraw news of the light. The book writhes in the clamp of hunger (written at speed, as it was, pre-breakfast, on the train to Brighton, each text one journey): knives, cutlery, fish, "a bouillon hive", "oxoed grit", "fat sugar that clogs the passage to any kind of paradise".

The Stumbling Block is the map, the shape of this urban garden from which the author (and his disciples) are about to be banished: ground constructed like a heart. Veins, the aorta, channels of blood, are constantly invoked. Needles that stitch the failing valves. "The shaping force," as Catling later admitted, "came from place." The book distils the essence as it now is, while summoning aspects that have passed out of reach: "the foundation of stillness is removed." The pages, blocks of black text, act like travel instructions, reports of mental journeys, alchemical prescriptions. "Without plan or direction they have begun to sleep a line." The dispossessed are channelled by a stone pillow. "In the gutters and elbows of curbs, in the approved architectural contrivances they have threaded themselves in a necklace cleated to ring a living, dreaming wall; a perimeter fence. Their expulsion has constructed a cage that concentrates the greed in its own bitter well." The visions that Catling offers are all made from the advantage of this barrier wall with its sealed gates, looking inward on a seething chaos. The "blocks" that he paraphrases – plinths, spirit benches, desert altars – are worked upon, chipped with language: until they tip, spill, gush, yield their water. That is the first quest. The "graphite font", at the book's opening, "has softened its mouth to hold water". At the conclusion: "a night thing, that sits on the heart . . . will sip from the ribs of guilt." The circular excursion has brought the poet back to his starting point; a stone, capable of satisfying thirst, also marks "the well of Joseph", identified in the uncollected poem, "Being here". The poet needs to leech his signature from the page: "the paper will drink any of the stains of . . . usage." Even the individual letters with which *The Stumbling Block* was printed will be melted down in a ladle, carried to the river at London Bridge and tipped in a silver stream into the racing tide: fusing at last into the object that the book defines.

Wounded in the tongue, Catling insists upon the shaman's right to draw artefacts from his own traumatized flesh. He invents a reverse archaeology, in which the maker returns his magical talismans to the earth. The assertions that illuminate the progressive sequences of *The Stumbling Block* operate as erasures. Conjurings, street fights, conspiracies: they are special and singular. They happen just as Catling reveals them. They will never happen again.

The second and more important quest is the pursuit of light, the provocation of blindness: "light in the eye of the needle grown solid with anger." Catling, in performance, bathes his tired orbs with ink, rubs them with chalk or dried semen. His face has a preternatural ability to remain blank, to absorb multiple personalities and soul-invasions: a canvas bucket in which summoned "others" come and go. The head is shaved and he's an Elizabethan magus. The bouffant helmet is restored and he's an Old Kent Road art spiv, a lecturer in heresy, a madman, a grotesque, a heavenly messenger. One wrong gesture and these masks are exposed as bad theatre. He's aware of that. His improvisations are thoroughly rehearsed (if only in the notebook). He'll work at buildings for as long as it takes to get his fix, recover the voices and gestures that will free him from the self-imposed task. "Mud and ink, paper and water are scoured into another projection." Eliminate by careful definition and the "primal eye" will "sense the light." Catling's creatures, the ones he impersonates, are "constructed spectres . . . almost strong enough to catch and drain the omnipotent cryptic grace of the block." When his acts of mediumship are successful, place bears no identifiable scars: "Lanterns of ice are offered to the early morning, light is stroked through their steaming chancels."

If the *The Stumbling Block*, Catling's attempt at "written sculpture" – exploiting the shifting transitional ghetto zone that wasn't quite Whitechapel, but was parasitical upon a city of business and surveillance – worked so effectively that it freed him from a landscape he had loved too long, allowing him to move elsewhere, then another, more severe task was soon to hand. Matt's Gallery, which had shown Catling's *Lair* in their space on London Fields, now had the use of an extinguished lighthouse at Trinity Buoy Wharf on the outer lip of the Isle of Dogs: "the flickering glacial rim of the new city". Immediate fascination gave way to days of inarticulate bile: the tower refused to communicate. Its charms were too dusty, too obvious. The radiant colony on the western horizon mocked his feeble strategies. I've rarely seen him sweat so hard to uncover the right path. He sensed that the building was "saturated in absence, a dark sodden kind". Solitary hours turned into weeks as he stared out at the river, toying with the notebooks, picking at the history of this abandoned promontory. (Gavin Jones, offered his docklands shot on a greasy cloacal slipway near the *Telegraph* complex, had his trembling heron-mound constructed in days: photographed, filmed for the *Late Show*, vandalised and destroyed, in the time it took Catling to sweep up the black dust of the loft, and pound it into ink. Jones was an Apache, a raider. Catling worked in sand, seeing the archetypal picture in the moment of its creation, before allowing it to be blown away.)

From the diamond-paned dome of the lighthouse's lamp-room, you could watch the procession of empty river buses on the shuttle to the City Airport. A vehicle would drive down to the jetty to meet them, and go away disappointed. Investment was draining into the mud. Half-finished flyovers dominated poisoned creeks. The only viable business in the area was the tea van which parked itself on Leamouth Road, to service lost salesmen, construction workers, and adventurous art drones who had heard rumours of the Catling manifestation. Cheeks bulging with bacon rolls, hot fat dripping down our shirt fronts, we fetched coffee for the artist while he squatted in his hutch, brooding on the installation which was billed to run from the 8th of November to the 1st of December, 1991.

It took time, but he got there. The notebook saw him through. He'd understood all along the sub-text to this show: how the developers, the Docklands underwriters, used art to pimp the territory, bring in the chattering classes. Make it appear that something was happening. He also knew that none of this mattered. His shtick was memory: raising a wind, creating the eidetic images that other people would carry away. He would vampirise empty places, conspire with them to redirect the expectations and fantasy-streams that visitors would transport to this site, the lighthouse. "The sounding board is other people's memory," he told Ian Hunt, "what they take when they go."

There would be no installation. Nothing would be imported and nothing would remain when he left. The paradigm of contemporary art practice. No other method works so well. The popularity of Henry Moore's bronze casts with industrialists and government agencies derives from their weight and imperturbability: you can't hack your name into them without the proper kit, and they feel as if, melted down, they'd be worth a few bob. These grave forms do not so much affect memory as displace it, decant their own weight, position themselves in our mappings of the city like railway termini.

Minimal adjustments were made: parabolic mirrors arranged like low tables, the wooden bays identified and readied for occupation. It was at Trinity Buoy Wharf that Catling finally ran the light to earth. He saw the tower as an extinguished eye, not a phallus. His texts, ground down from the dust and bone-flakes of the whispering loft, would replace the lantern (like Stan Brakhage pasting moths' wings and sections of leaf onto blank film). In the lamp-room itself, a circular steel "writing table" creaked and groaned with the effort of inscription. Catling went deep into character, removing his spectacles, cutting himself off from the procession of the curious. He ghosted from bay to bay mumbling his mantra, six coded retrievals from the notebook. Each one a hymn of regret: for sight and colour.

1.   . . . *memories, fluorescence showering into this lofty hutch. By its shimmering glow we see . . .*

2.   . . . *boulders which pounce and curve the light . . .*

3.   . . . *material sliced in the first beam . . . To see we must remember, wind the fluid back, suck it through the optic nerve, hold it in our breath where we can chalkily name it.*

4.   *The lectern shoulders against the beam . . .*

5.   *Nailed cones and rods scratch into the wave. Silked colours rent to white, they bleed tendrils . . .*

6.   *In this shaft of light, the ink cupped from here is red . . . It pumps its own light into a well where stars are: a parabolic night rafted in an iron sepulchre of day.*

His audience was admitted in small groups, twos and threes, by a doorkeeper. Catling droned on, five hours a day, for as long as anyone stayed in the building. He did not, as at the Serpentine show, come out of character. It was partly an Hogarthian freakshow, partly an audience with the oracle. The voice thickened and cracked. He performed through a heavy cold into fever, and back again. At weekends, the crowds came – until the wharf, "once the centre of waterway maintenance for the docks", was as busy as in its 1896 heyday. Several thousand signatures went into the visitors' book, making it a significant document in the archive of the area. The trip to the lighthouse (that mocking confusion with an AIDS charity, Virginia Woolf and other manifestations of plague and pestilence) became an important aspect of the show. Some people never got there and had a great time doing it. Others, lost in the desert hinterland, struck up unlikely acquaintanceships: Elton John's legendary percussionist Ray Cooper (last seen, photographed on the foreshore at Limehouse, modelling designer tat with his old mucker Steven Berkoff) offered a lift in his limo to a rain-drenched Dr Brian Hinton, poet, hedge-scholar, and apologist for that great lost guitarist (and bibliophile), Martin Stone.

At the Lighthouse illuminated ground that was trapped in torpid darkness. I found myself tracking the Grand Union Canal, the Limehouse Cut and the Lea, to arrive at the exhibition site by water. And then scarcely needing to go inside. Catling's performed presence was a generator of calm. It stopped the world, making it easy for casual visitors to drop into reverie, achieve the state where fiction was the highest truth.

The lighthouse signalled the beginning of the end for one period of Catling's work. He wouldn't find it easy to shake himself free of this "carcass of a cyclops, its eye extinguished and removed". By the time of his performance at the Bridewell Theatre in July 1994, he had been banished beneath the stage, exiled among water-pipes and rusty nails in the caretaker's cupboard: he *was* the Cyclops, "peering in the dark . . . throat knotted to a glass . . . without a true word to say." (Even the cover for the catalogue of this event, *Subversion in the Street of Shame*, depicted Catling with his eyes blanked by circular card labels.) He seems to have condemned himself to follow, and obey, a single beam: losing perspective and the ability to judge distance. His face has been folded. There is no nose. And his mouth is a sphinctal smudge, a gas hole. The performer is haunted and possessed by the presence he has summoned. Given the choice of roles, he has always been more Charles Laughton than Clark Gable: preferring the growl or the hump to the tights and padded codpiece. His favourite identification is with the blowsy, one-eyed drunkard, Rooster Cogburn, as manifested by John Wayne. Now he is tracked across London by the cyclops of Trinity Buoy Wharf, a dissatisfied articulation. A viral golem. (The poet Simon Perril in his essay on *The Stumbling Block* makes great play of this metaphor, the penalty of trading in "unanchored identity". "The Cabalist," Perril writes, "endows the Golem with life by the inscription of the word EMETH – truth – on its brow. When the clay creature has fulfilled its master's tasks it is dematerialised by the erasure of the first letter on its forehead, leaving the word METH – death.")

Catling's career can be thought of as having three phases. First: everything up to the Royal College. Grounding in South London; visits to museums (Horniman, Imperial War, South Kensington complex); expeditions to Dorset, South Coast, Highlands; creation of Sherlockian room as expression of personality (objects, found and made, books, stuffed animals, weapon sculpture); Maidstone and Walthamstow. Defensive magic. Role playing. Poe, Lovecraft, night cinema. English murder mystique. Work that celebrated a personal mythology (bomber pilots, natural history field studies, architectural excavations, fairground freaks, Dutch interiors, forensic anomalies, star charts, London, Maria Callas) and work that was intended to shock or offend dim sensibilities. "Between fists & cunts his/personality pivots", he wrote in his first book, *Necropathia*: before offering his responses to "earthworks", "tv loneliness", gangsters, sex criminals, suicides, insane asylums, bathing machines and "Siamese altar pieces".

The second phase, in my reading, runs from the Royal College to the conclusion of the Henry Moore Fellowship at Norwich. This is a period of very real achievement opposed by constant difficulties: of finding the space and time in which to work, procuring material, getting books into print. The pitch was still schizophrenic: the poet and the sculptor lived in different compartments, and both were alienated from, and somewhat embarrassed by, the performance artist. Marvellous books – *Vorticegarden*, *Pleiades in Nine*, *Das Kranke Tier*, *Vox Humana*, *The Tulpa Index* – appeared at regular intervals. But they were subliminal triumphs, unreviewed by literary clubmen, ignored by the art establishment. Catling's gifts, like those of Wyndham Lewis, made him a leper at both sets of tables. He continued as an object maker, often extending and making manifest themes that were sketched in the books of poetry. But there was a nagging sense of strain in all this, unresolved until the world caught up with him, and the restrictions and inhibitions of the Thatcher years cut him free.

The third phase was an arc of pure fulfilment: durational performances in buildings he had coveted for years (beneath the dome of the Tate Gallery, the British Museum Reading Room, Jack London's "Monster Doss House" in Fieldgate Street), books that were appreciated from the moment of their conception. Everything led towards the challenge, and public triumph, of the influential *Blindings* jamboree at the Serpentine Gallery. Catling was prepared, technically and emotionally, to conquer this flavourless space. It was a reprise of the lighthouse event in a kind of disenfranchised park restaurant. He would be always on show, surrounded by iconic texts and constructions that mediated between the building and the poet's incantations. Barefoot, this prophetic wideboy – Harry Lime with bunions – paraded in chalkstripe Harrods suit and dark glasses, reciting or raging, chatting to friends, or wandering off into the park. With the publication of the catalogue, in November 1995, the cycle would close: the poems written for the show, and revised in performance, would be available for study, no longer held like pebbles in the mouth. The secret power of the blinded monster, bastard son of Polyphemus, born in darkness, would be open to inspection. The Homeric Cyclops, a cave-dwelling shepherd, was cursed for scorning Zeus and his pantheon. He was a terrible mixture of strength (casual cannibalism) and deft tenderness, the care for his flocks. A giant undone by drink, by the sound of a fire-hardened olive stave being driven and twisted into his solitary eye: "The loud hiss that comes from a great axe or adze when a smith plunges it into cold water".

Ian Hunt, rhapsodising the show in *Art Monthly*, explains how each of Catling's holograph texts in the south gallery begins "by describing an injection of the eye with a fluid or suspension, to suppress vision in order to enlarge the definition of what seeing entails." The penalties of attainment. The cost of knowledge. The devices of benevolent masochism Catling inventories in the pursuit of wisdom. He moves across the city, haunting it like one of Wim Wenders' terrestrial angels, wings butchered by nail-clippers: in quest of the language formulae that will release him onto the next stair of enlightenment. The "here" that is repeatedly asserted in the texts is not the gallery, not Kensington Gardens, not London: Catling has given up any claim on those addresses, on the notion of place. He is offering himself as a wandering scholar and magician, ready to undertake some new series of projects that will surely invalidate every line of this awkward homage.

Last seen as a guide for a one hour bus tour of Oxford, part of the *Hidden Cities* programme, he chose to present himself in the guise of a dog. Hidden behind a screen of canvas at the front of the vehicle, he barked and howled. Yelping in terror as they crawled alongside experimental laboratories, or woofing in delight at the appearance of spectacularly long-legged female cyclists. His translation to fullblown donnish eccentricity was complete. And the dog, which is the sullen soul of London, was confirmed in its exile.

4.

He is a scrambler, and he delights in subverting his work's most resolute, confident, formal patterns and in putting his most exquisitely achieved effects at risk.

WS DI PIERO (ON ROBERT FRANK)

Catling is known, spoken of in a convenient shorthand as "the English Beuys". Hundreds will follow him into the crypts of churches, out onto Oxford earthworks. Thousands will process through public galleries. Fifty or sixty will read his books with close attention. Gavin Jones's Bracken House garden is an open secret, available to anyone with the will to find it. But what of those others? London is awash with deregulated shamans, equal opportunity visionaries set apart from the tribe. The years have been kind to them, ignoring them utterly, giving them something to kick against. They have been rescued from the confusion of patronage, grants, state-sponsored prostitution. Nobody gives a monkey's what they get up to, these flakes from the Puzzle Club, the memory-wipe generation with their vague hankerings after the glories of Punk cabaret. The Disobey mob. The toilet-club sitdown ravers. The unpublished of Stepney. They can't afford the time to read. New books are out of reach and the libraries are decanting their shelves to find the room for plague leaflets and martial arts promos. The solitary artist is an involuntary shaman – without a tribe, an outcast. S/he develops strategies of derangement, activates some small part of the map. (Like the performer and installation artist presently known as "Crow" – a fine shamanic moniker – with his Institution of Rot. Crow, tonsured, wide-eyed, an unearthed presence in Goth accoutrements, has customised a house in Corbyn Street, Crouch End. "Rot, decay, decomposition . . . that's what the Institution is about," he says, having lived for eleven years inside this decomposing metaphor. The city, with its possibilities of random meetings and discoveries, its gift of anonymity, is his space and his subject: when the man next door attempted to kill himself, Crow raided his doorstep. Many years later he exhibited the furred bottles of Gold Top as *The Suicide Milk*.)

Catling, with his years ducking and weaving through declining art school gulags, honed his ability for finding the unexpected, artists of stubborn individuality. (Not all of them in the bar. Not all of them bright-eyed popsies.) He picked up on rumours. He encouraged – by provocation – the most obtuse and singular elements. But he had one very unfortunate habit: he sometimes inflicted his discoveries on me. And he was almost always right; I would swallow the bait. I'd have to thank him for introducing me to Steve Dilworth's work, his eel-weavings and whalebone boxes, his crows crushed between sheets of glass. (Dilworth also cooked, as far as I can remember it, one of the great meals of my life: a tiny bird inside a fish inside a hare inside . . . Half the wild life of Gloucestershire washed down by copious drafts of whisky.)

Then there was Aaron Williamson. I tried to dig my heels in that time: a poetry reading above a pub in Hammersmith, a group of local amateurs with Aaron as guest. Williamson was a profoundly-deaf ranter with a reputation in Brighton. I refused point blank. Catling persisted. We went out for a drink somewhere to discuss it, and before I could back out we were on the bus. The poetastic out-patients were all that I expected: epic confessionals, bleak satires, modest refusals to read that segued into thirty minute intros. Aaron blew it all away. He was hair-raisingly good: intense, concentrated, savage, unrelenting. "Punk-mortem thug tulpas", Catling has called these texts. "Vengefully articulate language . . . an agile, writhing, tensile force that flickers between extremes."

So the prof was very much in credit when he asked if he could bring a photographer along – "he's all right" – to a film that was being made in Princelet Street. This lurcher with the Leica was a Catling tenant, sub-letting the rooms above the old synagogue in Heneage Street that had become, in their own way, a précis of post-Sixties modernism. (The windows looked out on architect Theo Crosby's stable conversion, but that was a small price to pay.) The original deal with the Bengali property owner must have been a golden one: it allowed Boyd Webb to gift it, at a nominal rent, to a catalogue of sculptors on the way up – and always the right ones, the ones who would appreciate, and make good use of, this magical set. The long room, with the director's desk that features in several of Webb's staged photo-compositions, enjoyed its own light: partly trapped from some earlier era, partly generated by its current occupiers. Alison Wilding lived there, then Catling, and now the photographer Marc Atkins. The room had shifted from a provisional domesticity to something rougher: less lived in and collaborated with than put to work, exploited. All the previous potentialities were redefined as: studio. The street door was locked and the bell went unanswered. There was no telephone. Atkins, a vegan (living on choc bars, crisps, Guinness), concentrated on meat: the female nude, light-sculpted, draped, posed against a shaded window. Flesh seen as soft stone. The adjoining kitchen, no longer a place of improvised meals and wine and family breakfasts, became a darkroom – as the photographer laboured over the texture of his unique prints; experimenting with different photographic papers, scratching at the negative, printing in such a way that his image would pick up the flaws of the wet board on which it was placed. An obsessive alchemy in which he himself would appear as a subject, hanging upsidedown among heavy folds in a debased classicism, or crawling in a Beckettian limbo towards a radiant slope of parrot cages or cans of cooking oil (scavenged props). Otherwise, he had no interest in what lay immediately outside his window, the incontinent clutter of the streets, so tenderly logged by the exiled Czech, Marketa Luskacova – who responded to the unselfconscious surrealism of the Club Row market as to a familiar dream. Atkins didn't want to know. He was repelled by the local. He thirsted for the universality of high art, unplaced, shaped in the studio of his skull.

This was the baggage, the lumber he brought to the house with the peeling pink door in Princelet Street. (Before arriving he had shaved Catling's head, as requested by the filmmakers. The grey wool lay on the floor of the studio for months, incorporated into shadowy compositions, swept into Crowleyesque heaps: like a lens fault, ectoplasm that couldn't be filtered out.) Standing outside, while incorporating himself into the group, the context of the film, Atkins found that his photographs were not subtractions from the general energy, but a very real addition. He was primed, by his Heneage Street experiments, to the mood of the project: documentary fiction, unreliable hypothesis giving way to fragmentation, confession, barbecued vanities. The director, Chris Petit, was risking what was left of his career by allowing himself to become involved with these people: non-actors barely capable of remembering who they were, but who couldn't stop talking about it. Shady locations. Overload of themes: biblio-paranoia, the legend of David Litvinoff (local colour adviser on the film *Performance*), the persistence of place, Sexton Blake novels composed by Flann O'Brien, a parade of marginalised and reforgotten writers and artists checking in – wrangled and harassed by the bookdealer known as Driffield. Robin Cook/Derek Raymond, Alexander Baron, Emnuel Litvinoff, John

Latham, Brian Catling, Aaron Williamson, Alan Moore, Tony Lambrianou, Martin Stone, Michael Moorcock: all talking each other down, all insisting on *their* version of the doctrine, at cross-purposes, tormented by history. The title, *The Cardinal and the Corpse*, came from one of the pulp novels O'Brien was supposed to have written – to show that he could. The commissioning editor at Channel 4, Waldemar Januszczak, who admitted to being "one of the most intelligent people in Europe", never got further than the credits. Who *were* these freaks? In his role as an avant-garde essayist, he had puffed John Latham as "perhaps the only genuine radical in British art of the post-war era", but seeing him on tape, a gaunt philosopher with an alien fire in the eye, he exclaimed: "lose the cadaver".

Atkins, an autodidact who tracked the culture at his own pace, had no such problems. Comprehensively underinformed about "lost" literature by his first-class degree from Cheltenham College of Art, his period at the Jan Van Eyck Akademie, Maastricht, his Rome sabbatical, he was dealing with a group as unknown to him as a culling of desert fathers. His was a hands-on approach. The photographs he took were not "stills", they were not intended to show off the actors, or the director in pensive mood. They were an impressive sequence that evolved into a parallel narrative: including ironic asides on the making of the film (shots I was never able to parley into the final cut). The texture of Atkins' prints was richer and blacker, more elegiac, than video tape with its inescapable thinness. Video is too eager to please, says too much. It "vacuums its subjects", as WS Di Piero says in an essay on Robert Frank; with the consequence that it "tends to flatten all the elements in a field to a single emotional valence." Frank wanted something more "operatic". The photographs taken for the *Cardinal*, using the sensibility derived from the studio work, have this mock grandeur. Catling, silver-mint head, stubble, cigar, embodies the Elizabethan magus, the Dr Dee clone, to a degree that is impossible on tape. Seen in colour, in an editing suite, he is the thing he is playing and also the other self, the actor, the performance artist. Photography lies with more conviction. It excludes. It concentrates essence. Within the frame of its formal properties, Driffield can exist in the same universe as the Kray foot-soldier, Tony Lambrianou. Cook is perched at a pub table in animated conversation, while Petit covers his mouth with a hand, in a gesture of erasure, to watch the same event on a hidden monitor. A white line, which harks back to Atkins' distressing of his prints, divides the composition – but is a natural form, the edge of a reflector board.

What I admire especially in these group compositions, and others taken in bars and the cellars of the Bridewell, are the complex, floating relationships Atkins reveals: a sinister *Las Meninas* interplay of watcher and watched. It's uncanny the way he is able to hit on instants of stillness; one figure raving, while the next turns to stare into the shadows, and a third notices, and stiffens before, the camera. And what doesn't matter is swallowed in velvet darkness. There is one print of which I am particularly fond, taken in a laundry room beneath an old swimming pool, two figures at the extreme edges of the frame, not looking at each other, or the photographer. A bare bulb catches the domed head of one of them, while the other is lit by streetlight creeping down through glass tiles. The rest is articulate gloom: diagonals from machines, blank doorways that lead away into unknowable passages.

The difficulty for Atkins, as for the shamanic artists (because he is not truly one of them), was how to pitch his work in such a way that he could get a living from it. Photo-journalism was not really an option, his prints didn't give up their meaning to those requiring an instant effect. Newspapers are after the shock of the familiar, the hit that we've seen time after time. They demand "strong" images without flaws in terms of focus and lighting. The operatic shades that Atkins favours are no use to them. Neither was generic photography much help: his nudes were too arty, too challenging, too dimly lit for the pornbrokers who like harsh print and all the detail they can handle, this side of cardiac arrest. If he shot a wedding group it would end up looking like *The Anatomy Lesson of Dr Tulp*. I helped him to get involved with portraiture, author heads. But this was not altogether successful. The strikingly moody snap of Petit taken for his Soho novel, *Robinson*, was rejected on the grounds that the author would be too easily confused with his creation.

But portraiture (combined with hiking) did open up the form which catapulted Atkins' work into all the paying broadsheets: the obituary tribute. First Robin Cook, who gave a great reading – the living, excited voice issuing from a skeletal frame – a few days before he died. And then the poet and teacher, Eric Mottram. I'd been asked for a brief, one page contribution, to a volume produced for Mottram's 70th birthday, *Alive in Parts of this Century*. My notion was that we would walk from Hackney to Herne Hill, that I would explain to Marc, on the course of this walk, who Mottram was, my memories of him, what he stood for – and then, on arrival, Atkins would take a single image. Text would be printed on one page and photograph on the next. Unfortunately, the editors liked a number of the options Atkins offered so much that they decided to use two of them: the contemplative Mottram first, then the laughter. The book was launched at King's in the Strand, where Mottram had taught for so many years, arranged so many readings. He was in fine boisterous form, enjoying the tributes and the company of his colleagues. A few weeks later he was dead, promoted into one of those figures the culture feels guilty about, giving their lives all the coverage that they denied to their publications. The contemplative portrait appeared everywhere, alongside fulsome praise for the "best known unknown poet in England." Now writers of a certain age, seeing Atkins arrive on the doorstep with his camera, make their excuses. The energy exchange is too intense. Leaving those marks on photographic paper, drains the life force. It's too risky a collaboration.

No other form of autobiography existed beyond the landscape and portraiture of the city: its weather, architecture, artists, rivers, canals, graveyards, signs, crowds, patterns of electricity and movement. To analyse all this, to spy on such secrets was to disqualify yourself from shamanic possibilities. Photography, on this epic scale, was too knowing. Too much hard evidence was left behind. Atkins tried to arrange the occasional show which he would advertise as a mental journey: the New York skyline intercut with Canary Wharf, a Heneage Street nude and a girl in Canada, clouds in West Wales, the Nevada desert. Robert Frank, trying to rid himself of the anguish of memory, the sentimental portfolio of achievement, asked a friend to drill holes through a stack of prints. Atkins, influenced by Frank, and drained by the sheer mass of city imagery boxed in his room, the weight of all that stone light, has started to deconstruct his catalogue: mix colour shots with strips from grander monochrome prints, with scribbled texts. But scraps of language are tautologous: there is already a powerful narrative element in the image. Each frame provokes the next, implies movement. Nothing is replete. The form is hungry. It encourages, depends upon, a restless urgency.

Atkins, growing up in a mining community (according to one version of his infinitely adjustable history), was subjected to Catholic pieties. Even the Cheltenham art students had their share of proselytising fundamentalists (this is harder to imagine). He became a determined materialist. His work, influenced by his tutor, Nigel Slight, was heavy with active contradictions: substantial spirits. A crowd of absences and negations, contrails, entrails, mud, paint: to evoke isolation. "Enjoined to/lap blood with mailed/pierced flesh and ripped/clean screams dancing/with greater though/lesser dimensional peers/a depiction of sad/seduction entombed within/the sheath of an eye." Narcissism and lethargy kept him brooding, motionless in a chair, before the need to be out, at work, reasserted itself. He says that he mistook the texture of *The Loneliness of the Long Distance Runner*, absorbed at age 14, for a prophetic message. To pull up short, drop out, refuse: instead of increasing the pace, devouring the territory. There was an additional contradiction, such as Robert Graves endured, in the worship of woman (in all her shifting identities): in that he was enforcing, through the energy of his rapture, a passivity. *The Man Does, Woman Is* conceit, which demands that the female manifests herself without movement, like a Windmill Theatre nude. An immanence, fecund but without imagination. This loving deactivation was a false trope. He knew that: the headless and hooded figures, the profane madonnas with their closed eyes, were replaced by contemporaries, by women in a hurry. With a life outside the studio, somewhere else to be. He took a few years to come to it, but it was a legitimate breakthrough: the city and its people were revealed as his true subject.

Atkins was, in many ways, the direct descendant of John Deakin, the best photographer of the feral Soho *demi-monde*. Like Deakin he second-guessed fate by committing portraits of not-quite-knowns, never-to-be-knowns, and the reforgotten. Poets. Who else but Deakin can we rely on for accounts of WS Graham, George Barker, Paul Potts, Oliver Bernard, John Heath-Stubbs? Who else but Atkins is working at it *now*? The faces that nobody wants to collect. He is gathering a fugitive archive, sleeping on pillows of it; up at dawn, prowling the streets, searching out the empty spaces that will reprieve him from the babble of portraiture. "London," as Deakin wrote, "is most personal in the half-deserted early morning or dusk – when it holds most promise and mystery."

There is no birth-certificate for Atkins. He willingly adopts heteronyms for different types of art practice. (Yes, he has read Fernando Pessoa.) Suffering from weak lungs and being summoned for an X-ray (at the time when he had been taking photographs for my *Radon Daughters* project), he gave the medics the name of SL Joblard (an invention loosely caricaturing aspects of a living sculptor). A reckless procedure: plunging into metafiction, sub-text, the fantasy world of spectres, doubles, half-resolved literary projections. Known humans parodied and vampirised, unformed incubi cruising for connections. Atkins was asked for the Christian name of a fiction who had no reality beyond his initials. "Steven", he replied (upping the stakes). I have the X-ray plate in front of me (HIGH KV/FILTER), with the rough draft of the Atkins essay behind it – prefiguring the photographer's formalist experiments, when he laid portraits printed on cellophane over pages of written text. The ribs are clouded in nebulous wisps that seem to shift as you watch them, nothing obviously malign. Placing the X-ray over the sellotaped map, taken from *The A to Z of Georgian London*, prepared according to John Hudson's instructions, the results are spectacular. The Joblard name – appearing at the bottom of the frame as "Even Joblard 18.11.92" – is aligned with the Dunstan chapel at St Paul's: the ribs and lungs are then thunder clouds, massed to east and west of Aldersgate Street, which runs through the centre of the composition like a bright spine. Lifting the plate sounds like a *Lear* storm, phony but effective. The orchards beyond Old Street are future cancers, nodules on the throat. The curious earthworks to the north of Ratclifs Layer are polyps, hair eggs.

The walks, out of all this, were healthful excursions. For both of us. Taking Marc from the tyranny of the darkroom, giving me a way to subvert what I thought I knew. Marching along the Thames, or cutting into the Surrey foothills, gave this book a form: removed it from the taint of the rehashed essay. Marc's photographs, in the end, didn't have to appear in the book (though I would be delighted if they did): they informed the text. I would look at key images for a long time before writing. Sometimes he made a record of inscriptions, or signs on walls, or memorial stones, that saved me the drudgery of trying to describe them in my notebook. (I was keeping my own photographic record, but Marc's was much more reliable.) His skill was to make himself redundant. I knew what he would take. I knew how it would look. He was collaborating on the formation of my prose. Sometimes I would notice one of his images, out there in the landscape, and wonder why he hadn't bothered to log it. I pointed out, as we came through Maryon Wilson Park, the way the dry grass formed an X on the opposite slope. Obligingly, Marc clicked his shutter. (The day started slowly, flat light, Charlton House Library closed as usual, and Mark had only taken nine shots by eleven o'clock. After the X things improved and he finished up with the usual three or four rolls to develop.)

Over the months, the prints have changed: different papers, sepia, near-brown. The quality has been consistent. The Tate & Lyle factory under a lowering sky, filtered for definition and menace (leading to a sequence of pure skyscapes). The last days of the Roebuck public-house on the corner of Durward Street: doomed as soon as photographed. The care that Atkins lavished on his inanimate subjects (however swiftly he operated) ensured that every image was an elegy. There was no point in hanging on any longer, better to collapse in a rubble heap, exist in memory. He would do things to make a picture that he wouldn't go near at any other time of his life: bugger his lungs by scuffling through the Rotherhithe Tunnel on foot, claw his way up church towers in the dark, put out on the river in the roughest craft with the craziest skipper, shake hands with Jeffrey Archer.

Photography at this level of intensity was also a way of focusing the shape of any prose speculation. Atkins would provide the defining image: the split head on the sepulchre at the entrance to Chingford Mount Cemetery, the stone angel that had become a tree in Kensal Rise. It didn't matter that I brought these things to his attention, or found them on some solitary expedition: I saw them as Marc Atkins photographs. I located them on his behalf. He was capable of expressing the essence of something I had tried to describe in a way that defied the possibilities of mere prose. I'd picked for years around a morbid fascination with the twin plaster dogs, the Dogs of Alcibiades, on their plinths in Victoria Park. They should symbolise something unpleasant, sentimental, and potentially perverse, that I could never quite locate. We trudged past them on the morning of our rainswept graffiti walk to Greenwich University, and I asked Marc to have a pop at the poodles. The light was grim and unforgiving. He had to sweat to trap the dogs on the absolute edge of his frame, to keep them both in the picture, and still contrive a composition that was not blank at its heart. And he pulled it off: the glistening wet road, haloes of diminishing electric lights on their poles, desolation. Printed on thick Japanese paper (his latest enthusiasm), the shot is timeless. It has everything I would love to invoke, and it grasps it in an instant. The head has been turned. The lens will be wiped and we'll walk on.

CINEMA PURGATORIO

*I am in the happy position of not being likely to be
forgotten never having been known.*

FRANCIS STUART

My brilliant career in cinema was over before it began, and there was
nothing brilliant about it. It didn't take very long, no more than ten or
fifteen years, to understand that the fantasy of making some kind of living while working on projects that would have, at least, the bite of
mainstream fiction, was just that. Film is ninety-nine percent hassle to
one percent fruitful accident. It's Russian roulette with thousands of
blanks and a single golden bullet. Grasp the basic equation and you
might still crack it. You might be the unique individual from the four
hundred who apply, brandishing their diplomas, first class degrees in
media studies, connections, self-evident genius, who gets taken on,
unpaid, to field the phonecalls in an empty office in Barons Court,
where several "in development" projects are waiting for seed money.
Where elements are juggled, dyke ramraiders balanced with Bengali
outworkers on a spree, with charismatic dysfunctionals, with whoever
or whatever blending of PC agenda will hit the BFI/Euro slush fund
on its blind spot. Because all are agreed that TV is kaput, not worth
slagging off; too sad for that. It's finished. As Chris Petit says, TV consists of "assembly, not cutting". Accumulation. Overload of dead
evidence. A sorry compromise between bent accountants and renegades living down their *Late Show* apprenticeship. Even insiders
sleepwalk with the bruised gaiety of the last days of the Russian
Empire; they know the fire is coming, but they don't know when –
and meanwhile nothing matters, they can get away with the most
breathtaking scams, work all the favours that will see them right in a
post-revolutionary world. This might explain, if nothing else does, a
few of those dazzling career curves: the surfing between novelist's chair,
commissioning editor's desk, National Theatre, steam-radio plug show.
It's comfortable rather than corrupt: this admirable persistence of the

271

jobbing craftsman constantly finding new ways to present the same old dog's dinner.

I was wrong from the start. I never got far enough into the business to have the option of selling out. My minimal contribution to the visual mythology of London is worth sketching only as a period piece, a cartoon that shorthands the obstacles overcome by more serious players.

I discovered the periodical *Sight and Sound* in the school library, and was, at once, addicted to a vicarious form of cinema. I read essays on films that I had never seen, made by directors I did not know. But, best of all, were the stills (whether taken from the films themselves, or re-staged, or photographed independently). From these emblems, these seductive and mysterious groupings, a fictional narrative could be implied. Even the heavy, glossy paper had an appeal that outlived the charm of the essays (as soon as I could understand them, as soon as I had seen enough of the films, I disagreed with the stance, the language, the prejudices). I realised that Lindsay Anderson, who sometimes wrote for *Sight and Sound*, and was beginning to be talked up in the film magazines, had also done time in this school. (Later, he went back there to shoot *If* – which disappointed me in its demonstration that the director had been unable to shake off, or destroy, the place and the imprinted attitudes he dressed in sad revolutionary rags. A career blighted by too much peevishness, not enough rage. Gavin Lambert – at school and at Oxford with Anderson, a fellow contributor to *Sequence* – though not much talked about, seems to have managed the thing, a life, with greater success: a sub-Isherwood Californian twilight, unspectacular screenplays and the occasional collection of tactful short stories or a novella, unnoticed with faint praise.)

Sight and Sound carried regular adverts for the London School of Film Technique. This wasn't Lodz, but you didn't have to learn Polish. At school I caught up with *The Seventh Seal*, *Seven Samurai*, *Day of Wrath*, *Rear Window*, Cocteau's *Orphée*, Bresson's *Un Condamné à Mort s'est Échappé*; *Peeping Tom*, *Hiroshima Mon Amour*, *Les Quatre Cents Coups* were bagged on local raids; and I hitched up to London for a crash course in Visconti, Antonioni, and the rest of the high-toned cultural baggage that could be hoovered up over a weekend spent in the darkness of the Academy, the Paris Pullman and various scattered Cameos and Classics. London was entirely subterranean; dropped off in somewhere improbable, like Ruislip, it was straight underground, emerging only to hit the next cinema or fleapit. A floor would be negotiated, usually in South

Kensington, Cromwell Road, Victoria, but we were on the move before it was possible to link up any of these map references. Without the film listings, London would have fallen apart. (Chris Petit, writing about Julian Maclaren-Ross, and describing how he developed his own psychogeography, confesses that he spent his spare time, when he wasn't watching films, chasing about the city ticking off significant locations. The list is intriguing: "a sinister park near Charlton Athletic football ground from *Blow-Up*; a crescent house and a riverside apartment in *The Passenger*; the house on the corner of Powis Square in *Performance*; the Covent Garden pub and Coburg Hotel in *Frenzy*.")

I cobbled together a film fan CV, completed the required script, and took myself off to Electric Avenue, Brixton, where the film school perched above a butcher's shop. The relief at escaping at last from all that healthy Cotswold air was extreme: the stench of exotic fruits and herbs, rancid meat, vinegar, musty paperbacks, linoleum, scent that made cats weep, had me hallucinating like a stylite. (After these years of confinement and repression, the hit from the school secretary's industrial perfume, her conceptual blondeness, made the knees buckle.) I was absolutely not at home, and comfortable with the anonymity, the markets, the terrible food, the unknown hills and valleys of South London, with their pollarded avenues, the careful curtains, the chapels and god hoardings, electrical repair shops and pet prisons. The cemeteries were bigger and had more life than most of the towns I knew. You could walk on a Sunday from West Norwood, where I lodged, through Streatham and Tulse Hill, Brixton and Kennington, to the river, to the Tate to see the Francis Bacon exhibition (stopping off on the return journey to pay your respects to Howard Hawks' *Rio Bravo* in Stockwell). I could meet a Thai friend, with whom I used to talk boxing and borrow his *Ring* magazines, to find him revealed as a poet, about to leave for Hong Kong and work experience with the Shaw Brothers, masters of martial arts exploitation cinema. His guardian, when I collected him from some Knightsbridge mansion, was horrified to discover that the pleasant schoolboy with whom she remembered chatting had evolved into a grubby and bearded, sub-human beatnik. (False assumptions, both.)

The London School of Film Technique had everything going for it, except any useful instruction in film-making, or opportunity to write/shoot/edit. (It's not a credit many people flash on their dust-wrappers. The respected critic, novelist, and dictionary compiler, David Thomson, is the exception.) The lethargy of the misnamed Electric

Avenue (great to see it again in Patrick Keiller's *London*) suited my case; the disinterest, the prevailing sense that film was something that was talked about, but didn't happen. I was free to spend time on my own researches – obscure poems, day-long wanderings, documentary photographs – and then to drop in to brew up some coffee, sit on the roof at the back of the butcher's shop, listen to the multinational chat. I was the only British student in the place, and the youngest by several years. The others, Egyptians, Malayans, Nigerians, had expectations. The diploma would fit them – especially if their fathers had political clout – to take over their country's film industry. The Americans and Europeans had more modest ambitions: a pleasantly dozy English interlude, followed by a job in the cutting room, on a newsreel crew, or a delayed return to real life.

There were muted rumbles of discontent, scenes in the secretary's office, justified complaints about the inadequate tuition (old lags from the Savile Club and unemployable technicians exercising their cynicism) – countered by yet another screening of *Metropolis* or *The Battleship Potemkin*. The titular head of the operation, Robert Dunbar, had a good reputation in the trade, but was rarely, if ever, seen. (He was, I suppose, a kind of Anthony Blunt figurehead, well-connected in the counterculture. His son, John – famous for being once married to Marianne Faithfull – ran the avant-garde gallery where John Lennon met Yoko Ono. His daughter, Jennifer, married the poet Edward Dorn. There's a frontispiece photograph in Dorn's pamphlet, *Manchester Square*, 1975, that showcases the whole troop.)

We didn't get to do much hands-on filming, after the Old Bill came around and confiscated most of the equipment. Certain members of the faculty – not Dunbar – had, apparently, got themselves webbed up with neighbourhood villains. Disputed provenance left the cupboards bare and porn moguls short of their second unit crews. Searching for film-stock to complete the course project, I came across a stash of *Definition* magazines, run from the premises, with philippics by distinguished ex-student Arnold Wesker. Was a marriage of convenience between literature and cinema possible? It didn't seem likely, even then, at the dawn of the era when the Royal Court playwrights were hoping to cut a deal with Woodfall Films; when Lindsay Anderson's and Tony Richardson's "Free Cinema", with its boys' clubs and funfairs, its night footage by Walter Lassally, earnestly strove to graft the English documentary tradition of the Thirties onto the provincial realist novels of the Fifties and Sixties. (You could make a case for Alan Sillitoe and Karel

Reisz with *Saturday Night and Sunday Morning*, or David Storey and Lindsay Anderson in *This Sporting Life*, but the only collaboration between equal partners was the troubled conjunction of Losey and Pinter.)

I think I realised, long before this, that I didn't have the temperament for the industry. I had no desire to serve my time as assistant glue-stirrer in a bureaucratic cutting room. Nothing else was on offer. I would never be competent to direct, the film we were labouring on proved that. Three essential qualities were lacking: an effective sense of structure (beginning, middle, end, in the correct order), the appearance of technical facility in all departments, and the ability to persuade, con, bully others into doing exactly what you wanted them to do, no matter how ridiculous it made them look. (This last, which seemed the trickiest aspect in those days, has now become second nature.) Neither would I ever get the angle of the baseball cap right, the way of slouching in a chair to watch the playback, or the video monitor.

I had the sense that it was time to retreat to further education, Dublin. This was a wise indecision, a good way of slowing down the inevitable: new light – soft, wet, grey. Willingly trapped between the hills and the sea, it could rain for months at a time. The culture was both urban and provincial: intelligent clerks, tweed cap poets with cowshit on their boots, horse-protestants, the unenlightened scum of the English public school system, American dropouts without the imagination or the means to reach Paris, Glasgow runaways, Liverpool painters, professional drunks, tribes of tinkers, barefoot children, showbands and barn-sized dancehalls, prostitutes with conversation who sat up all night drinking sweet tea, Incredible String Band floaters, sons of Brynners and Mitchums. The last bohemia. There was also a real town, going about its business, careful suburbs, grim estates, an infinity of cinemas. I, and several others, individually, and as a group, haunted them. Two or three a day: Rathmines to Drumcondra, Clontarf to Haroldscross. The projectionists had their foibles: at the Regal Ringsend, where we had come to admire Vittorio Cottafavi's *Hercules Conquers Atlantis*, the show began on time at five o'clock – but the doors weren't opened until the man who took the tickets arrived at quarter past. Reels were frequently shown in the wrong order. The cutting made Petit's *Chinese Boxes* look pedestrian: weird censorship excisions would have conversations stop and start at random, leap backwards and forwards like *Last Year in Marienbad* made with Rock Hudson and Doris Day. The projectionists would sample any nudity, cull the naughty bits for their private collections. Yet a film like Kubrick's *Lolita*, where the damage was all by implication, slid through untouched. Not for nothing did James Joyce invest in one of the first cinemas in the city.

Dublin seemed to have been programmed by the essayists of *Cahiers du Cinema* in their Hollywood nostalgic phase: seasons of Sam Fuller, Budd Boetticher, Nicholas Ray, Anthony Mann, Douglas Sirk, Vincent Minnelli, Don Siegel. Colour, landscape, lyricism. City speed. We devoured it, as an antidote to Yeatsian vapours, the careerist rhetoric of the Ulster poets. And we plotted films of our own.

I drew a horse in a sweepstake and, for the first time in my life, picked up a few quid when it won. This money went into a 16mm film to be shot in South Wales, cast of three, usual apocalyptic post-industrial back-drop, mood borrowed from Polanski's *Three Men and a Wardrobe*. The ruins of Morriston, the flaring smokestakes of Port Talbot, the Gower Peninsula, standing in for Poland – as Spain pastiched Arizona and New Mexico in spaghetti westerns. The cameraman on this inglorious folly was the other Tom Baker. He wasn't a future Dr Who but he did have some previous experience, and was thus roped in to light happenings and performances, to take photographs for magazines, or to provide a com-monsense view of our pretensions. The experience that Tom screened for us was an 8mm short, on which he had acted as cameraman for a school friend from Radley. This film was nothing like the scheme we had in hand: there was no symbolism, no sub-text, no homages. Straightforward action. An intruder breaks into a house and is hit on the head. That's about it. The quality lay in the *mise-en-scène*, smooth track-ing shots, cuts on action, reverse angles properly worked out, dramatic night lighting. Hungry violence. The director had enough money to act, in a small way, as his own producer. His name was Michael Reeves.

And here already you have the history of British cinema. There were two routes available: start in the ranks and work your way up (the long apprenticeships of Hitchcock, David Lean, Seth Holt), or begin with connections, family, some sort of income (Anthony Asquith, Michael Powell, Robert Hamer). Reeves might have combined the two strains. He had the privileged background and also the shop-floor training with Don Siegel and in Roman horror programmers. He could have had a career *maudit* like Holt, a nurturer of "forlorn projects", whose intimate biography would, according to David Thomson, "make a pretty picture of the razor lining to the film industry". (*If*, it should be recalled, was originally Holt's project, inherited by Anderson when the more expe-rienced director succumbed to alcoholism.) Or, it might have gone the other way, he could have become the real Michael Winner, a Winner with a talent for something more than survival.

We persevered, shuttling between Dublin and London (cheap stand-by flights out of Belfast in those days, less than a tenner). Tom stayed in Reeves's Knightsbridge cottage, just beyond Harrods, in Yeomans Row. (Nearby, I remember, was a shop or gallery that touted Russian icons.) The class of floor was improving. Tom delivered a car to the set in Rome. We scraped enough money together to begin a London film (awarding ourselves the University Film Society's non-existent production fund). Casting the female lead was tricky: productive conversations were held with Mandy Rice-Davies (going well until we came up against the question of a fee), with a fashionable model (soon to retire into animal welfare). We eventually started shooting in a basement in Cornwall Gardens. There was a perpetual irritation of schoolgirls fretting around the corner, in the hope of catching a glimpse of John Lennon and his customised Mini. Mornings drifted away setting up tracking shots, with tricksy reflections, in Battersea Park. There was a rather lame (mostly male) party in the Thai poet's flat. Mirrors and smoke and badly mimed decadence. Losey's *The Servant* was the presiding influence. A post-production budget was never found and the film was canned and deservedly forgotten.

Probably the only Dublin film worth retrieving would be a street documentary, *They*, photographed by Tom Baker, and cut to music by Van Morrison's original Belfast band – before receiving an improvised harmonica track by Peter (son of Larry) Adler. Who later provided the intro for Losey's *King and Country*. *They* consisted of lots of night driving, wet streets, vagrants, lunatics with agenda. Cafés, pubs, launderettes. The comings and goings of crowds, and loners, watched from a high Baggot Street window. I shot some footage for Tom and also did most of the editing, not having realised that the form I was most comfortable with only employed cutting in camera. The mechanical process of fitting scraps together was never satisfactory, rarely revealing a perfected organic form. I wanted a language such as that invoked by Jack Kerouac in his *Essentials of Spontaneous Prose*: "Not 'selectivity' of expression but following free deviation (association) of mind into limitless blow-on-subject seas of thought." Or the liberation Stan Brakhage discovered when his 16mm equipment was stolen from his car in New York and he traded the insurance payment for a secondhand 8mm camera, abdicating the possibility of expensive optical effects and superimpositions, living by whatever could be achieved in the act of composition. Those freedoms were still some way off.

We left for London. Tom took up residence in Knightsbridge as Mike Reeves's accomplice, conscience, sounding-board. A conspiracy of Englishmen, realists. Or so it struck me. A stubborn refusal to get carried away by visionary excess. Materialists, in the best sense. I could have envied that, but I was never comfortable with the step in from the well-dressed pavements, the small room with its lemon sofa, its reluctance to look inhabited. The house was perfect for a serious film-maker. It was as anonymous as a hotel room: a couple of Hopper prints, model cars on the mantlepiece, an active telephone. Tom's Dublin friends visited as tolerated ruffians, unwashed art cinema frauds, too dumb to accept the apotheosis of Don Siegel. I had seen, and appreciated, *Riot in Cell Block 11*, *Invasion of the Body Snatchers*, *Baby Face Nelson*, *The Line-Up*, but I had difficulty with the canonisation, accepting Siegel as *the* man. Mike Reeves' entire doctrine was based on that revelation. He had paid his way over to America, got Siegel's number, talked himself into a job as an assistant. He had identified the pure and absolute craftsman: swift, reliable, smart but lacking the responsibility of authorship, the horror of responsibility. Siegel, educated at Jesus College, Cambridge, was bright enough and tough enough to survive, to keep working, to perfect what David Thomson calls a career of "vindicated modesty". Reeves had something of that, enough to aspire to it as an ideal – but he recognised that he would have to subdue greater reserves of anger, a poetry of displacement and unease. A distaste for physical violence coupled with a penchant for staging violent resolutions.

Mike was generous enough to allow me to project the rushes of the latest and last of the 16mm films in his house. When he bothered to watch, he kept his comments to himself. There was some edge in the fact that he had chosen not to go to university, had settled straight down to the business. He read these insane London thefts – Streatham nocturnes, underground journeys, taxis, airports, canals, masks, colour chopping randomly to black and white – as undergraduate indulgence. But he didn't throw us out. He was putting together the package that would become his first substantial film, *The Sorcerers*.

I took a job in Walthamstow, the Technical College and School of Art, learning much more than I was able to teach: peddling that most discredited of non-options, Liberal Studies, to mods and skinheads, the future unemployed. I spent a lot of time listening to an exiled Hollywood editor: Jewish, political, bitter, unwell. Nobody seems to have told him that the blacklist was no longer in operation. That would have made it too easy, undone this most perverse of exiles. Saul could go on for hours: the only film he had to show for it was an endless protest march, placards, Albanian colour. He wasn't too interested in talking about the experiences that did intrigue me, his time working on skid row *film noir*. He had some connection with Irving Kershner's *Stakeout on Dope Street*. I'd seen it, quietly bleak – if unable to live up to that evocative title.

Saul gave me plenty of good advice about cutting my own film, all the proper information about "A" and "B" rolls (which I must do something about, one of these days). His own group of film students had spent a year not completing a monumentally dull documentary about Heathrow. The class lasted two hours. It took them most of that time just to get out there. Then it was dark. They finished with three or four minutes of the dimmest footage I've ever seen. It could have been shot in the Rotherhithe Tunnel.

Saul had the sense to take prolonged sick leave, and I inherited his job. I had the keys to the equipment cupboard. It didn't take many sessions to get rid of the trainspotters. They couldn't live with the freaks who did turn up, in droves: the throwouts from lower education, the psychopaths taking sculpture as an introduction to body carving, the "mature" students waiting for their genius to be recognised, the failed Hockneys and kitchen visionaries. I was in my element. Shoved film in their cameras and turned them loose. The term show went on for thirty hours. There were two genuine talents. One spent the entire year on an obsessive lyric project, travelling across London to his mother's flat on the far side of the river. Juddery train-window footage, skies, clouds; walks through Whitechapel, tracking in and out of the family delicatessen; and an endless, hand-held stagger across Tower Bridge, and up the steps to the flat – to present, as the audience are keyed up for some *Psycho* revelation, the old woman in her chair.

The other revelation was Brian Catling. Warhol performance cinema: a man, having been treated to the full spaghetti dinner, is dosed with pints of salt water; and then the camera rolls, holds steady through a reel of projectile vomiting.

Tom Baker, whose interests were moving towards an involvement with communal, mythopeic film-making, Stan Brakhage's *Songs*, was in the audience. He was slumming. He now had two major credits as a screenwriter, *The Sorcerers* and *Witchfinder General*; he was enough of a career cineaste to feel something like William Blake's grind of "nervous anxiety". The need to assert his independence, to escape from meetings,

279

discussions, rewrites. The revealed lunacy of rational men, whose trade it is to second-guess fate.

That first summer at Walthamstow I ran into problems of my own: a script I had written was accepted. As ever, this was a question of connections. Robert Klinkert, a Dutch cameraman I'd known at the film school, had been fishing around various European TV networks. WDR in Cologne bought my proposal for a documentary on Allen Ginsberg and the Congress for the Dialectics of Liberation, which was about to bring RD Laing, Paul Goodman, Stokely Carmichael, Gregory Bateson and a mob of floaters, spooks and activists, into Chalk Farm and Camden Town. I wrote an account of the affair, its comedies and its revelations, in a book called *The Kodak Mantra Diaries*, which I published myself in 1971. The best that can be said of the episode is that, one way or another, it shook up, tested, mangled and reset all the comfortable prejudices of the Dublin years. Ginsberg was troubled and charismatic. Talking to him for a few days, gave me material to think about for years. Also: I came out of this botched introduction to "real" film-making with enough money to move into a condemned terrace in Hackney (which is where I still am: the property having been redefined, under a new regime, as almost worth preserving).

A sniff of early success was fatal. It never happened again. Months – years – were wasted on a succession of increasingly improbable projects. I entered into a complicated correspondence with William Burroughs who was then conducting his flirtation with Scientology. The Ginsberg script had been assembled in two hours, after I got the phonecall from Klinkert. (The problems came when we tried to abide by these unreal improvisations) The mistake with the Burroughs fable was that I spent several months getting it right. The screenplay was adequately constructed, with just sufficient edge to make me want to see it done properly. Burroughs couldn't commit and the Germans, remembering the expense of dubbing over Ginsberg's obscenities, claimed that nobody in Cologne had ever heard of the author of *The Naked Lunch*.

I tried to work closer to home (and this must rate as the zaniest proposal of them all): I wrote an adaptation of the Anglo-Welsh poet Vernon Watkins' symbolist verse drama, *The Ballad of the Mari Llwyd*. A less cinematic text would be difficult to imagine. But Harlech TV in Cardiff had just been granted their licence to print money, and had taken Richard Burton on board. Naively, I imagined they might want to dress their piracy with a few low budget cultural throwaways. The shock came when they invited me down there. They loved the script and were eager to talk about it. I imagine that they were expecting some gnarled and mossy academic, not a dumb youth who was asked, as an opener, how much he'd like for his budget. The scam was blown. I realised, with mounting horror, that they expected me to front the production myself, deal with Welsh actors. I did a runner and still never set foot in Cardiff without checking over my shoulder for a *gorsedd* of auditioning bards with horse-skulls, ribbons and spades.

It was a relief to return to a proposal that Tom was putting together with Paul Ferris, who wrote the music for both Michael Reeves' features. They fancied a crack at a script for The Shadows. I would be an unseen grubber. I would do the treatment, Tom would tinker with it, and then go along with Ferris to present it to Hank and the boys in the gymnasium. The Shadows wanted, at this point, to be all-round entertainers, in their own right, free of their Dorian Gray, voodoo doll, godspieler. They were virtuosi of the suburbs, they worked out, they needed something more challenging than another prophylactic *Summer Holiday* with Cliff and Una Stubbs. They wanted the prestige of Dick Lester's cleverly contrived (lifted from the Maysles brothers), pseudo-documentary Beatles vehicle, *A Hard Day's Night*. Fat chance. Lester's sleight of hand allowed for the interplay of personality, without involving anything as time-consuming as the creation of roles, or fictional masks. My problem was that this bunch didn't have any obvious personality: spectacles, suits, grins – the rest was chipboard and dental cement. The obvious solution was science fiction. I've forgotten the detail: doubles, clones, cut-outs. Landing them in the boggiest and bleakest stretches of the West of Ireland, alien visitors wowing the fellaheen at cowshed dances – while the "real" Shadows arrive for a gig in Dublin. I'm glad I wasn't there for the handover to Hank Marvin.

Before I could get back to my reserve script (*Carry On K*: a travesty of Kafka's *The Castle*, in which the one straightman, the Kafka avatar, is perplexed and frustrated by a mob of English comic grotesques, all those demented music hall gargoyles), I was sucked into more Knightsbridge madness. Would we rescue a documentary, on "Mothers and Children", made in India by Bob Hope's adopted daughter? She'd embarked with a Californian friend on a Third World nightmare: near rape in the desert, a culture of bribes and bureaucracy they refused to understand, impounded equipment, inedible food, heat, flies, dysentery (and that was before they left the Bombay Hilton). An air-conditioned limo ran them out to a village where women and children were supposed to be readily available – but who could work in those temperatures? They picked up a couple of wobbly shots of kids on a homemade swing, and that was it. A showcase slot on an educational channel was waiting, and Bob required some tangible return on his investment.

Again, this was a right-school, who-you-know number. The disaster landed in the lap of one of the Astors, who had been at Winchester with Laurence "Renchi" Bicknell – who later lived in Dublin, and was involved in various of our enterprises. Bicknell was a painter and *voyant* (subject to occasional petit mal fits), who conceived and soliloquised notions of an expressionist puppet cinema, and meanwhile held down a day job making road safety films for a small Irish agency. There was something reassuringly surreal in the notion of road safety in Dublin. Driving tests were not required in Ireland in those days, and it was possible to pick up change parking cars for matrons who had shuddered in from the suburbs, but had no idea how to find reverse. Bicknell developed his technical vocabulary staging crashes. He was accepted and revered among the Mount Street bohos as a slightly weathered Cantab Rimbaud (in the blue jacket of a French labourer). He used to hang out with Pete Brown, had been to the Ginsberg readings at Better Books, and later got to know the Beat godfather in Liverpool. He didn't eat much, lived a life of radiant poverty and confusion, labyrinthine monologues, bursts of creative energy. He produced a lurid hardboard triptych based on Godard's *Pierrot le Fou* (which he didn't much like); iconic presences like blow-up film frames – distorted, gesturing, lips in industrial scarlet.

Bicknell, like so many others of that generation, saw cinema as a possible survival routine: the pensioned vision. He worked, for a time, as an assistant editor at the BBC, trying to rescue one of the worst of the *Sherlock Holmes* series. He crunched off-cuts of film to make the sound of a walk through autumn leaves. He salvaged directorial disasters: booms in shot, doors that opened the wrong way, sets that shook, mismatched costumes, slipping moustaches. And when the opportunity came to direct a 35mm short, he accepted it.

Andrew St John (who specialised in brokering hyphens, such as Barney Platts-Mills) was the producer. The film was set in Cambridge and based on a ballet production staged by Bicknell's mother. That was the hook for this potential art house programmer: nymphets against a heritage background. Cycle rides along the Backs. Changing rooms. Dance. English light. Music by Duke Ellington. A snappy title: *Mari's Girls*. The carefully assembled crew must be one of the most overqualified in the history of British cinema. David Hurn, a Magnum

282

photographer, to make the best use of the decision to use black and white stock. Chris Menges (a future Oscar winner for *The Mission*) as camera operator. Nic Knowland, responsible for lighting the luminous *Institute Benjamenta* for the Brothers Quay, as his assistant. Tony Jackson doing the sound. The result was as far as it could possibly be from our Ginsberg film: minimal content that looked exquisite, crisp sound, elegant cutting. There was only one problem. The Duke Ellington estate wouldn't sell the rights to the music, not for a viable sum. *Mari's Girls*, instead of being parcelled up for the film festival circuit, remained in the can, an unseen gem.

My attempts to find a bankable documentary subject grew increasingly hysterical. I was vetted by Stuart Montgomery of Fulcrum Press and then put in touch with Basil Bunting. Bunting, if there was a few quid in it, was game. I assured him that there was – and then ran out of change in the callbox. No television network in Britain had the slightest interest in the poet whose sonorous epic *Briggflats* was being belatedly puffed by Cyril Connolly.

I tried Graham Greene. They'd all heard of him, some of them were even beginning to collect his first editions. But Greene had always refused to appear on film. That was his stance and it was still accepted by commissioning editors (unaware that he was only waiting to be properly courted, that hours and hours of Greene skulking about, not-appearing-on-TV, were soon to be inflicted on us). The prohibition, the technical problem, was the challenge. I thought a piece constructed entirely in stills, like Chris Marker's *La Jetée*, might answer. Greene would then have to submit himself to an interview. He declined, his initials at the bottom of the letter provided by a secretary. (He was far too sharp to put holograph correspondence in the hands of some East End chancer.) I did meet the man, once, ten or twelve years later. Flasher's grubby white raincoat, collar turned up, looking like a hired impersonator: he bought a couple of underpriced Victorian detective novels from the book hutch I was sharing, under the Westway flyover, with the notorious Driffield and Greene's nephew, Nick Dennys.

Bicknell and I went back to Dublin, took some photographs, gathered material on a group of fragmenting bohemians: one was connected with post-Situationist groups in Germany, the Baader-Meinhof rump, one was hanging out with the Incredible String Band, others were making very determined efforts to lose themselves in the West of Ireland as *rentiers* peasants. We sent the script off to Godard. And to Apple. Then came back to unreality with the Linda Hope rescue mission.

Sessions convened in Yeomans Row. Baker, Bicknell and I teased out the sorry saga. Interviews were shot in a Chelsea flat near the river. Lunch breaks were taken in a media friendly bistro. I'd never before witnessed, at first hand, Californian grazing patterns. Linda couldn't make up her mind what to sample, ordered everything on the card, nibbled at a few scraps of leaf and pushed the rest aside. Then it was off to the Tropical House at Kew, cruising Notting Hill, Southall, Whitechapel for suitably winsome kids to be cut in. The phony travelogue was assembled entirely in London. I gather it went down quite well on the coast and was repeated several times.

I think we all knew the game was up. Mike Reeves had moved out of Yeomans Row and into the ambiance of *The Servant*, in a square off the King's Road. He was between projects, surfing on downers and sleeping-pills. He'd broken up with his girlfriend and was incapable, according to Baker, of talking about anything other than Don Siegel. He'd run *The Killers* for anybody he met at a poker game. Bicknell sub-let a house in somewhere we'd never heard of – De Beauvoir Road – that turned out to be borderline Hackney. Baker and I, wives and girlfriends, followed him. Tom still had hopes for a synopsis based on the "Troubles", Bonnie and Clyde in Belfast. Bicknell had been offered another impossible hack job.

It was our last commercial collaboration and we knew from the start it was going nowhere. One of the producers of the hippie musical, *Hair*, had acquired the rights to the Conan novels of Robert E. Howard. Steroidal rage in a dry-ice landscape of sword and sorcery, pillaged mythology: wimp's revenge sagas. I enjoyed them, when the moment came, bundles of gaudy paperbacks on which to binge – without guilt.

The Conan property was vertically stacked: the *Hair* man took time out at his Mediterranean villa and farmed the script to a screenwriter with enough clout to carry a credit. This "name" obviously had a raft of projects in development, so he employed a legman, a hustler, to dig out wannabes who would work below the line, in the hope of future employment, or some minor on-screen acknowledgement ("additional dialogue"). The legman met Renchi in the lift of a hotel, took a fancy to him, and put him on the team. At which stage, I became involved. We divided up the Conan books and went away to read them and come up with separate synopses.

The first one took three days. This seemed too quick, so I wrote another: an epic of improbable movement and exotic violence, occultism and bogus libertarian politics (completely out of key with the pitch of the source material). Renchi wasn't ready with his part, which he was working on with his wife, Judith. We postponed the first script conference for another week – when the Bicknells duly delivered their pages. An amazingly detailed, intricate, layered mapping, with drawings and symbols and footnotes, which carried the thing about one-third of the way into the credits sequence. I was embarrassed by the superficiality of my fullblown narrative, and tried to hide it away. At this point, wisely, Judith dropped out. Bicknell and I carried on for months, in London and at a cottage in North Wales (breaking off to watch an ectoplasmic Dylan at the Isle of Wight on an antique TV set, to shoot 8mm trial sequences of our own, and to deal with head-lice picked up on an adventure playgroup documentary we'd made in Paddington).

Renchi doodled and challenged my tendency to find easy solutions. The story grew denser and denser, a dim and primitive consciousness travelling across cultures and continents to arrive at Egypt, initiation and maturity. This was all very well, a useful exercise – but we were only being paid £100 each. The script had to be finished. It could have gone on forever, refined and improved to the point where it would have been an unnecessary exercise to make it. We handed over the finished folder, took our money, heard no more. Years later, watching *Conan the Barbarian* on television, I was amused to notice that the screenplay (by those heavy-hitters, John Milius and Oliver Stone) included odd scenes, such as the early one in the cave, that were virtual paraphrases of our long lost original.

Communal life in Hackney (explorations of East London, the riverside and the Lea Valley) led to a complete revision of our notions of cinema. We stopped wasting time cobbling together complicated descriptions of events that would never happen. We stopped hassling other producers and got back to making films. A comprehensive Brakhage programme (*Dog Star Man*, *Metaphors of Vision*, *Songs*) at the National Film Theatre helped to convince us that there was another way. We picked up a couple of secondhand 8mm cameras and started on a diary that was to last for about eight years. The diary coincided with the establishing of a base in Hackney, gardens recovered and planted, bucolic meals, portraits of friends, journeys, agitprop, childbirth. Techniques of multiple superimposition, single-frame cataloguing, allowed swathes of material to be squeezed economically on to a three-minute roll of outdated stock. (We could control the speed of projection – so that feature-length meditations could be produced for a few pounds.) Inevitably, this is a form of chamber cinema, watched by those who compose it. But the subject/object problem was partially overcome, as the camera passed from hand to hand. There were obvious difficulties: lack of sound, repetition of basic material, hermeticism, the inability to shift from the lyric, the sketch, to some harsher and more challenging form. It was a worthwhile experiment, taken in conjunction with a similar attitude to publication. Books could be produced when we were ready to produce them, on a small scale, allowed to find their natural audience (about four hundred readers at peak). It wasn't a definitive solution, but it served its time. The Bicknells and Tom Baker left London for a large country house outside Alton in Hampshire, a shot at community life of a more formal and demanding kind. The film diary petered out. I experimented with various fictions, using the short-hand techniques I'd learnt: basically, creating a situation, letting it run and shooting it, in a documentary style, as it progressed. Very few retakes, no rehearsal, no reverse angles, edited in camera. When the Bolex finally fell apart, I let it go. Renchi had bought himself a video camera, which was never much used. That era was over.

Writing these notes dusted off suppressed memories. There had been a more personal script back there among the industrial castoffs. I'd shown the first quick draft to Mike Reeves, then worked on it, between stints on other things, odd jobs in warehouses and breweries, always, I suppose, with Reeves in mind. I tried to give the main character the bleakness that I saw in his protagonists, the restless frigidity. My man worked (no surprises here) as a film lecturer. He had his leftist pretensions, constantly trying to push his students into collaborating on Brechtian fables. He's paid very little and lives on his wife's private income. To break out of this cycle of dependency, he takes a night job as a porter in a near-brothel in Finsbury Park. This is a dump where East End gangsters can hide out, or play cards, after killings or major hijacks; a convenient location for Trade Unionists to meet their mistresses, or be serviced by prostitutes.

The man is taken up by one of the hotel's clients (who, he subsequently discovers, is also the owner). He's asked, for what he assumes are purposes of blackmail, to film an adulterous couple in one of the rooms through a two-way mirror. He agrees. The woman, of course, is revealed as his own wife. Very soon he is implicated in even murkier events. There's an accidental killing. A corpse to be disposed of, and – in the script's only prophetic aside – an elaborate gangland funeral in Chingford Mount.

There probably wasn't enough pace, enough structured violence for

Mike; too much ambiguity, too much chat. I meant to get the finished script to him, but, by then, the connection was broken. We heard that he'd taken an overdose and killed himself. He'd made three features. The critic Dave Pirie wrote of *Witchfinder General* that "no film before or since has used the British countryside in quite the same way." It was, he said, "one of the most personal and mature statements in the history of British cinema." Reeves was about to start shooting a film loosely based on Edgar Allan Poe's *The Oblong Box* when he died. He wasn't quite twenty-five years old.

2.

"I can't stand to think about him waiting in the room and knowing
he's going to get it. It's too damned awful."
"Well," said George, "you better not think about it."
ERNEST HEMINGWAY, *THE KILLERS*

9.9.95. I wanted, before moving on, to check my memories of Michael Reeves and his films with Tom Baker. Tom was still out there on the Hampshire estate, still living in the squash court. He'd done a good job on it, made a kind of deck, accessed by steep stairs with no banister rail; a window had been put in that gifted the room with soft autumnal light, and offered a view of the clocktower, old stables and the high red wall of the kitchen garden. (A minor royal had lived here once. A raised platform had been built to help the Queen Mother get into the bath. Then the house declined to a prison camp, and a partly inhabited burden on capital.) Inherited occasional tables and comfortable low chairs (riskily set on the edge of the unprotected drop) slummed, without stress, alongside plain pine, tomato plants, bowls of velvety blue flowers, paperback books, a large ginger cat. The apartment was blessed with everything that mattered: space, light, distant greenery, silence. Such a privileged depth of it – the absence of horns, hooters, alarms, music, screams – that mere townies declined at once into a narcoleptic coma.

Tom was unchanged: a modest, tawny presence, slightly crinkled, nervously rotating a biro cap in his dirt-encrusted hands. He didn't find decisions easy – driving to work at a steady 35 miles an hour gave him palpitations at every road junction. The squash court room had settled for being permanently unfinished, a patchwork of sanded planks, chipboard, holes: unresolved alternatives. A copy of the *Financial Times* was neatly folded at the corner of the table, a seasonal feature on Lord Archer clearly visible. Tom purported to "love numbers", their purity, their lack of ambiguity. He'd like to dabble in the market – if these numbers were not attached to the unpredictable mess of human-run companies, businesses that go belly-up. Tom received a copy of Will Hutton's *The State We're In* (a book that has successfully achieved that status, something to be given away): it was one of the few hardbacks on show. Baker's stance was, he said, repentantly rightwing. Independence, self-sufficiency, being left alone to build your cabin. Tom was a movie sentimentalist, a theoretical redneck who wouldn't kill a dead mosquito. His ethic didn't come from Sir Keith Joseph but from Henry Fonda in Delmer Daves' *Spencer's Mountain*. He wanted to be around to watch the leaves change colour.

Tom had grown up in the same Berkshire village as Mike Reeves: civil servants, ex-colonials, widows living on their dividends. Detached houses with generous gardens, backing onto woodland. This is where Reeves made his first 8mm films. Tom was the actor – pursued through the trees, crawling through ponds, dragging a gashed leg to a lonely phonebox. Then it was Tom's turn. He wrote some romantic trifle about an artist and his model, canalbank walks, pigeons fluttering in church lofts. Reeves dutifully shot it.

From the start, it seems, he was a driven man. Film was his only outlet. It was what he was going to do, no debate. The next short was the one I remembered, the break-in. The Reeves stock company was already being forged in Deep England. The hero was Ian Ogilvy, who ends up screwing a broken bottle into the villain's face. Which was the stock Reevesian preoccupation: the apparently decent, "normal" citizen pushed to locate the evil within himself, to absorb and reciprocate all the venom of his oppressor. (Mike was sufficiently exercised by the 8mm version, tracking on a tea-trolly, to make the story again in 16mm, hiring a massive crab-dolly from Samuelsons.)

With Baker in tow, he barged into various offices in Wardour Street. After this, Tom decided that perhaps Dublin wasn't such a bad option. Reeves should have joined him but gave up his place to work as an assistant on an Irving Allen production, *The Long Ships*, which was being shot by Jack Cardiff in Yugoslavia. Eye-patched Richard Widmark as a bloodlust Viking. Sidney Poitier as the leader of the Moors. International co-production butchery. Mayhem with a travel brochure background. Reeves got his name on the screen. Then he saw *The Killers*.

It happens to plenty of directors: one film obsesses them, one director. Truffaut with Hitchcock. Lindsay Anderson with Ford. Petit with Fassbinder. Reeves with Don Siegel and *The Killers*. The germ of everything he attempted is in that one experience. The steely blue look of the shot-for-TV train. Lee Marvin's sharkskin suit (reprised in John Boorman's more effectively psychotic *Point Blank*). The willing victim played by John Cassavetes (doing the jobbing work that funded – and perhaps influenced – projects of his own, such as *The Killing of a Chinese Bookie*). Even Ronnie Reagan, when he could still remember the lines, faked it as Angie Dickinson's sugar daddy, the mobster in the tower. (While Reagan spent the next few years trying to buy up and destroy prints that might give the voters the right idea, Reeves was hiring and re-hiring a 16mm version for private projection.)

The news of the Kennedy assassination came through while Siegel was on the floor with *The Killers*. He described that day: "A loud, piercing scream from Angie cut through the announcer's voice. I rushed to her as she started to topple . . . I grabbed her in my arms and carried her into a small dressing room . . . There was complete confusion and grief at the studio . . . One wise guy, a gaffer and a member of the John Birch Society, wanted to work out the day . . ."

With enough family money to afford it, Reeves left for Hollywood, and called Siegel from a payphone. Don was a civilized man, intrigued by this pleasantly spoken, upper-crust English kid. Maybe he could still out-cult the Rays and the Fullers. He let Mike stay in his guesthouse and even carried hospitality to the extent of allowing him to direct a few tests he was making for Elvis Presley: a parade of jailbait ingénues and crooning models. This was the film-buff footnote that has Reeves cast as Siegel's "assistant". The two men got on well enough together – poker and cigars – for the American to visit his protégé in London.

Rome was the obvious progression, an active scene – Californian TV dropouts, freaks, hustlers, money-laundering flesh peddlers. Casting calls for everything from *La Dolce Vita* to spaghetti westerns, muscle beach mythology, and horror porn. Reeves used his experience on *The Long Ships*, the fabulous connection with Siegel, the convenient private income, to talk his way into covering a few sequences on *The Castle of the Living Dead*. He then chipped in enough cash to secure his first solo directing credit, a schlocky programmer that budgeted at £14,000. Briefly visible in Kilburn, *Revenge of the Blood Beast* was a Barbara Steele vehicle, whose pitch was blatantly signalled in its Italian title: *La Sorella di Satana*. Steele was an irresistible masochist icon: a dark madonna for excitable Latins, glamorous gash for phlegmatic British raincoats.

I've never managed to see *Blood Beast*, but Tom – whom Reeves chauffeured into darkest North London – makes a very favourable report. He thought that Ian Ogilvy was involved, but remembered, on the positive side, a low comedy of terror with all the stock paraphernalia: Van Helsing, Transylvania, period motorcars, a creature from the swamp. It sounds rather like a companion piece to Polansksi's *Dance of the Vampires*.

What next? Rome was a place of rumours, café propositions, phonecalls. Reeves entered into negotiation with schools of Soho sharks, happy to slap palms with a talented auteur who had the key to his own piggybank. He asked Tom to come out, to deliver a motor.

Baker found himself sitting in on some major league shmoozing, anecdote-weavers who made the Ancient Mariner look like a dummy. He was swept in and out of restaurants and bars, mopping up meatballs in thick tomato sauce, as Paul Maslansky conjured marvellous possibilities out of the air (before breaking off to fight in the Six Day War). For Maslansky, it was actually going to happen. He motored on. He hit the cash cow with the *Police Academy* numbers. A fitting reward for a master of bullshit.

Baker and Reeves discussed possible scripts. One afternoon, Tom was sitting alone in a "delightful" little studio, frequented by Fellini, around the back of the Colosseum. He was enjoying the vines, the courtyard, the peace of it all, when Michael Klinger, an East End face with a chain of cinemas and an interest in several stripclubs, burst in. "What are *you* for?" he barked. Wrong question. Tom had vague hopes of working on the forthcoming Reeves movie as an assistant, or of contributing to some future script, or of going back to Ireland, or . . . He went back to Ireland. Klinger, together with Tony Tenser, was to play a real part in London cinema of the Sixties. The media tended to depict them as hairy-knuckled heavies. But they had the last laugh, trotting around the festival circuit, picking up prizes for producing *Repulsion* and *Cul-de-Sac*.

One of the busier flim-flam artists on the loose was a character called Pat Curtis. He was working small miracles on behalf of his prize stock, the former beauty queen and dentist's receptionist, Raquel Welch. He sprayed out press releases, thought up ever more extravagant demands, in order to assert her status. He fancied becoming a producer. A workable conjunction was in place: Mike Reeves (with half the budget), Tony Tenser's Tigon Films, and Pat Curtis. Find the right property and they were up and running.

A story by John Burke, the prolific "noveliser" (see most Pan film books), took Reeves' fancy. The title, *Terror for Kicks*, was awful, but he liked the hook: an elderly and discredited hypnotist has developed a machine that allows him to gain control of a chosen subject's mind. He is then able to experience vicariously all the sensations that he directs his creature to enjoy: an escalating cycle of "kicks". The perfect metaphor for cinema. (As Kathryn Bigelow recognised when she recycled it for *Strange Days*.) Complacent voyeurism turned back on itself – with the bonus of being free to stage a procession of fights, beatings, rapes, murders, and car chases. All that was needed was a name to put above the title, a name that would identify the product on offer.

Reeves wasn't short of bottle. He flew straight out to Spain, hoping to snare Boris Karloff. The veteran horror star, ex-Uppingham School, was happy to chat to another public school fellow – even if the bounder didn't have much interest in cricket. Anything would be an improvement on recent labours, such as *The Ghost in the Invisible Bikini*. A deal was struck. The film, under its new title, *The Sorcerers*, would budget at £25,000; out of which Karloff would take £11,000. He also insisted upon revisions to the script, which not only made him, in some senses, a co-author, but also the man responsible for bringing an unlooked for dignity and depth to the proceedings. The one-dimensional notion of an evil genius (yet another crazed scientist) getting his rocks off by plugging into the under-financed dregs of swinging London was unacceptable to Karloff. He wasn't prepared to walk through it and pick up the cheque. There was enough gravitas in his hardwon screen persona to inspire the novice director – who was happy to make adjustments to the outline. The hypnotist must not be irredeemably evil, evil from the start. He would battle with his wife, admirably played by Catherine Lacey, lose ground, suffer, feel aroused in defeat, and achieve a final act of sacrifice.

Tom trailed along with Reeves to visit Burke's Fulham basement. He helped with a few pages of the script and went back to Ireland before shooting began. He was pleased to discover that he'd been given a full credit. *Sorcerers* is, I think, thematically, the more complex and interesting of the two major Reeves features. It's obviously nothing like as lyrical or ambitious as *Witchfinder General*. Its horizons are pinched and mean. There's none of the fluidity and investment in landscape: *Sorcerers* remains resolutely stopped down, locked in the skull, an unacknowledged and genuine contribution to London's covert filmography. There's a strong element of spiritual autobiography in the pitch, homages to a lost catalogue of memories – *Peeping Tom*, early

Hitchcock, *Repulsion*, forgotten second features, Edgar Wallace and Edgar Lustgarten. A way of seeing the aimless lifestyle of West London that fitted the budgetary restrictions of a frenzied shooting schedule.

Karloff, right from the start, cruising the pavements, arguing over advertisements with a newsagent, is an architectural creation: all greys and tired browns, homburg, long coat. The cheap set from which he operates with his wife belongs in the Thirties, in *Sabotage*. The very notion of the hypnotist is a Hitchcockian translation from German expressionism. It's salutary to be reminded, in those days of Dick Lester, *Darling* and *Modesty Blaise*, that such low-lit, suburban gravy tins could still exist. While he stays within the studio world, a cupboard off the Goldhawk Road, Reeves is comfortable. He's doing what he does best: manipulation of objects and persons. The world is obedient, the light can be controlled, day is night.

Outside, running headlong into the chaos of streetlife, the Carnaby Street decadence the supplements were busy underwriting – an amphetamine rush of photographers, hoodlums, rag trade wideboys, media pimps, countercultural bandits – he loses it. The club scenes have escaped from some Cliff Richard revivalist number: 'coke' is cola, extras twist like zombies, nobody knows what to say. They smoke instead. There's no language. The dialogue never rises above the functional in any of Reeves' films; awkward stage directions spoken aloud, bubble talk to shift the characters to the next scene. Karloff snares Ian Ogilvy – more than ever the director's alter ego – by spotting him toying with an existential hamburger. The doc's out to find a "pill popper" type eager for wild psychedelic experiences. Ogilvy, who has a propensity for leaving his chums at the pub door and announcing that he needs to be "alone", off for a solitary walk, is excused on the grounds of his "bloody artistic temperament". The restlessness, the non-job (sitting in a junkshop that has no buying customers), the apparent means to do whatever he wants to do, is a sympathetic caricature of Reeves' own dilemma. Ogilvy is a smoother Reeves with terminal angst, other-directed, driven to contact the violent, risk-taking aspects of himself. The motorbike burn-up from *Sorcerers* is paralleled by the cross-country gallops of *Witchfinder General*. (Orthodox uppercrust hobbies.)

There is no time in this Stevensonian fable to engage with the psychogeography of the city: that was left to foreign eyes, to Antonioni, Polanski, Jules Dassin, Joseph Losey. And to the hairy men of the underground. But Reeves was good enough to share a poetic sense of place with those masters: the episode of the night swim in the Dolphin

Square pool, when the old couple, left at home, enjoy the sensation of water rippling over their hands, as Ogilvy and his girlfriend plunge, plays nicely against Skolimowski's municipal London bath scenes from *Deep End* – which were in fact shot in Munich. (It's curious too how Elizabeth Ercy, as the feckless crumpet, the one in the crochet dress, a non-actress of resonant superficiality, is made to assume a wistful French accent that echoes Catherine Deneuve in *Repulsion*: the madwoman in the South Kensington bedsit.)

Otherwise, it's very much the London of dark heritage: riverside Ripper alleys, White City car chases, the shadow of a police helmet on the warehouse wall. As in *Blow-Up*, there's an awkward scene in an antique shop. Ogilvy has to endure a camp timewaster in a leather cap – who, like all the bit players, comes straight out of central casting: the kvetching Yiddisher snackbar man, the rabbiting cabbie, the Ortonesque cop with raincoat and pipe. The interest is in the vivid demonstration of the Reeves thesis: how Ogilvy, with his DJ name ("Mike Roscoe"), is pushed from ennui towards unmotivated acts of violence; how there is no redemption, no way of sidestepping fate. It may be Cliff and the Shadows "Out in the Country" on the Dansette, but, beyond the bamboo blinds, the neon is as sick as only Michael Powell or Hitchcock can make it.

Karloff should have been grateful to Reeves for rescuing the final act of a notable career, spent in gracefully living down to his exotic pseudonym. Putting the experience of working with an intelligent and committed young director behind him, he submitted himself to Peter Bogdanovitch's debut feature, *Targets*, held that pushy exercise in urban paranoia together, and went out gloriously: a triumph for the reforgotten.

Tom Baker, who was only casually involved with *Sorcerers*, played a major part in the scripting of *Witchfinder General*. I believe that the film's success lies in the tension between Baker's Utopian permissiveness, his feel for the countryside, and Reeves' demonic fatalism. The film, a loose account of the career of Matthew Hopkins, a hunter and punisher of witches at the time of the English Civil War, finds its way into the dictionary of horror films – when, in truth, it is nothing of the sort. It's a Suffolk western, a British cowboy picture: with extreme and painful scenes of mutilation, torture and execution.

The methodology of this production had much in common with such diverse future titles as Patrick Keiller's *London* and Chris Petit's *Radio On*. In no case was the generating idea written out, enough was held back for the immediate occasion of the shoot: the excitement of the present tense was preserved. So many films die as proposals, as more and more of the murky material that has to be discovered and dealt with – as the payoff for undergoing all this stress – is dredged out, talked through, de-energised. Reeves, with the moderate success of *Sorcerers* behind him, and with those masters of exploitation, AIP, taking an interest, was free to structure the film in his own way. Vincent Price, the campy Corman aesthete, had agreed to play Hopkins. Scenes had to be written in to accommodate television names of the time: Patrick Wymark of *The Power Game* as Oliver Cromwell, Wilfred "Steptoe" Brambell as a horse-trader. But, otherwise, Reeves and Baker were able to construct a story to fit entirely with their own preoccupations.

The high spot for Tom came when the two men, on a whim, took a late train out of Liverpool Street into Suffolk. Reeves looked across the flats lands and said: "This is what it's been about all along." They roamed East Anglia in a hired car, stopping to examine odd buildings that took their fancy, constructing a pack of mental polaroids. The narrative grew out of their discoveries. The redbrick houses with their leaded windows at the start of the film suggested a difficult uphill tracking shot, leading towards the execution of the supposed witches. Reeves liked strong openings. He amazed me once by declaring his admiration for Michael Winner's *I'll Never Forget What's 'Is Name*; Oliver Reed smashing up a desk with an axe. The freshness that is still to be felt, even viewing *Witchfinder* on television, comes from this reversal of standard industry procedure. Reeves and Baker didn't write their script and then hand it over to location finders, they made a journey, allowing the spirit of place to enter the dictation. So much of the landscape around the prehistoric flint workings of Grime's Graves was (and is) in the hands of the military – who were prepared to have Ian Ogilvy and Nicky Henson galloping over their ranges. It's a nice conceit to imagine these recreated ghosts of Cromwell's New Model Army careening around camouflaged earthworks, strategically planted conifers and golf bunkers for trigger-happy nuclear strike crews.

Neither Reeves nor Baker had an interest in the occult, in mass psychosis, demonology. Reeves inhibited Vincent Price's usual cataleptic excesses, while allowing the sidekick, Robert Russell, to give full play to his psychotic proclivities. The menu of rapes and tortures is orchestrated with an eye on the American drive-in market. Painful as some of these scenes are (poor old Maigret, Rupert Davies, being run to exhaustion around a table), they didn't satisfy Louis M. Hayward of AIP, who took a screen credit for devising the odd sadistic refinement.

But the reasons why the film still lives in the memory are the qualities that Dave Pirie isolated: English ground, English weather, movement through nature and the seasons. Film as a journey, as a very particular shape – embellished with cruel cuts, such as the dissolve from waves crashing on a stone beach in North Norfolk (when the king has apparently escaped) to the orange flames of the witch-burning at Lavenham. (A scene whose force is somewhat diminished by the anachronistically white teeth of Paul Ferris, the composer, going heroically over the top in a minor part.)

Nobody other than Pasolini in his account of Chaucer's *The Canterbury Tales* (or Michael Powell with his odd wartime fable, *A Canterbury Tale*) has demonstrated the same affection for the play of sunlight on stone, rooks in the trees, evening fields. There are several scenes, unassertively presented, that have the inevitability of the highest art: Price riding up a track alongside a line of poplars in the dusk with his packhorse, like an evocation of Don Quixote; or Hilary Dwyer strolling beside a millstream, a golden interlude before the next bout of savagery.

Credit for the placement of these shots should go to Baker, but they were finely executed by John Coquillon – who went on to shoot another flawed but authentic elegy in Sam Peckinpah's *Pat Garrett and Billy the Kid*. Peckinpah enjoyed the American advantage: that his character actors – Slim Pickens, Chill Wills, Jack Elam and the like – had faces full of bad weather, corrupted dignity. They were replete with broken narrative, the mythology of all those other trails and bars and campfire rivers. (Peckinpah's invasion of the West Country for *Straw Dogs*, also photographed by Coquillon, finds the inherited Reeves yokels as ready as ever to celebrate their heritage of idiocy, incest, and ritualised buggery.)

The fruitful tension that existed between the very different philosophies of Reeves and Baker became clear as *Witchfinder* moved to its bloody conclusion in Orford tower. Baker had written a final scene something in the mood of Bergman's *Seventh Seal*; Price would ride out to a gipsy camp, near the seashore, or a river. He would have some link with these nomads, but would betray them – to end up hanged and abandoned, when the travellers move on. The film's narrative would then have completed its circle. We would be left, as we began, with a sacrifice made to the land.

But Reeves was having none of this, he improvised a darker climax – descending the spiral of the tower's stairs into a satanic chamber.

Natural light was excluded and the young woman driven to the point of madness, before Ogilvy, the director's surrogate, hacked Price to pieces. The ordinary man was capable of absolute evil. By his actions, he was revealed to himself.

Witchfinder opened to brisk business. The critics were indulgent. Future projects had to be rapidly assembled. Where Michael Powell with his excursion into the English macabre, *Peeping Tom*, found himself excluded for many years from the company of decent Wardour Street pornographers, brokers and moneymen, Reeves, by staying within the genres of horror and landscape heritage, was lauded, invited to join the club. He had achieved everything he wanted – and with his own repertory company: his friend Tom Baker to take care of research and legwork, a superb cameraman in Coquillon, Paul Ferris who ploughed some of his fee back into getting the score just right; even actors, like Ogilvy, with whom he was comfortable. Producers were coming to him, they knew that he had the touch.

Michael Klinger reappeared on the scene. Enthused by the box office success of Arthur Penn's *Bonnie and Clyde*, he challenged Reeves to come up with an English story that featured "plenty of Thompson sub-machine guns". Baker, a prophet before his time, suggested Belfast, or Dublin in the Twenties. Reeves was sympathetic, but it was getting more and more difficult to persuade him to commit himself. He left Yeomans Row, split from his girlfriend, and moved to Chelsea. He wasn't eating – and had never, in any case, had a meal in his own house. He was using a lot of pills: Valium, lithium, barbiturates. He had trouble sleeping and trouble talking about anything except his own problems – and Don Siegel. Any new faces that came into his orbit were given a forcible induction course in *The Killers*. Freelancers, ex-pats, actors with scripts, vampiric hustlers: they leeched on to him. He was drifting into the climate of the last reel of *The Servant*. Tom Baker, who was physically rather the type of one of those Losey young men, James Fox or Michael York, had moved away; pissed off that some recent acquaintance, poker pal, had been handed the Irish project.

Baker got a job doing rewrites for a 20th Century Fox TV series. He had to bring in his pages to one of Hitchcock's tough matrons, a script doctor who made him stand at the desk, while she checked his work. A red tick in the top righthand corner meant that he'd earned £17. No mark, no payment. He thought he could, just once, turn some work Reeves' way – but Mike sneered at the idea of demeaning himself for the box. Television was for upstarts (Spielberg) or has-beens (Seth Holt), hacks who couldn't cut it. Tom could patch up these paranormal quickies on his own. He could sit through production meetings in Grosvenor Square, where the English end of the operation trembled before the highly polished brogues of an American hatchetman who had been sent over to make sure that the parent company was getting value for money.

The new Reeves film was going into production on a Monday. Coquillon was photographing it. Hilary Dwyer and Rupert Davies were back – with Vincent Price and Christopher Lee as the headliners. The script took its title, *The Oblong Box*, from Poe, and its shock effects, its mythology, from Jack the Ripper, Burke and Hare, and Gaston Leroux's *Phantom of the Opera*. But, as Baker (now living in Kentish Town) heard, it wasn't to be. Reeves died that weekend of an overdose. Tom doesn't believe that it was suicide. He thinks it was an accident, confusion, drink, tiredness.

Baker gave up the unequal struggle and dropped out of commercial cinema soon afterwards. For a few years, he made 8mm "songs" – superimpositions of trees, meadows, his family. They were insistently optimistic, autumnal. He moved to Hampshire, worked on the estate and survived by selling some of his organic product locally. Things were difficult – until he took a job as a gardener for a wealthy family who lived a few miles down the valley. This led to such apparent anomalies as reverse commuting: using a Range Rover to drive back into London to plant a few beds for the "King" of Greece and his wife, before returning, each night, to the country.

Tom took me over to see the estate. Rain was falling steadily, without venom. He didn't care for it, this business of getting wet. Should we shelter? Or should we go back to the car? To take his mind off it, I asked after the names of some of the flowers. He couldn't remember. He knew all the first letters, but that instant card indexing system was gone. For him, as for all of us. From the treeline at the top of the hill, on the far side of the manmade lake, with its island and exotic birds, we could look back at the house. Tom doesn't have a camera anymore. He might borrow one – if he goes to Maine to see the leaves turn. I'd got used to calling on Marc Atkins. We had to let the evening close in unrecorded. It was a great moment of stillness, most of the small mansions tucked discreetly into folds of the landscape, hidden in copses; a scene imagined by Baker, but unwritten. No need for that. He'd outgrown the irritation that still possessed me.

3.

*"I only remember Robinson . . . the Doctor micturating in the
Seine at dawn . . . Myself, I'm only an ex-sailor, I have no
politics, I don't even vote."*

JACK KEROUAC, *CÉLINE*

Robinson and London. The first problem is finding a name for the
principal character; which is rapidly followed by the difficulty of nam-
ing the film itself. Patrick Keiller remembers Kafka, his fabulous
assertion that the name Robinson does not exist in Ireland. (Perhaps
acquiring it through marriage is permitted. Or perhaps the current
president disproves the old state, the mythical island that Kafka was
invoking. Or perhaps the doctrine fell apart with Anne Bancroft's stockings in *The Graduate*: when that shamefully lush adulteress was permitted
to appear in the picture houses of O'Connell Street.) At any rate,
Robinson suited Keiller's purpose: a minor character ("who else would
sleep in his shoes?") rescued from Kafka's *Amerika*, Defoe's Crusoe – displaced, condemned to internal exile on his return from an epic sea
voyage. All Keiller had to do was to place the name of the city, his subject, in bold type and it was done. **London**: a film.

More than that, *the* film of its period – essay, document, critique,
poem. A modestly ironic epitaph to Conservatism and the destruction
of the city. A triumph, as Keiller sees it, for the dictatorship of the suburbs and suburban values. (Although John Major, with the patented
anonymity of that name, seems to embody suburbia, warm beer, long
shadows, cycling spinsters, he has in fact a far more exotic provenance:
an inner city hustler with an Angela Carter background. An idiot savant
with a peppery temper. Being nothing in himself, having no programme beyond the hucksterism of the gangster, he symbolises
nonentity. A national waxwork – like Catherine Deneuve on a medal-
lion in France.)

Keiller's training was as an architect and he taught, part-time, for a
number of years at Walthamstow. And later at Plaistow. I listened to him
describe this period with considerable unease. He brought it all back:
spasmodic attendance, the scouting around local parks, markets, back-
waters. English cinema can't escape from that grim fortress in
North-East London: Ken Russell, Peter Greenaway, Brian Catling as
students, and now Keiller on the staff. A retrieval from this period of his
life is to be found in *London*, when the narrator speaks of Robinson's

job teaching at the University of Barking, and the camera lingers on the glistening mud of the Channelsea River at Three Mills. It takes a lot of usefully wasted half-days to locate *that* vision. Keiller explains that in those days he was in a gay relationship; the kind, perhaps, that is alluded to in his *London* script.

In the tradition that Chris Petit proposes, Keiller can be seen as the epitome of part-time man. A bit of teaching, some architectural work, film on the side: until the balance tips favourably, and the side becomes the entire surface. (All the others did it: Lindsay Anderson with his theatre work and commercials, David Hare and Christopher Hampton with their plays, Jarman with art and gay politics, Greenaway as a cultural Euro token, Petit with fiction and journalism. Making films is a public hobby, an indulgence.) After 1982 there was no more architectural work, so Keiller concentrated on developing his own kind of cinema. It was economic. He could do it pretty much on his own. He didn't need synch sound. It looked arty, but had spirit, rough edges. It might have been designed to appeal to the managers of production funds, the BFI, Channel 4 in its earlier and more progressive phase.

He was interested in the exploration of architectural space, which is a real difficulty in films without characters as a foreground (the cinema of Antonioni). He was also intrigued by Surrealist texts, Czech modernist poetry, the implications of psychogeography. He had a fondness for literary detection, sniffing out places where writers and painters had lived – preferably European writers. Apollinaire, Rimbaud, Alexander Herzen. Where Petit, freshly arrived in London, spent his weekends (from a job in telephone sales) tracking down the locations where notable films had been made (thereby constructing a narrative of his own, an anticipation of his future cut-up project, *London Labyrinth*), Keiller set himself to accurately identify the original sites of Impressionist paintings. Pissarro in Lower Norwood. The railway bridge. The search, triumphantly concluded, gave Keiller the material, the sense of the particularity of that place, that went into his 1983 16mm short, *Norwood*. A cul-de-sac that took his fancy was imagined as the hideout for a runaway criminal. The film was posthumous, the reverie of a dead man. Keiller had only to wait for the light. The soundtrack, the language, would be added (invented) later. The technique was the one he had developed at the time of his first film, *Stonebridge Park*: shooting with self-imposed restrictions, then devising a contradictory narrative. For *Stonebridge Park* Keiller made two long handheld tracking shots over a footbridge, his own voice tells the colourful tale of a motor trader who dips his hand in the till.

Keiller had begun as a *flâneur*, wandering the underdescribed quarters of the city, taking slides, not as examples of architectural style, but because these places seemed to have a story of their own. Of course, the "found" buildings had no idea that they had been lost until Keiller nominated them. What changed was not the layout of a vanished London, but Keiller's map of it. He assembled a personal scrapbook: a democracy of image and text, word and picture. Neither was in the service of the other. Now in film he was creating a style based upon the shooting of moving stills, slides that could be held long enough to allow him all the narrative exposition that he wanted. (He indulged his affection for Surrealism by coming to live, with his partner, in West Norwood. He kept his spirits up by imagining a future artistic colony. I understood what he meant: West Norwood was my first London home, I'd stayed there throughout my period at the Brixton film school.)

This blend of the exotic and the homemade that Keiller successfully produced on minimal funding endeared him to the committee men, the shufflers of synopses. Even the critic Alexander Walker, who contemptuously referred to the Catholic-educated Petit as a "recidivist", became dewy eyed when rhapsodising Keiller's *The Clouds*: "Cuts through history and geology to get to the inner mystery of time and space". Backed by a sympathetic producer, Ben Gibson, and promoted by the great facilitator of contemporary English cinema, Keith Griffiths, *London* was given the green light. The budget, underwritten by Channel 4, was around £180,000 (half a dozen frocks for Cilla Black). Keiller, with his painstaking method of assembly, went over by £20,000 – which ate up most of the receipts of a very successful festival and small-house release. Such films, it seems, can only exist by permission from above. Small establishments doling out limited credit can therefore control and refine the level of criticism. The justified anger in *London* is tempered by its weary and dandified tone, epitomised by Paul Scofield's bollocks-in-a-vice delivery.

When the script landed on Griffiths' desk, he remarked at once the coincidence in the name Robinson – how it immediately suggested the parallel work on the city undertaken by another leading director from his stable, Chris Petit. Petit's Soho novel, recently extracted in *Granta*, was called *Robinson* as a gesture in the direction of Céline. The fantastic city of *Guignol's Band* (acknowledged by Godard) lay buried beneath the surface of Petit's swift and functional prose. Griffiths, explaining this, found himself a keeper of secrets, a power broker whose triumphs would be unnoticed by the man on the Clapham omnibus, the studio audience for *Have I Got News For You*. He would authenticate as many Robinsons as could be found. Without fuss, this beard-stroker scuttled about Europe, encouraging, talking up, making connections. Keiller, Petit, the Brothers Quay, Jan Svankmajer: he curated all of them, acceptable subversion. He was one of the few people sharp enough to understand Keiller's fluid metaphors: how the Robinson from Kafka's *Amerika* would recall the Czech author's preoccupation with Charles Dickens, his tempering of barbarism with decadence. The great paranoid never went to America. His book opens with an imagined voyage. He aspires towards a condition of exile, perverse comedy. Keiller's film would have all of that, a documentary fiction shot, for convenience, over one year. A fiction that would pass at first sight for an extended *Look at Life*, those colours, flags and parade grounds, rivers and gardens. Begin where you like.

Patrick Keiller's *London* is not your London, it's not the city of the commuter, the person who knows where s/he is going. His discoveries belong to the stalker; they are unexpectedly public as well as poetically obscure. A memorial ceremony for Charles I or a Portuguese driving school in Vauxhall. It doesn't matter that when he was filming, out there with Julie Norris, he didn't walk. With all that camera equipment to schlep about, it's not surprising. He needed the tripod. His film is constructed from views, animated postcards (Eastmancolour sympathetic to the violent reds of buses and uniforms). The fiction walks instead, that's the glory of it. We don't need to know what we do not see. We willingly play the game and stroll alongside Robinson. Every journey is a narrative, a homage to ghosts from the past, and a measured commentary on the follies of the present. Keiller decided against a simple first person monologue, opting instead to use Robinson, as Céline used him, as a representative of fate; a fictional device to strike attitudes, or take risks, that he wouldn't inflict on the essentially passive narrator.

The metropolis, its shrines and suburbs, rivulets, open spaces, rituals and ceremonies, are investigated by innocent pilgrims, Bouvard and Pecuchet reborn, who are never to be seen – but whose footsteps are anticipated by Keiller and his "reconditioned newsreel camera", an Eclair Cameflex. This was a conscious attempt to visualise the city as a whole: an ethnographic home-movie. "Since *Blow-Up*," Keiller said, "no one had made a decent film in London." That might be stretching the case, but it was easy to understand what he meant. No one had approached the topography of the city with that level of care. No one could afford to spend six months meandering across South London, with a style journalist in tow, trying to pinpoint the patented weirdness of Maryon Park in Charlton. Where the colours didn't suit Antonioni, he had them repainted. He treated the streets as a studio. He wanted them set-dressed before he began. Like Blake he had no time for unvarnished nature. Keiller didn't enjoy that kind of budget, the status of the privileged artist. He was, or pretended to be, a kind of artisan: disenfranchised, queasy, a tourist on his own turf, regurgitating guidebook information, standing back in the crowd. An untrustworthy witness. He knows too much. If he were more visible, it would be in somebody's interest to hang him – as a warning – like Roberto Calvi under Blackfriars Bridge.

Keiller stares at London with autistic steadiness. It discomforts us, we are not used to it. He freezes still lifes, arrangements of municipal flowers, swirls of brown riverwater. When some gatepost or doorway takes his fancy he gazes at it with the abstracted longing of an out-patient at a discontinued bus stop. This is not how television, with its programmed restlessness, behaves. This is like the very beginning of cinema, when an audience was thrilled by watching the representation of a train arriving at a station. Keiller's long-focus lens, his cool voyeurism, is almost too exciting. We begin to breathe freely, to accept the slow pulse of these rhythms. We're ready for Warhol's cataleptic account of the Empire State Building. We're ready to brood on stone until we become stone, until the granite enters our veins. Keiller is shooting surveillance films with a postcard camera – and then overlaying banal, but beautiful, images with a frisky emigrant text.

The film is a quiet provocation, provoking reverie, honouring accidental survivals (such as the London Stone in Cannon Street); reciting legends in a tone of indulgent disbelief. It aspires to the form of an epistolary novel, a fabulation backed by congeries of improbable fact. The narrator, returning from a seven-year exile, an accidental Odysseus fleeing from the excesses of Thatcherism, decides to take a leisurely inventory of the city's consciousness, to attend significant events – parades, bomb scares, carnivals; to indulge in fantasies of escape. (The shock of this return must be like the one the cultural historian Patrick Wright describes at the opening of *On Living in an Old County*, when he came back from Canada in 1979 to find himself "reeling with distance from a society which seemed to be making not just a virtue but a new set of principals out of hindsight." Indeed, the experience of *London* is not dissimilar to that of a crash diet of Wright essays from the *Guardian*: scepticism, celebration of Englishness, the polemic that is half in love with the thing it denounces.)

Paul Scofield, that most pared-down and tranquillised of Lears, is the narrator, the voice in the head; a syrup to smooth over authorial distemper. He is describing an absence, a necropolis of fretful ghosts, a labyrinth of quotations: not so much the ruin of a great city as the surgical removal of its soul. The casting of Scofield as the narrative voice (always a difficulty for Keiller) signals an exhausted integrity; it is abundantly clear that this is an actor, a tone, a method of phrasing, and not the narrator himself. Scofield is a distancing device. The monologue of the year is given as a performance – detached, convalescent, camp. He knows so many inconsequential facts. He regurgitates the city's history like a cabbie rehearsing "the knowledge", or a motormouth crimper (Scofield's stage barber from *Staircase*, dispenser of healing unguents). The man is too old for the adventures he is claiming, too careful; he uses English with such absurdist precision, it's like a second language. (Keiller loves language schools. The first day's shoot was at the Montaigne. The colours of the letters on the wall reminding him of a packet of Kodak film.) "Be-zaar", says Scofield. And bizarre it is. Anecdotes rinsed like mouthwash, then swallowed.

"A journey to the end of the world." That's how it begins. An immediate (but unintentional) invocation of Louis-Ferdinand Céline, the laureate of millennial Britain; present but rarely named. A blitz-culture Betjeman with a beret and a foul yellow cigarette. *Voyage au bout de la nuit.* ("The greatest French movie ever made," said Jack Kerouac. About the book.)

Keiller's narrator, a ship's photographer, is coming back to spend time with his reclusive, and possibly dying, former lover: Robinson. Who is marooned (Crusoed) in Vauxhall, once a pleasure garden and now a posthumous Soviet, cut off from central funding, or any hope of social regeneration. ("His income is small, but he saves most of it.") Robinson will never be seen. He's a rumour, a virus: the excuse the narrator uses for talking to himself. A cruise liner (located by Keiller's most useful production manager, Jacqui Timberlake), a creamy berg, completes its stately progress through Tower Bridge and into the archives of London cinema. (Cabins accurately priced at £4,000 per week. A good enough budget for a film shot on the hoof.)

The incoming vessel (no visible crew) is always a threat (Dracula at

Whitby), while the downriver cruiser (Bob Hoskins in John Mackenzie's *The Long Good Friday*) is merely boastful and self-deluding. He's there to show off the Olympia & York skyline. No way out. Tower Bridge, like so much of London, is now a museum of itself, held together by frequent coats of paint. You can buy a ticket to watch wax-works operate the gleaming Victorian machinery. But the bridge is also the most convenient of establishing shots – anything beyond it is waste-land, unworthy of attention. It opens Jules Dassin's *Night and the City*. It salutes Hitchcock's return from exile in *Frenzy*; one of the last films (based on Arthur La Bern's novel *Goodbye Piccadilly, Farewell Leicester Square*) to draw on the rich midden of London's sub-cultural fiction, terse proletarian narratives of lives on the criminous margin. Tower Bridge, used as the London logo, is invariably taken head-on. John Wayne in *McLintock!* – with the redundant exclamation mark that aligned it with cops/capers/car chase television – did try to cross the river. But the only genuine engagement with the structure, as anything but a prop, came with the student film of the Walthamstow visionary, and his epic quest to reach his mother's council flat on the Bermondsey shore (childhood acquaintance with Tommy Steele).

Perhaps the optioning of Alexander Baron's *The Lowlife* as a vehicle for Harry H. Corbett (never made) was the end of it, this flirtation between subversive literature and mainstream cinema. Now buying an upmarket property is bidding for a graphic novel (Alan Moore, Neil Gaiman) rather than an unreconstructed ZAP!! POW!! KERPLONKK!! comic strip. Or perhaps the Nicolas Roeg/Donald Cammell *Performance* was the final decadent flare: an original screenplay using authentically sub-terranean material transmitted by the louche figure of David Litvinoff, a novelist *manqué*. Litvinoff was too busy living to write. He made tapes instead. His life was a book, the forerunner for an age of ghosted gang-land memoirs.

Hitchcock struck an eminently practical attitude towards all this. "I don't read novels, or any fiction. I would say that most of my reading consists of contemporary biographies and books on travel," he informed Truffaut. Jack Trevor Story, the backbone of the Sexton Blake Library, never recovered from Hitchcock's transfer of his first book, *The Trouble with Harry*, from its original scrubby heathland to autumnal Vermont. The paltry sum for which he let the property go was a grievance to the end. But when producers grew bored with metropolitan lowlife fables, publishers also lost their nerve and simply airbrushed certain areas from the map. For ten or fifteen years there was no Hackney, no Stratford

East, and Whitechapel existed only if it included another nomination for the identity of Jack the Ripper. Emanuel Litvinoff (half brother to David) managed to bring out his sketches from Cheshire Street and Brick Lane, *Journey through a Small Planet*, by agreeing to deliver a heavyweight Eastern European trilogy.

Tower Bridge: Hitchcock's camera swoops through the span and along the river in a conspicuous display of budget. Keiller's Cameflex never moves, moves only *between* shots – the unrecorded drive to the next set-up. Much of the film-maker's time is spent in waiting: for the light, the boat on the river, Concorde brushing the rooftops. This enforced period of meditation, making no sense economically, is what gives *London* its quietest poetry. Vision is earned: the streets south of St Paul's, eddies of lost time that Atkins and I took so many weeks to locate. Keiller's long focus stare is a charm against frenzy (the culture of speed and Hitchcock's malign virtuosity). Movement becomes a function of voice, and voice an instrument. As a mode it is estranged from industrial cinema with its basis in montage: Hitchcock's fondness for anachronism is revealed as nostalgia for the era of the good murder, the silk tie strangler. Keiller's separate takes (different angles, lenses, distances) on the same subject are a way of articulating space. He is careful to avoid the soft edges of standard television documentation, with its gentle dissolves and palliative (and meaningless) zooms. He cuts straight, or goes to black. The chapter headings read like a book.

Frenzy, exploiting the last rites of Covent Garden as a working market, is infected by a Europhobic terror of alien cuisines, trays of unwashed immigrant fruit, exotic vegetables. The leather elbow patches of La Bern's ex-bomber pilot – a tribute to his faded gentility – once filmed (they have to be new) become raffish, retro fashion. Anna Massey, fleeing from the career crisis of Michael Powell's *Peeping Tom*, is distrait, nibbled to essence, a Giacometti maquette. She has been cast perversely against type as a perky barmaid, a one-night-stand victim.

She inhabits the silence of a public-house that has been muted, stripped of its resonance. ("I had lunch with Hitch in his office," Powell wrote in *A Life in Movies*. "Silent movies are a dead duck, Micky.") The silence of Powell's film within a film, the 16mm of the amateur, the fanatic. A snuff movie shot by a cameraman with a bayonet tripod who sees London as a closed system, a labyrinth.

Keiller defines this silence, the absence of debate, as a conspiracy of the suburbs, an attack on metropolitan life by small-minded provincials, careerists distrustful of the liberties of the café-bar, the aimlessness of the *flâneur.* He quotes Alexander Herzen, his "motivating source", a stranger who saw London life as a discipline of solitude: "One who knows how to live alone has nothing to fear." The city offers itself up to poets and exiles, men of silent watchfulness, visionaries (Rimbaud and Verlaine) wandering through the iron forests of the docks; opium smokers, dreamers, dowsers of invisible energy patterns. Or, more comfortably, those who are able, like Monet, to take a suite at the Savoy. Lord Archer in his penthouse. John Bellany in his hospital bed. The soul of the place lends itself to reverie, but has an antipathy for cinema. Bureaucratic weather inhibits it. You have to watch the clouds like Constable to snatch that instant of revelation, beams spilling out of darkness. Skies like a hangman's hood.

Any future London cinema must take its lead from the school of Keith Griffiths, from Petit and Keiller, and become a cinema of vagrancy. There's no longer time for the laying of tracks, the crane, the cherry-picker: obsolescent industrial technology (to be viewed at the Museum of the Moving Image on the South Bank). Truths about a city divided against itself can only be uncovered, so Keiller believes, through a series of arcane pilgrimages, days spent crawling around the rim of things. Expeditions that fail to discover any trace of Sherlock Holmes in Vauxhall or Poe in Stoke Newington – but which stumble instead on the transcendent oddity of airport perimeter roads, Ikea warehouses, neutral buffer zones between town and country. Landscapes of the id, such as riverside Shepperton, that have developed – from long exposure to the presence and the fiction of JG Ballard – their own peculiar microclimates.

London cinema in its pomp was a creature of the suburbs – that's where the studios were. Names like a Betjeman litany: Borehamwood, Bray, Pinewood, Elstree. That's where a phantom metropolis, a mental city like Blake's Jerusalem, could be built; civic dignity reduced to plasterboard. Canary Wharf is the contemporary version: an Anton Furst set for a superhero-as-newspaperman movie.

Mutating revengers, menageries of werewolves, Fu-Manchu, Frankenstein's monster, Dracula's favourite daughter, Jack the Ripper, Mr Hyde: they stalked from these sheds like a regiment of liberated animal experiments. A second London, with a roof over its head, and buildings with no volume, was laid out in the Green Belt. A day-for-night mirror world of dreadful busyness, thoroughfares of scuttling raincoats and umbrellas, greasy trilbies, paste teeth. A city in which the crowd is assembled from overexcited extras who refuse to be anonymous, and who are always inserting bits of unnecessary business. This polis is devised for the convenience of remote voyeurs (with their names printed on the back of their canvas chairs). Social classes are divided by strictly enforced faultlines: even clippies on the buses sound like Sloane Rangers on laughing gas. Half-hunters can be checked against regular 9am hangings.

This London, at its peak on either side of the Second World War, was a good place to escape from: the crazy angles of its post-Expressionist architecture provoked flight. Its boundaries were established by the distance a fugitive could run in attempting to avoid the consequences of a crime he had not committed. Arthur Woods' *They Drive by Night* (based on a novel by the excellent James Curtis) is a paradigm of the genre. Emlyn Williams, with his endemic head cold, and looking like an incomplete dissolve between Charlie Chaplin and Nigel Lawson, is the innocent on the lam – determined to prove that the countryside is never more than a few badly-woven tussocks and a clapboard truckers' shack in a perpetual thunderstorm.

City of artificial night: serpentine tracking shots, that marry interior and exterior scenes, drift down rain-splashed alleyways and into basement clubs, or wrestling halls, or climb perpendicularly into the windowless flats of chorus girls. Gashes between buildings, lesions in the brain. The Gerald Kersh novel, *Night and the City*, vividly expresses this mood. "He saw London as a kind of Inferno – a series of concentric circles with Piccadilly as the ultimate centre." Jules Dassin's translation into film is inventive and dynamic, mixing psychologically perceptive set design with a notably vivid account of the geography of post-war London.

Richard Widmark in flight, in cold sweat terror, impersonating Kersh's anti-hero Harry Fabian, scrambling over clinker mounds, dodging along the riverside, anticipates Kerouac's Shroudy Stranger, the future age of Céline when Robinson would come into his own. The title (that cursed name) would descend from the mysterious American poet Weldon Kees (and his parasite Simon Armitage) to Christopher Petit and Keiller; from Kerouac and Burroughs (who made an excursion to visit the disgraced writer in Meudon) to Jonathan Meades and his Pygmy hunt in *Pompey*. Petit is well aware of the genealogy. His novel *Robinson* opens with paired quotations from Ballard and Kees ("Robinson alone at Longchamps, staring at the wall."). Petit's book, an unmatched (and largely unnoticed) exercise in literary and cinematic archaeology, represents the junction point where lost fiction converges with lost cinema. So successful was this shotgun marriage that the novel instantaneously disappeared into a black hole of its own making.

In *Robinson* Petit manages, beyond his homages to Graham Greene, Maclaren-Ross, Mark Benney and Kersh, to pay his respects to a legendary *habitué* of the Coach and Horses, Robin Cook. ("Robin behaved badly before anyone else did." Jonathan Meades.) Cook, between wives, and taking time out as a labourer in a vineyard in France, decided to reinvent himself as a novelist, to construct London as a city of illegitimate memory. He relied on his experience as a night driver, minicabbing drunks to dislocated estates. The result, the Derek Raymond "Factory" series, spiced Edgar Wallace B-Feature picaresque with extract of Krafft-Ebing. They were acclaimed by a Camden Town cult audience who prided themselves on reading the unreadable, stomaching any horror that would have their neighbours in Hampstead throwing up in their gardens. (*I Was Dora Suarez* was the one book in recent times that had the poet David Gascoyne gagging.) Psychopaths on the loose in apocalyptic weather. The past like an acid flashback. The stench of a victim's vomit down the front of your suit. Naturally, these novels, with their Gothic representations of a dream city, were filmed. In France.

When Cook and Petit, English romantics (public school, military, colonial), were drawn, closer and closer, into the heart of the maze of smoke, Keiller made his excuses and left – to navigate the source of the River Brent. Had he been a poet, *London*'s narrator confesses, Brent Cross shopping centre would have been his inspiration. At last the camera moves, floats upwards on an escalator, gazing dreamily on plashing fountains, a Mogadon crowd numbed by the muzak of the spheres. The narrator speaks of noticing a "small intense man" reading Walter Benjamin, for all the world like a card-carrying Cambridge poet. The instant of empathy is an illusion. The spectre vanishes into Willesden. Could it have been Petit on a shopping spree? Or Dennis Nilsen? (Or Ferdinand from Céline's *London Bridge*? "Whoosh! . . . I race along! . . . Willesden! . . . There's the house, I spot it!")

Beyond Brent Cross, Ikea, the bloated hangars of consumerism, London loses its grip. Keiller can wait, crouching in the stubble like an anchorite, for meaningful movement in the clouds. He has already told us so much. Now he'd like to persuade us to forget. There is more history here than any one man can bear. The film-makers have to pass through Mortlake without acknowledging Dr John Dee – the point of departure for Derek Jarman's punk Elizabethan *Jubilee*. Keiller knows about the Tradescants, Ashmole and the mysteries of Lambeth, but he also understands that one film doesn't have to say everything.

London, a lacuna at its centre, is a termite concourse for passengers in transit. The only cinema appropriate to its spiritual aridity is a cinema of surveillance. Let the city shoot its own suicide: unedited, mute, a procession of silent traffic, headlights like torches. If you are noticed, you will be eliminated. This is a cinema that has outgrown its audience.

Visiting Keiller meant another trip to Oxford. It transpired that, like Catling, he lived in a tributary avenue off the Cowley Road. NO FREE/PAPERS/PLEASE pinned to the door. And no need for them, the house was stacked – like a potential David Mach – with mounds of the *Guardian*. The life of the artist was compartmentalised between the domestic and the cultural. Keiller was pegging out children's clothes in the kitchen. Later we were able to talk in his front room, which is dominated by two Steenbeck editing machines, cans of film and maps from his current project, *Robinson in Exile*, which will make a number of Defoe expeditions around the country. The journey will begin in Reading: Beckett, Wilde. And on to describe a sort of spiral shape, a snail shell, that is pinned to the wall. As with this book, I thought, it can all be reduced to a basic pictogram.

When I took my leave, noticing the wooded hills on the southern horizon, it was still spitting down with Tom Baker's rain. It hadn't stopped in a week. It was the only way to keep the film-makers indoors. Petit, with his moody Polaroids, would actively enjoy these conditions. But when I visited him in Golders Green the sun was as bright as a funeral.

4.

It is quite rare to meet interesting people in Golders Green.
AIDAN HIGGINS, *THE BIRD I FANCIED*

Petit camps on the other side of the road, downhill from Evelyn Waugh's childhood home, the one with the blue plaque. He's three flights up, well beyond the carpetline. The anonymous Thirties (or is it Fifties?) block is set back from North End Road. Off-the-peg Bauhaus: service flats with no service. A solitary armchair carefully placed in the foyer. An antiquated lift that nobody seems to use. There's not a living soul to be seen in the late afternoon. Free papers – the kind Patrick

Keiller refuses to accept – pile up outside the entrance. Visitors have to lean down to hit a buzzer, press their noses against an evil silver grater – and shout for admittance.

The flat has found its ideal tenant. It has all the space of an undressed film set, a lavish bachelor pad stripped bare by bailiffs. (Which turns out to be the case: a couple of gay kiters vanished into the twilight, leaving Petit with a monstrous TV and video kit, before shipping out a pantechnicon of undocketed electrical goods.) The novels on the Ikea shelves are so crisp and bright that you'd guess that their owner reviewed books (or stole them) for a living. The discerning visitor makes straight for the copy of Patricia Highsmith's first novel, *Strangers on a Train*, and discovers that it is the correct American first edition, in dustwrapper, with a presentation inscription to "Christopher Pettit". Indicating that they weren't best buddies, and that Petit used his period as film editor of *Time Out* to prepare the ground for future survival strategies as a bookdealer.

A large colour poster for Wim Wenders' *American Friend* (inspired by Highsmith's *Ripley's Game*) and a Gavin Jones oil painting of creamy orange clouds. A rack of CDs. A bright rug. A ruff of Hamlet cigar stubs smouldering in a glass ashtray. There's room here for one of those characteristic Petit tracking shots that would explore the entire gaff – kitchen, bedrooms, corridor – before coming to rest in the old-fashioned bathroom. Then cutting to the desk at the window, the Apple Mac, the fat Irish thriller Petit has been working on for years. The windows are protected by a device that looks like the inner gate from a lift. Across the street, stretching high above the roofs is a set of spooks' aerials that delight the film-maker. They are known, he tells me, as "photovoltaic scanners". Urban paranoia made manifest. The watcher watched

This Irish book, *The Psalm Killer*, is going to be a big one. Petit has made a close study of the genre, balanced all the elements, found the right form. It's an economic necessity, he has to pull it off. The maps and charts are spread out. He's even changed his mind and made a few trips to Belfast. His back's gone – he's spent so long in that chair – but the book is almost finished. The omens were good, right from the start: poking through the dreck in the Oxfam shop in Kingsland Road I found a paperback by the Welsh poet Jon Manchip White called *The Robinson Factor*. It was a tale of the Troubles that ghosted, in pulp form, Petit's thesis: conspiracy, torture, double-dealing, unreliable history.

What was absurd was that one of the most gifted film essayists of his generation was driven to this drudgery to keep his nose above water; condemned to the treadmill with the rest of us hacks. Petit has an uneasy relationship with television's commissioning editors. "Within a fractured narrative, populated by minor and often inconsequential characters, the force of the images of landscape and weather are striving to construct a different emotional way of looking at the world." As his producer, Keith Griffiths, expressed it in his essay "Anxious Visions". These qualities do not endear themselves to either of the dominant documentary schools: the fraudulent fly-on-the-wall (manipulative while aspiring to neutrality) or pictorial print journalism with its mediating narrative voices, its "balanced" parade of witnesses who cancel each other out in a babble of meaningless soundbites.

Petit had, on their terms, an early success with *Suburbs in the Sky*, a charming tribute to air hostesses. More recently, entrusted with a companion piece on bank managers, Chris blew it. He went for poetry, mantic images of factory estate clearing-houses. Night tracking shots: the coming information superhighway that will leave the former pillars of suburbia in a state of trauma. It's a bleak prospect. Air hostesses can have their fling (like chalet girls) and then retire on their memories. Nobody cares if bank managers end up howling in a secure ward. But Petit's intimations of breakdown, self-delusion (with inserts of appropriately futurist locales), were not appreciated. He was called in to recut. The only film he could work on without problems from upstairs was a new version of Michael Powell's *Battle of the River Plate*, shot with his son, and a collection of plastic models, in the bathroom.

Chris Petit's film career spans that amorphous period between the suicide of Michael Reeves (the close of those Sixties pirate productions) and the institutionally approved chamber cinema of Patrick Keiller. Reeves insisted on a landscape subservient to the drive of his narrative (Tom Baker remembers with awe the way he stood under a beech tree in the rain orchestrating a troop of Cromwell's cavalry, none of them at home in the saddle). Keiller makes his journeys first (having written enough material to secure funding), and then formulates a finished text. Petit is perhaps the most troubled of the three: stuck with a subject, the dictation of a script, while secretly wanting nothing more than to let the camera run on the clouds. Gipsying around North London, from Hampstead to Willesden, to Belsize Park, to Golders Green, he established himself as the archivist of suburbia. The example of Julian Maclaren-Ross was always in his mind (or, more vividly, Robin Cook):

the night return from Soho. Metropolitan life (of café, pub, cutting-room) reinvented in isolation.

Petit's London was overlaid with European cinema. He worked in telephone sales (taking orders from Josephine Hart) and arrived at *Time Out* that way, soon moving sideways to take over as film editor (1973–1978). Good days for the job: film was being more written about than made, and the former listings magazine still had a patina of credibility (it had replaced the defunct *IT* and *Oz*, *Frendz* and *Red Dwarf*). The task was to make consumption inconspicuous, to give the appearance of edge to questions of aesthetic consumerism. To use a leavening of gay or leftist politics to soft-peddle the purchase of a futon, or a cinema ticket. The office tolerated a squabble of future movers: Dave Pirie (an enthusiast for Michael Reeves), Jonathan Meades (dropping in to pick up a dining partner), Richard Rayner. These men might influence you to take a ride out to Kilburn to tick off *Revenge of the Blood Beast*, but they were not perceived as bona fide journalists. Nobody was going to offer a transfer to the Street of Shame. Petit understood that watching films with a bunch of cloistered cynics – who were never going to offer him a seat in the back row – was not a career for a mature human being. Meanwhile, expenses were good and he got to travel: in Munich, at the end of a sympathetic interview, he passed a script he had been working on over to Wim Wenders. Word went out that the script had been spotted under the director's arm at the Edinburgh Festival. It took him a year or so to read it, but the response was positive. Why didn't Petit direct it himself?

Radio On. A strong title. A beginning that labelled Petit for all time as a maker of angst-laden road movies. Wenders co-produced and lent his camera operator, Martin Schäfer. The BFI kicked in and Keith Griffiths came on to the scene. It didn't seem to concern anyone that Petit had never made a film in his life, had no technical training, and had never even shot a roll of portentous 16mm. Margaret Thatcher had just stormed Downing Street, the "can do" age of the fanatic was upon us.

What *Radio On* proves is that much of the mystique of the director, the long apprenticeship, the epic difficulties in setting up a project, are phantasmagoric. Petit had a chat with the right man at the right time and walked into it. Like Reeves, he wanted to pit himself against English landscape, work with weather. Unlike Reeves, he had no particular interest in a narrative armature. What he understood – from such films as Wenders' *The Goalkeeper's Fear of the Penalty* – was that he should "apply his own experience to film"; that it was permissible to watch a jukebox for the entire duration of a song. He had certain defining images to work with (a shot of feet in the bath) and what went in between could sort itself out. He thought of a journey made between London and Newcastle, but settled in the end for Bristol – a city he knew well from his student days. He went scouting with Schäfer, drove him to some typically featureless Petit field in Wiltshire and asked how he would shoot it. Schäfer took his time, banged a pylon into the middle of his frame, and the putative director knew at once that he'd got the man for the job.

Radio On is music and weather, a pair of interesting German women, a bottled-up squaddie, a cameo by Sting, Silbury Hill; Weston-super-Mare as Lord Archer never imagined it even in his darkest moments; a Bristol hotel and flyover unmatched in British cinema for their power of poetic displacement. Nothing that engages our attention actually happens, but the film is superbly shot. It's already, at the start of Petit's career, an essay in paranoia, anxiety, tension, restlessness – relieved by twilight reverie, drowned visions through a car window, quarries in the rain, night cities. It is a film of emotional equivalents. You have to grant it a pluralist sense of time. You are encouraged to let go, let the attention waver, drift with the music. (Petit secured an assignment tracking Germany for provocative sounds on behalf of *Melody Maker*, made contact with Kraftwerk, talked to Bowie in his perverse Berlin period – a reprise of the Francis Stuart novel, *The Pillar of Cloud*. He picked up on Wreckless Eric – who would, in a later incarnation, play graveyard gigs with Martin Stone. He wasn't impressed by The Police, but grasped that Sting was very shortly going to be a global marketing point.) The soundtrack was the pitch. It was easier than writing dialogue.

The film played the festival circuit and Petit travelled with it. He toyed with the idea of another road movie: this time taking two women, Lisa Kreuzer (from *Radio On*) and Marianne Faithfull (from her Lots Road squat), to Scotland. It didn't happen. Too many other ghosts were already out there, ahead of him or behind him: Barney Platts-Mills with *Private Road* (expunged from the record books), Bruce Robinson (*Withnail and I*), Peter Whitehead on an estate rented by Howard Marks to receive a drug run from Colombia. Think of Whitehead's non-film, with all the paraphernalia of production (except film stock), as the one that got away. The story that Petit never made.

The best option for Chris seemed to be to involve himself with the only internationally marketable local product, the mystery story. He read yards of Christie – thinking of her formulaic (and heartless) plots in terms of Fassbinder. (Did Fassbinder's *Chinese Roulette*, with Anna Karina, influence the title, or dominant mood, of Petit's *Chinese Boxes*?) He institutionalised himself with PD James – and was unlucky enough to earn the right to direct *An Unsuitable Job for a Woman*. It's ironic that this would be the first truly English subject undertaken by the most English of directors. (*Radio On* was a European film made in England, a German romantic sensibility seeing the buildings of West London, the road out, in a way that they had not been seen before: there is one "wipe" near Heathrow that is so profoundly un-British in its fluidity that Petit should immediately have been asked to return his passport.)

Unsuitable Job, a standard industrial product, was a painful experience for Petit. He was landed with a vanity script that brought with it a couple of wealthy amateurs who wanted to buy into the business. He found himself dealing with half a dozen status-seeking producers, the full inertia of a union crew, chancers flogging Rolexes from suitcases, Anton Furst (pre-*Batman*) designing megalomaniac sets, wells deep enough to call for Jacques Cousteau, actresses who auditioned effectively and then got swept away in the hubris of make-up. Added to which, Schäfer expressed his discomfort at working in this unsympathetic atmosphere by a monumental go-slow: it took him forever to underlight the lightless interiors. Petit accepted the project because he found *Unsuitable Job* the least offensive item in the James canon (no Dalgleish and his Byronic sensibilities to flatter). He thought he would have the freedom Reeves enjoyed with *Witchfinder General* to describe the Suffolk landscape. If any place on earth was designed for Petit's camera, it was the Fens: slate clouds, no horizons, a network of suicide ditches. The logistics of the production forced him to make do with a Berkshire gravel pit. (He saved the location research, the exhilaratingly grim afternoons staring at manifest nothingness, for his novel *Robinson*. And the death of Cookie, one of the finest scenes he never directed. "We arrived at Denver Sluice as the light came up on a landscape that looked like a child's unfinished drawing: a huge sky bisected by the line of the land, the network of canals – oily as sluggish mercury in the coming light – converging on the sluice whose churning waters sounded disconcerting and alien in such inanimate surroundings . . . I watched him, framed in the windscreen, while he found his camera positions. He finally settled on a stretch of canal bank identical to the rest, apart from a solitary, thin sapling . . . He talked me through the shots again, gabbling them off. 'We've twenty minutes at the most before full daylight.'")

PD James, given over to Petit and Schäfer, is an unnerving

experience. Like Anglia TV in a power cut, dubbed into Norwegian. Like some tight-jawed Ibsen family saga of sexual guilt, self-slaughter, lipstick on photographs of the dead. The metaphor of the bottomless well stands in for the fjord. Billie Whitelaw looks as if she can't wait to get back to something lighter: such as Beckett's *Not I*. The rest of the cast are all interchangeable members of the Guard family. Dominic, in particular, turning out as badly as his unfortunate childhood in Losey's film of *The Go-Between* would have led you to expect (the foreknowledge that he would be transformed into a costive Michael Redgrave). Schäfer's interiors were so dim that there was nothing to do except stare out at the dripping foliage in the overgrown garden. Petit's refusal to provide covering shots resulted in some notably abrupt cutting; characters met, parted, fucked, brooded at windows, like a pack of badly wired ferrets. Dame Phyllis, reeling out from a viewing, was heard to remark, with characteristic charity, that she felt "it was the director's film".

Messing about with PD James was an act of lèse-majesty which resulted in a long banishment: Petit's subsequent feature films would be made, virtually back to back, in Germany. The first, *Flight to Berlin*, was an original story by Jennifer Potter, intended for a Paris shoot. Difficulties with the unions meant making a last-minute switch to Berlin. Potter admitted that, because she was "very much a novice", she based the character played by Tusse Silberg on herself. The emotional complications were worthy of Nabokov. And my own grasp of this film is unreliable: it appears fairly frequently on television, but too late at night to be sure if you've seen it or dreamt it. The phantom microsleep of motorway driving, nanoseconds or lifetimes, before you jerk back to consciousness in the glare of an oncoming juggernaut. Lisa Kreuzer was there again, and Paul Freeman from *Unsuitable Job*, and – how the hell did he get involved? – Eddie Constantine as a gesture in the direction of *Alphaville*. Schäfer was now impossible, tinkering prodigiously with inkies, taking a week to light each set-up. The nightmare is an anthology of all Petit's preoccupations up to that point in his career, unravelling in a plot that threatened to become endless: another flight of stairs, another bar, another face on loan from a forgotten movie.

Jennifer Potter, a fine novelist who had not yet begun to publish, had perhaps the greatest investment in this fabulation. (Petit, along with the poet Hugo Williams, was credited with the working screenplay.) Potter, who was married to Petit, touched on the background to the affair in a powerfully written piece for the *Guardian* Women's Page ("A German

Love Story"). She details her response to the director's dalliance with the German lead from *Radio On*. "If I'd been born a man, she was just the sort of woman I would choose." And now there was another engagement with the actress who was, as it were, playing Potter's autobiographical role in *Flight to Berlin*. A woman she met once in the kitchen of her old home and didn't care for. There was a very real sense of permutations and alliances, combinations and conspiracies, that infected the mood of the film. The situation demanded a Fassbinder to orchestrate it, provoke some dreadful conclusion.

Petit, very sensibly, went straight on to Palace Pictures and *Chinese Boxes*. I believe that it's his best work; shot fast and tight, with urgency and barely controlled hysteria, the thriller achieves the status of prophecy. Robbie Coltrane, in a role that is both a nudge and a wink at Orson Welles in *The Third Man* and a rehearsal for the name part in Petit's future novel *Robinson*, is given a minatory speech in which he foresees the coming chaos that will follow the demolition of the Berlin Wall. "The German Spring," he growls. "We'll be overrun by sleazo commie gangsters." If you want political vision, the news six years ahead of itself, read gash fiction; keep your eye on lost midnight movies.

I think of *Chinese Boxes* as Petit's first colour film. Both *Unsuitable Job* and *Flight to Berlin* were shot in colour, but conceived in monochrome. There is nothing in British cinema that achieves the transcendent gloom of Martin Schafer's grey on grey photography for *Radio On*. The freedom a twelve-man crew gave Petit to work fluidly and fast. He did his best with the two subsequent features to turn colour into black and white: he repressed it, stopped it down, keyed it against the zombie performances that he required of his actors. To play the lead in a Petit film was to accept voluntary redundancy. It was like joining the Foreign Legion. Petit didn't like rehearsals, motivation chat: he sat David Beames down and dosed him on everything he could find that had Robert Mitchum in it. Sleepwalkers with attitude, that's what he demanded.

Chinese Boxes had a new cameraman, Peter Harvey, but – more importantly – it had an editor from the Wenders company. Fred Srp not only had a surname that dispensed with vowels, he took his prejudice against them to the extent of breaking every rule of smooth cutting. Srp loved the harshness of chopping dialogue on the consonant. The basic units of grammar in the film are extraordinary: a close shot of a woman's high heels in a pool of artificial light, a jump back, a door behind her opens, light floods in. Close-ups of drinkers in an afterhours bar, arms and shoulders meshed: sick neon, bad skin. Srp keeps the narrative moving in lurches and glides, unexpected angles, the excision of indifferent linking material. But this time the story holds together with the logic of a cold turkey nightmare. Petit exploits the physicality of the American actor, Will Patton, and the corrupted intelligence of the Germans (Gottfried John, Adelheid Arndt). The subject is made for him: layers of untrustworthy information, a countertext of jukebox romanticism, the sexuality of hungry ghosts; paranoia, perversion, the city.

No film that opens with a drunken Gottfried John waving a bottle of Mezcal (shaking up the secret worm) and promising the keys of the city can fail. Within seconds Petit himself appears, at ease in his own fiction, leather-jacketed, firing a gun out of a car window in an underpass. The story, pages delivered by pony express, on the day of shooting, from L. Kit Carson, self-destructs as it speeds along: drug mules, bathroom deaths, phonecalls, beatings, broken bones, cars. But Petit isn't doing a *Made in USA*, his film isn't a lecture, a critique, an essay on form. *Chinese Boxes* is much closer to the famous definition of cinema delivered by Sam Fuller in Godard's *Pierrot le Fou*: "Love . . . Hate . . . Action . . . Violence . . . Death . . . In one word Emotion." Only the conclusion would have to be excised: Petit's film is the antithesis of emotion, or the far side of it; a *mise en scène* that seeks to explain its absence.

The highlight of *Chinese Boxes* is a white-on-white shootout in a pulp paper yard (pulp fiction made manifest). Action, theatrically and effectively staged, years before Tarantino, by a man who was conditioned by Gaston Bachelard, Robert Walser, Peter Handke, not video takeaways. *Chinese Boxes* is yet another version of the Petit labyrinth: keep picking at the layers until you achieve an unsatisfactory resolution that takes you back to where you started.

The film was so good, so self-contained, that it disappeared almost immediately. It was granted cult status before it had its first public viewing. A *Moving Picture Show* special on the ponytails at Palace Pictures ignored it. Petit was not so much blacklisted as snowpaked, whited out of the reference books. (David Thomson's *Biographical Dictionary of Film* has no entry for Petit, or Keiller, or Reeves. They don't exist.) Petit drifted into voluntary limbo, an office without a job at Palace Pictures. The lost years fictionalised in *Robinson*.

The breakaway publishers Bloomsbury offered a project – writing a history of Soho. It was at this point that I met Petit, on the end of a telephone. He became a leading customer for erased London fiction. Poor bugger, he found himself taking part in the chain; having to chase Mark Benney titles that had already moved on to Charing Cross Road at inflated prices. (The book cellars of Cecil Court also had a role to play in the hallucinogenic mirror-world of *Robinson*.) Petit rapidly assembled a major Soho bibliography: Benney, Kersh, Robin Cook, Maclaren-Ross, Wrey Gardiner, Alexander Baron, John Lodwick, Jack Trevor Story, Wolf Mankowitz, Bernard Kops, Frank Norman, Fabian of the Yard, gangland memoirs, the death of Freddie Mills. He kept a few dealers from the poverty line. There was one problem: he couldn't write the book. It would only work as fiction, an absorption of the original material, re-energised in a fast moving narrative of pursuit, "moral decay and sexual collusion".

Chatting to Petit, as an excuse for not getting back to work, it soon became evident that he had very good taste (it agreed so closely with my own): Céline and the reforgotten London writers in fiction, J-P Melville and other odds, sods and marginals in cinema. Petit wrote with much greater clarity, less wildness, than I did: I couldn't see how his novel would fail. Which shows why I'm not working as a publisher's reader. *Robinson*, though its prose was sharp enough to be extracted in *Granta*, remains an insider's book. A book that works best in extracts, teasing without resolution. It's close to Ballard, not as visionary or compulsive as *Crash*, but better constructed and richer than *Concrete Island*. A terse novel rather than an extended story.

The germination of *Robinson* was an incident (or non-incident) in a pub: Petit taking a dislike to a man standing at the bar, a face that reminded him of someone else. He couldn't stomach the way the man talked, the gestures he made. It started there. (Just the sort of alcohol fuelled epiphany that occurs – between invention, false memory and quotation – at the interface where second-hand literature meets uncommissioned cinema. Poking through a box of books at a sale in the North of England, I found a slightly tired copy of Aidan Higgins' *Helsingør Station & Other Departures*, marked down to £1.00. A palimpsest of previous sticky labels revealed that it had been tried at £12.95, £4.99 and £2.99 before finding its ultimate purchaser: me. The clincher was a dustwrapper quote by Chris Petit: "The sort of writing that looks random . . . He goes hunting the literary equivalent of snipe, and gets bull's-eye after bull's-eye, making it look easy, until you have a go."

Honouring the principle of random selection, I flipped the pages and found myself in a pub "down from Jack Straw's Castle, patronized by queers and queer-bashers" at the head of the road where Petit now lives. Higgins is drawn to an old soak with "odd ale-coloured eyes" whom he mistakes for William Trevor. Also to be found at the bar was the most buoyant of the lost novelists. It took the man years to realise that he *was* lost, that his life had mutated into *Krapp's Last Tape*: "Jack Trevor Story the thrice-bankrupt one . . . firing down double brandies in the company of adoring young floozies.")

Petit's novel is very much like that. The pub at the centre of the Soho world, where he could drop in and check on his model, Robin Cook, was the Coach and Horses. Higgins' pub, which he insists is not to be confused with the Coach and Horses ("a Young's house near Hampstead tube station, patronized by the fancy") is called the Coach and Hound. *Robinson* is not a film, nor is it one of those overwritten *roman à clef* novels about film-making, stuffed with misapplied technical terminology. But it does have an ex-film director's grasp of essentials, strong cuts, close-up detail. "The click of his shoes: metal quarters on the heels." "The sugar cubes were pitted where I'd pissed on them, and when the urinal flushed itself automatically they floated."

Petit's narrator, like Patrick Keiller's, keeps his distance from *Robinson* – who is the energising force in the narrative. The man drifts through Soho, escaping from a fading marriage, seeing Robinson as his fate and his salvation: a Harry Lime fixer, a bad father, a Clerkenwell Fassbinder drawing him into a conspiracy of night drives, hotel sex, pornographic epics. The weather of the city. Even the geography of the streets is tilted. He is as likely to walk into a De Quincey apocalypse as a Graham Greene church. Soho is seen as an alternate Atlantis, an underwater kingdom.

> *Death by drowning became Robinson. I associated him with water, because of his description of Soho as a rat-run, with its suggestion of ships. During the wrecked nights . . . I fancied I saw schooners moored in the streets . . . masts higher than the rooftops, a harbour in the square, the streets running off its backwater creeks. Sometimes Soho was the ship itself, sometimes the raft to which I clung after being swept overboard.*

Yet again the launch of a new career was somehow botched and Petit moved further underground: into television. The hunger and the anonymity of the form might have been invented for him. He started somewhere near the top – with Miss Marple, a Barbados freebie – and worked his way resolutely down, and out.

Petit saw Christie's *A Caribbean Mystery* as an exercise in point-of-view, an exorcism of his colonial childhood. The original hotel where Dame Agatha stayed was still around, reminding the director of military barracks in Malaysia. He listened every evening to Donald Pleasance and TP McKenna doing the anecdotes in the bar while he worked out the next day's diagonal tracking shots. He succeeded admirably in de-heritaging Christie, offering instead a bleak existential fable – with Barbados appearing about as inviting as Canvey Island in an acid rainstorm. Further scripts, episodes of *Morse* or Ruth Rendells, were not biked around for his approval.

He gave up drama for documentary: a short essay on JG Ballard for *The Moving Picture Show*. Fighting hard to avoid the author interview and the chorus of talking heads, Petit started to play with crash demonstrations, Ballard's raw material. His documentaries moved closer and closer to found footage: off-cuts, bin ends, insolvent surrealism. A piece made for one of BBC2's terrible "themed" evenings (on *Weather*) can be seen, in retrospect, as the beginning of the end. Numerous re-edits were attempted, a balance had to be found between the charmingly off-beat (crop circles, fish falling from the sky, thunder phobics) and an engagement with foaming millennial visionaries (bunkered artists, madman linking the Great Storm to the collapse of the financial markets).

Too late to bale out: *The Cardinal and the Corpse* found Petit sending for a "freak wrangler" to keep Robin Cook, John Latham, Brian Catling, Alan Moore and a raft of counter-cultural revenants in order. This was grave robbery on an epic scale. A roll call of the ungrateful dead, each man busking his own argument with the past: a discredited revision of London's psychogeography. It ends with the bookdealer Driffield burning all his unsold treasures on a sewage beach in the Isle of Sheppey. Martin Stone, who was discovered to be alive and well and toothless in Paris, wrote the music and delivered the obsequies.

After that nobody was going to trust Petit with cameras and a crew, he was banished to an editing suite – where he constructed two very significant London films. *Surveillance*, made for *The Late Show*, lasted about ten or eleven minutes, and was a shifting collage of superimposed neutral imagery. Haunting and prophetic, this was the first English film on an important subject: post-human cinema. Home movies made by machines. Dictated confessions in real time. But, unlike Michael Klier's feature-length compilation *The Giant*, Petit was forced to "heat up" his footage, run a few whispered observations – contradict his own thesis.

London Labyrinth, the equivalent of Keiller's *London*, was not well received by its sponsors. (Where Keiller would show the architectural aftermath of an IRA bomb, Petit would cut in a clip from the Dick Emery show: an explosive device on a bus confused with a lunch box. Proving that successful comedy often anticipates future newsreel coverage.) Petit wrote a piece for *Sight and Sound* called "Flickers". It consisted entirely of present-tense images from favourite films: an epic of fragments, arbitrary dissolves. "Lee Marvin walking, low angle, through LAX in *Point Blank*; footsteps like gunshots. The sound of wind in trees in *Blow-Up*. Driving shots through the windscreen in *Vertigo*." *London Labyrinth* was just like that: home movies, John Betjeman, Ken Loach bikers, suburbs, underground trains, clips from plays, strippers auditioning, Fu Manchu riverside conspiracies. Cinema in meltdown. The end of the night. An abdication of involvement. Robinson in his cutting-room – like Dr Mabuse – recomposing history from endless reels of documentation and fantasy. Patrick Keiller, passing through Ridley Road market on his pilgrimage to Stoke Newington, sees its multiculturalism as a beacon of hope. His long-focus lens foreshortens the crowd into a swimming mass of spermatozoa: productive chaos. Petit, shooting a scene for *Weather* in the same location, depicts a solitary preacher, a black ranter holding up a punctured plastic globe. Rubbish blows about his feet. Nobody listens as he screams, warning of the coming rain.

Marc Atkins rang me to announce that there was to be a showing of *Radio On* at the Whitechapel Gallery, open to allcomers, gratis, without card or qualification. We went along there at the conclusion of one of our walks. There was quite a decent turnout, a poetry reading crowd – about twenty-five souls. Two or three gave up before Petit had finished his first tracking shot around the dark flat. Thereafter, it was a steady trickle. A vagrant made the best of it, snoring in the front row, with plenty of space to stretch out. The scene where Beames encounters the squaddie in a pub provoked a couple of laughs: the cutting made it look like an obtuse gay pick-up. Sting was recognised. And then, as the car rolled into Bristol, the rest of them decided they'd rather sit in a doorway, and take their chances with the weather in the streets. Four of us stuck it out to the finish, the stone quarry: East London's defiant apocalyptics, squareheads crazy enough to insist on devouring their free lunch to the final knuckle.

PD James, making a rare visitation to a blighted metropolitan zone, downriver of Tower Bridge, wrote a very useful book; a book that I am still happy to draw upon. That was back in 1972. Title? *The Maul and the Pear Tree*. (It could cost you half a ton to send a booksearcher out to locate the first edition. Treble that if you employ Driffield.) The book was co-written with TA Critchley of the Police Department at the Home Office, where James then earned her crust as a Principal in the Criminal Policy Department. (Plenty there, you might think, to keep a lively intelligence occupied. No danger of a shortfall in criminal policies.) James had already produced four well-received mysteries, but this was her first work of non-fiction (apart, obviously, from interdepartmental memos, annual reports and the like).

The Maul and the Pear Tree was a spirited, effectively researched account of the infamous Ratcliffe Highway Murders of 1811; an account that offered, as an additional benefit, when the compulsory gloating over the lurid specifications of these crimes was accomplished, a persuasive sketch of the districts of Shadwell and Wapping in their maritime pomp: brothels, grog shops, provisioners – the bustle and fret of a crowd in perpetual motion; oysters at midnight, drunks to be fleeced or pressed, news from abroad, the bartering of exotic animals. All of this restless activity "bounded to the south by London's dark blood stream, the Thames". A working river and a community that existed only to exploit it. How offensive, how alien to James' conservative sensibilities, this licence, these maggots in the wound: the absence of order. The English murder mystery is essentially concerned with good housekeeping, imposing structure on chaos; identifying a villain who is given the choice of committing suicide, or being dispensed with, off-stage. *The Maul and the Pear Tree* was a sabbatical, an opportunity for James to cruise the wild side, binge on heritage Dickens – and all within the conventional form of a documented criminal investigation. She had merely to pay her respects to Thomas De Quincey's essay "On Murder Considered as one of the Fine Arts", to defuse its excesses, and she was released from all moral obligation.

The case saw James at the height of her powers: a fastidious dabbling in horror, the bright forensic eye swooping on irrelevant detail. The frustrating aspect was that there was no villain to be unmasked, no Adam Dalgleish to twitch a nostril in righteous indignation. The supposed murderer, John Williams, may have been staked through the heart at the crossroads (Cannon Street Road/Cable Street), but his skull went missing. It was out there, a trophy, under the counter of some pub, implicated in Masonic or occult ceremonies, fondled as a totem of power by gangsters and brown brogue fascists.

Now, more than twenty years after her original modest raid on the riverside, James was ready for a grand return. She would invent a crime more suited to the spirit of Olympia & York, the new principality of Docklands. A crime that could be solved, dealt with, written out (like the problems of the Canary Wharf transport infrastructure). Old Wapping would then be definitively erased, struck from the map; no decent, right-thinking citizen would ever have to visit there again.

What James (or her researchers) discovered was too dismal for mock-Victorian fiction. Property pirates, tarted-up boozers revising their own legends, gloomy speculators in revamped cellars, wretched art trading on the cusp of entropy, media fortresses bristling with surveillance cameras and razor wire: loose money. What vitalising crime (a sacrificial murder to restore the dead ground) could be visited on a territory whose boundary markers were properties owned by Lord Owen and David Mellor? An attempt had to be made to appease her disgruntled audience after that turkey *The Children of Men* (stacks of which were appearing in remainder shops everywhere). James had read about the problems of East London. She sat on all the relevant tribunals dishing out Arts Council doles. The subject – the badlands on the wrong side of St Katharine's Dock – was contemporary (eight or ten years off the pace), but it had been leeched of its fictional zest by genre hacks (Sax Rohmer or Seamark's *Down River*), by current sharpies such as Kim Newman (*The Quorum*), by the endless exploitation of the Canary Wharf skyline as a convenient television shorthand for dim-witted futurism. The predatory energy of Wapping's lowlife past had been transported upstream by Dalgleish's impersonator, Roy Marsden, for his annual Long John Silver show at the Mermaid Theatre in Blackfriars. James was left with a cold trail: dubious quotations, a London Dungeon of wax-work crimes exhibited in genuine locations. Her novel was destined to become the final testament of Thatcherism (like *Edwin Drood*, it should have been left unfinished).

Original Sin is a virtual reality parable enacted in an empty set, a set defined by architectural models – so that even James's traditional ingénue, Mandy the Temp, in her "fab" gear, seems to be trying to catch the eye of Gavin Stamp. A silly parade of deaths and suicides announces the dissolution of the golden age murder mystery: Agatha Christie forcefed a diet of Pevsner and the patriotic humbug of Kenneth Baker's latest Faber anthology. (The freakish logic of these blood-on-tweed crossword puzzles can only be managed, so James asserted on a radio programme, by a middle-class audience serviced by middle-class detectives. Summer vacation fiction. Consoling reading for troubled times, produced by professional amateurs: academics, country clergymen, doctors, lawyers. Or steely, independent women beavering away at one of the few options open to them.)

What left this particular reader uncomfortable was James' tendency to editorialise, colonise her narrative with pronouncements from Smith Square. It's too much like enduring one of those episodes of *The Archers* where extracts from the Countryside Code and some pest husbandry brochure are spliced into a saloon-bar monologue. Two of James' coppers can't sit down for a swift half without debating the morality of capital punishment. "I happen to believe that the death penalty does deter, so what I'm saying is that I'm willing for innocent people to take a greater chance of being murdered so that I can salve my conscience by saying that we no longer execute murderers." (Give credit to a fat-neck, commie stomper like Mickey Spillane. He integrates his rabid politics within the deranged psyches of his characters. His prose screams and sweats. No sub-text. What you read, as your lips move, is what you get.) James' robotic humanism suggests that the author has donated far too much of her time to literary festivals, book gabble, the smokeless backrooms of power brokering. She could even be said to have invented a new form of fiction, conducting the promotional interview within the novel. The phobia about the Thames flooding through the Greenwich Foot Tunnel which is suffered by the wimpish Frances Peverell signals an obvious autobiographical prompt (obligingly picked up by John Walsh of the *Independent*, who can gaze down from his openplan office on the relevant section of the river). *Original Sin* has to be worked over like a crib for an author profile. You daren't skip-read for fear of being ticked off by the fastidious Commander Dalgleish for misquoting Jane Austen. The culture comes from a time warp: garlands of Eng Lit as memorised by a conscientious 16-year-old from the Cambridge High School for Girls.

Despite (or because of) all this, *Original Sin* has been a notable success as far as that marginal community, the purchasers of hardback novels, are concerned. Dame Phyllis is back where she belongs, at the top of the charts, after a nationwide publicity tour that swept her from a lunchtime engagement at Hatchards in Piccadilly to an evening spot in Birmingham – and then, on successive days, a progress through Manchester, Norwich, Cambridge, Chester, that might have had Lady Thatcher reaching for the whisky decanter. With her unfailing good humour, the Dame did an Archer, pitching product, defacing title pages – slid across ready-opened by deferential managers – with a neat, black signature. Punters, publishing flotsam in tight red suits, local press stragglers: all were treated with courtesy, all were equally "dear". (The Jamesian "dear" is the Ackroydian "darling".) Old fashioned virtues still work. Reviewers purred and obediently recycled the plot survey cobbled together by the relevant Nicola: "a puzzle of extraordinary ingenuity and complexity . . . characters who will remain in the mind." The freshness of the riverside setting was stressed and the obsequious hacks fell over themselves to make the book sound as exotic as Thomas Burke's Chinatown. (The one exception, Hugo Barnacle, exposed *Original Sin* as very unoriginal detective fiction by stressing the slapdash craftsmanship, the evidence doctored in the best tradition of Agatha Christie, and a plot lifted straight from Margery Allingham.)

Chris Petit did well to single out *An Unsuitable Job for a Woman* as a PD James novel that might effectively translate into his favoured brand of cinema: overgrown fairytale garden, English skies, metaphorical weather. More importantly, he avoided an encounter with the creepy and prophylactic Adam Dalgleish, costive poet and occasional filth: a narcissist addicted to solo amusements. "To lunch alone in a strange place . . . was a rare pleasure. There would be no time for a solitary walk or for exploring an interesting-looking church." (Even when she gives Dalgleish a rest, James favours the same solipsistic masculine types. Theo Faron, the disengaged Oxford don in *The Children of Men*, is made to paraphrase the Byronic policeman's sentiments: "Normally he would now begin planning his route with care; a good pub for an early lunch, an interesting church to visit, a detour to take in an attractive village." The England of John Major's Orwellian fantasy: "interesting", "attractive", uninhabited.)

If he doesn't watch it, Dalgleish will find that he's just the sort of versifier to be taken up by the disciples of Peter Fuller, Ruskinite bother boys. As a high profile poet with atrophied tastes (and a good tailor) he belongs out there in the Fens, silhouetted against lowering skies, straining to escape the inconvenience of some vulgar stiff, hot to inspect the rood screen of another John Piper church. Villagers, estate dwelling proles, will insist on having themselves raped and murdered (social engineering), so that suspicion can fall on middle management boffins or aristos who nurture a shameful secret. Think of Dalgleish as Philip Larkin (sans bicycle clips and pocketline ruined by the bulge of bondage magazines). Larkin made over for a transatlantic Burberry advertisement. Larkin imagined by Barbara Cartland, all scowls and piercing hawklike glances.

Descriptions of wholesome outdoors mayhem between consenting adults thrive during periods of social upheaval. There's nothing like an authentic hunger march, or a poll tax riot, to upgrade the country house murder mystery. The Thirties have long been acknowledged as the period of the lethal spinster (a clean Dorothy Sayers, or a Christie in dustwrapper, will set you back a few hundred pounds). Those great ladies were the only writers ever likely to be block booked for honours. As a coven they are equivalent in status to the theatrical knights of our own day: an easy and popular dispersal of trinkets to demonstrate the scale of any government's interest in the arts. Margaret Thatcher famously "rereads" Frederick Forsyth and makes small noises about Jeffrey Archer. New Labour has to rub along with Ken Follett (and keep the Pinters, Hares, McEwans and Mortimers for the silver service dinner circuit.)

The Golden Dagger dames specialised in the creation of parallel worlds where bluestockings or rural busybodies stood alone against a conspiracy of social climbers, artsy-fartsy pinko bohemians, garlic-breathed gigolos, Hebrew financiers and allround wrong 'uns. (They echoed the Spenglerian doctrine of High Modernism, keeping chaos at bay by swatting TS Eliot's "jew" from the sill.)

At the still centre of the classic English murder mystery is a sanctuary where the plot-so-far can be recapitulated over a leisurely luncheon; where a well-connected amateur can lobby the professionals, schmooze with the unbuttoned judiciary, pull rank. PD James' Cadaver Club is just such a place, a worthy successor to the Diogenes. "The lamb had arrived, pink and succulent and tender enough to be eaten with a spoon." In England it is still the Cadaver Club, bib and braces, not any internationalist conspiracy of Masons and Mafia, that sets the world to rights: warmed-over prep school grub, a starched ex-matron to dish it up. (And also, when arranged by private treaty, to dish it out. Witch hazel for throbbing bottoms.) "All the volumes of the *Notable British Trials* are on display, as is the rope with which Crippen was hanged. ("A trifle morbid, perhaps, but barbaric is going a little far.")

Conrad Ackroyd, with his blue plaque moniker, is the member who signs Dalgleish in. As soon as the Commander has finished miming his invariable prune-lipped disapprobation of the club's morbid memorabilia, he shuts up and listens to Ackroyd, who "although he could be facetious, was seldom dull." The old queen was, after all, "one of the most notable and reliable gossips in London." Ackroyd, like Mrs Demery the Cockney char, is a "turn", the liveliest thing in a sensationally turgid book. His surname, taken in conjunction with the club's "few first editions of Conan Doyle, Poe, Le Fanu and Wilkie Collins", is enough to invoke, by conditioned reflex, the Agatha Christie cornerstone, *The Murder of Roger Ackroyd*. Or, as Derek Raymond frequently proclaimed, paraphrasing Edmund Wilson, "who gives a fuck *who* killed Roger Ackroyd?" Raymond, attempting in *The Hidden Files* to define the "black" novel in which he specialised, glossed the Jamesian school as "pretentious crap for the well-heeled middle class market". A conventional putdown by a man, quite reasonably, distancing himself from his disadvantaged background as an Old Etonian with a family pile in greenest Kent. Raymond was just the kind of tight-skinned wideboy given a cameo by Christie, before being discovered in a golf bunker, his skull smashed and his trousers held up by a – surprise, surprise – *genuine* regimental tie.

Class confusions continue to dog English fiction. Peter Ackroyd, a scholarship boy, and brilliant processor of information, who talks – with poetic licence – of his childhood in the shadows of Wormwood Scrubs, followed James into riparian London. But *Dan Leno and the Limehouse Golem* has none of the procedural longueurs of *Original Sin*. While successfully masquerading as front-desk Hatchards Literature, *Dan Leno* is soon exposed as a rattling good yarn, a revived shilling shocker. Ackroyd's detective is a marginal presence, cohabiting in Pooterish domesticity with a nice young man. The narrative isn't burdened with the tedium of a convincing topography, or nostalgia for lost decencies. Like an Edwardian masher, Ackroyd exploits Limehouse, in best yellowback style, as a spicy backdrop. A labyrinth of permissions. The far side of the glass in a Wildean opium den. Mr Hyde's funny night out. He has a genuine relish for music hall, the London crowd: stinks and songs and shocks. The execution by hanging of a female artiste, a child of the streets, is like a scene cranked in a penny slot-machine. These wharves and slipways are not overwhelmed by liturgical gloom, but lurid with torchlight; gamey, wet-mouthed, obliging. Sites of sexual tourism, they sweat with greasepaint, horseshit, moonshine on the razor's edge.

(Meanwhile Derek Raymond's old mucker, Mark Timlin, has taken it on himself to carry forward the campaign against Jamesian detective fiction by means of the class argument. Timlin, a former rock roadie, a dogtrack figure in a blue crombie overcoat, lurked with effect at Raymond's shoulder: part minder, part inheritor. A sense of threat always present in that abstracted and watchful silence. Nobody could guess, with any accuracy, the moment when he would flip and wreck the bar. Nick Sharman, Timlin's South London PI, "ex-cop, ex-doper", works the interface where "the mob clash with rock 'n' roll's godfathers". Not so much hardboiled as pre-digested. Streatham steakhouse fables. A kebab skewer in the eyeball. Sharman has made it onto television, where the dark reveries of Raymond's "Factory" novels – frequently optioned – never get further than being a conversational gambit at funerals and book launches. It was left to Timlin, the survivor, to give Dame Phyllis a bit of a slap for her innocent remarks about the primacy of the well-educated sleuth.)

Original Sin, it must be said, does for Wapping what the Docklands Development Board did for the Isle of Dogs. Commander Dalgleish arrives on set exuding "the moral rigour of Torquemada" – as John Walsh put it – at the head of a positive discrimination posse (one troubled Jew, one feminist orphan), to sort out some bother in a publishing house so surreal in its work practices that it's almost believable. James has always been most comfortable with in-house crime, the bunkers of the Establishment, the vertical hierarchies of hospital, nuclear power plant, research laboratory. (It's a relief when her titles aren't lifted from the Book of Common Prayer or Palgrave's *Golden Treasury*.)

In *Original Sin* the only substantial character is a fake Venetian palazzo that overlooks the old pirates' hanging dock, and is serviced, whatever the state of the tide, by a private riverbus. There is something not right about this building – apart from the fact that there isn't, and never was, anything remotely like it in Wapping. It offends the spirit of place. Andrew Davidson's illustration for the Faber hardback depicts pastiche cladding that has more in common with Terry Farrell's MI6 extravaganza than any structure between the Town of Ramsgate and the Prospect of Whitby. Neither do Davidson's looming tower blocks fit the scene; they speak of artistic licence, a wholesale displacement of the Lambeth nexus: Tintagel House, Camelford House, Lord Archer's apartments as the only floor in Alembic House with darkened windows.

Now the book begins to make sense. James has folded the London gazetteer; her Wapping is a pale tracing of spook's Lambeth. (Coming back over Southwark Bridge at the end of one of our *Lights Out* walks, I discovered an even better model: a pillared phoney, with its own dock and steps up from the river, built for the "Communality of the Mystery of Vintners" by Wates Properties Limited. The side of this property that faces Upper Thames Street has been let to Chase Manhattan, Chase Investment and the Sumitomo Corporation. Japanese gentlemen in pale grey suits waving for taxis. But the river frontage is empty, mock marbled, expecting the imminent arrival of James' fictitious Peverell Press.)

Publishing is sick. Quill pen nostalgics, labouring at their high desks in fear and trembling, at the incursions of Murdochian brutalism, decide to take the soft option by committing suicide in complicated ways, or by arranging to have themselves strangled – with draught-excluders stuffed down their throats (presumably to stop them screaming "red herring"!). These macabre diversions don't hobble the dialogue, which comes in two forms: sponsor's messages and awkward plot summaries. What PD James does *not* do is the police in different voices. Toff or plod, male or female – the same ex officio paragraphs. A slender yarn has been basted in gravitas until it drags itself along like a ruptured Victorian three-decker. Wilkie Collins by correspondence course. Themes of the moment (marginalia to catch the eye of the think tank) – AIDS, urban regeneration, yobs on the loose – are chucked at the screen in the hope that some of them will stick. ("Don't talk to me about unemployment. They may have been unemployed but they could afford expensive motor-bikes, and two of them had cigarettes hanging out of their mouths.")

The narrative, after several pages of convoluted actuarial prose, comes to life with a clap of scene setting worthy of Enid Blyton and the Famous Five. "He was wearing a yachting cap set well back on a mop of black curls and his eyes were bright slits in the weatherbeaten face." The strain of delivering a text worthy of the censorious Dalgleish brings forth a gush of generic clichés that would be inoffensive in a work with fewer pretensions. ("His eyes were narrow, sleepy under heavy lids, but they were eyes which missed little and gave nothing away.") Edgar Wallace, who could dictate yards of this flannel to a harem of secretaries, before scooting over to Deauville, didn't feel the need to blather on about how "the criminal justice system has favoured criminals for the last forty years." Find 'em and shoot 'em. Next case. Systems of criminal injustice, interminable trials, bent briefs, judges climaxing as they reach for the black cap, the early morning drop: they are the lifeblood of British fiction, the inspiration for hundreds of duff plays. Don't knock it.

But the creator of *Sanders of the River* wasn't stuck with a hero who is increasingly embarrassed at being spotted in a romance he would never permit his housemaid to take out from Boots' Library. Dalgleish's cameos are now as unconvincing as Charlton Heston's hairpiece. He models himself on the Duke in *Measure for Measure*, travestied in priestly drag, hanging around the stews and rat holes to sneer at a city going to buggery. It's not hard to like Dalgleish, it's impossible. The higher he rises, the more insufferable he becomes. Which is James' major achievement: that one of the great and good, a woman universally admired, a diamond geezer, should prove capable of imagining such an unmitigated herbert. Dalgleish peaked too soon, in a landscape James caught as well as any living writer: Ely, the Suffolk coast, darkness everywhere. Empty churches, disappointed lives. Turnip rot, icy quag, incest. Modest Sapphic alliances, inactive adulterers picking over the Polaroids in the attic. Hope represented by some feisty young woman with decent A-levels and an aureole of hair tumbling around her shoulders.

Dalgleish thinks best in motion. The London of *A Taste for Death*, with its underlit vestries and fetid canals, is a city seen through the curved window of a "claustrophobic" Rover. The Commander, favouring his alabaster profile, stares out in silence – as he himself is gazed upon by the devoted Kate Miskin: a fetishistic bonding of voyant and voyeur. "She saw in his face a look with which she was familiar; a stern withdrawn self-absorption as if he were stoically enduring a private pain." Elective haemorrhoids. There are stickily obsessive descriptions of seat-belts, driving gloves, "sensitive hands lying lightly on the wheel." It's a rare event for the now deified AD ("probably the most intelligent detective in Britain") to patronise public transport. He did, once, let the train take the strain, but that was strategic, so that he could, like John Major, boast of how he had "settled down to re-read Trollope's *The Way We Live Now*." The true test of an author who is definitely "one of us" is to be "re-read" and never risked as a novelty. No politician would confess to reading Trollope for the first time. That would be as bad as buying your own furniture. Potboiling serial fiction is fine as long as it's Victorian.

Thinking of car journeys, there is a much recycled story of Dame Phyllis being chauffeured through Middle England to some book bash in the company of Will Self. (Why didn't Petit audition that cast for one of his road movies?) They pass a village cricket field and James, amiably making conversation, asks the professionally saturnine ex-junkie if he plays? Self grunts. "Rugby, dear?" No reply. Self and James are parodic versions of Dalgleish and Miskin. Better, in those circumstances, to keep shtum.

Will Self, a few years down the line, will be ideal casting as Dalgleish. But it's not the bone structure, the lazy television translations, that worry me; no, it's the fact that Dalgleish is supposed to be a poet. Who on earth would publish him? Conglomerates don't care for the word "poetry", they speak of sales peaking at a few hundred copies. Yet this part-timer, this civil servant, is known to the entire readership of England. Politicos, fellow spooks, suspects under interrogation: they've all kept up with his output. And he seems to be handsomely rewarded for it. I'm sorry, but that's pushing suspension of disbelief too far: unless it's a cute way of laundering Secret State blood money. You hear these rumours explaining some of the crazier advances. The sort of figures that scuppered Sinclair-Stevenson.

Dalgleish the versifier is better known than Roy Marsden. Which must be why Marsden picks up all those authoritative voice-overs. Oral harassment. A poetic of toiletries and DIY. Most versifying coppers have been something short of officer class: Edwin Brock, John Arlott in his Hampshire youth. You can understand that: pounding the beat at night, up on the toes, cup of tea and a scribble in the black notebook. Time to synthesise the free-flowing, random impressions of a long solitary walk. But Dalgleish in his auto, never a moment to himself? The dude's too grand somehow for an anorexic Faber paperback. Perhaps he is sponsored by CH Sisson at Carcanet? Right credentials. With his melancholia, austerity, his Hardyesque predilection for landscape, I see him as a stablemate for Donald Davie. What does he write *about*? Obviously, the job helps: "His next book of poems contained that extraordinary one about a murdered child." A touch of Ted Hughes or Tony Harrison? Surely not. Meditations in strict metre, closely resembling pared-down paragraphs by PD James.

> *A wide expanse*
> *of heavily sun-speckled water*
> *which, as she watched,*

was flicked by the strengthening breeze
into a million small waves
like a restless inland sea.

English poetry. Poetry as a hobby, conferring sensitivity on the man of action. When James talks of poets and poetry, as she frequently does in *Original Sin*, the eyes of her readers cloud over; they flick the pages to find the next killing. With the best will in the world, it's hard to swallow Gabriel Dauntsey – with a couple of pamphlets back in the Forties, when he was shaping to be World War II's Wilfred Owen – as the "advertised star of the evening" at a pub show, "off the Waterloo Road." I've been to that show, seen the audience of five wannabes clutching their bulky folders and waiting for their turn. The drunks who thought it was quiz night. There is no collective memory that embraces poets. That's what makes them such monsters of ego: they are hanging grimly to an identity that everyone else is hellbent on denying. "Sorry, who?" Being an English poet is serving a life sentence as Hitchcock's "wrong man". You are the only one who knows your name, what you've done. Even the bloke who organised the evening has no idea why you've come and has absolutely no intention of paying for the privilege of your company.

Derek Raymond (aka Robin Cook) was, like PD James, fascinated by poetry. He was one of the leading lights of another establishment, the Compendium mob, favourite copy for rude-boy journalists. A Cook tribute was the contemporary equivalent of the apprentice's passing-out ceremony. In both cases you were likely to finish up legless in a Clerkenwell dustbin. Cook was known as the great survivor, the boho X-ray: for his funeral piss-up at the French they dug out a terrible oil painting, a ghost train frightener, and hung it on the wall. (In Petit's *Robinson* the Cookie character talks of himself in the third person, which is about right. Robin's anecdotes, mesmerising to his audience, were of equal fascination to their inventor. He reported on his past life as on a well-loved video. Given a sympathetic prompt, he would yarn at length in a brisk, telegrammatic present tense. Petit spices this with some of Julian Maclaren-Ross' military swagger. "Cookie's general philosophy was simple, and got simpler in the course of his third bottle of wine. Life divided into those who were good sports and those who weren't. Marriage, on the whole, was not good sport, though plenty of good sports married and it was with them that Cookie formed most of his liaisons. 'Wife at home, bored. Husband knackered by a two-way journey up to the city. Bob's your uncle.'")

Cook was always game, always up for it: photocall in the Coach and Horses, black beret, untipped French cigarette, leather jacket, skin like Tutankhamen. He was made to pose indoors, his back to the street, curls of smoke dressing the composition. The wiry fitness of a workman, a roofer bright with cognac. A cashiered dandy. A charmer. A lowlife ace shot from a low angle (the photographer couldn't trust himself to stand upright). Dame Phyllis, on the other hand, budget reflecting status, gets to pose in polo neck and cashmere overcoat on the foreshore at Wapping.

Now, sadly, it's official. Derek Raymond is dead. Cook had preceded him in 1971, after the publication of *The Tenants of Dirt Street*. The Seventies were lost years for anyone who could remember the Chelsea Set. It was far too soon for the formation of a Robin Cook appreciation society. His was a name whispered by obnoxiously hip bookdealers and journalists who envied the apparently footloose lifestyle. Cook manifested in France, drudging in a vineyard as a day labourer: his name fought over by a shlocky airport novelist (a medical horror dystopian) and a diminutive, but perky, Scottish politician. Jonathan Meades noticed how, at this time, Cook referred to himself as if he were already deceased; as if those picaresque adventures had happened to someone else. Which is how Derek Raymond came into being as a master of the posthumous narrative. His Factory novels are the troubled dreams of a man in the graveyard. A vanished England is invented in exile. Raymond was, in his own way, as much of a romantic as Shelley. Perpetual rain, rucks in New Cross boozers, flesh rotting beneath the floorboards of rooming houses: an out-of-the-body experience from the start. Sexton Blake ghosted by Jean-Paul Sartre. The "general contract" Raymond called it, the vulture on your epaulettes. Poetry and death. Like PD James, he was fond of a good quotation: TS Eliot, or sometimes Auden. Jamesian themes abound in his work, the country going down the khazi – but from a different point of view. From the taproom floor, the one-bulb Kilburn bedsit. The crusted lavatory bowl. (Raymond is the kind of bolshie motormouth whose interrogation Dalgleish would leave to his Jewish sidekick.) The wounded loner kicking against the heartless crowd: that's his theme. Bad music migraines. A 24-hour nightmare.

Cook was hooked on philosophy, always diving into Henrietta Moraes' drum for a bit of a barney about logical positivism; paying his respects to his old flame, Veronica Hull, and her novel, *The Monkey Puzzle*. ("A student of philosophy's journey to disenchantment . . . to Soho, where poets, painters, intellectuals and bums gather in the community of drink.")

The Factory novels are monologues of erasure, frisky with despair. Cook never shook himself free from the romance of the Spanish Civil War, Esmond Romilly. The good die young. The dead are good. That's his sentimental side. Old chums who bought it prematurely were always with him. He was affectionate even in his hatreds. Gust, the psychopath in his final novel, *Not Till the Red Fog Rises*, spends his time in prison mugging up on Dylan Thomas. It's a winning foible – allowing your characters to share your own literary tastes.

But Raymond, as he insists in *The Hidden Files*, was first and last a writer: "Writing is what I understand by living." He didn't do committees, or reviews, or visible charity, or panel games. If he had ever joined anything, he'd long ago lost his membership card. He couldn't sit through a tribute to his latest novel on the BBC's *Kaleidoscope* without shooting out of the studio for a drag. (That's when I suspected something might be wrong. He looked much as he had for years, fit and lively, but he had trouble getting through his second lager. He refused a third. The quack, so he told me, had warned him to stop drinking. And he'd stuck with it. He'd switched to Guinness. But the energy level was good. He cheerfully agreed to meet Marc Atkins and to let him shoot a portrait.)

Cook's honours (like those of David Gascoyne) were all foreign, kept in his sock drawer. He was a premature European, shunted – iffy suitcase in hand – from border post to border post: Spain, Greece, Italy, France. A typically postwar career, long past its sell-by date. The Irish novelist Francis Stuart was another who had a gift for transience, being in the wrong place at the right time: Berlin in Year Zero ruins, Canning Town when the docks were dying. The Forties and Fifties were better times for a gentlemanly vagrant: Stuart might have to scratch a subsistence living as a warder at the Geological Museum, but Victor Gollancz continued to publish his gambler's fiction. A yellow jacket novel every couple of years: John Cowper Powys revised by Simenon. Dostoevsky interpreting a Jack Yeats horse fair. Triumphant perversity. Cook had many of the same qualities. As did Stuart's friend, the ex-Boat Squadron, book-a-year man, John Lodwick. They lived abroad whenever they could, the better to focus on the re-invention of a fabulous homeland. Masters of selective amnesia: the inheritance of

James Joyce – who could concentrate on mapping Dublin only from the safety of Trieste.

The posthumously published Raymond novel, *Not Till the Red Fog Rises*, moves with the unforgiving urgency of Cook's favourite video, the Brian De Palma/Al Pacino remake of *Scarface*. ("Remember, Tony, every day above ground is a good day.") Frenzy that stays on the cusp of losing it. The vindicated desperation of the best American pulps: Jim Thompson, David Goodis, William Irish. Depression literature that is sure enough of its ground to substitute hallucinatory nightmares for consoling fables. Stripped-down fate tales: sorry characters, doomed from the start, trapped within the confines of strict genre discipline. Deliver your pages, hold the attention of a jaded editor or butt out. Orphan books written to be abandoned. Dream logic without the luxury of revision. (The best you could hope for was that Orson Welles, talking longdistance to a potential producer, playing for time on an airport telephone, would notice a title on the paperback rack and turn it into *A Touch of Evil*.) Even the dustwrapper of *Red Fog* pastiches the sort of cover illustration that sold hundreds of thousands of Gold Medal or Lion books. It doesn't make reference to any specific incident in the story (the artist would have had to waste time reading it), but gloats instead over a topheavy blonde who is spreadeagled in compromising conjunction with two fat pistols, an empty tumbler and a scarlet blanket.

Unlike Commander Dalgleish with his pregnant silences, there are no worries about Raymond's characters playing mute in the motor. They rabbit like speed freaks, speech bubbles of rancid vernacular. They represent Cook's recall of his nights as a minicab jockey: the lunar deserts of Willesden and Deptford, other people's paranoia crackling over the intercom – the voices of the restless dead. With the author's foot hard down, the plot of *Red Fog* is advanced by the classic Raymond Chandler device of sequential confrontation: aphoristic head-to-heads every time Gust ducks into a bar, or seeks out an old (and soon to be extinguished) flame.

The novel attempts to twin London with Moscow, Warsaw, East Berlin: the revenge of Petit's "sleazo commie gangsters". Raymond insinuates his feverish pulp-porno dementia into a sub-Eliotic wasteland. Fifties hoods (as depicted by Fabian of the Yard), the heavy mob from Poland Street, brassy tarts, incompetent hitmen: an anthology of urban myths to plague Gust, the dead man, the fugitive on licence from hell. (No serial killer movie can now be released in America without its complement of quotations from Dante.) The book reeks with the stench of excrement. "Busybodies . . . I shit 'em." "Eyes the colour of old shit." "Dry sphincter where he took her doggy fashion." "The shit'll come flying out of you." "Nose filthy . . . covered with shit." "Wouldn't give you the skin off his shit." "Ten thousand kinds of shit and I'm in it all." Incontinence as the universal condition. Swampy armpits. Flypaper flesh. Psoriasis. Colostomy bags. The khaki drip and dribble of leaking bowels, liquid fear. Raymond believes that we are all, one day, going to visit that apple-green room "where people wait to be told if it is cancer."

Rogue X-ray machines people the city with chemotherapy aliens, slapheads. The protagonist of any "black" novel has no choice but to get the business done before "quitting his shape". And with what relish Raymond outlines that business in an escalation of spellbinding set pieces. There's a shootout in a Chinese restaurant that matches anything in *Scarface*. Gust, with £17,000 in fifties tucked into his pockets, is forced to sleep rough in Soho Square – having no change for the buses.

"Democracy these days is just a show". Derek Raymond was the laureate of these special-needs non-citizens, self-mutilating bounty hunters. That's what got him going, abnormal brain chemistry. Anything that would explain this compulsion to write. *Dead Man Upright*, the last of the Factory novels, was an essay in psyhopathology, not a thriller. PD James, representing enlightened Conservatism, took a very different view of her craft. She had no truck with freaks. "Motiveless murders don't interest me. I can't see the fascination for serial killers like Dennis Nilsen. Nobody knows what motivates them. They're just mad, bad and dangerous to know. They're not susceptible to logic."

Logic? James' fiction, beginning with a bleakness to equal Raymond's, has given way to the institutionalised anonymity of a government white paper. The language is cryogenic, left too long on ice. Crime, James seems to be saying, is generated in chaos; in bad manners, misquotation, modernist architecture. State intervention will not cure our ills. We must trust ourselves to the disinterested justice of a superior being, a poet/policeman who keeps his thoughts to himself and drives with his gloves on.

Someone called Cookie was also involved . . . but
does not remember it.

WILLIAM BURROUGHS, *MY EDUCATION,*

A BOOK OF DREAMS

I'd heard the rumours about Robin Cook being in hospital, tests on his liver, and I'd assumed that he wouldn't be able to take part in the week of readings that I was helping to organise at the Bridewell Theatre (off Fleet Street). I rang his agent Maxim Jakubowski at the Murder One bookshop. "No, it's absolutely impossible," he confirmed. "He won't be taking on anything like that for months." Regretfully, I planned an evening that would would have to make do without Cook at the top of the bill. There was still a generous dose of London's subterranean literature on offer: Patrick Wright introducing (and gently interrogating) Emanuel Litvinoff, Chris Petit (with a bank of TV monitors) curating the Soho bibliography of *Robinson*, while I would act as straight man to John Healy, prompt him through a career retrospective, before he delivered an extract from *The Grass Arena*.

I was discussing the programme with Paul Smith of Disobey (who were sponsoring the show) when Cook rang. He was out of hospital and feeling well up to speed and ready for action. Of course he'd be there. Wouldn't miss it. Liver hard as slate, according to the quack. No surprise, ha! Wouldn't dream of having anyone sent to pick him up. Make his own way. Staying with the writer John Williams and his family while he convalesced. Marvellous! Can't wait.

This was excellent news, the bill was revised. (No problem there, Paul didn't believe in sending his catalogues to the printers until about three days before the off. The boxes would be delivered along with the audience. Exciting – as long as you dispense with trivia such as proof reading and getting the right photos alongside the right authors.) Litvinoff would open and Cook would do a bit of chat with Petit and then close with a short reading. I'd been to Cook's readings before and usually came away feeling sorry for the poor sod who had to follow him. He was the reverse of the trembling and intense poet, devoured by false modesty, who stops and starts, and then goes on forever. Cook breezed through a couple of anecdotes, before letting rip with a practised riff from one of the Factory novels.

I checked again that Cook was up to it and told him he needn't arrive until the interval. But he insisted, he wanted to be there from the off. The voice was as animated as ever. Paul wasn't quite so sure: he'd seen Cook's *Dora Suarez* performance with the musicians James Johnston and Terry Edwards and found it "odd". The tone too plummy. He was sympathetic and ready to be convinced – unsure whether the big crowd had come along for Cook or for the sounds.

There was a good audience for the first night at the Bridewell and Litvinoff was in full flow. Meetings with Canetti, alchemical investigations, John Lehmann and wartime poetry, trips to Russia, East End life and fictions: Wright took him through all of it. Cook hadn't checked in and Petit, curiously, had gone home to change. John Healy was pacing up and down like a condemned man. From time to time, he would lay down his carrier bag, lean against a pillar and rehearse a nervous gesture which involved undoing, and doing up, his belt buckle. Carol, the woman who ran the place, was hysterically bright. She was convinced that the church authorities who controlled her lease were going to step through the door just as Healy exposed himself, or Stewart Home spat out one of his expletive-undeleted routines. My worry was: how were we ever going to put the cap on Wright and Litvinoff? Manny was like a ghost returned from limbo. Initially unhappy (after his experience of *The Cardinal and the Corpse*) at being associated with this lowlife trash, these shysters and ganefs, he was carried away by the responsive audience – who were amazed to find that he was alive and well and still hammering at the typewriter.

Then Cook's cab drew up. I could see the street from where I was sitting. At first, I didn't know who it was. I could see the cabbie holding the door for nobody to get out. There was almost nothing there. Cook was a beret resting on a skull; enormous eyes, all pupil; neck like a lizard. If Spielberg's ET monster had stayed on earth, lived, acquired intelligence, hung out for decades in the Coach and Horses, this is how he might have looked. Memento mori made flesh. Jeffrey Bernard without the pique. You'd struggle to make the connection between the Marc Atkins portrait in the catalogue and this slowly advancing apparition. The old Cook, the Cook of three months ago, was wasted but spry; lean, sharp-eyed – not much changed from the Sixties sharpie. Long hair covered the ears. A black polo neck. The beret stylishly perched on the crown of the head, where it now enveloped it like a malignant mushroom. Something else was missing: the untipped cigarette. Cook sauntered in, hands in pockets.

There was a moment of panic. Petit, in his performing suit, hadn't returned. Litvinoff was still cruising. I found Paul Smith. Cook would have to go straight on, we couldn't ask him to hang around. We had a quick chat and I took him to the pub on the corner and left him with a few of his mates. I was getting ready to stand in for Petit, while Smith tried to signal Wright to wrap it up.

It worked. Petit manifested. Cook was fetched from the pub and gave the performance of his life. The voice was there, it sang. He told the old stories as if for the first time. He had the audience eating out of his hand. Even Litvinoff, who insisted on staying, was moved. "He's a real writer." Cook had chosen his texts with great care, talked the selection over with John Williams. Everybody knew it was much more than a reading. They were watching a man deliver his own funeral oration.

Cook read from *He Died With His Eyes Open*.

I dreamed I was walking through the door of a cathedral. Someone I couldn't distinguish warned me: "Don't go in there, it's haunted." However, I went straight in and glided up the nave to the altar. The roof of the building was too high to see; the quoins were lost in a dark fog through which the votive lamps glowed orange. The only light came through the diamond-shaped clear panes in the windows; it was faint and cold . . . There were no pews or chairs, just people standing around, waiting. No service was in progress. Knots of men and women from another century stood about, talking in low voices . . . Then my waist was held by invisible hands and I was raised from the floor; at the height of the roof I was turned slowly parallel with the ground and then released so that I floated, immobile and face downwards, far above the people whose faces I could make out in the half-dark as a grey blur, staring up at me . . . I descended quietly, of my own accord, and landed lightly on the spot from where I had been taken, whereupon I walked directly out of the building without looking back.

A few days later Cook was dead, liver cancer. The audience in the Bridewell wouldn't have needed to have the news confirmed. They understood the privilege of the occasion, the life in that thin voice. More than any other English writer, Cook's quality was his special relationship with death. He visibly brightened, his attention was fully engaged, when you asked him to talk about the Factory novels as posthumous dreams. A busier and more mundane Swedenborg, he communicated with those he had known, and still knew: the ones whose faces were made from shadows. "They are always there," he said, being filmed in the City Airport; his double reflected out over the choppy waters.

I went with Marc Atkins to the memorial service in Kensal Green. Step through the gates and the ground is immediately familiar. You recognise these places as old friends when you meet them for the first time. It was a pleasant morning; we had half an hour to put on and wandered through the labyrinthine paths. We met Mike Hart from Compendium, coming towards us, making his circuit from the other entrance. Pyramids and stone mansions whose original pomposity had been weathered by long indifference into something more democratic: a sanctuary for wild nature, a trysting place for work-experience vampires. Irrelevant memory doses. Boasts and titles and meaningless dates.

I spotted one particular stone angel that had to be photographed: a robed hermaphrodite tangled in the bare Medea branches of a tree. The image was entirely mythical. The tree devoured the stone like a recollection of dry fire. Like Actaeon, the voyeur, turned into a stag: trapped, as it were, by the wonder of a sight unexpectedly encountered. Like Ezra Pound's obsession with the girl who becomes a tree.

> The tree has entered my hands,
> The sap has ascended my arms,
> The tree has grown in my breast –
> Downward,
> The branches grow out of me, like arms.

The angel's hands were gone, her face was hidden; the branches spread out above her like electrified hair. Her wings, tangled in the thicket, were a useless decoration. Marc snapped away busily: an icon that I would have to work hard to justify.

There was a full house in the crematorium, standing room only: the kind of social mix – writers, riffraff, perfumed ladies with too much kohl, respectable gents in inherited suits – that you'd find, late afternoon, in one of Cook's drinking haunts. Mark Timlin read from *The Hidden Files*. Cook's brother Julian – same voice, better clobber – brought him back to life in a parallel version: what Robin might have been if he'd gone straight, played by the rules. John Williams spoke, quietly, about Cook's last days – fleshing out what we had merely suspected. Business as usual, to the end. Bessie Smith and TS Eliot wrapped it up. "Go, go, go said the bird . . . One.end, which is always present."

Petit saw Cook's wake at the French as a useful summary for the last rites of Soho bohemia: he pitched it that way to the *Independent*. Marc was on a loose commission to get the picture. Innocently, they imagined that he'd be able to line up the whole mob in a single team photograph. Many of the folk from Kensal Green would never make it back to London proper. This was as close as they'd ever come to the country-side. The whiff of the Grand Union Canal had them reaching for the smelling salts. Some looked as if their powers of invention had been entirely used up in getting to the right venue on the right day. Others were so skeletal and waxy, it wasn't worth arranging a ride home. They had only to be matched with the right sepulchre, lifted onto an empty plinth. This, properly, was where they belonged. Hip flasks were much in evidence. Small groups formed and broke. Nothing to say. Nothing to be done. They touched, shook hands, moved away. If Cook was not immortal, what hope for the rest of the unregistered dead?

Marc and I, together with Gerry and Pat Goldstein, went off in search of a minicab. Not our part of town, but the upper reaches of the Harrow Road are worth visiting – if you want to feel good about living in Hackney. If you have a taste for social anthropology. Gerry and Pat are one of the great metropolitan double acts, overlapping, stereophonic yarns, memories, questions: they know everybody, have met every writer, mover, face – at least twice. A chance encounter and, next time, there they are on your sofa. They've read everything too: their appearance at some ravaged bookstall asking for . . . Colin MacInnes' London novels, Maclaren-Ross, Gerald Kersh, Anna Kavan, Cormac MacCarthy . . . signals the next cult. They are bibliographic litmus paper, strikingly dressed in styles (well-cut swagger coats with padded shoulders and tight belts for Gerry, and tailored suits of the kind that Christine Keeler reserved for her court appearances for Pat) that can't quite be placed: vaguely mod, vaguely clubland. Gerry grew up with Malcolm Mclaren in Stoke Newington and Stamford Hill. ("Goldstein was an intellectual Jewish *flâneur* straight out of Alexander Baron's London novel, *Low Life*." Jon Savage, *England's Dreaming*.) He was a longtime advocate of Mervyn Peake (friend of his daughter Clare), and therefore a champion also of Michael Moorcock. David Litvinoff was close to him, as was Sandy Lieberson, the producer of *Performance*. Gerry was a passionate enthusiast, and liable, from time to time, to the odd paranoid outburst. "Since you've been knocking around with that Petit, you're turning into fucking Martin Amis," he once yelled at me down the phone. (Yes, he knew Amis in his guitar-strumming Chelsea coffee-bar days.)

Harrow Road doesn't go in for cabs. What's the point? It would be like setting up a rank in the middle of the graveyard. Anyone who has washed up here is in it for the duration. But we persevered; Gerry's lips were dry, flecked with foam, he wanted a fizzy drink. Pushing north-west to the borders of Harlesden, we finally found a trashed launderette that claimed to run a few cars as a front for some far more complex operation. A big black guy, his spectacles held together with masking tape, led us along the street towards a wreck that had obviously been rejected at the breaker's yard.

I was going to be paying, so I grabbed the front seat. Marc, all six foot six of him, squeezed in between the Harold Pinter and Lady Antonia Fraser of Shepherd's Bush. The driver had no idea where Dean Street was, but – as his car wasn't going to make it that far anyway – what did he care?

The tyre blew just as we hit Westway. There was no spare. (There was no window on the passenger's side, come to that. A few cursory strands of sellotape.) We paid our man off (to his utter amazement) and trans-ferred to the underground – which carried us into a tunnel and then stopped. Marc's not happy in tunnels at the best of times, but with Gerry and Pat in spate, on either side of him, he was in no shape to go to work with his camera when we did eventually arrive at the French.

The bar was packed with very sober drunks. There was a general rush to get a few drinks in, to catch up, become part of an event that was not happening. It was like celebrating a "not proven" verdict – under the eye of that terrible Cook portrait. John Williams and his family had seen to the smooth running of the crematorium service, now there was no one in charge. Timlin worked his corner. Maxim Jakubowski was here and there, attending to business. Malcolm Mclaren, a watchful presence, strategically unguarded, was reunited with Pat and Gerry. The two film-makers who had presented the best television portraits of Cook, Chris Petit and Paul Tickell, guardedly assessed the prospects of the Factory novel scripts ever getting the go-ahead. John Healy, in crisp, open-necked shirt, stood on the pavement outside, nursing an orange juice. The truth is that these were semi-professionals, irregulars, fringe media drifters paying their dues, looking for connections, the inside story. The true gargoyles, the intravenous vodka hawks, the blotting paper soaks who usually barnacled the bar, were pacing it. What was the rush? In an hour or two the amateurs would be wet-eyed, standing rounds, issuing dinner invitations.

Marc couldn't hack it. He works best in his own time: in the studio, or wandering the city. Not this. The afternoon was dim (nothing to recall the great days of John Deakin, or Willy Ronis with his beautiful barmaid caught in a beam of sunlight). The whole mob were too self-conscious, too well aware that this was supposed to be the end of an era. Groups came together, passed out cigarettes, shouted for another drink, parted. If they emptied their pockets, they'd still be stone cold sober. An edge of desperation and repressed violence was evident. The ones cruising for copy decided to cut their losses. The gargoyles repossessed their territory. The perfumed ladies with the kohl and the scrapyard jewellery, laddered stockings and tart's heels, found their space, made their connections.

And riding calmly through all of it were the relics of Cook's family: wives, children, brothers and half-brothers. Julian Cook, with his unnerving resemblance to the dead man, had the best of it. He seemed to have absorbed the disembodied spirit. Glass in one hand, large cigar, arms around two women, he swam through the sweating survivors, making up a party to go on elsewhere.

Marc and I walked back to Hackney. He worked overnight in the darkroom, but he knew that what he had was of no use of the *Independent*. Lost faces in the half-dark. No Robin Cook. No story. He'd have to settle for another obituary portfolio.

3.
"I thought you were supposed to be in Paris?"
"I am in Paris."
EXCHANGE BETWEEN DAVID HEMMINGS
AND VERUSHKA, *BLOW-UP*.

I refused to cede the imagination of the riverfront to PD James. There had to be a final site to visit that would expunge the horror of the fraudulent Wapping palazzo from *Original Sin*. I'd had my eye for some time on Charlton House, according to Bob Gilbert (in *The Green London Way*), "one of the most determinedly overlooked buildings in London". I'd walked there two or three times (by myself, with my wife on a crisp Boxing Day, and with Atkins) – but didn't feel that I'd cracked it.

Connections were made, views admired. You could come in by river to the Thames Barrier. You could cross on the Woolwich Ferry and battle down the bleak Woolwich Church Street. You could stroll over, along the crest of the hill, from Greenwich. I'd done all of them and I was still not satisfied. Charlton Park was coded with obscure monuments, acorns on plinths, scorpions in relief, astrological signs, eroded dates and inscriptions. There was an orangery, supposedly designed by Inigo Jones, that had declined into a Gents Toilet (decommissioned). There was an uncared-for mulberry tree that claimed to be "the first planted in England in the year 1608". Broken sentences. Revealed fragments.

Charlton House is, as Bob Gilbert says, "built in the shape of a shallow H with an impressive tower on either flank topped with a cupola and spire". The building is Jacobean, completed in 1612 for Adam Newton, tutor to Prince Henry, the eldest son of James I, by an unrecorded architect; thought by some to be John Thorpe, builder of Holland House, Kensington. Prince Henry, who died at the age of eighteen, was the emblematic centre of a group that included Newton and Inigo Jones (who lived for a time at Cherry Orchard in Charlton). We were drawn, as disciples of Frances Yates, to consider this circle that grew up around Prince Henry as being in the spirit of the "Rosicrucian Enlightenment"; being somehow a downriver equivalent of the court of Frederick, Elector Palatinate, and his wife, Henry's sister – the "Winter" king and queen.

On our Boxing Day stroll, my wife and I found the house closed up. We enjoyed the prospect across the park, the red brick with stone dressings, the liquorice stick chimneys, the walled gardens, and the west frontispiece which Pevsner calls "the most exuberant and undisciplined ornamentation of all England". The stone heads were not benign: snarling lions, horned men, petty demons, protruding tongues, upward thrusting flowers. An arch on the grass in front of the house had been surrounded, for its own protection, by a wire fence – making it seem toxic and forbidden. The house, and its meaning, was obscured by its current disguise as a Community Centre: "Children's toy library, dance groups, bridge, craft classes, tenants associations, chess, spiritualist church, T'ai Chi, Royal British Legion, photographic club, support groups, race and health projects, weddings, seminars and disabled access." Racks of pamphlets were visible through a window , on the east side.

St Luke's warm redbrick church in Charlton Village was also closed. There was a monument to Sir Adam and Lady Newton by Nicholas

Stone. There was also a memorial to Spencer Perceval, the only British Prime Minister to have been assassinated: so far. The church grounds gave a splendid view, across the gravestones, to the Thames, and the distant Canary Wharf: for years it had been a landmark, a fixed point on which ships, negotiating the bends of the river, could take a bearing.

We came back that afternoon along the escarpment to Greenwich. But still I was dissatisfied. By summer (29.6.94), I was ready to take another shot at it. Now I was on a quest for the missing Sions (signs), references that had been making themselves known on all our riverrine expeditions: Syon House, the Sions of Twickenham, Zions everywhere. There was even a legendary self-published book by a local Charlton historian, Ron Pepper, that proposed a direct link between Adam Newton and the occult-political society, the Prieuré of Sion. It wasn't an easy book to track down. I hoped that the library in Charlton House would have a copy.

Yet again, when Atkins and I arrived, insufficiently disabled, access was forbidden. A film crew had taken over the building. Caravans, baseball caps, plates of hot grub being dished out, period costumes hanging limply over fences; the library closed and the stairs guarded by a canvas waistcoat.

We cut inland, towards the foothills. Horn Fair Field: uncovered that myth – the horns came from the ox, a symbol of St Luke, not from the miller cuckolded by King John. By the seventeenth century the fair was established on St Luke's Day, the 18th of October. A procession took place, meandering from Bishopsgate to Charlton, by way of Cuckold's Point in Bermondsey; three times around the church and across to the field for the proper business, riot. (The counter-procession would, in due course, go from Bishopsgate into Whitechapel to celebrate the liberties of the London Hospital.) London was mapped by these drunken and licentious cross-town scrambles, borough to borough, sacred site to sacred site: relics of saints, drums and beribboned phalluses. The walk, responding to astrological prompts, laid down narrative trails that should still be respected.

We pushed on, across meadows and ungrazed terraces; London was lost in a heat haze. We were consoled by the oddity of the triangular folly, Severndroog Castle; the sudden turn in a path through the woods that gifted us with an anamorphic view, a sheer drop to a spread of complacent, blue-grey suburbs. Eltham Cemetery was a good point from which to turn for home.

Coming back over the ridge and downhill towards Woolwich Old Town, Atkins was frisky, aroused by a foxy lady striding towards us in a seethrough skirt: he broke into a rush of Tourette's syndrome puns. The distant river gave us a destination. Waiting to cross out of Eglinton Road into Herbert Road, I found what we had been looking for: elegant tile lettering in a frame, a building marked for demolition. The curved pillar of a public-house, two surviving words: **SION ANTS**.

(We located Sion College, on the Embankment, next to Unilever House, when we were walking towards Whitehall on the day of the Conservative Party leadership election. We got our heads around the door but were refused admittance. Neither was a future appointment possible. Stewart Home in his provocative pamphlet, *Conspiracies, Cover-Ups & Diversions*, states that "Prince Charles is temporarily using the library of Sion College as a London venue for occult activities . . . The premises are shared with the City Livery Club, making it an important centre of ruling class activity . . . Dr Thomas White who founded Sion College is notorious among conspiracy theorists as both a mason and a black magician. Among other indications of lodge activity still evident in the library are three masonic chairs." In Home's outrageous interpretation, Charles heads a lodge that has broken away from P2 to set up its own "Greek rite"; ceremonies involving child sacrifice and ritual sodomy. The Prince's public concern with modernist architecture apparently masks an obsessive interest in psychogeography: a temple is to be established within the pyramid that tops Canary Wharf. And control over the great Greenwich leyline reasserted. The signal for the success of Charles' occult conjuration will be the grant to the Royal Borough of the funds to carry through all of its preposterous Millennial proposals.)

This was the last excursion in the book: I'd even taken the trouble to ring Charlton House a few days beforehand to establish that the library *would* be open. We were back where we started when we set out to plot the graffiti, walk the **V**: Victoria Park, the canal, Isle of Dogs, Foot-Tunnel, Greenwich. Same Italian caff for breakfast. The boats to the Thames Barrier weren't running yet, too early; so we decided to stroll on, up the hill, and over Blackheath to Charlton.

A dull, overcast day: Marc had restricted himself to no more than three or four photographs (another attempt to produce a convincing image of St Alphege). Now Atkins was suffering. After being out on the road all these months, he'd acquired the aches and pains that I'd dispensed with: medial ligament trouble, headaches, the compulsive annotation of detail. He was taking the images that I only thought about. I didn't need to speak.

A funfair was pitched on Blackheath, ghost houses and horror hoardings. Borrowing Marc's camera, I was the one taking the photographs. I think we both knew, even then, that it was all too easy. Secrets never yielded themselves to mild grey mornings and full stomachs. It was no more than I expected when the woman at the coffee stall in Charlton House told us that she was sorry but the library was closed today, they'd rung around, but they couldn't find anyone to come in. Forget it. We made no attempt to explore the stairs and the upper chambers; we walked east across the park, never looking back.

I haven't mentioned Maryon Park yet, although it's a very important element in the psychic landscape. Maryon Park was the reason I came to Charlton in the first place: to see where Antonioni had filmed *Blow-Up*. In the Sixties the kick lay in finding it at all, the atmosphere was unique but the park didn't connect with an area of London that I knew. It had been briefly colonised by European art cinema. Gradually, through further expeditions in more recent times, I worked out how Maryon Park gave way to Maryon-Wilson Park, to Charlton Park, to the Horn Fair Field. Charlton House was occupied by members of the Maryon and Wilson families until Sir Spencer Maryon-Wilson sold it to the Council.

Coming into Maryon Park from Woolwich Road, as I did when I made my original investigation, is uncanny. It plays directly into the film, into the very specific sound of wind in the trees. (An effect that Antonioni had first exploited towards the end of *L'Avventura*.) Something you can't fake by rustling film stock in a bin. An amphitheatre, a wooded bowl, with tennis courts at the centre. An old Chinaman in a white raincoat sitting on a green bench, a newspaper folded in his lap. Steep steps that run up to the tree-shaded lozenge of ground on which David Hemmings (as the photographer) sees Vanessa Redgrave setting up whatever it is that happens; the crime that is revealed (or created) when the film is developed, the contact sheet examined, and single frames are enlarged and distorted – until they develop their own momentum. They revise the past, narrate a murder which might never, otherwise, have happened. It is the neurotic voyeurism of Hemmings, his insistence on achieving a state of meaning and control, that proposes a tragic explanation. Whoever cuts the film, cuts history.

Antonioni took a lot of trouble to identify this enclosed meadow, to see it as the essence of his film. The incident in Julio Cortazar's short story, *Las babas del Diabolo (The Devil's Spittle)*, on which the script for *Blow-Up* is based, takes place on a *quai* in Paris, and describes a "narrow escape": an amateur photographer catches a middle-aged woman and a youth as they are involved in an intense and ambiguous conversation. The narrator, telling his story, sees only what the photographer sees: the railings, the harsh sunlight, the late-morning shadows. An apparently straightforward arrangement of light and form. The episode, frozen and carried away, blown up to the size of a small cinema screen in his studio, suggests a complex resolution. There is another watcher, an elderly man in a car, who comes briefly forward to remonstrate with the woman. The photographer makes sense of these theatrical fragments – shocks himself – by deciding that the woman is a pimp, the boy a male prostitute, and the elderly man a client. He therefore becomes (or the narrator forces him into that role) the director of his own fantasy. He's engaged in all the traditional tasks of cinema: shaping and constructing a script, casting, shooting, editing, post-production. He picks a respectable, smartly-dressed woman who *could* – because he orders her to do it – play a procuress (Genevieve Page in Buñuel's *Belle de Jour*?), a youth that appeals to him (Dominic Guard, too old for *The Go-Between*, too young for *An Unsuitable Job for a Woman*, or James Fox, Terence Stamp as *Billy Budd*). He plays games with reality by deciding to take the part of the man in the car. The closed window reflects the photographer: a more innocent version of himself. The photographer's intervention, his decision to click the button, has changed time.

Paris described by an Argentinian becomes the London of Antonioni: somewhere exotic, dangerous – and misunderstood. The director's partner, Monica Vitti, the one who did not disappear in *L'Avventura*, was playing *Modesty Blaise* for an exiled American, Joseph Losey. Vanessa Redgrave would perform the Vitti role with confused conviction; less mystery, less of the submerged comedienne. A strong woman who finds herself taking her shirt off ("it looks even better on a man") in the wrong story.

The grass platform in Maryon Park is one of London's more seductive secret theatres. You stand there and astonishing fables tempt you. This terrace, with its view of the river (rigorously excluded by Antonioni), was first surveyed by the Egyptologist, William Flinders Petrie, in 1891. (Petrie was born in Maryon Road.) Later excavations in 1915 revealed a Romano-British settlement covering $17\frac{1}{2}$ acres: a double bank and ditch surrounding a group of hut dwellings.

Antonioni, accompanied by his script-writer Tonino Guerra, was hauled backwards and forwards across London by the journalist Francis Wyndham (one of those fascinated by the Kray Twins and the gangland mythology they were actively helping to create). Style magazines, and the colour supplements which were just getting into their stride, were using iconic images by hustlers such as David Bailey that linked fashion, rock and villainy. (Hairdressers who could double as bullion blaggers.) Thus condemning the fastidious Italian director to stand forlornly around at grim speed-freak parties and catatonic raves; to trawl pubs and clubs on the Richardson's patch, to sample scrapyard chic. One such party is reported in Gore Vidal's "memoir", *Palimpsest*. The Tynans threw a bash to celebrate the Labour Party's electoral victory. Guests included Marlon Brando, Richard Harris and Michelangelo Antonioni. Brando tried to get Tynan into the bathroom. "The evening," Vidal boasts, "made such an impression on Antonioni that he made a film of it, *Blow-Up*." If Antonioni was to turn himself into a multinational brand name, he had to exploit London, its excesses and sub-cultural freaks, as Fellini had exploited Rome for *La Dolce Vita*. His moment of genius was in allowing himself to be found by Maryon Park, by making the most significant contribution to an anthology of vanishings. Whatever happened on the grass terrace had to leave no visible trace behind it. (And here Antonioni did slip up. You can still find the flakes of dark green paint with which production designer Assheton Gordon "dressed" the wooden fence. He recomposed the setting so that it could look more like itself.)

Francis Wyndham had written a piece called "The Modelmakers" for the *Sunday Times* Magazine, alerting Carlo Ponti to commission Bailey to make a short film called *The Photographer*. Bailey ("David Bailey makes love daily") was a famous predator, used to snacking on anyone who posed for him. He had recently signalled his interest in moving upmarket by marrying Catherine Deneuve (the frigid prisoner of a South Kensington flat in Roman Polanski's *Repulsion*). Bailey (along with Michael Cooper, the heroin addict and suicide, who shot the *Sergeant Pepper* sleeve) became one of the models for the David Hemmings character in *Blow-Up*. The part was originally intended for Terence Stamp, once a lover of Jean Shrimpton, Bailey's famous protégée. Or so Stamp thought – until Antonioni saw Hemmings in Andrew Sinclair's adaptation of Dylan Thomas' *Adventures in the Skin Trade* at the Hampstead Theatre Club. Stamp, who was very much up for the role, "had begun a minute study of Bailey, Donovan and Duffy, even to the extent of imitating their hand movements and improvising the tune he would hum under his breath in the darkroom." The loss of a role for which he was born (or so he felt) was a turning point in Stamp's career: from now on he would be an inanimate clotheshorse, all cheekbones and flaring nostrils, one of those lost Buddhist, rag trade aesthetes who drink a cup of tea very prettily, and pay for it by appearing in top-dollar adverts.

The photographer was not a figure reserved for Antonioni. The voyeur with the telephoto lens, who "invents" crimes with which he can counter ennui and sexual repression, goes back to Hitchcock's *Rear Window* (1954) – based on a story by William Irish, himself an alcoholic and a hotel room prisoner. Neither was Antonioni the first director to base a film on a contemporary practitioner: Stanley Donen had Richard Avedon on set to coach Fred Astaire for *Funny Face* (1957). They were caught together by Magnum photographer David Seymour. By the Sixties, cinema was haunted by a Brechtian urge to expose itself, play games with appearance and reality. The photographer was everywhere, on screen and off, from Godard's *Le Petit Soldat* to the paparazzi of *La Dolce Vita*. The darkest reading was Michael Powell's *Peeping Tom* (1960). His photographer uses a 16mm movie camera, but the voyeurism is undiluted. *Peeping Tom* is a sealed system, *Blow-Up*'s dark unconscious: London as a labyrinth, not a landscape. David Hemmings is only comfortable in movement. Carl Boehm is an alien, incapable of accepting external reality until he has got it down on film. Bailey, in a rare moment of revelation, described himself, Nikon in hand, as "a three-legged phallus". Carl Boehm was a phallic assassin, spearing his victims with a spiked tripod, as he tracked forward into the final close-up.

Even in England, Antonioni was following in the wake of one of our great institutions: Michael Winner. Winner's *The System* (1964) was one of a cycle of "rebel" youth, yobs at the seaside, exploitation flicks. Most of them starred Oliver Reed. *The System*, like Losey's *The Damned* (1962), was no exception. Reed and Winner were made for each other. The difference between English and Italian cinema is the distance between Oliver Reed's flaring nostrils and Marcello Mastroianni's world-weary smile.

The System focused on the rootless life of a beach photographer. Reed was plucked from his natural habitat, grimacing in Hammer horrors, to be lit by Nicolas Roeg (on his way to *Performance*). In the cast was another coming actor: David Hemmings.

These superficial connections become more and more intriguing: as if all the writers, directors and actors were trying to nail the times in a single story. A story that could not be told until Antonioni located Maryon Park: that one covert strip of grass, with its sentinel trees, its wind chorus, its doorway into other worlds. Reed was there again, for a crude *Blow-Up* rehearsal, in Guy Hamilton's *The Party's Over* (1963) which was written by the excellent crime novelist Marc Behm. Hamilton would be promoted to serious industrial product with the Bond films; *The Party's Over* was his single stab at a sociological document.

John Barry, who had written the jukebox fillers for an earlier essay in the same vein, *Beat Girl* (1960) – which featured the compulsory cameo from Oliver Reed – provided the score: before moving on with Hamilton to serial Bondage and conspicuous wealth. (He sold that riverside apartment in Alembic House to a youthful Conservative politician, Jeffrey Archer.)

Blow-Up viewed as a video in 1995 provokes an overwhelming urge to rush the tape to the cutting-room for emergency amputation: lose those appalling rag day students, the tennis court mime, most of the secondary performances. Hack it to the bone: some urban driving, some interplay in the studio, the park. Reduce it to essence, to Cortazar's original story. Antonioni has invested everything in David Hemmings as the narrative hook. And he's good, he makes the strange dialogue (filtered through the director's questionnaires, Argentine prose, translations into French, into Italian, back into English by Edward Bond) sound almost plausible. He's stupid, but sharp; lethargic, but driven. An austere narcissist. A puritanical decadent. A tourist on his own territory: he visits clubs and dope-flops patronised by rock trash and bent aristos as if he were seeing them for the first time. (Jimmy Page busking away with the Yardbirds. A good customer, a mate of Martin Stone. Stone used to keep him supplied with Aleister Crowley manuscripts.) Hemmings, a deracinated moralist, thirsts for experience, images that will offend. Despite himself, he becomes a latterday Mayhew – responsive, like most photo journalists to the obvious (whatever can be pitched at know-nothing picture editors). Picaresque squalor, blown fashion, a commercially viable underground culture. Antonioni's locations are genuinely found, a mapping of surreal expediency and not the tired old favourites from the back catalogue. The vagrants' shelter from which Hemmings emerges – and which is the start of my version of the film, after I've eliminated all the tedious cross-cutting with white-face extras – is not, as might be expected, in Whitechapel or Kennington, but in Consort Road, Peckham Rye. Near the spot where Blake saw his tree of angels.

The "irony" of this counterpoint, fashion shoots and lowlife authenticity, is needlessly laboured – but accurate. Bailey was always "going back to his roots" to produce bad art shots of weather in the streets. Don McCullin, a tougher craftsman with a much truer eye, mixed frontline carnage with reports on teenage gangs. The incest of photographers photographing photographers begins to pick up momentum. Interiors for *Blow-Up* were shot in the studio of fashion ace John Cowan, although the Hemmings character drew most of his external characteristics from Bailey. (Antonioni arranged for Bailey and Duffy to be interviewed at length. With Terence Donovan, they had been turned by colour supplement scribes into a representative triad: in the same way that Antonioni, Fellini and Visconti, were a convenient shorthand for Italian cinema.)

Hemmings laying out his photographs for his caption-writer in an Italian restaurant is a direct reference to *Goodbye Baby and Amen, A Saraband for the Sixties*, which Bailey put together with journalist Peter Evans. The book was the usual mix of Krays and Shrimptons, moody streetscapes, high contrast crones, poverty glitz. The manager and power-broker to whom Hemmings defers, frequently recoursing to that prophetic toy, a prototype car phone in the Roller, is called "Ron". (We'll put aside the fact that he does appear from time to time, and is impersonated by Peter Bowles, and grant him a crueller identity. And recall those hard-edged Bailey portraits of the Twins, the sugary wedding photos from Broadmoor. The cruising photographer, the *flâneur* with an agenda, reports to the gangster: that is the psychic map of Sixties London. Michael Moorcock reminisces about Reg Kray putting the bite on him in a D'Arblay Street coffee-bar, in quest of a mutual acquaintance and a deal that had gone sour. He says that, for the first time, he "understood fear"; his knees locked, his bowels spasmed. The friend was not seen again.)

Marc Atkins, a McCullin enthusiast, watched the video with me; I was interested in his technical comments. He identified Hemmings' camera as a Nikkormat, a precursor of the Nikon. He laughed aloud at the speed with which the shots of the park were processed. "Fibre paper", he said. "It would take me six months to produce that quantity of prints." But I willingly suspended disbelief at this point: the revealed structure of the park commanded its own momentum. The choirs of hallucinatory lensmen.

What do we have? Hemmings, in Cowan's studio, impersonating (allowing himself to be possessed by) the spirit of Bailey. Antonioni's cameraman Carlo di Palma, under instruction, in a set-dressed park, shooting Hemmings. As is Don McCullin, on assignment, who is doing a location report story. McCullin's image of Hemmings, snooping behind a specially painted fence taking *his* shot of the distant crime, is reprinted in *Magnum Cinema* (*Photographs from 50 years of movie-making*). Beautiful grey sheen on the jacket – which is not, of course, visible in the filmed version. Interestingly, although brash supplement colours are one of the principal qualities of *Blow-Up*, Marc Atkins remembered it as being in black and white. This might be because that is how he sees the world, rarely working in colour; or, more probably, because the passage that most engaged his attention was the production of the monochrome prints – the editing, enlarging of details, the pinning to the wall.

David Hemmings, trapped in the claustrophobia of Cowan's studio, developed a "master and servant" relationship with Antonioni. Hemmings gave life, and a rough edge, to the Italian's self-conscious voyeurism (as Jeanne Moreau rescues an overly symbolic pilgrimage across the wastes of Milan in *La Notte*). Yet again I see the psychotic weather of one film being transmitted to another, and then another: *The Servant* to *BlowUp* to *Performance*. Coded accidents. Actors vampirised by the nonentities they impersonate. Paranoid plots evolving through generations of cinema, the thousand nights of Scheherazade. Sarah Miles from *The Servant*, with her breathy schoolgirl laugh, stroking Hemmings's hair. Hemmings as an energised avatar of James Fox and Michael York. (The pale jeans and blue shirt of the public schoolboy released into Chelsea. Tom Baker in Dublin, very much of this type, sent out to photograph Gents' Toilets along the quays for a spread in the University magazine. Michael Reeves shooting tests in Hollywood for Elvis Presley jailbait.)

Restlessness. The film's jaunt across the city. "I haven't even got a few minutes to have my appendix out." Hemmings, perpetually dissatisfied, is "looking for landscapes". Trying to find the one place that haunts his imagination, trying to invent a crime that will fit it. The arbitrary London of the surrealist, the alien, the speed-freak. The poet David Gascoyne always dreamed of this fantastic metropolis, a geography assembled from a "collection of descriptions of London by foreigners". They see what we miss. They are not distracted by notions of class, the tedium of public transport. They are on holiday, or on the run. A visionary hit, then out: Céline, Kerouac, Polanski, Godard. Gascoyne in the Thirties was as excited by the notion as Patrick Keiller is today. "Dostoevsky, Rimbaud and Verlaine", he wrote in his journals, "Strindberg, Alain-Fournier – they were all in London at one time or another – (and Gustave Doré, and Van Gogh) – and all have left some sort of record of their impressions, which are naturally strange, only half-recognisable, like a dream of a place one knows. I particularly like Alain-Fournier's appreciation of the suburban villas of Chiswick and Kew, and of the atmosphere of London summer Sunday afternoons at the beginning of the century, and his saying that of all towns, he would prefer London to be unhappy in."

Isn't this precisely what Antonioni defined: a park that is unresolved, in time-shift, late summer? An openair theatre from which all traces of the ritual performers have been erased? A copse of trees undiscovered by Pissarro as the setting for a Kokoschka sacrifice? *Murderer, the Hope of Women*. Because it is the woman, in this case, who is most agitated; most deeply implicated in the crime. The absurd body of her victim, when Hemmings discovers it – in a municipal park that stays conveniently open at night, when he is not carrying his camera – is as rigid as the John Major waxwork at Tower Bridge. (Can a corpse be *too* stiff? This one is the spitting image of George, one half of the Spitalfields double-act: the stained glass coprophiles.)

Even Hemmings, dipping his fingers in the sauce, talking with his agent over an Italian lunch, knows that the small meadow, and the light that is unique to that place, is what should close his album. "I got something fab for the end. In the park. It's very peaceful and still. I think it's best for the end to be like that . . . I've gone off London this week, it doesn't do anything for me." (I should, if I had the discipline, close *Lights Out* on that note. A few yards of grass about which it is possible to be silent.)

Stop/start the video. Go over the blow-ups, as Hemmings does. Go over Marc's photographs. "What a wanker," he says, watching Hemmings swoop after pigeons, writhe and twist to find an angle. "I'd never pose like that." But he would. I've got the snaps to prove it: shots of Atkins photographing the grass arena in search of traces of Hemmings impersonating Bailey. Bent like a contortionist. (Probably the old Chinaman on the bench was recording me from behind his newspaper.)

One morning, passing through Spitalfields, on our way down to the river, and the walk to Putney, and Mortlake and Chiswick, we spotted a grotesquely overmanned crew shooting an underimagined commercial. Café life: a redhead at an outside table being made-up by a blonde in a black romper suit. The tan-jacketed male lead lounged about, bored and frowning, while he waited for his turn with the powder. Traffic skidded past the yellow plastic cones. A mob of white T-shirts tried to look busy. Reading the director's name on a folding canvas chair, I nudged Atkins forward: BAILEY. (I've got the master shot of Atkins taking his snap.) Bailey was the oldest person on set. He had become the man Carlo Ponti wanted him to be, the film-maker who should have been given his first feature at the time of *Blow-Up*.

The official stills photographer, in grey paint-smeared jeans, like Hemmings as he emerges from the doss house, was taking shots of the portly director, not of the models. A mobile phone was clipped to his belt. They all had these holsters – except Bailey. Atkins, I see from my colour pic, is wearing a satchel: in which the photograph of the river that will be left in Alembic House for Lord Archer is clearly visible. (He also seems, perhaps in homage to Mike Goldmark, to be wearing a baggy T-shirt and shapeless black tracksuit trousers.)

There is no keeping these memory thieves off the territory. Every photograph distorts the flow of time. 21.10.94: I received a letter from Paul McNally at M-OCEAN Pictures Limited. "This may be old news to you but I found this Beatles photo session at Wapping Old Stairs very interesting – McCartney chained to the dock wall and Lennon playing 'dead' . . . The session was part of a 'Mad Day' organised by Don McCullin on 28th July 1968. The other locations were St Pancras Old Church and Gardens, Old Street roundabout, Farringdon Road, St John's Wood, Highgate and Notting Hill."

So these were the bodies found at the fictional Wapping publishing house in PD James' *Original Sin*.

And now the fear was becoming real . . . Suddenly there was a wild scream and she started, but it was only a seagull. The bird swooped above her, perched for a moment on the railings, then winged its way downriver . . . The strap strained down to the puckered surface of the water, and beneath that surface something was just visible, something grotesque and unreal, like the domed head of a gigantic insect, its millions of hairy legs stirring gently in the tide . . . At the end of the strap was a human body. As she gazed down in horror the body shifted in the tide and a white hand rose slowly from the water, its wrist drooping like the stem of a dying flower.

McCullin, fresh from his *Blow-Up* assignment, was capturing the Beatles as they posed their way in a psychic progress across London –

like one of the mappings in Alan Moore's graphic novel, *From Hell*. (I got a call from Alan. He had hired a recording studio on the riverside in Wapping where he was working on a demo tape that he wanted me to hear. In his breaks he'd been wandering the foreshore and had found several "significant" objects. The piece he played me was called *Litvinoff's Book*. "Off to a looking-glass house . . . They say two can keep secrets – if one of them's dead.")

The list of locations from McNally's letter read like the contents page of *Lights Out*: Aidan Dun's New Jerusalem at St Pancras, George Jeffrey's book-stalls at Farringdon Road, one of the gateways to the mysteries. McCullin's photographs were uncanny: Paul McCartney, shirt off, posing with a chain on the foreshore, at the very point where a character from my novel *Downriver*, Dr Adam Tenbrucke (whose suicide was based on a real death), attaches himself to the wall and waits for the tide.

The Beatles, it seems from the account in McNally's photocopy, directed themselves. McCullin followed and shot whatever he wanted. They arrived in the late afternoon, "parking their cars in Wapping High Street." The photographer, taking time out from chasing wars, turned his carrion camera on the antics of a group who found it increasingly difficult to be in each other's company. "John and Yoko then went away briefly and returned for more Beatles tomfoolery on the steeply sloping concrete bed. John played dead, while George wore his specs and Ringo felt John's forehead . . . Then came the last sitting: John, wearing McCullin's battle jacket, lay down on the ground as Ringo, George and Paul stood behind him."

(At this point in the narrative, when a number of themes were threatening to come together, cohere, lift towards some awful conclusion, the doorbell rang. It was Atkins, leading a wolf-dog on a string, and carrying two prints. Successive versions of the same image: a sneering David Bailey in his baseball cap, stubbled, sweaty, suspicious of the strange lens poked into his face. Bailey had dark rings under his eyes. He looked like Hemmings – his photographic "evidence" stolen, his studio trashed – when he returns in daylight to Maryon Park, to find that the body has gone. To see the wind, the shaking tree, the grass: *as it is*. Unphotographed and unphotographable. The moment when cynicism turns to ice, when he loses it, and gains in exchange a dreadful self-knowledge.)

The important occasion came when Antonioni visited Maryon Park for the first time, when he recognised its potential. (Antonioni "follows"

Chris Petit, the solitary wanderer, who arrived in Charlton on a quest to find the *BlowUp* location. As he describes it in his essay, *Newman Passage* or *J. Maclaren-Ross and the Case of the Vanishing Writers*, the presence of the future director, with his urban anxieties, influenced the shape of Antonioni's unformulated project: the hanging figure from *An Unsuitable Job for a Woman*, the morally corrupt businessman, the unforgiving skies of *Radio On*. "I made my own map of the city." The stranger, reading London as a dream, is guided to a patch of ground – enclosed, protected – that will serve him. That is already replete with undisclosed fictions. David Gascoyne, a few miles upstream, years before, had anticipated the coming war: "Went up into the Park, where I fell asleep lying in the sunshine in one of the enclosures, and had mad dreams.")

The figure of the distinguished elderly man (rumoured to be a guest appearance by Michael Redgrave) who is drawn into the secret meadow by a transparently coltish Vanessa Redgrave came to look, as I re-ran the video, like the photographs of Antonioni himself (in the large prints hung on screens in the Festival Hall as part of the *Magnum Cinema* exhibition). Only the corpse doubled for John Major. And Hemmings at the fence, holding up his camera, has his free eye *open*. He is posing, not shooting. Redgrave was being un-directed to give a Monica Vitti performance: the "ungainly comedienne" that David Thomson discovers. But Antonioni had leased her to Joseph Losey, so that she could be paired with Terence Stamp in *Modesty Blaise*. (And photographed alongside him by Eve Arnold.) The same Stamp who so badly wanted the part of the photographer. The Stamp who copied David Bailey's hand gestures. The mystery is resolved. The figure in the bushes, the undisclosed assassin, is Stamp. He can kill the director – who has agreed to an assignation with his mistress, so that she can be shown this wonderful English location – and, at the same time, implicate David Hemmings. After collaborating in Antonioni's artistic suicide, Stamp will then fade quietly into the shadows of the international money market (*Wall Street*), futurist megalomania (*Alien Nation*), Virgin Atlantic commercials – until he is exposed as a bespoke version of the man that he once shot in the park. A grey Mr Arkadin. A lethargic Kane.

I started to pore insanely over my photographic files: the sequence I took with Anna, my wife, on Boxing Day, and the place as it was when I made my first excursion, and then the walk with Atkins in the summer of '94. The frames began to bleed and mix. Bare winter trees, strong diagonal shadows. A sunburst into the lens. Cropped turf. Lush grass with a path cut through it. The photographer stooping and staring. Trees and bushes overgrown, thick enough to hide regiments. The flakes of dark green paint on the fence. The steps where Redgrave challenged Hemmings. The enclosure was an eye. Every movement was watched and recorded. Seasons could change as you walked across the grass. Bushes flowered and died.

We came in, on the day of the failed Charlton House excursion, from the other direction; down through Maryon-Wilson Park. Marc took the photograph of the X on the hillside, and I imagined that we had returned to the point from which we started: the given word. The **V** of the walk (Hackney to Greenwich and home through North Woolwich), the **O** of the Maryon enclosure, and now the **X**, **VOX** again. ("Noughts in their crosses/Ice in their eyes." David Gascoyne.) *Blow-Up* shifted to "BlowJob"; a licence for that which is unobserved, the excitement of risk between the man in the suit and the girl who persuades him to visit such an obscure site.

We didn't take the usual steep steps. I decided, on a whim, to climb the quarry. Noises stranger than any of the effects in Antonioni's film were coming from the edge of the scrub woods at the quarry's foot. A trio of respectable, middle-aged women scrabbling for stones, filling their Littlewoods carrier bags with pebbles. "For the dogs," they said. "The dogs love them."

We walked the ridge on a forbidden path, sat down in the sunlight – the sky clearing over the river – to enjoy the view of the Thames Barrier. Atkins shading his eyes. The tattoos on his arms: F & O. It was a very good spot to let it all go. A squirrel ran along the fence, hopping effortlessly from post to post. I wanted one final shot at the Charlton House mystery. We'd get the boat back down to Greenwich and I'd comb the town until I found some trace of Ron Pepper's elusive document. (One more photograph for the collection as we passed through Antonioni's paddock: a ruined, wooden-frame tennis racket hidden in the grass. The alternative ending to *Blow-Up*. Antonioni shot two versions: Hemmings picking up an invisible tennis ball and returning it to the mimers, and Hemmings picking up a real ball from a phoney game. This was the racket. And the pun. Brown grass, tinder dry, with the scorch marks of a recent fire.)

We found the information in the last place we expected it. The girl in the tourist office at Greenwich *had* heard of Ron Pepper, she was almost sure of it. Not a book, a "weird" article. It might still be checked out in the local history library in Mycenae Road.

So it was up the hill and back to Charlton. But first we ducked into the passageways of the market to see if any of the print shops had an engraving of Maryon Park or Charlton House. Interesting things in the cheap boxes, tear-outs, architect's plans, follies, but not what we were looking for. Then we came across the inevitable out-to-lunch shop, locked, with a window display that had us both reaching for our cameras. A blown-up Roque map of the riverside from 1745, Greenwich to Woolwich, with an empty gilt frame on chains: creating a portrait of a choice section. Charlton House to Maryon Park and the "Hanging Woods". We stood in the narrow passage, pressing our noses against the glass to memorise the details. The V of the paths through the tight curls of woodland made a pubic mound. A gash. The heights that we had been obsessively exploring had a name: "Mount Whoredom". A resort of the Woolwich Militia, the river rats.

They were very helpful at Mycenae Road; courtesy without an inquisition. The copy of Ron Pepper's 31pp pamphlet, *Charlton House — A "Hidden" Mystery?*, had been bound in black boards. Were there further copies for sale? Unfortunately not, they had all disappeared. This was the one and only.

I sat at a table, between a local genealogist and a man checking the shipping records, and began scribbling. I wanted to copy the whole thing. ("One Saturday evening in October 1983 . . . we accepted an invitation . . . to spend a couple of hours with a psychic sensitive to check out if 'anything was there' . . . Those who accept the possibility of tapping into 'something' will not be surprised to learn that this is what happened — on the main stairs where, it turned out from later research, over the years people have experienced feelings of unease, fear or a sense of wrongness.") I was hooked on the craziness, lost in admiration for a man who had actually been able to get as far as the stairs of this building.

After ten minutes, with writer's cramp setting in, and Atkins back from his prowl around the gallery on the ground floor, his usual phonecalls, it struck me that there might be a photocopier available. Of course. No problem. I walked away with Pepper's entire text in my hands. Sir Adam Newton: "a Scot who spent some part of his early life in France, passing himself off as a Catholic priest . . . returned to Scotland about 1600 and was appointed as tutor to the young Prince

Henry, heir to the throne . . . Newton was described as 'a man of considerable learning' . . . who, although a layman, was installed as Dean of Durham."

A good authentic *Holy Blood & Holy Grail* preamble. Pepper was a traditionalist. He wasted no time in drawing in Ralegh and his circle, and the death of Prince Henry of a "mysterious fever". ("Headaches and buzzing in the ears . . . delirium . . . raving convulsions" . . . curtains.) Then it was on to Charlton House itself, the structure and ornamentation, the demons of the porch.

It was clear that Atkins and I would have to make one last attempt. We slogged along the escarpment as if we were on a treadmill (with a drum of revolving scenery). And, miraculously, having cracked the book test, everything was opened to us. The woman at the table waved us towards the stairs. We could go into any room in the house.

The malign staircase is constructed with square columns on which are the figures which Pepper describes as "devil heads"; wolves and horned creatures attributed to Bernard Jansen, and carved according to Newton's specifications. There are also four-legged obelisk forms – like instruments on which you might perch a camera. The wooden heads yawn and jeer. They contradict all the community activities that happen around them: the disabled dancing, the righteous seminars.

We were alone in the panelled upstairs galleries, sunlight streaming through the west window, burnishing the polished deck. We examined the allegorical panel in the White Room: *The Triumph of Death*. We searched the fireplace in the Wilson Room for the "upward piercing flower" that repeats a motif from the west porch. Looking down on the Horn Fair Field, we brooded on Pepper's notion that this was "an ancient place of worship", a place that had for centuries been the conclusion of a pilgrimage out of the City of London. ("Large groups of participants apparently travelled down river . . . landing at Cuckold's Point . . . to march in procession to Greenwich and Charlton, with horns of different kinds on their heads . . . Many indecencies were committed.") The local historian concludes that this was a "holy place", familiar to "shamans dressed in antlers and animal skins". Cernunnos, the horned god, had appeared here "in various guises over thousands of years . . . as Herne the Hunter, the Green Man and Harry-ca-Nab."

The quality of the light was such that Atkins asked me to sit, to pose for a photograph, on a raised platform at the end of the White Room. The day had been warm enough to justify a David Bailey cap. Let him show it. I would leaf through the rest of Pepper's essay while I waited for my shadow to fall, as he wanted it, across the reflection of a long window.

How would Pepper conclude his yarn? How would he rescue us both from this infinitely extendible narrative? "Associates of Newton would have included such men as . . . Sir Walter Ralegh, Robert Fludd, John Florio, John Dee and Christopher Marlowe." In other words, all the usual suspects. ("For those who read symbolism into local natural scenery, the House overlooks the great U-shaped Thames meander – a pair of horns?") And then we arrive, as we had to, at "a secret organisation known as the Prieuré de Sion". Our old friends, the Sion Ants. No conspiracy thesis is complete without them. Isaac Newton, of course, was a Grand Master. And descended from "ancient Scottish nobility".

Well, that brings it closer to home. A summer-house, with gargoyle decorations, in the grounds of a property that belonged to my wife's family, at the time of our marriage, had, by tradition, been used by Newton. Pepper is as fond as I am of these arbitrary leaps. "It also," he states with breathtaking optimism, "makes for a possible family relationship with Adam Newton . . . The potential relevance of this falls into place with a reference . . . to the Sinclair family (originally St Clair) whose domain was at Rosslyn in south-east Scotland, only a few miles from the former Scottish headquarters of the Knights Templar . . . In a charter believed to date from 1601 the Sinclairs are recognised as 'hereditary Grand Masters of Scottish Masonry' . . . Could there then be a family connection, linking the Newtons across the generations, with a secret network . . . part of the wider Prieuré de Sion web?"

Why not? I can think of worse places to live. Let's boot out the meditation classes and the Vietnamese lunch clubs and repossess the gaff. Atkins would make an impressive skinhead butler. Let's go for the *Remains of Day* scenario. Dump all this wearisome travelling across London and enjoy the fruits of a good library, a well-stocked cellar, rosy twilight on the skulls of stone demons.

Tom's most well, now, and got his bullet around his neck on a watch-guard for a watch, and is always seeing what time it is, and so there ain't nothing more to write about . . . But I reckon I got to light out for the Territory . . . I been there before.

MARK TWAIN, *THE ADVENTURES OF HUCKLEBERRY FINN*

```
┌─────────────────────────────────────────────────────┐
│          ACKNOWLEDGEMENTS & SELECT                  │
│                 BIBLIOGRAPHY                        │
└─────────────────────────────────────────────────────┘
```

Thanks to Marc Atkins for keeping a photographic record of these journeys, for good-humoured company in the towers and tunnels. Looking back on his prints reassures me that none of this can really have happened. The images incite a prose text that will keep pace with them. And to Neil Belton, my editor, respects for his nice judgment of the moment when sub-text begins to choke the life from the primary growth, when there is altogether too much blood on the authorial knuckles.

Commissions from Jean McNichol of the *London Review of Books* launched me on some of the more fruitful digressions.

Skating on Thin Eyes: A Walk

For the dirt on tagging, my thanks to Will Sinclair – who also made available a short video (*Graffiti Forever*, 1995) produced with Max Votolato.

For information about the complexities of Kurdish politics in Hackney, my thanks to Emma Sinclair-Webb. Emma also talked me through the map of the relevant homelands and interpreted my collection of snapshots, the posters and signs from the walls. John the Barber (Cambridge Heath Road) weighed in with a number of vivid anecdotes.

Richard Makin gave up his time to curate a private view of his installation at the University of Greenwich.

Louis Aragon. *Paris Peasant*. London, 1971.
Cyril Arapoff. *London in the Thirties*. London, 1988.
Alexander Baron. *The Lowlife*. London, 1963.
Susan Buck-Morss. *The Dialectics of Seeing: Walter Benjamin and the Arcades Project*. Cambridge, Mass. 1991.

363

Alan Burns. *The Angry Brigade*. London, 1973.

Gordon Carr. *The Angry Brigade, the Cause and the Case*. London, 1975.

(Daniel Defoe) James Sutherland. *Defoe*. London, 1937.

(Defoe) AJ Shirren. *Daniel Defoe in Stoke Newington*. London, 1960.

Peter Fuller. *Marches Past*. London, 1986.

Wolfgang Gortschacher. *Little Magazine Profiles: The Little Magazines in Great Britain 1939–1993*. Salzburg, 1993.

Stewart Home. *Neoist Manifestos*. Stirling, 1991.

—— *Red London*. Edinburgh, 1994.

—— *Neoism, Plagiarism & Praxis*. Edinburgh, 1995.

Michael Hunter. *The Victorian Villas of Hackney*. London, 1981.

Paul Joyce. *A Guide to Abney Park Cemetery*. London, 1984.

Patrick Keiller. *London* (a film). 1993.

Grace Lake. *Viola Tricolor*. Cambridge, 1993.

—— *Bernache Nonnette*. Cambridge, 1995.

Tony Lambrianou. *Inside the Firm (The Untold Story of the Krays' Reign of Terror)*. London, 1991.

Richard Makin. *the curve of forgetting*. London, 1992.

—— *forward*. Cambridge, 1995.

Alfred Métraux. *Voodoo*. London, 1959.

Thomas Pynchon. *V*. New York, 1963.

—— *The Crying of Lot 49*. London, 1967.

Tom Raworth. *A Serial Biography*. London, 1969.

Peter Riley. *Royal Signals*. Cheltenham, 1995.

Elizabeth Robinson. *Lost Hackney*. London, 1989.

Iain Sinclair. *Downriver*. London, 1991.

—— *Radon Daughters*. London, 1994.

Ian Thomson. *'Bonjour Blanc', A Journey through Haiti*. London, 1992.

(Victoria Park) Michael Hunter (& others). *Parks & Open Spaces in Hackney. A Report by the Hackney Society*. London, 1980.

Patrick Wright. *A Journey through Ruins (The Last Days of London)*. London, 1991.

The Dog & the Dish

Elements of the canine sermon, in an earlier form, appeared as "Isle of Dogs" in the *London Review of Books*, Vol. 12 No. 9, 10 May 1990.

A brief account of the gangland funeral appeared as "Ronnie Kray Bows Out" in the *London Review of Books*, Vol. 17 No. 11, 8 June 1995.

Alexander Baron. *King Dido*. London, 1969.

William Blake. *Complete Writings*. London, 1969.

William Burroughs. *My Education (A Book of Dreams)*. New York, 1995.

Duncan Campbell. *The Underworld*. London, 1994.

Brian Catling. *The Stumbling Block Its Index*. London, 1990.

Albert Donoghue (& Martin Short). *The Kray's Lieutenant*. London, 1995.

Andrew Duncan. "Brian Catling: shared psychosis in the penetralia of the collective imaginary." *Angel Exhaust*. Issue 11, Winter 1994.

James Ellroy. *The Big Nowhere*. New York, 1988.

—— *American Tabloid*. London, 1995.

Scott Ely. *Pit Bull*. London, 1990.

Frankie Fraser (& James Morton). *Mad Frank*. London, 1994.

Robert Graves. *The White Goddess*. London, 1948.

Reg & Ron Kray (& Fred Dinenage). *Our Story*. London, 1988.

Reg Kray. *Born Fighter*. London, 1990.

—— *Thoughts (Philosophy & Poetry)*. London, 1991.

—— *Villains we have Known*. Leeds, 1993.

Ron Kray. *My Story*. London, 1993.

Emanuel Litvinoff. *Journey through a Small Planet*. London, 1972.

—— *A Death out of Season*. London, 1973.

Barry MacSweeney. *The Tempers of Hazard*. London, 1993.

Eric Mason. *The Inside Story*. London, 1994.

James Morton. *Gangland, London's Underworld*. London, 1992.

John Pearson. *The Profession of Violence*. London, 1972.

Charlie Richardson. *My Manor, An Autobiography*. London, 1991.

Iain Sinclair. *Lud Heat*. London, 1975.

Billy Webb. *Running with the Krays (My Life in London's Gangland)*. Edinburgh, 1993.

Robert Westerby. *Wide Boys Never Work*. London, 1937.

John Williams. *Into the Badlands*. London, 1991.

Bulls & Bears & Mithraic Misalignments

I am grateful to John Hudson for supplying me with some of the fruits of his Elias Ashmole research, for clues that are followed up in this essay. And to Alan Moore for keeping me up to date, instalment by instalment, with *From Hell*, his epic account of the morbid side of the late Victorian imagination.

Sections of the essay, in earlier versions, were published by the *London*

Review of Books ("Bad News"), Vol. 12 No. 23, October 1990, and by the *Critical Quarterly (*90's Fictions*)*, Vol. 37 No. 4, Winter 1995.

(Elias Ashmole) CH Josten. *Elias Ashmole. His Autobiographical & Historical Notes, his Correspondence, & other Contemporary Sources Relating to his Life & Work.* 5 vols., Oxford, 1966.

(Ashmole) Michael Hunter. *Elias Ashmole & his World.* Oxford, 1983.

Michael Ayrton. *Golden Sections.* London, 1957.

—— *The Minotaur.* London, 1970.

Sylvia Bogdanescu. *The Life & Times of St Dunstan-in-the-West.* London, 1986.

Jorge Luis Borges. *Labyrinths.* New York, 1964.

Edward M Borrajo. *Catalogue of the Collection of London Antiquities in the Guildhall Museum.* London, 1908.

John Bossy. *Giordano Bruno and the Embassy Affair.* London, 1991.

Edward Wedlake Brayley. *Londiniana; or, Reminiscences of the British Metropolis.* 4 vols., London, 1829.

TJ Chandler. *The Climate of London.* London, 1965.

AE Daniell. *London City Churches.* London, 1896.

Alexander Davidson. *The City Share Pushers.* London, 1989.

Eric de Maré. *Wren's London.* London, 1975.

Edward Dorn. *Way West.* Santa Rosa, 1993.

Al Dyos & Michael Wolff. *The Victorian City.* 2 vols., London, 1973.

TS Eliot. *Collected Poems 1909–1935.* London, 1936.

Geoffrey Fletcher. *Offbeat in the City of London.* London, 1967.

Robert Frank. *Moving Out.* New York, 1996.

EO Gordon. *Prehistoric London, Its Mounds & Circles.* London, 1925.

Rigby Graham. *Michael Ayrton.* Uppingham, 1987.

Graham. *Monotypes.* Uppingham, 1994.

Warren Grynberg. *The Square Mile (The City of London in Historic Postcards).* Glos., 1995.

Anthony Hilton. *City Within a State (A Portrait of Britain's Financial World).* London, 1987.

Luke Howard. *The Climate of London (Observations 1806–1830).* Revised & enlarged. 2nd edn., 3 vols., London, 1833.

Howard. *Barometrographia.* London, 1847.

Will Hutton. *The State We're In.* London, 1995.

Ralph Hyde (introduces). *The A to Z of Georgian London.* London, 1981.

David Jones. *The Anathemata.* London, 1952.

Peter Laurie. *Beneath the City Streets (A Private Enquiry into Government Preparations for National Emergency).* Revised edn., London, 1979.

TC Lethbridge. *Gog Magog, the Discovery & Subsequent Destruction of a Great British Antiquity*. Cambridge, n.d.

Howard C Levis. *Bladud of Bath, The British King who Tried to Fly*. Bath, 1973.

Parry Marshall. *City of London, An Illustrated Pocket History*. London, 1947.

WH Matthews. *Mazes and Labyrinths: A General Account of Their History & Development*. London, 1922.

Alan Moore. *From Hell*. Baltimore, 1994.

Roy Porter. *London, a Social History*. London, 1994.

Peter Redgrove. *The Black Goddess & the Sixth Sense*. London, 1987.

Richard Sennett. *Flesh and Stone (The Body and the City in Western Civilization)*. London, 1994.

TC Stewart. *The City as an Image of Man*. London, 1970.

Jack Trevor Story. *Little Dog's Day*. London, 1971.

Walter Thornbury. *Haunted London*. London, 1865.

Henry Walker. *Stamford, with its Surroundings*. n.d (c.1912).

Esme Wynne-Tyson. *Mithras, the Fellow in the Cap*. London, 1958.

X Marks the Spot

Thanks to Aidan Dun for guiding Marc Atkins and myself around the *Vale Royal* patch. And to Mike Goldmark for, among other things, digging out the Thomas Hardy poem.

Some of this material ("Mysteries of Kings Cross") appeared first in the *London Review of Books*, Vol. 17 No. 19, 5 October 1995. The section from *Red Eye* was originally published in the *Grosseteste Review*, Vol. 7 Nos. 1–3, Summer 1974.

Pete Brown. *Let 'em roll Kafka*. London, 1969.

Michael Crick. *Jeffrey Archer, Stranger than Fiction*. London, 1995.

Aidan Dun. *Vale Royal*. Uppingham, 1995.

Robin Farquharson. *Drop Out!* London, 1968.

Allen Fisher. *Place*. London, 1974.

David Gascoyne. *The Sun at Midnight*. London, 1970.

—— *Collected Journals 1936–42*. London, 1991.

Bob Gilbert. *The Kings Cross Cut (A City Canal & its Community)*. London, 1985.

WS Graham. *The Night Fishing*. London, 1955.

John Healy. *The Grass Arena, An Autobiography*. London, 1988.

Michael Horovitz. *Children of Albion (Poetry of the "Underground" in Britain)*. London, 1969.

Chris Jenks. "Watching Your Step: The History & Practice of the *Flâneur*." *Visual Culture*. London, 1995.

Tim Powers. *The Anubis Gates*. London, 1985.

Arthur Machen. *The London Adventure or the Art of Wandering*. London, 1924.

Barry MacSweeney. *Brother Wolf*. London, 1972.

Jean-Nicholas-Arthur Rimbaud. *Prose Poems from the Illuminations*. New York, 1946.

Peter Whitehead. *Wholly Communion*. London, 1965.

Charles Williams. *The Region of the Summer Stars*. London, 1944.

Lord Archer's Prospects

Thanks to Lord Archer for his permission to view and photograph his Alembic House property, the art trophies and the prospects of the river. Thanks to Dick Humphreys of the Tate Gallery's Education Department for passing on many fruitful hints and for smoothing our way to explore the outlying areas of the empire, the domes, wards, and prison remnants.

Krzysztof Z Cieszkowski let me have a copy of his very useful essay on "Millbank before the Tate". And Carol Williams, passing through London at just the right moment, brought to light the curious experiments involving the spiderwort plants. And thanks to Paul Burwell, deftest of pilots, for the upriver voyages.

An extract from this essay appeared first in *Tate (The Art Magazine)*, Issue 9, May 1996.

GL Apperson. "The Tradescants' Museum." *Bygone London Life (Pictures from a Vanished Past)*. London, 1903.

Jeffrey Archer. "The Devil's Audience with Jeffrey Archer." *The Printer's Devil*. Issue G, 1995.

John Aubrey. *Aubrey's Brief Lives*. Edited by Oliver Lawson Dick. London, 1949.

Julian Barnes. *Letters from London 1990–1995*. London, 1995.

William Burroughs. *Electronic Revolution*. Cambridge, 1971.

Angela Carter. *Wise Children*. London, 1991.

Catherine Caulfield. *Multiple Exposures (Chronicles of the Radiation Age)*. London, 1989.

David Caute. *Joseph Losey, A Revenge on Life*. London, 1994.

Krzysztof Z Cieszkowski. "Millbank before the Tate." *The Tate Gallery Illustrated Biennial Report*. London, 1986.

Alex Constantine. *Psychic Dictatorship in the U.S.A.* Portland, Oregon, 1995.

Stephen Dorril & Robin Ramsay. *Smear! Wilson and the Secret State*. London, 1991.

Marianne Faithfull. *Faithfull*. London, 1994.

Joy Hancox. *The Byrom Collection (Renaissance Thought, the Royal Society & the Building of the Globe Theatre)*. London, 1992.

Sadao Ichikawa. "The Spiderwort Strategy." *Bio-Dynamics*. Summer 1978.

Prudence Leith-Ross. *The Story of the Tradescants*. London, 1985.

John McEwen. *John Bellany*. London, 1994.

Arthur MacGregor. "A Magazin of all Manner of Inventions" (Museums in the quest for 'Salomon's House' in seventeenth-century England'. *Journal of the History of Collections*. 1 no 2, 1989.

(Howard Marks) David Leigh. *High Time (The Life and Times of Howard Marks)*. London, 1984.

Isadore Meschan. *Synopsis of Roentgen Signs*. Philadelphia, 1963.

Charles Nicholl. *The Chemical Theatre*. London, 1980.

Rosemary Nicholson. "A Museum of Garden History." Off-print, *Period Home*, Vol. 4 No.2., n.d.

Leonard Reed (with James Morton). *Nipper (The Man Who Nicked the Krays)*. London, 1991.

AE Waite. *The Alchemical Writings of Edward Kelly*. London, 1893.

Peter Wright. *Spycatcher*. Australia, 1987.

House *in the Park*

Thanks to Rachel Whiteread and to James Lingwood (of Artangel) who commissioned an essay on the *House* event, and its fallout. And thanks to the two Rachels, Whiteread and Lichtenstein, for time spent talking about their work. Stewart Home, apart from answering a number of questions, has been a constant supplier of transgressive leaflets and black propaganda newsprint.

An earlier (and briefer) version of "*House* in the Park" was published in *House* (London, 1995), a collection edited by James Lingwood and

Rachel Whiteread. Some of the Stewart Home material appeared first ("Who is Stewart Home?") in the *London Review of Books*, Vol. 16 No. 12, 23 June 1994.

Richard Allen. *The Complete Richard Allen*. 3 vols., Dunoon, Argyll, 1992–1994.

Peter French. *John Dee, the World of an Elizabethan Magus*. London, 1972.

Stewart Home. *Pure Mania*. Edinburgh, 1989.

—— *The Festival of Plagiarism*. London, 1989.

—— *Defiant Pose*. London, 1991.

—— *Black Mask & Up Against the Wall Motherfucker*. London, 1993.

—— *No Pity*. Edinburgh, 1993.

—— *Conspiracies, Cover-Ups & Diversions*. London, 1995.

—— *Cunt Lickers Anonymous*. London, n.d. (1995).

—— *Analecta*. London, 1996.

—— "Gender, Sexuality & Control." *Smile*. Issue 11, n.d.

Anon. (Home, Fabian Thompsett & others). *The London Psychogeographical Association Newsletter*. (From: LPA, Box 15, 138 Kingsland High St., London E8 2NS) Of particular interest to this essay: Issue No. 2 ("Omphalos under Fire!"); Issue No. 5 ("Housey! Housey!"); Issue No. 6 ("Smash the Occult Establishment"); the unnumbered single sheet "Nazi Occultists Seize Omphalos"; Issue No. 13 ("Isle of Dogs Leyline Bombed").

(Home) Larry O'Hara. *Stewart Home: the Fascist's Flunkey*. Single sheet polemic. London, 1996. (With further statements from the "Anti-Deception Committee". BM Box 4769, London WC111 3XX)

The K Foundation. *Money, A Major Body of Cash*. Single sheets loose in black folder. Vienna, n.d (1994).

Rachel Lichtenstein. Series of postcards from *Ner Htamid* exhibition. n.d.

Adam McClean edt. *A Treatise on Angel Magic*. Grand Rapids, MI., 1989.

Kimerly Rorschach. *The Early Georgian Landscape Garden*. New Haven, Conn., 1983.

Patrick Wright. *The Village That Died for England*. London, 1995.

The Shamanism of Intent

Thanks to Gavin Jones and Brian Catling for making themselves available for interview, for the time they gave up to discuss their work, the guided tours of studio and bunker.

The bones of this essay first appeared in *The Shamanism of Intent (Some Flights of Redemption)*, the catalogue of an exhibition at the Goldmark Gallery, Uppingham, 1991. Some of the Gavin Jones material was first published ("Gavin Jones, Painter: A Brief History by Flashlight") in *Modern Painters*, Vol. 4 No. 4, Winter 1991. An earlier version of some of the Catling material ("A New Vortex: The Shamanism of Intent") first appeared in *Modern Painters*, Vol. 4 No. 2, Summer 1991.

Material relevant to this essay was exploited in several films: "Three Sculptors" (written by Iain Sinclair, directed by Saskia Baron) for BBC2's *Late Show*, 22/11/91; "Photographing Whitechapel" (written by Iain Sinclair), for BBC2's *Late Show* 26/5/92; and "The Cardinal and the Corpse" (written by Sinclair, directed by Chris Petit), 1992, for Channel 4's *Without Walls*.

Marc Atkins & Anet van der Elzen. *Masses Lacing Masses*. Hertogenbosch, Netherlands. 1992.

—— (Brian Catling, Nigel Slight & others). *Blind Montage*. Hertogenbosch, Netherlands. 1992.

Max Beckmann. *On my Paintings*. New York, 1988.

Stan Brakhage. *A Moving Picture Giving & Taking Book*. West Newbury, Mass., 1971.

Brian Catling. *Lair*. London, 1987.

—— *Soundings, A Tractate of Absence*. London, 1991.

—— *Future Exiles*. London, 1992.

—— *The Blindings*. London, 1995.

(Catling) Liz Brooks. "Of Knowing & Haunting the World: the Gnostic Art of Brian Catling." *Performance*. No. 65/66, Spring 1992.

(Catling) Ian Hunt. "Spread Table, Spread Meat, Drink, & Bread. An interview with Brian Catling." *Parataxis*, No. 4, Summer 1993.

(Catling) Simon Perril. Draft typescript for essay/lecture on "The Stumbling Block". Cambridge, n.d (1993).

(Catling) Ian Hunt. "Being Here (Locating Brian Catling)". *Art Monthly*, No. 180, October 1994.

Paul Celan. *Selected Poems*. London, 1972.

Crow. Black folder: press-cuttings, photographs, postcards. The Institution of Rot. London, 1993.

Steve Dilworth. *Acts of Faith*. Illustrated catalogue of work, with photographs by Beka Dilworth. Stornoway, Isle of Lewis, 1992.

Edward Dorn. *Hello, La Jolla*. Berkeley, 1978.

Mircea Eliade. *Shamanism, Archaic Techniques of Ecstasy*. London, 1964.

—— *Rites and Symbols of Initiation*. New York, 1965.

Daniel Farson. *Soho in the Fifties*. London, 1987.

Carl Hiaasen. *Double Whammy*. London, 1988.

Markéta Luskačova. *Photographs of Spitalfields*. London, 1991.

Robin Muir. *John Deakin*. (Selected photographs and essay). London, 1996.

Christopher Petit. *Robinson*. London, 1993.

JH Prynne. *Aristeas*. London, 1968.

(Prynne) Simon Jarvis. "The cost of the stumbling block." *Parataxis*, No. 4, Summer 1993.

Peterjon & Yasmin Skelt. *Alive in Parts of This Century: Eric Mottram at 70*. London, 1994.

Paul Smith ed. *Subversion in the Street of Shame*. Catalogue for events at the Bridewell Theatre (Robin Cook, Chris Petit, Emanuel Litvinoff, Alan Moore, Brian Catling, John Healy etc). London, 1994.

Michael Tucker. *Dreaming With Open Eyes (The Shamanic Spirit in 20th Century Art & Culture)*. London, 1992.

Aaron Williamson. *A Holythroat Symposium*. London, 1993.

Cinema Purgatorio

Thanks to Tom Baker, Patrick Keiller and Christopher Petit for their time and hospitality.

Some of the Keiller material ("London, Necropolis of Fretful Ghosts") appeared first in *Sight and Sound*, June 1994.

Principal films:

Patrick Keiller. *London*. Koninck/BFI, 1994.

Christopher Petit. *Radio On*. BFI/Road Movies, 1979.

—— *An Unsuitable Job for a Woman*. Boyd's, 1982.

—— *Flight to Berlin*. Geba/Road Movies/BFI, 1984.

—— *Chinese Boxes*. Palace Pictures/Road Movies, 1981.

Michael Reeves. *The Sorcerers*. Tigon, 1967.

—— *Witchfinder General*. Tigon/American International, 1968.

Bibliography:

Laurence Bicknell. *Relations*. London, 1973.

Louis-Ferdinand Céline. *Journey to the End of the Night*. London, 1934.

—— *Guignol's Band*. New York, 1954.

—— *London Bridge*. Normal, Ill., 1995.

James Curtis. *They Drive by Night*. London, 1938.

Edward Dorn. *Manchester Square*. London, 1975.

Keith Griffiths. "Anxious Visions." *Vertigo*, Winter 1994.

Aidan Higgins. *Helsingør Station & other Departures*. London, 1989.

Franz Kafka. *Amerika*. New York, 1946.

Jack Kerouac. *Céline & other Tales*. Pacific Red Car (pirate edn) 1985.

Gerald Kersh. *Night and the City*. London, 1938.

Arthur La Bern. *Goodbye Piccadilly, Farewell Leicester Square*. London, 1966.

Jonathan Meades. *Pompey*. London, 1993.

Richard Murphy. *Sixties British Cinema*. London, 1992.

Christopher Petit. "Newman Passage *or* J. Maclaren-Ross & the Case of the Vanishing Writers." *The Time Out Book of London Short Stories*. London, 1993.

Michael Powell. *A Life in the Movies*. London, 1986.

Don Siegel. *A Siegel Film (An Autobiography)*. London, 1993.

Iain Sinclair. *The Kodak Mantra Diaries*. London, 1971.

Jack Trevor Story. *The Trouble With Harry*. London, 1949.

David Thomson. *A Biographical Dictionary of Film*. London, 1995.

François Truffaut. *Hitchcock*. London, 1968.

Alexander Walker. *Hollywood, England (The British Film Industry in the Sixties)*. London, 1974.

Vernon Watkins. *The Ballad of the Mari Llwyd*. London, 1941.

Patrick Wright. *On Living in an Old Country*. London, 1985.

The Cadaver Club

An earlier version of some of the PD James material ("The Cadaver Club") was first published in the *London Review of Books*, Vol. 16 No. 24, 22 December 1994.

Peter Ackroyd. *Dan Leno and the Limehouse Golem*. London 1994.

Anon. "Poussin Holds the Key." *London Psychogeographical Association Newsletter*, No. 9, 1995.

Michael Baigent, Richard Leigh, Henry Lincoln. *The Holy Blood & the Holy Grail*. London, 1982.

—— *The Messianic Legacy*. London, 1986.

Alain Berala (intros). *Magnum Cinema (Photographs from 50 years of movie-making)*. London, 1995.

Robin Cook. *The Tenants of Dirt Street*. London, 1971.

Cook as "Derek Raymond". *He Died with his Eyes Open*, London, 1984.

—— *I was Dora Suarez*. London, 1990.

—— *The Hidden Files: An Autobiography*. London, 1992.

—— *Dead Man Upright*. London, 1993.

—— *Not till the Red Fog Rises*. London, 1994.

Thomas De Quincey. "*On Murder Considered as one of the Fine Arts*". *The Collected Writings*, New & Enlarged Edition, Vol. XIII, Edinburgh, 1890.

Chris Ellmers, Alex Werner. *London's Lost Riverscape*. London, 1988.

JS English. "*. . . And all was Light*" *The Life and Work of Sir Isaac Newton*. Lincoln, 1977.

Bob Gilbert. *The Green London Way*. London, 1991.

Veronica Hull. *The Monkey Puzzle*. London, 1958.

PD James (with TA Critchley). *The Maul & the Pear Tree (The Ratcliffe Highway Murders of 1811)*. London, 1971.

—— *An Unsuitable Job for a Woman*. 1972.

—— *Death of an Expert Witness*. 1977.

—— *A Taste for Death*. 1986.

—— *Original Sin*. 1994.

—— *The Children of Men*. 1992.

Henry Lincoln. *The Holy Place*. London, 1991.

Don McCullin. *Unremarkable Behaviour, An Autobiography*. London, 1990.

Jonathan Meades. *Peter Knows What Dick Likes*. London, 1989.

NH Merton. "The Hidden Hand of the Jesuits in the Death of Diana Sinclair." *Crown Against Concubine (The Untold Story of the Recent Struggle between the House of Windsor and the Vatican)*. Exeter, 1994.

Henrietta Moraes. *Henrietta*. London, 1994.

Kim Newman. *The Quorum*. London, 1994.

Ron Pepper. *Charlton House – A "Hidden History"*. Privately published, 1985.

Frederick J Pohl. *Prince Henry Sinclair, His Expedition to the New World in 1398*. London, 1974.

Ezra Pound. *Selected Poems*. London, 1959.

Jon Savage. *England's Dreaming, Sex Pistols and Punk Rock*. London, 1991.

Andrew Sinclair. *The Sword and the Grail*. London, 1993.

Gore Vidal. *Palimpsest*. London, 1995.

INDEX

refresh yourself at penguin.co.uk

Visit penguin.co.uk for exclusive information and interviews with
bestselling authors, fantastic give-aways and the
inside track on all our books, from the Penguin Classics
to the latest bestsellers.

BE FIRST

first chapters, first editions, first novels

EXCLUSIVES

author chats, video interviews, biographies, special
features

EVERYONE'S A WINNER

give-aways, competitions, quizzes, ecards

READERS GROUPS

exciting features to support existing groups and
create new ones

NEWS

author events, bestsellers, awards, what's new

EBOOKS

books that click – download an ePenguin today

BROWSE AND BUY

thousands of books to investigate – search, try
and buy the perfect gift online – or treat yourself!

ABOUT US

job vacancies, advice for writers and company
history

Get Closer To Penguin . . . www.penguin.co.uk